Wittgenstein: Lectures, Cambridge 1930–1933

This edition of G.E. Moore's notes, taken at Wittgenstein's seminal Cambridge lectures in the early 1930s, provides, for the first time, an almost verbatim record of those classes. The presentation of the notes is both accessible and faithful to the original manuscripts, and a comprehensive introduction and synoptic table of contents provide the reader with essential contextual information and summaries of the topics in each lecture. The lectures form an excellent introduction to Wittgenstein's middle-period thought, covering a broad range of philosophical topics ranging from core questions in the philosophy of language, mind, logic, and mathematics, to illuminating discussions of subjects on which Wittgenstein says very little elsewhere, including ethics, religion, aesthetics, psychoanalysis, and anthropology. The volume also includes a 1932 essay by Moore critiquing Wittgenstein's conception of grammar, together with Wittgenstein's response. A companion website offers access to images of the entire set of source manuscripts.

David G. Stern is a professor of Philosophy and a Collegiate Fellow in the College of Liberal Arts and Sciences at the University of Iowa. His publications include *Wittgenstein's* Philosophical Investigations: *An Introduction* (Cambridge, 2004) and *Wittgenstein Reads Weininger* (co-edited with Béla Szabados, Cambridge, 2004).

Brian Rogers is an attorney in Los Angeles. He has a PhD in philosophy from the University of California, Irvine and has published in journals including *The Review of Symbolic Logic* and *Nordic Wittgenstein Review*.

Gabriel Citron is the Ray D. Wolfe Postdoctoral Fellow in the Department of Philosophy and the Anne Tanenbaum Centre for Jewish Studies at the University of Toronto. He has published in journals including *Mind* and *Philosophical Investigations*.

Wittgenstein Lectures, Cambridge 1930–1933

From the Notes of G.E. Moore

Edited by
David G. Stern, Brian Rogers,
and Gabriel Citron

CAMBRIDGE
UNIVERSITY PRESS

CAMBRIDGE
UNIVERSITY PRESS

University Printing House, Cambridge CB2 8BS, United Kingdom

One Liberty Plaza, 20th Floor, New York, NY 10006, USA

477 Williamstown Road, Port Melbourne, VIC 3207, Australia

314-321, 3rd Floor, Plot 3, Splendor Forum, Jasola District Centre, New Delhi - 110025, India

79 Anson Road, #06-04/06, Singapore 079906

Cambridge University Press is part of the University of Cambridge.

It furthers the University's mission by disseminating knowledge in the pursuit of education, learning and research at the highest international levels of excellence.

www.cambridge.org
Information on this title: www.cambridge.org/9781108730198

© Cambridge University Press 2016

This publication is in copyright. Subject to statutory exception and to the provisions of relevant collective licensing agreements, no reproduction of any part may take place without the written permission of Cambridge University Press.

First published 2016
First paperback edition 2018

A catalogue record for this publication is available from the British Library

Library of Congress Cataloging in Publication data
Names: Wittgenstein, Ludwig, 1889-1951. | Moore, G. E. (George Edward), 1873-1958.
Title: Wittgenstein : lectures, Cambridge, 1930-1933 : from the notes of G. E. Moore / edited by David G. Stern, Brian Rogers, Gabriel Citron.
Description: New York : Cambridge University Press, 2015. | Includes bibliographical references and index.
Identifiers: LCCN 2015020032 | ISBN 9781107041165 (hardback)
Subjects: LCSH: Philosophy. | Moore, G. E. (George Edward), 1873-1958.
Classification: LCC B3376.W564 A5 2015 | DDC 192—dc23 LC record available at
https://lccn.loc.gov/2015020032

ISBN 978-1-107-04116-5 Hardback
ISBN 978-1-108-73019-8 Paperback

Additional resources for this publication at www.wittgensteinsource.org

Cambridge University Press has no responsibility for the persistence or accuracy of URLs for external or third-party internet websites referred to in this publication, and does not guarantee that any content on such websites is, or will remain, accurate or appropriate.

Contents

Acknowledgements	*page* vi
Editorial introduction	ix
Synoptic table of contents	lxi

Lectures, Cambridge 1930–1933
From the Notes of G.E. Moore

Lent Term, 1930	3
May Term, 1930	39
Michaelmas Term, 1930	65
Lent Term, 1931	101
May Term, 1931	137
May Term, 1932	155
Michaelmas Term, 1932	175
Lent Term, 1933	225
May Term, 1933	305
Appendix: Moore's short paper on Wittgenstein on grammar	367
Biographies	379
Moore's abbreviations	385
Bibliography	389
Index	399

Acknowledgements

Gabriel Citron originally began work in 2008 on an edition of Moore's lecture notes from May Term, 1933. When David Stern and Brian Rogers became interested in editing the full set of notes in the summer of 2009, Tom Baldwin – Moore's literary executor – suggested that the three of us collaborate on the project. Each of us contributed equally to an initial transcription of the notes from the manuscripts and to the formation of procedures for editing and presenting the notes. All three editors made substantial contributions to the conversion of that initial transcription into the finished text and the writing of the editorial introduction, but the order in which the editors' names are listed reflects the relative degrees of input. David Stern and Brian Rogers did the bulk of the conversion of the initial transcription into a final text, with help from Gabriel Citron, and then all three shared in reviewing and polishing the edited text. Brian Rogers edited the diagrams and took primary responsibility for editing the logical and mathematical portions of the text. David Stern did most of the work in writing the editorial introduction, biographies, and footnotes, with some portions initially drafted by Brian Rogers and Gabriel Citron. He also obtained colour scans of the manuscripts and is responsible for their appearance on the Wittgenstein Source website.

Many people have been extraordinarily generous in helping us to produce this volume. We would especially like to thank: Tom Baldwin, Moore's literary executor, and Perry Moore, Moore's heir, for permission to produce an edition of Moore's notes; Tom Baldwin and Josef Rothhaupt, for encouraging the three editors to collaborate on this edition; Hilary Gaskin, our editor at Cambridge University Press, for encouraging us to take on this ambitious project, for her advice at several stages of the work, and for her support over the years, even as we asked for a number of deadline extensions; the Syndics of Cambridge University Library for kind permission to reproduce the images in this volume and the companion website; the American Philosophical Society, Franklin Research Grant, and the University of Iowa Arts and Humanities Initiative for support of David Stern's travel to Cambridge University Library and for funding acquisition of high-resolution scans of Moore's manuscripts from the Library; the School of Social Sciences and the Department of Logic and Philosophy of

Science at the University of California, Irvine for support of Brian Rogers's travel to Cambridge University Library; the Old Members' Trust, University College, Oxford and the E.O. James Bequest, All Souls College, Oxford for support of Gabriel Citron's travel to Cambridge and for purchasing scans and photocopies of research materials; librarians at Cambridge University Library for repeatedly scanning Moore's lecture notes, and for help at every stage of the way, including suggesting using an ultraviolet light to read words damaged by glue; David McKitterick and Jonathan Smith, at the Wren Library, Trinity College, for help with questions about texts, and access to both Wittgenstein's *Nachlass* and student notes taken at his lectures; Alois Pichler and Michael Biggs, for their expert advice on image editing; the Wittgenstein Source website for offering to host online images of the source manuscripts; and the University of Iowa Obermann Center for Advanced Studies for sponsoring a Summer Seminar on this book.

We would also like to thank all of the following for their assistance with questions about editing the text: Tom Baldwin, Michael Biggs, Simon Blackburn, Katie Buehner, Bill Child, David Citron, Mauro Engelmann, John Forrester, Arthur Gibson, Naftali Goldberg, Jane Heal, Wolfgang Kienzler, Jim Klagge, Gregory Landini, Mathieu Marion, Michael Nedo, Alex Oliver, Lydia Patton, Alois Pichler, Tom Ricketts, Josef Rothhaupt, Joachim Schulte, Hans Sluga, Jonathan Smith, Carrie Swanson, Kai Wehmeier, and the participants in the 2015 University of Iowa Obermann Summer Seminar. Of course none of these people are responsible for any errors that remain.

Editorial introduction

1. Overview

When Wittgenstein moved to Cambridge in January 1929, he was returning to the place where – over fifteen years before – he had studied under Bertrand Russell, engaged in discussions with G.E. Moore, and begun to develop his early philosophy. Since completing the definitive expression of his early thought in *Tractatus Logico-Philosophicus*, Wittgenstein had spent several years away from philosophical pursuits. Returning to Cambridge and re-engaging in philosophical activities marked a significant new phase in his philosophical career. This phase is now known as the 'middle Wittgenstein' – as it occurred between Wittgenstein's 'early' work, associated with the *Tractatus*, and his 'later' work, most strongly associated with the *Philosophical Investigations*. While these years were once regarded as merely a period of transition between Wittgenstein's early and later work, scholars have now begun to recognize its distinctive philosophical character.

Upon returning to Cambridge, Wittgenstein received a research position at Trinity College and immediately began to draft new philosophical writing. The next few years were very productive, resulting in a great quantity of writing, some of which has since been published as *Philosophical Remarks*, *Philosophical Grammar*, and *The Big Typescript*. In January 1930 Wittgenstein also began to give lectures, in which he further developed the themes of his ongoing research. Among those who attended these lectures was his old friend and long-time discussion partner, G.E. Moore. This volume contains the notes that Moore took of Wittgenstein's 1930–1933 Cambridge lectures. These notes not only provide a remarkably thorough and detailed record of Wittgenstein's first few years as a lecturer but also offer us a new perspective on the middle Wittgenstein.

While other accounts of Wittgenstein's lectures from this period have been published, Moore's notes as they appear in this volume are the fullest and most reliable record of what Wittgenstein said in those classes of the early 1930s. After Wittgenstein's death, Moore summarized his lecture notes in a series of articles entitled 'Wittgenstein's Lectures in 1930–33', published in *Mind* between 1954 and 1955.¹ The vast majority of that essay consists of Moore's summaries of what Wittgenstein said and his critical evaluation of the views he attributes to Wittgenstein, rather than direct quotations from his lecture notes. Moore's original notes provide access to this material in Wittgenstein's own words, including extended discussions of topics that receive scant attention in Moore's essay.²

Two sets of lecture notes taken by students have also been published: notes taken between January 1930 and May 1932, compiled by Desmond Lee,³ and notes taken between October 1932 and May 1935, compiled by Alice Ambrose.⁴ Compared to these accounts, Moore's lecture notes are much more comprehensive, often including whole topics that are missing from the student notes. Furthermore, both the Lee and Ambrose volumes involve substantial editorial reconstruction of the original student notes. This volume instead presents Moore's notes in their original form with very little editorial intervention. We have neither added words to Moore's original notes nor rearranged their order. This volume thus provides for the first time an almost verbatim record, in note form, of what Wittgenstein said in his seminal lectures of the early 1930s.⁵

Moore's notes also include a record of his own reactions to the lectures. In the margins and blank pages of his notebooks, Moore recorded a number of reactions to what Wittgenstein was saying. He also added some responses when he revisited the notes to prepare his *Mind* articles. Moreover, in one case, Moore actively contributed to a class by reading aloud a short essay he had written in response to Wittgenstein's use of the term 'grammar'. Moore's philosophically significant comments are reproduced as footnotes to this volume, and his essay on 'grammar' is included as an appendix.⁶

The remainder of this introduction is structured as follows. Moore's presence at Wittgenstein's lectures is placed in the context of their philosophical relationship in Section 2, which also provides information about

---

¹ Reprinted as chapter 6 of Wittgenstein 1993.
² See Section 5d of this introduction for a detailed comparison of Moore's published essay to his original notes.
³ Wittgenstein 1980.   ⁴ Wittgenstein 1979.
⁵ Section 3e of this introduction describes these student notes in further detail; Section 7 sets out our editorial policies.
⁶ See Section 5 of this introduction for further discussion of Moore's reactions to the lectures.

the character and atmosphere of the lectures. The chronology and main themes of the lectures are outlined in Section 3. Because these themes are also discussed in Wittgenstein's philosophical writings from that time, those writings are briefly described in Section 4. A survey of Moore's ways of responding to the lectures is provided in Section 5. Section 6 discusses the significance of Moore's lecture notes and how they contribute to a broader understanding of Wittgenstein's philosophy. Finally, Section 7 sets out the editorial policies that have been used in the production of this edition.

2. Wittgenstein and Moore in Cambridge

a. Moore and Wittgenstein, 1912–1929

G.E. Moore and Ludwig Wittgenstein became acquainted in 1912, not long after Wittgenstein had first arrived in Cambridge to study philosophy with Bertrand Russell. Moore, already one of the most distinguished philosophers in the country, soon came to feel that the undergraduate Wittgenstein was not only 'much cleverer at philosophy than I was' but also 'much more profound, and with a much better insight into the sort of inquiry which was really important and best worth pursuing, and into the best method of pursuing such inquiries'.[7] Moore must have formed this high opinion of Wittgenstein very quickly, for Russell wrote in a letter to Ottoline Morrell in March 1912 that 'Moore thinks enormously highly of Wittgenstein's brains – says he always feels W. *must* be right when they disagree. He says during his lectures W. always looks frightfully puzzled, but nobody else does.'[8] Russell reported that Wittgenstein also thought highly of Moore, having told him 'how much he loves Moore, how he likes and dislikes people for the way they think – Moore has one of the most beautiful smiles I know, and it had struck him'.[9]

In October 1912, Wittgenstein briefly attended Moore's psychology lectures, but 'expostulated violently', Moore recalled, because Moore was 'spending so much time in trying to find the meaning of and refute Ward's view that psychology differs from physics not in subject-matter but only in point of view. He said that what I ought to do was give my own views and not attack other people's. After that he ceased to attend my lectures but was quite friendly, coming to see me in my rooms and

---

[7] Moore 1968, 33. In Flowers 1999, 1 149; 2016, 1 153.   [8] Monk 1990, 42.
[9] Monk 1990, 42–3.

inviting me to his.'[10] Moore and Wittgenstein would meet at least twice a week, often for several hours, not only for philosophical conversations, but also to discuss music and poetry, two of the great loves of Moore's life. Moore 'had a pleasant tenor voice and would sing at length to Wittgenstein ... or they would perform chamber music together, Wittgenstein, as usual, whistling one part'.[11]

Founded in 1878, the Moral Sciences Club has been the principal venue for the discussion of philosophical papers at the University of Cambridge since the late nineteenth century. In November 1912, Wittgenstein won a vote that changed the rules of the Club in far-reaching ways. Moore was elected chairman, with the power to 'act as a kind of dictator at the Moral Sciences Club', as he put it upon first hearing of the plan.[12] Moore continued to serve in that role for most of the time until his resignation on grounds of poor health in 1944. Other changes implemented in 1912 included a rule that papers should be limited to seven minutes, and that there would be supplementary meetings, not open to those with an MA.

In early October 1913, Wittgenstein moved to Norway, to write up the results of his work with Russell and to continue his research undistracted. He had originally thought of moving to the far north of Norway, but after learning that the inn he had in mind would be closed for the winter, he chose to stay in Skjolden, a small village at the head of Sognefjord, the longest fjord in Norway. Early in 1914, Wittgenstein put a great deal of effort into persuading Moore to visit him. Eventually, and at the request of his Cambridge friends, Moore agreed to come.[13] He arrived towards the end of March 1914, and stayed for two weeks. While he was there, Wittgenstein dictated a series of notes, setting out his new ideas about logic, the distinction between showing and saying, and Russell's theory of types.[14] Wittgenstein asked Moore, on his return to Cambridge, to find out if he could submit the dictated manuscript as a BA thesis. Moore enquired, and wrote back that it would need to be supplemented with notes and a preface. Wittgenstein exploded at what he felt to be the absurdity and injustice of the thesis regulations, and sent Moore a violently angry letter.[15]

---

[10] McGuinness 1988, 141.   [11] McGuinness 1988, 142.   [12] McGuinness 1988, 143.
[13] Nedo 1993, 18. In Flowers 1999, 1 36; 2016, 1 38.
[14] 'Notes Dictated to Moore in Norway, April 1914'. In Wittgenstein 1979a, 108–19. See Monk 1990, 101–2; McGuinness 1988, 197–9.
[15] Wittgenstein 2012, 73. See Monk 1990, 103–4; McGuinness 1988, 199–202.

Moore was so deeply affected by Wittgenstein's outburst that he did not reply and avoided contact with him for the next fifteen years.

In August 1914, a few days after the outbreak of the First World War, Wittgenstein joined the Austrian army as a volunteer. During the next few years he not only continued his work on the ideas he had dictated to Moore that spring but also wrote on religion, ethics, the will, solipsism, and the self, among other topics, ultimately filling at least three notebooks. The book we now know as the *Tractatus* was completed in the summer of 1918. Near the end of the war, in early November, Wittgenstein was taken prisoner by the Italians. He was in the Monte Cassino prisoner-of-war camp from January 1919 to August 1919, when he was discharged. He returned home to Vienna, convinced that he would do no more philosophical work. After completing a teacher-training programme, he spent the first half of the 1920s teaching in small village schools in the region. In 1921 his *Logisch-philosophische Abhandlung* (Logico-Philosophical Treatise) was published in the final volume of Ostwald's journal *Annalen der Naturphilosophie*. It was translated into English, principally by Frank Ramsey, and published in 1922 as *Tractatus Logico-Philosophicus* – a title that had been proposed by Moore. Wittgenstein's career as a teacher ended in the spring of 1926; in the summer of that year, he began work as an architect on a house for his sister, Margarete Stonborough, a project that was to occupy him for the next two years.

In January 1929, three months before his fortieth birthday, Wittgenstein returned to Trinity College, Cambridge, after more than fifteen years away from the university and more than ten years away from full-time engagement in philosophy. By chance, Moore happened to be on the train from London to Cambridge which carried Wittgenstein on the final leg of his return journey. Thus Wittgenstein's relationships with Moore and with Cambridge were rekindled at the same time. Moore was to play an important role in this new phase in Wittgenstein's life.

As the author of the *Tractatus*, Wittgenstein returned to Cambridge as something of a philosophical celebrity. Officially, however, he was enrolled as an 'Advanced Student' reading for a PhD, with Frank Ramsey as his supervisor. Indeed, he and Ramsey met more than once a week for intense philosophical discussion. Moore later thought that the prospect of those conversations with Ramsey was a significant motive for Wittgenstein's return to Cambridge.[16]

---

[16] Wittgenstein 1993, 46.

By June 1929, Wittgenstein was running out of money, so Moore and Ramsey applied to Trinity College on his behalf for a grant. Ramsey wrote that he had been 'in close touch' with Wittgenstein's work, saying that Wittgenstein 'began with certain questions in the analysis of propositions which have now led him to problems about infinity which lie at the root of current controversies on the foundation of Mathematics'. Ramsey was impressed by Wittgenstein's progress and judged that 'he will probably do work of the first importance'.[17] On 18 June, Wittgenstein was awarded a PhD for the *Tractatus*; Moore and Russell had acted as Wittgenstein's examiners earlier that month. In his report, Moore described the thesis as a 'work of genius'.[18] The following day, Trinity awarded Wittgenstein a grant for the remainder of 1929.

In the months that followed, Wittgenstein showed clear signs that he wanted to engage a wider audience. In July 1929 he presented a paper on generality and infinity in mathematics to the annual meeting of the Mind Association and the Aristotelian Society in Nottingham.[19] In September, plans were announced for an introduction to Wittgenstein's philosophy, to be written by Friedrich Waismann.[20] In November, Wittgenstein read 'A Lecture on Ethics'[21] to a Cambridge society known as 'The Heretics'. In December, he had the first of a series of meetings with Moritz Schlick, the leader of the Vienna Circle, and Friedrich Waismann, at which Waismann took detailed notes that were later read to the Vienna Circle.[22] The meetings took place during the long breaks between Cambridge terms, which Wittgenstein usually spent with his family in Austria; the last of these meetings was in July 1932. In January 1930, he gave a short talk on 'Evidence for the Existence of Other Minds' to the Moral Sciences Club,[23]

---

[17] Quoted in Wittgenstein 1993, 48. [18] Monk 1990, 272.

[19] He had initially intended to present his paper 'Some Remarks on Logical Form', which was published in the conference proceedings (Wittgenstein 1993, 28 ff.), but rejected that paper almost as soon as he had submitted it.

[20] McGuinness 1979, 18. In Flowers 1999, 2 165; 2016, 1 452. The book began life as an exposition of the *Tractatus*, but as Waismann continued to work on it during the early 1930s, it developed into a book on Wittgenstein's subsequent ideas. See Baker 1979, Wittgenstein and Waismann 2003, and Schulte 2011.

[21] See Wittgenstein 1993, 36 ff., and Wittgenstein 2014.

[22] Waismann's notes are in Waismann 1979. The meetings began in 1927, but the first meeting of which we have a detailed record took place on 18 December 1929.

[23] Klagge 2003, 333.

and in May 1930, he gave a lecture on 'The Foundations of Mathematics' to the Trinity Mathematical Society.[24]

It is not surprising, then, that around this time Wittgenstein also formed the desire to give a regular lecture course at the university. In October 1929, the Moral Science Faculty – in accordance with Wittgenstein's wishes – invited him to present a course of lectures for the Lent term of 1930. When Richard Braithwaite conveyed this invitation and asked under what title the course should appear there was a long silence, after which Wittgenstein responded: 'The subject of the lectures would be philosophy. What else can be the title of the lectures but Philosophy.'[25] In future years, Wittgenstein's lectures were regularly listed under that title in the *Cambridge University Reporter*. In 1932–1933, he also gave lectures on topics in the philosophy of mathematics, under the title 'Philosophy for Mathematicians'.[26]

b. Wittgenstein and Moore, 1930–1933

On 17 January 1930, all those who wanted to attend Wittgenstein's first lecture course gathered in Braithwaite's rooms to agree on times for a weekly lecture and discussion class. It was decided that the lectures would take place from 5 to 6 p.m. on Mondays and that a discussion class would also be held from 5 to 7 p.m. on Thursdays. Both the lectures and discussion classes were initially held in an ordinary lecture room in the University Arts School. Shortly after the course began, Raymond Priestley offered his set of Fellows' rooms in Clare College for the discussion classes. According to Moore, the discussion classes lasted at least two hours, and after the lectures were moved from the Arts School to Wittgenstein's rooms in May 1931, they began to last at least as long as the discussion classes.[27]

---

[24] Klagge 2003, 362; Wittgenstein 2003, 373–4; Wittgenstein 2012, 186.
[25] Monk 1990, 289.
[26] Moore does not seem to have attended these lectures. All of his notes are from Wittgenstein's other lectures and discussion classes, although Wittgenstein did discuss topics in the philosophy of mathematics in them from time to time. See also Ambrose's notes for the 1932–1933 lectures on 'Philosophy for Mathematicians' in Wittgenstein 1979, 205–25; Young 1981, 63–4; Klagge 2003, 344–5; Wittgenstein 2012, 207.
[27] Wittgenstein 1993, 49. For further discussion of this move and its significance, see Section 3b.

Those who were present at Wittgenstein's lectures in the early 1930s included other Cambridge dons, graduate students, and undergraduates. Attendance at Wittgenstein's lectures during these years varied more than it did later on, as Wittgenstein had not yet adopted his later policy of insisting that only those who would attend regularly could take part. Some of the dons who attended Wittgenstein's lectures and classes for at least parts of the period covered by this volume – in addition to G.E. Moore – included I.A. Richards and Richard Braithwaite. Some of the students who attended the lectures and classes for at least parts of this period included Alice Ambrose, Julian Bell, S.K. Bose, Karl Britton, Maurice O'Connor (Con) Drury, A.C. Ewing, Reuben Goodstein, David Guest, John Inman, D.G. James, John King, Desmond Lee, Margaret Masterman, J.B. Nansen, A.J. Shillinglaw, Francis Skinner, C.L. Stevenson, Raymond Townsend, Harold Ursell, W.H. Watson, and L.C. Young.[28]

Wittgenstein's first lecture was scheduled for Monday, 20 January. Two days earlier, Wittgenstein had been sitting by Ramsey's hospital bed in Guy's Hospital in London; Ramsey died the following day on Sunday, 19 January, at the age of twenty-six. Wittgenstein's lecture went ahead the next day, as scheduled, nonetheless. Arthur MacIver, a student who was present, observed that Wittgenstein seemed terribly nervous.[29] Wittgenstein wrote in his diary later that day: 'Held my first regular lecture today: so, so. I think that it will go better next time. – if nothing unforeseen comes up.'[30] And indeed, MacIver observed in his diary that Wittgenstein's next lecture, one week later, did go better. Wittgenstein struck him as much more assured, although MacIver also had the impression that the lecture was completely without a plan, and that Wittgenstein was circling over the same ground as before. At this second lecture MacIver took a few notes, but in his diary, he wrote that notes from such a planless lecture could only be 'memoranda for private reflection', and that 'no genuine record' was possible of such a course of lectures.[31] This was a common theme among

---

[28] For further information about attendance at the lectures during these years, see Klagge 2003, 340 ff. It is not always clear exactly when a given person began to attend and when they stopped doing so within the general period.

[29] McGuinness 2016, 229.

[30] Translation from Klagge 2003, 341; Wittgenstein MS 107, 247. The Wittgenstein *Nachlass* is available in Wittgenstein 2000, which is currently being replaced by an online edition available at www.wittgensteinsource.org.

[31] McGuinness 2016, 232.

those who began attending Wittgenstein's lectures; Alice Ambrose recorded in her journal for her first term that 'I felt that I was hearing a lecture in which there were gaps, such as intermittent deafness might produce.'[32] Indeed, in the late 1930s and afterwards, Wittgenstein would usually begin the year by warning his students 'that we would find his lectures unsatisfactory, that he would go on talking like this for hours and hours and we would get very little out of it'.[33]

Despite these difficulties, Moore attended the lectures regularly and took extensive notes. Moore's assiduous note-taking was such a prominent feature of Wittgenstein's classes that it was even mentioned in I.A. Richards's description of the lectures in his poetic satire, 'The Strayed Poet'.[34] Moore later recalled that 'at the lectures, though not at the discussion classes, I took what I think were very full notes, scribbled in notebooks of which I have six volumes nearly full. I remember Wittgenstein once saying to me that he was glad I was taking notes, since, if anything were to happen to him, they would contain some record of the results of his thinking.'[35]

Throughout his teaching career, Wittgenstein used his lectures as an opportunity to engage in original and spontaneous philosophical investigation. The recollections of his students provide vivid descriptions of his approach to lecturing. Norman Malcolm, for example, recalled that his

> only preparation for the lecture ... was to spend a few minutes before the class met, recollecting the course that the inquiry had taken at the previous meetings. At the beginning of the lecture he would give a brief summary of this and then he would start from there, trying to advance the investigation with fresh thoughts. He told me that the only thing that made it possible for him to conduct his lecture classes in this extemporaneous way was the fact that he had done and was doing a vast amount of thinking and writing about all the problems under discussion. This is undoubtedly true; nevertheless, what occurred in these class meetings was largely *new* research.[36]

---

[32] Ambrose 1972, 13. In Flowers 1999, 2 263; 2016, 2 550.
[33] Gasking and Jackson 1951, 76. In Flowers 1999, 4 143; 2016, 2 1037.
[34] Quoted in Monk 1990, 290.   [35] Wittgenstein 1993, 49–50.
[36] Malcolm 1984, 23–4. In Flowers 1999, 3 60–1; 2016, 2 620. Malcolm first attended Wittgenstein's lectures in 1939, but his description also applies to Wittgenstein's methods as a lecturer in the early 1930s.

Desmond Lee, who attended Wittgenstein's lectures and discussion classes from 1930 to 1931, remembered the lectures as 'very informal', and

liable to break off into discussion. He had no kind of system or technique, but simply talked about problems that were in his mind, the method (in so far as there was any method) being entirely discursive, with constant refinements and clarifications – rather on the lines of *Philosophical Investigations*. The discussions were not so very dissimilar from the lectures ... Though Wittgenstein preferred discussion to lecture as being less formal and allowing a train of thought to be followed more easily, he completely dominated any discussion in which he took part, and these discussions associated with his lectures were largely a monologue, the problem being to find a question or problem to get him started and to provide an occasional interjection to keep him going.[37]

Thus, when Wittgenstein spoke of Moore's lecture notes as a 'record of the results of his thinking', he was referring, not only to his discussions of the latest topics he had been working on in his manuscripts, but equally to the new ideas that arose during his lecturing and in his discussion with members of the audience. Indeed, the open-ended and unscripted nature of Wittgenstein's lectures is one reason that Moore's thorough notes are so important.

Wittgenstein was particularly sensitive to who was in attendance, for members of the audience played a key role in the success or failure of the lectures. As G.H. von Wright recalled:

He had no manuscript or notes. He *thought* before the class. The impression was of a tremendous concentration. The exposition usually led to a question, to which the audience were supposed to suggest an answer. The answers in turn became starting points for new thoughts leading to new questions. It depended on the audience, to a great extent, whether the discussion became fruitful and whether the connecting thread was kept in sight from the beginning to end of a lecture and from one lecture to another.[38]

Wittgenstein especially depended on Moore in this way; Desmond Lee recalled that 'he relied on [Moore] a good deal to help in his discussion classes by making the comment that would set or keep the ball rolling'.[39] Moore was the audience member best able to appreciate Wittgenstein's

---

[37] Lee 1979, 214. In Flowers 1999, 2 191; 2016, 2 479–480.
[38] von Wright 1984, 15–16. In Flowers 1999, 1 73; 2016, 1 76–77. Like Malcolm, von Wright was not present at Wittgenstein's lectures in the early 1930s.
[39] Lee 1979, 218. In Flowers 1999, 2 195; 2016, 2 483.

efforts and help to move the discussion forward. Karl Britton, who attended Wittgenstein's discussion classes from November 1931 to May 1932, recalled that there was a general consensus among those in the room that Wittgenstein was primarily addressing himself to Moore:

> Moore used to come to these seminars: he occupied the only comfortable chair and was the only one permitted to smoke. We felt that Wittgenstein addressed himself chiefly to Moore, although Moore seldom intervened and often seemed to be very disapproving. Sometimes the lecturer appealed to him, but my recollection is that Moore's replies were usually very discouraging indeed. At all events we had the impression that a kind of dialogue was going on between Moore and Wittgenstein, even when Moore was least obviously being 'brought in'.[40]

Wittgenstein was glad that Moore was attending his classes; in April 1932 he expressed doubts to a friend that anyone else in the room understood him: 'My audience is rather poor – not in quantity but in quality. I'm sure they don't get anything from it and this rather worries me. Moore is still coming to my classes which is a comfort.'[41]

The lectures were often an intense experience for Wittgenstein and the attendees alike. Karl Britton's description of the atmosphere of these classes is probably the most detailed that we have:

> Wittgenstein spoke without notes but knew very well what he wanted to discuss and what he wanted to 'put across', though sometimes he seemed to change his mind on some point while he was speaking. Sometimes the proceedings began with a short paper in which one of the senior members would attempt to sum up the conclusions reached at the end of the previous meeting: and it was characteristic of the situation that Wittgenstein would be terribly dissatisfied with the statement produced. In discussion he would ask questions: and the one who volunteered an answer was liable to be his interlocutor throughout much of the two hours. On the whole, Wittgenstein was tremendously impatient in his discussion: not impatient of the raw newcomer to philosophy, but of the man who had developed philosophical views of his own. Wittgenstein talked often standing up and walking excitedly about – writing on the blackboard, pointing, hiding his face in his hands. But the most characteristic of all his attitudes was a very quiet, very intense stare – suddenly adopted and leading to a slow deliberate utterance of some new point. Very often he got thoroughly 'stuck': appealed in vain to his hearers to help him out: he would walk about in despair murmuring 'I'm a fool, I'm a fool'. And such

---

[40] Britton 1955, 1071. In Fann 1967, 56; Flowers 1999, 2 205; 2016, 2 491.
[41] Wittgenstein 2012, 203.

was the difficulty of the topics he discussed, that all this struggle did not seem to us to be in the least excessive.[42]

Alice Ambrose, who started attending Wittgenstein's lectures in October 1932, similarly recalled that 'Wittgenstein worked very hard in lectures, sometimes with perspiration streaming down his face, despite the fact that his small stove, in which for one term he burnt quite ineffective coke, gave off an imperceptible heat.'[43]

Wittgenstein's and Moore's philosophical relationship in the early 1930s was not limited to Moore's attendance at Wittgenstein's lectures and discussion classes. In 1930 Wittgenstein attended Moore's Saturday morning discussion classes; Drury noted at the time that this led 'to a very lively exchange between Moore and Wittgenstein'.[44] Moore was also chair of the Moral Sciences Club during these years. Wittgenstein frequently attended the Club's meetings from early in 1929 to the May term of 1931. Fania Pascal remembered Wittgenstein as 'the disturbing (perhaps disrupting) centre of those evenings. He would talk for long periods without interruption, using similes and allegories, stalking about the room and gesticulating. He cast a spell. The expression on Moore's face as he listened patiently and attentively was tolerant, impressed, but also questioning.'[45]

In a summary of his diary entries for 1929, Moore recorded that Wittgenstein visited him 'about once a week'[46] during term-time. It was these regular meetings which prompted Wittgenstein to reflect, in late 1930, on his relationship with Moore. In a diary entry for 7 October 1930 he wrote:

I have occasionally thought about my strange relationship with Moore. I respect him greatly & have a certain, not inconsiderable affection for him. He on the other hand? He esteems my intellect, my philosophical talent highly, that is, he believes that I am very clever but his affection toward me is probably *quite* inconsiderable ... I asked Moore today whether he is glad when I come to see him regularly (as in the previous year) & said that I will not be offended whatever the answer turns out to be. He said that it wasn't clear to himself, & I: he should think it over & inform me; which he promised to do.[47]

---

[42] Britton 1955, 1071. In Fann 1967, 56–7; Flowers 1999, 2 205–6; 2016, 2 491–492.
[43] Ambrose 1972, 15. In Flowers 1999, 2 265; 2016, 2 552.
[44] Drury 1984, 109. In Flowers 1999, 3 198; 2016, 2 786.
[45] Pascal 1979, 27 and Rhees 1984, 16. In Flowers 1999, 2 224–5; 2016, 2 511. The meetings Pascal attended were in 1930.
[46] Moore's diary notes for 1929.   [47] Wittgenstein 2003, 51–3.

Nine days later Moore gave a characteristically disarming and honest reply to Wittgenstein, which Wittgenstein duly recorded: 'Moore later answered my question to the effect that while he does not actually like me, my company nevertheless does him so much good that he thinks he should continue to keep it. That is a peculiar case.'[48] This candid exchange, however, did not end Moore and Wittgenstein's close friendship, or their regular meetings. In her memoir of Wittgenstein in 1932–1935, Ambrose recalled that Wittgenstein 'used Moore as a touchstone to test his own clarity of thought and exposition … he respected Moore greatly and had discussions with him at 86 Chesterton Road [Moore's home] once a week during term, on a day Moore specially set aside for him.'[49] Indeed, even in 'his final year as a professor Wittgenstein used to visit Moore about once every fortnight'.[50]

After the May term of 1933, Moore stopped attending Wittgenstein's lectures. After a few meetings of Wittgenstein's lecture class the following term, Wittgenstein decided that the class was too large, and that he was unable to go on lecturing as he had done before. Instead, he chose a small group of students to whom he would dictate what became known as the *Blue Book*; meetings took place twice a week, and the first instalment was dated 8 November.[51] Copies of this material were then provided to the larger group and formed the basis for discussion, marking a new stage in Wittgenstein's teaching at Cambridge.

3. Moore's notes on Wittgenstein's teaching, 1930–1933

a. Moore's lecture notes: a chronology

Moore took notes at each of Wittgenstein's regularly scheduled philosophy courses, between January 1930 and May 1933. Unlike what he wrote in his philosophical notebooks, Wittgenstein's lectures were explicitly intended to introduce his current way of thinking to people who were unfamiliar with it, many of whom were philosophical novices. In Moore's six manuscript notebooks, we have a remarkably careful and conscientious record of what Wittgenstein said at the time. As Moore himself put it in the introduction to his articles on the lectures, written twenty years later, he had 'tried to get down in my notes the actual words he used'.[52] These

---

[48] Wittgenstein 2003, 59. [49] Ambrose 1972, 14. In Flowers 1999, 2 263; 2016, 2 551.
[50] Malcolm 1984, 56. [51] See Smith 2013. [52] Wittgenstein 1993, 50.

notebooks provide us with both the most comprehensive and the most accurate record that we have of those first few crucial years of Wittgenstein's teaching in Cambridge and how he presented his developing thought to his students.

Moore later said of his notes that he thought they were 'very full',[53] and he did capture an enormous amount of what Wittgenstein said. But in order to achieve this he frequently had to use incomplete sentences, often writing in note form. We have not attempted to complete these partial sentences because one of the great values of these notes is the unmediated access they give us to what Moore wrote down at the time. This results in a text that in some places takes a little getting used to – especially in the initial lectures, where Moore is at his most telegraphic.

Any summary of Moore's notes on Wittgenstein's lectures is bound to be selective and inevitably calls for debatable decisions about what matters most. Nonetheless, we believe many readers will be helped by a sequential outline of the main themes of each lecture, and so we have provided a synoptic table of contents. Most of the entries are either quotations of key words and phrases from Moore's notes, or paraphrases of them.

When Moore later summarized the content of his three years of notes in a series of articles published in *Mind*, he divided the notes into three distinct groups. Group (I) contained his notes for the last two terms of the 1929–1930 academic year, Lent and May 1930.[54] Group (II) consisted of his notes for the 1930–1931 academic year, namely Michaelmas 1930, Lent 1931, and May 1931. Group (III) included his notes from the end of

---

[53] Wittgenstein 1993, 49.

[54] The three Cambridge University terms are arranged as follows: the academic year begins with Michaelmas Term (7 October to 5 December, during the years that Moore attended Wittgenstein's lectures), which is followed by Lent Term (approximately 14 January to 14 March), and then Easter Term (around 19 April to 10 June). However, Moore normally referred to Easter Term as May Term, and we follow him in this. While it was still a widely used alternative name in Moore's day, it has since become much rarer. The Michaelmas and Lent terms are sixty days long (eight weeks and four days), while the May term is ten days shorter (seven weeks and a day). Strictly speaking, these terms are known as 'full terms' and are only three-quarters of the length of the corresponding 'university terms', which start a little earlier and end a little later. As the full terms are the only units that concern us in what follows, we will ignore this distinction and simply talk of the three terms. Lectures are usually scheduled for the duration of each term, with the exception of the May term, in order to allow time for final examinations. Wittgenstein ordinarily taught for the first six weeks of the May term.

the 1931–1932 academic year, taken during May 1932, and those for the full 1932–1933 academic year: Michaelmas 1932, Lent 1933, and May 1933.[55]

Moore considered his way of organizing the material a natural one, but also one of some importance for his overall interpretation of the notes, as it provided a framework for his discussion of changes in the views he attributed to Wittgenstein. It is also a convenient structure for considering the broader context of the development of Wittgenstein's writing and teaching in the early 1930s.

Because the *Philosophical Remarks* is a careful selection of Wittgenstein's writing up to the spring of 1930, one can find passages in that book that cover many of the topics addressed in Wittgenstein's lectures for Group (I), often in strikingly similar ways. For the same reason, even though the source material for *The Big Typescript* was not completed until a year after the end of the period covered by the Group (II) lecture notes, there are extensive parallels between the issues discussed in the notes from Groups (II) and (III) and the material in that book.[56]

b. 1930–1931: Groups (I) and (II)

Wittgenstein usually gave eight weekly lectures during the first two terms of the academic year and six during the last, shorter, term. There was also a separate discussion class later in the week for each week that he lectured. During this period, Moore took notes at the hour-long lectures, but not the discussion classes, which normally lasted for two hours.

In the notes for Groups (I) and (II), the start of the notes for each lecture is frequently marked by a Roman numeral at the head of the page. For three of the first four terms (Lent 1930, Michaelmas 1930, and Lent 1931) the notes are numbered from one to eight.[57] The record for the May terms is not quite so well organized, but it is clear Moore was almost always present and taking notes.[58]

---

[55] For a discussion of the gap in Moore's notes between (II) and (III), see Section 3c.
[56] See Section 4 for further discussion of the relationship between these books and Wittgenstein's writing at the time.
[57] The only gap in Moore's record for these terms is for the fourth week of Lent 1930, when the lecture was rescheduled and folded into the discussion session. See 4:17 for further discussion.
[58] Those for May 1930 include at least five sets of lecture notes, and probably a sixth. There are five numbered lectures, namely the first four, and the sixth. However, Lecture 4 is

The lectures in Group (I) can be divided into two roughly equal halves. For most of the first seven lectures of the Lent term, Wittgenstein discussed topics in the philosophy of mind, philosophy of language, and philosophical logic, topics that he returned to in greater detail in Group (II). Halfway through Lecture 7, Wittgenstein began to talk about questions about the infinite, and for the remainder of that academic year, he focused on issues in the philosophy of mathematics and logic.

A central concern, not only in this first set of lectures, but throughout all three groups, is the difference between science and philosophy, and the particular character of Wittgenstein's own approach to philosophy. This is briefly touched on in the opening remarks to the first two lectures and discussed in much more detail in the first lecture of each of the first two terms of Group (II).[59]

Roughly speaking, the great majority of the lectures in Group (II) contain a more detailed exploration of some of the topics that had been outlined during the first half of Group (I). After the opening lecture of Group (II) on questions of method, Wittgenstein devoted most of the year to issues in the philosophy of mind and language arising out of the question 'What is a proposition?'. Both the notion of a grammatical system and the idea that a proposition is characterized by rules of grammar, play a leading role in the subsequent discussion.

Towards the end of the second academic year, Wittgenstein moved his lectures and classes to his rooms in Trinity College. Moore's summary notes for May Term, 1931, include the cryptic remark, 'New kind of lecture, May 4.' This is explained by John King, as follows: 'I well remember that Wittgenstein suddenly broke off his first lecture and turning to Professor Moore enquired whether it would be in order and acceptable to the authorities if in future we met in his rooms ... He had never liked the formality of the lecture room, and his manner and style were more suited to a more intimate and less conventional approach. Moore said he saw no objection to such a move, and thereafter we met in Wittgenstein's rooms.'[60] King recalled that after the move 'note-taking was not so easy,

---

roughly twice as long as the others, and there is a page break about halfway through, which probably marks the start of Lecture 5. See 4:66 for further discussion.

[59] See the second half of Section 6 for some further discussion of what Wittgenstein had to say about his philosophical method at the time.

[60] Letter from J.E. King to Desmond Lee. In Wittgenstein 1980, xii. King states that Wittgenstein's rooms at the time were at the top of Whewell's Court, but this is almost

and lecture and discussion tended to merge'.[61] Furthermore, after the first lecture of that term, Moore abandoned his practice of using Roman numerals at the start of each lecture. For the next year and a half he only dated some sets of notes, so it is not always possible to identify the start of each set of lecture notes for those terms.[62]

c. 1931–1932: after Group (II) and before Group (III)

There is a gap in Moore's tripartite scheme between the end of (II) and the beginning of (III), which corresponds to the first two and a half terms of the 1931–1932 academic year. When he wrote 'Wittgenstein's Lectures in 1930-33' in the early 1950s, Moore thought he must have stopped attending the lectures in Michaelmas 1931, 'for some reason which I cannot now remember'.[63] In fact, no lectures were listed under Wittgenstein's name in the *Cambridge University Reporter* that year. Wittgenstein had written a letter to Moore in August 1931, saying that he did not intend to give any formal lectures 'as I think I must reserve all my strength for my own work'.[64] Indeed, between July 1931 and May 1932, Wittgenstein went on to write over 750 pages, filling three large manuscript volumes. In the summer of 1932 he used those volumes to dictate material that was used in *The Big Typescript*.[65]

Nonetheless, Wittgenstein did hold an informal discussion class once a week during the 1931–1932 academic year. Moore attended the class, but did not take notes during the first two terms. In doing so, he was continuing his previous practice of taking notes in the lectures, but not the discussion classes. However, John King's notes from those terms make it clear that most of those classes covered broadly similar topics to those of the previous year.[66]

---

certainly a mistake. Moore, who kept a detailed diary, dated Wittgenstein's move to Whewell's Court to the start of Michaelmas Term, 1931 (Wittgenstein 1993, 49).

[61] Wittgenstein 1980, xii.
[62] For May 1931, the last term of Group (II), there are only three dates in the notes: 27 April, 4 May, and 1 June. King and Lee confirm that meetings for this term 'appear to have run from April 27th to June 1st' (Wittgenstein 1980, xvii). The intervening lectures are not numbered. However, if one counts each page break as indicating a new lecture, there are six sets of notes. See 6:6, 6:7, and 6:11 for further discussion.
[63] Wittgenstein 1993, 49. [64] Wittgenstein 2012, 193.
[65] For further discussion of Wittgenstein's writing at the time, see Section 4.
[66] Wittgenstein 1980, 65–108.

d. 1932–1933: Group (III)

As we have seen, Wittgenstein only held discussion classes during the 1931–1932 academic year. But on 13 May 1932, halfway through the May term, Moore began to take notes again and continued to do so for the remaining two meetings of that term.[67] It appears that by this point, Wittgenstein had moved away from the more open-ended discussion format that Britton described, as he was now discussing fairly technical topics in the philosophy of mathematics and setting out ideas that he must have worked out at some length beforehand. Substantial portions of the notes from those three classes during the second half of May closely parallel the discussions of inductive proof, periodicity, and the infinite in the last two chapters of *The Big Typescript*.[68] These were still discussion classes, inasmuch as they were informal meetings that were not part of the official University lecture list. However, the notes make it clear that Wittgenstein was presenting technical material in a format that must have required extensive board work, so it is easy to see why Moore thought, twenty years later, that he had 'resumed the practice of attending the lectures'.[69]

Moore's last year's worth of lecture notes are considerably longer than those from the previous three academic years put together.[70] While the notes for each meeting are often longer and more detailed, the principal reason we have so many more notes from this stage of Wittgenstein's teaching is that towards the end of Michaelmas 1932, Moore began to take notes during both of the weekly class meetings.[71] By this point it looks as if there was no longer a clear distinction between lectures and discussion

---

[67] Wittgenstein's diaries show that he taught six Friday afternoon classes that term; Moore's notes are for the last three.

[68] Detailed references are provided in the footnotes to those lectures.

[69] Wittgenstein 1993, 49.

[70] The notes for the first five and a half terms take up about 33,000 words, for an average of a little under 1,000 words per lecture. The notes for the last three terms run to about 46,700 words. The notes from the end of Michaelmas 1932 average 1,160 words for each date; for Lent and May 1933, the figure is a little over 1,280 words a meeting.

[71] In Moore's essay on Wittgenstein's lectures, he stated that he only took notes at the lectures, but not the discussion classes (see Wittgenstein 1993, 49). This is clearly true of Groups (I) and (II), but the dating, quantity, and sheer number of separate sets of notes from the 1932–1933 academic year show that he did take notes during all, or almost all, of the dates when discussion classes were scheduled in Group (III) after the middle of the Michaelmas term.

classes, as there seem to have been comparably detailed lectures during both of each week's scheduled meetings. It is difficult to say which of the twice-weekly notes from mid-November 1932 to May 1933 may have come from a discussion class, rather than a lecture, as the great majority of these sets of notes are longer than most of those from previous years.

There are no dates or indicators of breaks between sets of notes from a single day's lectures for the first half of Michaelmas 1932; they are followed by six sets of notes, including notes from both the Mondays and Fridays of the second half of November.[72] It seems likely that Moore only took notes at the first class meeting of the week for the first part of the Michaelmas term and returned to dating his notes when he began taking notes at both meetings each week.[73] In our numbering of the lectures, we assign an Arabic numeral to each week of the term. When Moore took notes in just one class in a given week, that set of notes is assigned the appropriate Arabic numeral. However, when Moore took notes at both meetings in a given week, we append an 'a' or 'b' to the week's Arabic numeral, to distinguish the two classes. For the last two terms of that year, Moore continued this practice of dating each set of lecture notes. We have sixteen sets of notes for Lent 1933,[74] and twelve for May 1933.[75]

The topics covered in Group (III) are considerably more diverse and wide-ranging than those of previous lecture courses. To some extent, these changes may be due to a shift in Wittgenstein's approach to teaching, already signalled by the 'new kind of lecture' that Moore noted after the move to the more informal setting of Wittgenstein's rooms the previous spring. The dwindling distinction between lectures and discussion classes may also have played a part, in that instead of lecturing for an hour a week Wittgenstein was now teaching twice a week for two hours or more. In addition, Moore had also become more experienced at taking notes under these circumstances and more familiar with Wittgenstein's methods of teaching.

---

[72] 7, 14, 18, 21, 25, and 28 November. Moore clearly dated the start of each of the last five sets of notes; the first set of notes probably dates from 7 November, but alternative hypotheses cannot be ruled out. See the footnote to the start of Lecture 5 for further discussion of dating.

[73] The five dated sessions from the end of the term take up about 5,800 words; the undated material that precedes it is roughly the same length, which suggests that we probably have notes for about five of the other eleven meetings that term.

[74] The notes cover each Friday and Monday from Friday, 20 January to Monday, 13 March.

[75] The notes are from Friday, 21 April to Monday, 29 May.

As he had done at the start of the previous lecture series, Wittgenstein discussed a variety of issues in the philosophy of mind, philosophy of language, and philosophical logic in Michaelmas 1932. Some of the topics are familiar, such as his treatment of different conceptions of meaning, definition, and propositions, and his discussion of tautologies and rules of inference. However, he also discussed topics at length that he had only mentioned in the past, including questions about the difference between mere bodily motion and action, and an extended exploration of the distinction between reasons and causes. The last two lectures of the term are devoted to a critique of Russell and the *Tractatus* on generality.

During the first three weeks of Lent 1933, Wittgenstein discussed the philosophy of mathematics. Beginning from the idea that the proof of a mathematical theorem alters the rules of grammar, he concentrated on questions about proof. Wittgenstein returned to the *Tractatus* during the fourth week, when he focused on the Tractarian conception of logical analysis and atomic propositions. After a brief discussion of the philosophy of time, he devoted most of the rest of the term to a new set of closely related topics in the philosophy of mind: questions about inner experience, privacy, the visual field, the meaning of 'I', idealism, and solipsism.

The notes for May 1933 begin with a discussion of meaning and verification, symptoms and criteria, grammar, rules and use. The lectures for the last five weeks include wide-ranging discussions of topics in the philosophy of religion, ethics, aesthetics, and psychoanalysis. Wittgenstein did not write much on these topics elsewhere, and these lectures are often more nuanced, careful, and detailed than what he did write. That term is also notable for the unusually detailed discussions of Freud, Darwin, and Frazer, and in particular, Wittgenstein's critique of certain presuppositions at work in Freud's psychoanalysis, Darwin's theory of emotion, and Frazer's anthropology, which in turn inform broader reflections on the relationship between science and philosophy.

e. Moore's lecture notes compared with the lecture notes taken by students

Moore was not the only note-taker at Wittgenstein's lectures in the early 1930s. Desmond Lee took notes from January 1930 to June 1931; John King took notes from October 1930 to May 1932. Alice Ambrose took notes starting in October 1932 up to the end of May Term, 1935. Almost fifty years later, Lee and Ambrose each edited volumes based on their respective sets of lecture notes. Lee not only made use of King's more extensive notes, but also much shorter notes taken by R.D. Townsend and John Inman.[76]

While both Lee's and Ambrose's published versions of their notes are in roughly chronological order, those editions clearly involve substantial editorial reconstruction, selection, and rearrangement. Where it is possible to compare the record for specific lectures, Moore's contemporaneous notes are much more detailed, and often significantly different. For instance, King and Lee's published lecture notes for Lent 1930 are less than two-thirds the length of Moore's, even though King and Lee include a few extra notes from later discussions and expand their notes into complete sentences, while Moore's are often telegraphic and compressed. For May Term, 1930, Lee only took notes for three meetings, whereas Moore's cover at least five. If we compare just the three lectures at which Lee was present, Moore's notes are over twice as long. Similarly, the King and Lee coverage of the 1930–1931 academic year is about two-thirds the length of Moore's notes for that period.[77] If one compares the unpublished student notes from 1930–1931 with the published texts, it is striking how much difference there is between the telegraphically worded notes and the polished published version, with all the gaps filled in. Perhaps the most striking difference of all, however, is that the published version of Ambrose's notes for the 1932–1933 academic year is much less than half the length of Moore's notes for that period, over 30,000 words less than Moore's 48,000.[78] Moore's notes are not simply more detailed than the published student notes for those years; rather, Moore's notes contain whole discussions that cannot be found in the current editions of Wittgenstein's lectures from the early 1930s.

---

[76] All the notes for the 1930–1932 volume have been given to the Wren Library, Trinity College. Ambrose's notes appear to have been sold to a private buyer, and no information about their current location is readily available.

[77] Moore's notes for the first two academic years amount to roughly 30,000 words; the published student notes from that period are just over 18,000 words long.

[78] Wittgenstein 1979, 3–40. Moore's notes for the last three terms he attended cover more class meetings than those for the first five terms combined, because he began taking notes at not only the lectures, but also in the discussion classes that were held later each week. They are also, on average, longer and more detailed than those for the first two years. There are about 47,000 words in Moore's notes for that final year, compared to just under 18,000 words in the published student notes.

In addition to being longer and more comprehensive, Moore's notes are probably almost always more accurate. For a number of reasons, he was in the position to best understand the lectures. First, unlike any of the other note-takers, Moore had a long-standing personal relationship with Wittgenstein, and they shared a significant philosophical history. Second, Moore was a mature and experienced professor of philosophy, while the other note-takers were still students: King and Lee were undergraduates, while Ambrose, who had earned her first PhD at the University of Wisconsin in 1932, was working on a second PhD with Moore and Wittgenstein. Third – and closely related to the previous two points – Wittgenstein seems to have directed the lectures specifically at Moore.[79]

As well as being significantly redacted, the published student notes of these lectures have sometimes also been heavily edited, rearranged, and tidied up. Lee and Ambrose take a very free approach to their source material, extensively rearranging, modifying, and selecting from it in order to provide as readable a version as possible. Cora Diamond's edition of *Wittgenstein's Lectures on the Foundations of Mathematics, Cambridge 1939*, which is based on four sets of notes, adopts a similar editorial policy.[80] This is certainly one effective way of collating multiple sets of notes, or of turning a rough set of notes into a readable text (though see Geach 1988 for an alternative method). However, using this editorially heavy-handed method leaves the reader in the dark regarding which words and passages were taken down at the time and which were reconstructed many years later, with no indication as to where material judged to be repetitive was left out or consolidated, or indeed, when material had actually been added during editing to smooth out the final reading. As Diamond concedes with disarming honesty in her editorial introduction, 'choices had to be made with no adequate basis in any version'.[81] Publishing Moore's notes in their original form allows us to avoid these problems.[82]

f. Moore's lecture notes as a publication of Wittgenstein's

In his memoir of Wittgenstein, Norman Malcolm reported that Wittgenstein was furious with those who said that he kept his post-*Tractatus*

---

[79] For further discussion of Moore's relationship to Wittgenstein at the time, and his role in the lectures, see Section 2b.
[80] Wittgenstein 1976.   [81] Wittgenstein 1976, 8.
[82] See Section 7 for further discussion of our editorial policies.

philosophy secret, for 'he had always regarded his lectures as a form of publication'.[83] It may be thought that Wittgenstein was thinking primarily of the *Blue Book*, dictated during the 1933–1934 academic year, and the *Brown Book*, which dates from the following year, both of which circulated privately, in mimeograph or typescript copies, and were widely read by British philosophers in the years before, and immediately after, the publication of the *Philosophical Investigations*. However, it seems clear that Wittgenstein did in fact consider all of his lectures to be a form of publication. He told Casimir Lewy 'that "to publish" means "to make public", and that therefore lecturing is a form of publication'.[84] Moore's notes are, therefore, the closest thing that we have to an authorized record of these earliest 'publications' of Wittgenstein's later period – his 1930–1933 lectures.

4. Wittgenstein's philosophical writings, 1929–1933

In order to appreciate the value of Moore's notes of Wittgenstein 1930–1933 lectures, it is helpful to consider the other records of Wittgenstein's thought from that period – and in particular Wittgenstein's writings. Wittgenstein returned to philosophical writing when he came back to Cambridge in 1929. The next few years were a time of transition between his early and his later work, and are of great interest for anyone who wants to understand the development of his thought. The manuscripts from 1929 record his first steps away from the *Tractatus*; by the end of 1936, he was at work on an early version of the *Philosophical Investigations*. Wittgenstein was a prolific writer during these years, and many, though not all, of the topics discussed in Moore's lecture notes are also discussed at length in his philosophical writings from those years.

On 2 February 1929, Wittgenstein began writing – in the first of a series of large, hard-bound manuscript volumes – a sequential record of selected work in progress, often culled from smaller first-draft notebooks. Wittgenstein's principal posthumous publications from the early 1930s, the *Philosophical Remarks*, *The Big Typescript*, and *Philosophical Grammar*, were constructed by selecting, and then rearranging and revising, material taken from these volumes, and also involve a substantial editorial contribution.[85]

---

[83] Malcolm 1984, 48.   [84] Lewy 1976, xi, note 1.
[85] For further discussion of how Wittgenstein's editors have shaped perceptions of his writing, and the construction of the books published under his name after his death, see Kenny 1976 and 2005, Hintikka 1991, and Stern 1996.

As almost all of Wittgenstein's manuscript volume entries from these years and Moore's lecture notes can be precisely dated, it is possible to systematically compare and draw connections between what he said in his lectures and what he wrote at the time.[86] Indeed, the connections between his lectures and his writings at the time and in later years are so extensive, and far-reaching, that we only provide a very brief summary of this relationship here.

With the exception of some writing from the mid-1930s, around the time when he was working on *The Blue and Brown Books* and shortly afterwards, Wittgenstein almost always wrote in German. There are some notes in English in his *Nachlass*, the papers that he left to his literary executors, that appear to have been written in preparation for lectures; the most extensive of these date from the 1935–1936 academic year.[87] A handful of similar remarks date from 1931,[88] but no one remembers his making use of notes at any of his university lectures.

The sequence of manuscript volumes that Wittgenstein began in February 1929 continued through eighteen such volumes, until 1940. From the first, this writing usually took the form of 'Bemerkungen', a term usually translated as 'remarks'. These could be as short as a single sentence, or as long as a sequence of paragraphs stretching over several pages. The beginning and end of each remark was marked by a blank line separating it from its neighbours. Most of the volumes of remarks from 1929 and the early 1930s are a sequential, dated record of remarks, many of which were first composed in smaller notebooks.

The manuscript volumes played a number of different roles in Wittgenstein's philosophical writing. First of all, they served as a diary-like record of new work. Later on, he used the manuscript volumes to rewrite, rearrange, or criticize his own earlier work. The manuscript volumes also served as a source from which he would select remarks that he would dictate to a typist, thus yielding several carbon copies of a chronologically ordered typescript, one of which could then be cut up,

---

[86] Thanks to the detailed indexes to the *Philosophical Remarks* (Wittgenstein 1964) and *The Big Typescript* (Wittgenstein 2005) in the Vienna edition of Wittgenstein's writing from this period (Wittgenstein 1993–), it is very easy to date each of the remarks in those books and track any given remark's context in the source manuscripts.

[87] Wittgenstein 1993, chapter 10.

[88] See MS 155, 36v–38r (quoted in Wittgenstein 1993–, vol. 3, vii), Klagge 2003, 343, and also MS 155, 39v–42r, 84v–85r; MS 153b, 5r, 30r, and 38r.

rearranged, and retyped to produce a topically organized draft. The typescript that was later cut and rearranged to yield the book we now know as the *Philosophical Remarks* was produced in this way while Wittgenstein was in Vienna in March and April 1930, drawing on the first three volumes and part of the fourth, during the break between the Lent and May terms in 1930.[89]

The rationale for the rapid production of this typescript of selections from his work up to that point was that Wittgenstein had spent almost all of the grant Trinity had awarded him in the summer of 1929, and evidence of progress was needed if a case was to be made for renewed support. To this end, Moore wrote to Russell in March 1930, asking Russell to look at Wittgenstein's recent work, and Russell reluctantly agreed to take on this responsibility. Wittgenstein visited Russell in mid-March, and again in late April, when he gave Russell a copy of the typescript he had just dictated. Over these two visits they spent a total of five days in discussion during which Wittgenstein 'explained his ideas'.[90] Russell wrote a letter of support to the Council of Trinity College in May 1930, which, supplemented by a letter from J.E. Littlewood, secured a further short-term grant.[91] Russell reported that the typescript 'would have been very difficult to understand without the help of the conversations'.[92] Russell emphasized the role of the notions of space, grammar, and nonsense in Wittgenstein's new philosophy, and also the extent of Wittgenstein's new work on the philosophy of mathematics, including his work on infinity, possibility, and mathematical induction. Russell concluded:

The theories contained in this new work of Wittgenstein's are novel, very original, and indubitably important. Whether they are true, I don't know. As a logician who likes simplicity, I should wish to think that they are not, but from what I have read of them I am quite sure that he ought to have an opportunity to work them out, since when completed they may easily prove to constitute a whole new philosophy.[93]

---

[89] The source typescript, selected and dictated from over 800 pages of writing in the manuscript volumes, is TS 208 in von Wright's catalogue of the Wittgenstein papers. The *Philosophical Remarks* (Wittgenstein 1964), the topical rearrangement of that chronological record, is TS 209. TS 210, dictated from the remainder of volume four, was produced shortly afterward. All of this material is available in the Bergen Electronic Edition (Wittgenstein 2000); much of it has also been published in the Vienna edition of Wittgenstein's writing from the early 1930s (Wittgenstein 1993–).
[90] Wittgenstein 2012, 183.   [91] Wittgenstein 2012, 187.   [92] Wittgenstein 2012, 183.
[93] Wittgenstein 2012, 183.

Subsequently, Wittgenstein cut up a carbon copy of the typescript and glued a selection of those remarks into a large office minute book. In December, that volume, the *Philosophical Remarks*, served as a fellowship dissertation, resulting in a five-year fellowship from Trinity College, which was ultimately extended to the end of the 1935–1936 academic year. G.H. Hardy and J.E. Littlewood, the two leading mathematicians in Britain at the time, served as dissertation examiners in addition to Russell.

Wittgenstein made no further use of the selection of remarks from his first three and a half manuscript volumes after it had served its purpose in securing his fellowship. He gave his copy of the *Philosophical Remarks* to Moore.[94] In the following year, Wittgenstein continued writing new remarks in the manuscript volumes at a similar, if slightly slower, pace. Between August 1930 and July 1931 he completed the fifth and sixth manuscript volumes. In the summer of 1931 he began work on a similar typescript of selections from these new remarks.

However, Wittgenstein had retained copies of the source typescript for the *Philosophical Remarks* that he had dictated during the spring break of 1930. In the next stage of his work, during the summer of 1931 and most of the 1931–1932 academic year, he returned to that typescript, a chronologically ordered selection from the material he had written in 1929 and early 1930. In this 'Wiederaufnahme',[95] or 'resumption' of his remarks in volumes seven to ten, Wittgenstein carefully worked his way through the first three-quarters of that typescript, in effect providing a remarkably close re-reading of his own writing from 1929. Wittgenstein quoted extensively from the typescript, often writing passages word for word, sometimes pasting in fragments cut from a copy of the typescript. In other places, he revised as he rewrote, and often engaged in running commentary or criticism.

In the summer of 1932, Wittgenstein once again dictated selected passages from his recent philosophical writing, adding to the typescript he had begun the previous summer. Drawing on the complete set of typescripts from his first ten manuscript volumes, Wittgenstein cut them up and rearranged them by topic. Although the book we now know as *The*

---

[94] Moore passed it on to Wittgenstein's literary executors after Wittgenstein's death.
[95] The German term is Wolfgang Kienzler's, who has written an extensive study of this stage of Wittgenstein's work (1997, chapter 2, briefly summarized in Kienzler 2001). The English translation is Joachim Schulte's (1998, 380), which seems preferable to Kienzler's own term, 'second staging' (2001, 127). See also Paul 2007, 158 ff.

Big Typescript was not actually typed up until the summer of 1933, by dictation from that collection of cuttings, almost all the remarks in it had been composed by the end of the 1931–1932 academic year. Almost immediately, Wittgenstein began to write additions and revisions on that typescript, and to plan more than one far-reaching rearrangement and rewriting of the opening chapters of that book, ultimately published as *Philosophical Grammar*.

While the *Philosophical Remarks*, *The Big Typescript*, and *Philosophical Grammar* are carefully composed, they never reached a polished and final form, and are too dense and intricate to be easily accessible. In fact, all three of these books are best understood as works in progress that were never completed, or as selections and rearrangements from the source manuscripts. On the other hand, Wittgenstein's Cambridge lectures during those years were given with the intention of engaging an audience in a setting where very little could be taken for granted, and where most of those present were philosophical novices. We might expect, therefore, that an accurate record of those lectures would be an extremely valuable introduction to his thought at the time.

5. Moore's responses to Wittgenstein's lectures, 1930–1955

Moore's notes of Wittgenstein's Cambridge lectures are valuable for their thoroughness and accuracy. However, Moore was far more than merely an accurate note-taker. He was a colleague of Wittgenstein's who had his own philosophical reactions to the ideas that Wittgenstein was developing. His notes also contain many of Moore's responses to the content of Wittgenstein's lectures. Moore's comments are recorded in a number of places, often intimately interwoven with the notes themselves.

a. Moore's comments and markings alongside the lecture notes

Even in the course of transcribing Wittgenstein's lectures into the six manuscript volumes, Moore was not simply an amanuensis or a recorder of Wittgenstein's words. In addition to lecture transcriptions, Moore's notes also sometimes include his own reactions, questions, and clarifications. Comments that are clearly in Moore's own voice rather than in Wittgenstein's can be found throughout the lecture notes. For the most part, Moore wrote his lecture notes on the right-hand pages in his notebooks. The left-hand page was left blank, giving him space for occasional remarks of his own. Occasionally he speculated about what Wittgenstein meant by a given remark, or tried to give a concrete example of a more abstract point of Wittgenstein's. Sometimes he noted where he thought Wittgenstein had made a mistake or gone wrong. These comments and markings provide some record of Moore's initial response to Wittgenstein's later thought at its early stages of development.

In addition to brief verbal remarks, Moore also marked his notes in other ways. He indicated words or passages that had attracted his attention with underlining and crosses in the margin. He often put question marks next to phrases or passages that he thought mistaken, did not understand, or could no longer read. He added page numbers indicating cross-references to related passages and drew lines to bring out connections. He carefully wrote out words that were barely legible.

In these comments and markings, we have a record of two sets of distinct interactions on Moore's part with his lecture notes. The first set indicates Moore's immediate reactions to Wittgenstein's lectures and gives us some insight into what Moore was thinking at the time. The later additions show him organizing and cross-referencing the notes. The first was contemporaneous with the lectures themselves, and can be found in the short comments, clarifications, and criticisms Moore added either during the lectures or shortly after. The second occurred twenty years later, when Moore revisited his notes in order to work on his articles for *Mind*, and in so doing, added further responses in the form of comments, underlining, and markings of various kinds. On occasion, we see the later Moore struggling to recall or work out what Wittgenstein had said twenty years earlier. Thus, the notes include contributions from three authors, as it were: principally Wittgenstein in the early 1930s, but also Moore in the early 1930s and Moore in the early 1950s.

It is sometimes difficult to tell when these comments and markings were made, but they can often be dated by means of the handwriting and the medium. Those comments and markings that are in precisely the same thickness of pencil, and same style of writing, as the lecture notes on that page, were almost certainly made during the lecture. Some more reflective comments may have been made shortly after Moore got home from the lecture, or after a follow-up conversation with Wittgenstein a few days later. Other comments and markings, such as those written in ink, or in a much more shaky hand, were certainly made two decades later – in the early 1950s – when Moore was re-reading his old notes in preparation for his *Mind* articles.[96]

b. Moore's summary notes

Before writing the articles for *Mind* in which he tried to summarize his lecture notes, Moore first wrote over a hundred densely packed pages of remarkably detailed and painstaking 'summary notes'. These appear to be the product of two successive re-readings of the entire set of lecture notes. One set of summary notes contains Moore's quotations and paraphrases of every passage in the notes that caught his attention as he worked on his articles; a second set is more selective, concentrating on those remarks that have a bearing on Wittgenstein's conception of grammar. These summary notes attest to the remarkably thorough and conscientious approach that Moore took to the project of sifting through his lecture notes for posterity. For the most part, they set out key points in Moore's record of what Wittgenstein said, either word for word, or in a very close paraphrase. Occasionally, Moore's 'summaries' are particularly interesting, either because his summary brings out points that are not explicitly present in the source material, or we see Moore articulating a critical response to Wittgenstein. These selections are included in the footnotes, preceded by the phrase 'Moore's summary notes'.

c. Moore's paper for Wittgenstein's discussion class

Some of the meetings at Wittgenstein's discussion classes during 1931–1932 began with a short paper by one of the senior members.[97] In February 1932, Moore took on this role. His paper, on Wittgenstein's use of the expression 'rules of grammar', is included as an appendix to this volume.[98] Moore was initially scheduled to give a short talk in the class on Friday, 19 February. The class had to be cancelled, and the talk was

---

[96] In Section 7b we discuss our editorial policies concerning these additions of Moore's to his lecture notes.

[97] Britton 1955, 1071. In Fann 1967, 56 and Flowers 1999, 2 205; 2016, 2 491. Quoted above (in Section 2b).

[98] The manuscript is part of Cambridge University Library's collection of Moore's papers, and was first published as 'Wittgenstein's Expression "Rule of Grammar" or "Grammatical Rule"' (Moore 2007).

postponed to the following week. In a letter from Wittgenstein to Moore, dated Monday, 22 February, he wrote: 'I look forward to hearing you on Friday. I'm sorry I wasn't well enough to hold my class last Friday.'[99] Moore presented a short paper which he later summarized as follows:

> I did not understand how he was using the expression 'rule of grammar' and gave reasons for thinking he was not using it in its ordinary sense; but he, though he expressed approval of my paper, insisted at that time that he was using the expression in its ordinary sense ... I still think that he was not using the expression 'rules of grammar' in any ordinary sense, and I am still unable to form any clear idea as to how he was using it.[100]

Moore's drafts of this essay can be found on seven pages of manuscript notes in his papers, catalogued under the title 'Wittgenstein's use of "grammar"'. The first five pages, the 'revised version', are a heavily revised draft of the text of Moore's talk, rewritten in the week provided by the cancelled class; the last two pages are the conclusion of an earlier version of the talk, which had been drafted in time for the cancelled class meeting on 19 February.

Moore did not record Wittgenstein's response in the discussion class, although in his diary he noted that 'In February am writing paper for Wittgenstein, which he praises on March 1.'[101] However, John King did take notes in the class, and we have included both the original text of his notes for that day, and the edited version of those notes produced by Desmond Lee, immediately after the text of Moore's paper.

d. Moore's essay on Wittgenstein's lectures

Moore's best-known philosophical responses to Wittgenstein's lectures are contained in the series of articles that he published in *Mind* in 1954 and 1955 – a few years after Wittgenstein died – based on the notes he had taken.[102] These articles take the form of an overall summary and analysis of the development of Wittgenstein's views on a number of topics during the course of the 1930–1933 lectures. However, they provide relatively little

---

[99] Wittgenstein 1995, 253. We follow Rothhaupt's reconstruction of this episode; see Rothhaupt 2007, which also discusses the manuscript's historical, biographical, and philosophical context.
[100] Wittgenstein 1993, 69.   [101] Moore's diary extracts, Add. 8330.1.5.
[102] Wittgenstein 1993, 45–114.

direct quotation from Moore's notes and are rather selective in the topics that they cover. Moore's essay is primarily an expository and critical analysis of what he understood Wittgenstein to be saying in his lectures, rather than a direct report of what Wittgenstein said. Furthermore, these discussions of Wittgenstein's lectures provide rather more coverage of the earlier lectures than they do of the last year that Moore attended, despite the fact that almost two-thirds of his original notes are from that latter period. Not counting the opening pages of Moore's first piece for *Mind*, which provide some historical background, the published articles comprise a little over 30,000 words of summary and analysis, while the original lecture notes contain approximately 80,000 words and over sixty diagrams and illustrations. Indeed, Moore repeatedly warned the readers of his *Mind* articles that he could not 'possibly mention nearly everything, and it is possible that some of the things I omit were really more important than those I mention'.[103]

Thus, while Moore's *Mind* articles do not give readers direct access to his notes of Wittgenstein's lectures, they do an extraordinary job of organizing and systematizing Wittgenstein's sprawling discussions. In addition to systematizing, Moore also tracks the development of Wittgenstein's positions on various matters and the use of some of his technical terminology. Moreover, Moore often offers his own views on what Wittgenstein said. Sometimes he points out inconsistencies or peculiarities in Wittgenstein's claims, or points out where he thinks that Wittgenstein was incorrect. Sometimes he expresses doubt as to whether he understood what Wittgenstein was trying to say, and sometimes he even tries to make seemingly implausible claims of Wittgenstein's more plausible by offering possible interpretations of what Wittgenstein may have meant.

The articles give a palpable sense of Moore puzzling through Wittgenstein's developing thought.[104] Moore's magisterial survey of his notes deserves to be read carefully by anyone interested in Wittgenstein's lectures during those years. The publication of Moore's original notes in this volume should not be regarded as a replacement for Moore's essay. In fact, there is surprisingly little overlap between the two. While Moore does of course quote from his notes in the essay, for the most part Moore's essay

[103] Wittgenstein 1993, 50. See also Wittgenstein 1993, 92 and 110.
[104] Some of the entries in Moore's *Commonplace Book* also show him grappling with various of Wittgenstein's later ideas during the period from the late 1930s to the early 1950s. See Moore 1962, under index entry for 'Wittgenstein, L.'.

is analytic and synoptic, and takes the form of a critical exposition and evaluation of the central ideas that he attributes to Wittgenstein during those years.

6. The significance of Moore's notes on Wittgenstein's lectures

In his essay on Wittgenstein's lectures, Moore began his summary of the 'chief topics' as follows:

First of all, in all three periods he dealt (A) [pp. 51–87][105] with some very general questions about language, (B) [pp. 87–92] with some special questions in the philosophy of Logic, and (C) [pp. 92–97] with some special questions in the philosophy of Mathematics.[106]

Moore then indicated what he considered to be the principal new topics in the final year:

Next, in (III) and in (III) alone, he dealt at great length, (D) [pp. 97–103] with the difference between the proposition which is expressed by the words 'I have got tooth-ache', and those which are expressed by the words 'You have got tooth-ache' or 'He has got tooth-ache', in which connexion he said something about Behaviourism, Solipsism, Idealism and Realism, and (E) [pp. 103–108] with what he called 'the grammar of the word "God" and of ethical and aesthetic statements'.[107]

Finally, Moore touched on a few significant topics which did not fit neatly into this overall scheme:

And he also dealt, more shortly, in (I) with (F) [pp. 108–109] our use of the term 'primary colour'; in (III) with (G) [pp. 109–112] some questions about Time; and in both (II) and (III) with (H) [pp. 113–114] the kind of investigation in which he was himself engaged, and its difference from and relation to what has traditionally been called 'philosophy'.[108]

Moore uses this framework to develop a detailed survey and summary of the main views, and changes of view, that he attributes to Wittgenstein over the course of these lectures. This topical organization provides the overarching structure within which Moore quotes from, summarizes, and reviews his lecture notes in the remainder of the essay. In constructing his

---

[105] Page numbers in square brackets are our additions, indicating the pages in Moore's essay (in the Wittgenstein 1993 reprint) where those topics are discussed in further detail.
[106] Wittgenstein 1993, 50.   [107] Wittgenstein 1993, 50.   [108] Wittgenstein 1993, 50.

discussion of Wittgenstein's lectures in this way, Moore gives the leading role to, as he puts it, 'some very general questions about language', which not only come first, but occupy well over half his essay. Moore begins this part of his essay by emphasizing that Wittgenstein said more than once that he did not regard language as the subject-matter of philosophy, and that he only discussed questions about language because 'he thought particular philosophical errors or "troubles in our thought" were due to false analogies suggested by our actual use of expressions; and he emphasized that it was only necessary for him to discuss those points about language which, as he thought, led to these particular errors or "troubles"'.[109] Nevertheless, as a result of Moore's focus on Wittgenstein's views about language, a great variety of quite specific questions in the philosophy of language, mind, knowledge, logic, and arithmetic, which might equally well have been considered in their own right, are instead sifted for the light they cast on Wittgenstein's views about meaning and grammar.

The approach Moore takes in his essay leads him to present Wittgenstein as making many more positive philosophical claims than we actually find in the form of explicit statements of doctrine in the lecture notes. Precisely because Moore's exposition is much more systematic and better organized than the lecture notes, it can give the reader a misleading idea of what actually went on during those meetings. Paradoxically, Wittgenstein's open-ended discussion in his lectures, and his fragmentary and piecemeal remarks in his writing, inspired Moore, his most attentive listener in the early 1930s, and Waismann, his appointed expositor during those years, to produce summaries of his philosophy at the time. Those summaries are simultaneously impressively faithful, in terms of their assembling his various sayings and writings into an orderly set of philosophical theses, and deeply misleading, in that they make his teaching seem much more conventional and systematic than it actually was.[110]

Moore's lecture notes show that many of the lectures had a free-flowing, off-the-cuff character. We get to see Wittgenstein working through his thoughts in a setting in which he could take very little for granted. We see which topics Wittgenstein chose to present to his students and how he

---

[109] Wittgenstein 1993, 51; see also 114.
[110] Similarly, Lee and King's lecture notes from the early 1930s in the Wren Library, Trinity College are strikingly different from the polished version that Lee produced many years later.

developed them; we see him set out his reservations about the *Tractatus* and his changing approach to the questions that occupied him at the time. The lectures were an opportunity for Wittgenstein to try out and explore ideas, many of which made their way into his later writings in a more polished, but often substantially different, form. There is very little, if any, of the dialectic between different voices that is characteristic of much of Wittgenstein's post-*Tractatus* writing in Moore's lecture notes. The principal voice in these notes is that of Wittgenstein the teacher, setting out ideas that he wants to convey to his students or debate with Moore.

During the early 1930s, Wittgenstein was constantly coming up with new ideas, and almost as quickly, repudiating those ideas, or radically reinterpreting them. In August 1934, Waismann wrote to Schlick that

> He [Wittgenstein] has the great gift of always seeing things as if for the first time. But it shows, I think, how difficult collaborative work with him is, since he is always following up the inspiration of the moment and demolishing what he has previously left out ... But all one sees is that the structure is being demolished bit by bit and that everything is gradually taking on an entirely different appearance, so that one almost gets the feeling that it doesn't matter at all how the thoughts are put together since in the end nothing is left as it was.[111]

One example of the rapid development of Wittgenstein's views in the early 1930s is the case of the 'verification principle'. In Wittgenstein's conversations with members of the Vienna Circle in the late 1920s, he introduced the notion of a principle of verification: the idea, roughly speaking, that the meaning of an empirical claim consists in what would confirm or provide evidence for that claim. Carnap's memoir speaks of 'Wittgenstein's principle of verifiability'.[112]

Maurice Cornforth recalled that immediately after his arrival in Cambridge in 1929, Wittgenstein attracted a circle of young students and that he

> proceeded to tear all our preconceived ideas to pieces. He taught that no proposition had meaning unless one could demonstrate what experiences would verify it; and everything which could not be verified (this is, most propositions which philosophers believed) he attacked as meaningless metaphysics, or as he expressed it, 'nonsense'.[113]

---

[111] Wittgenstein and Waismann 2003, xxviii.
[112] Schilpp 1963, 45. See Stern 2007 for further discussion of Wittgenstein's relationship to Carnap.
[113] Guest 1939, 95.

Indeed, in early 1930, both Moore and Waismann recorded Wittgenstein as saying that 'the sense of a proposition is the way in which it is verified'.[114] But by April 1933, Wittgenstein said this 'only meant "You can determine the meaning of a proposition by asking how it is verified"' and went on to say 'This is necessarily a mere rule of thumb, because "verification" means different things, and because in some cases, notably including the case of first person self-ascription, the question "How is that verified?" makes no sense.'[115]

Most interpreters of Wittgenstein's writing and teaching in the early 1930s have approached that material with the aim of assessing his movement away from the *Tractatus* and towards the *Investigations*. However, Wittgenstein's thought was changing rapidly during the first half of the 1930s, and his writing from this period should not be seen simply in terms of a transition from the earlier to the later philosophy. While this talk of 'transition' or 'development' may appear to be a neutral description of this phase of his work, it lends itself to thinking of Wittgenstein's philosophy as structured in a certain way, as developing *from* a starting point *to* an end point, *from* the early philosophy *to* the later philosophy, or *from* the *Tractatus* *to* the *Philosophical Investigations*. The work done in between will then be seen as a matter of his taking a path that leads away from the earlier masterpiece and towards the later one. Joachim Schulte frames this interpretive difficulty in the following terms:

> A general problem of reading and interpreting Wittgenstein [is] that it is enormously difficult to read a text as a complete and unified work and at the same time as a transitory stage within the author's oeuvre as a whole. Early or intermediate stages will appear as something superseded by later insights. The first and last versions will be allotted special status while what happened in between will appear to be of minor relevance.[116]

For this reason, it is particularly difficult to give one's full and undivided attention to any one part of Wittgenstein's work from the early 1930s, without seeing it as an intermediate step between a well-known point of departure and an equally familiar destination. Indeed, in addition to the danger Schulte identifies in the passage quoted above, that of seeing the

---

[114] Wittgenstein 1993, 59, based on 4:18; Waismann 1979, 79. Further development of the view can be found in the *Philosophical Remarks* (Wittgenstein 1964). See §§59, 150, 160, 225, 232.
[115] Wittgenstein 1993, 59, based on 8:58.   [116] Schulte 1998, 380.

intermediate stages as superseded by later insights, we must also take care to avoid the complementary pitfall of approaching the lectures from the early 1930s purely as a source of early formulations of central ideas in the later work. This interpretive 'frame' has prevented readers of this material from appreciating the extent to which it comprises a remarkable variety of different approaches. In places, Wittgenstein explores ideas that he would later develop, and in other places he explores ideas that he would later reject. In some places, he sets out methods and techniques that are very different from those characteristic of Wittgenstein's later philosophy in general and of the *Philosophical Investigations* in particular.

In a discussion of the relationship of Wittgenstein's teaching during 1932–1935 to his earlier and later philosophy, Alice Ambrose observed that both of the standard approaches to Wittgenstein's philosophy – the one-Wittgenstein view on which 'Wittgenstein's concerns, earlier and later, are conceived as being the same' and the two-Wittgensteins view that there is a 'discontinuity between the *Tractatus* and the *Investigations*' – 'ignore the iconoclastic ideas which came out in lectures, dictations and discussions' during those years.[117] To regard Wittgenstein's philosophy as fundamentally continuous is to fail to recognize that a 'quite new conception of philosophical statements was being formulated, and was illustrated in the treatment of certain problems'.[118] But to see Wittgenstein as the author of two very different philosophies, an early one set out in the *Tractatus* and a later one in the *Investigations*, still has the effect of pushing the work he did during those years out of sight, she contended. If one only reads the lecture notes, dictations, and other writings from that period for those places where he criticizes his own earlier work, or moves towards his later philosophy, one will miss much of what is most interesting, and distinctive, about his teaching in the first half of the 1930s.

Ambrose's remarks about the years during which she was a student of Wittgenstein's are equally applicable to the overlapping period during which Moore attended his lectures. But even among those who agree with Ambrose about the importance and distinctive character of this phase of Wittgenstein's work, there is very little agreement about *which* aspects of his teaching, or writing, during the first half of the 1930s constituted his most important insights, or significant contributions. However, there can

---

[117] Ambrose 1972, 16–17. In Flowers 1999, 2 266–267; 2016, 2 553.
[118] Ambrose 1972, 17. In Flowers 1999, 2 266; 2016, 2 553.

be no doubt that during the early 1930s, Wittgenstein repeatedly emphasized the importance and distinctive character of his philosophical method. The final section of Moore's essay on Wittgenstein's lectures sums up what Wittgenstein had to say there about matters of method. Moore was 'a good deal surprised' by some of the things Wittgenstein said 'about the difference between "philosophy" in the sense in which what he was doing might be called "philosophy" ... and what has traditionally been called "philosophy"'.[119]

In his first lecture of the 1930–1931 academic year, Wittgenstein maintained that philosophy was going through a fundamental change – a discontinuity in the development of human thought comparable to chemistry developing out of alchemy, or to Galileo's founding of dynamics. Because a method had been found, 'now, for the first time, there can be skilful [philosophers]'.[120] However, 'we are not accustomed to – have not been trained in – sort of thinking that is required in philosophy'.[121] While philosophy remained extremely difficult, Wittgenstein thought there was no longer any room for personal expression, as there had been in the past. At the end of the notes for the day, there is a striking summary of this line of thought:

Philosophy is reduced to matter of skill: but it's very difficult to acquire any skill.

You can't acquire it by hearing lectures: only way is to discuss ...

It doesn't matter whether I tell you the truth or not: because the method is found.[122]

This was a theme that not only played a particularly important role in Wittgenstein's teaching and writing during those years, but was also central to his own understanding of the difference in philosophical outlook that separated him from Moore. Indeed, according to Ambrose, Wittgenstein told her 'that he had a method of going about doing philosophy which Moore lacked'.[123] In his autobiography, Moore addressed the question of his philosophical relationship to Wittgenstein by saying that Wittgenstein had not only made him more circumspect, but also that Wittgenstein's method was very different from his own:

---

[119] Wittgenstein 1993, 113–14.
[120] 5:2. See also Lee 1979, 218. In Flowers 1999, 2 195; 2016, 2 483.   [121] 5:1.
[122] 5:2–3.
[123] Ambrose 1972, 14. In Flowers 1999, 2 263; 2016, 2 551. This passage is from the ellipsis in the quotation from Ambrose at the end of Section 2b.

How far he has influenced positively anything that I have written, I cannot tell; but he certainly has had the effect of making me distrustful about many things which, but for him, I should have been inclined to assert positively. He has made me think that what is required for the solution of philosophical problems which baffle me, is a method quite different from any which I have ever used ...[124]

But what, precisely, was Wittgenstein's method? Moore observed that Wittgenstein 'did not expressly try to tell us exactly what the "new method" which had been found was. But he gave some hints as to its nature.'[125] In his summary of those 'hints', Moore emphasized Wittgenstein's statements that he was not trying to teach any new facts, but rather to provide a 'synopsis of *many* trivialities' with the aim of removing 'our "intellectual discomfort"'.[126] Apart from that first lecture in October 1930, Wittgenstein offered few further explicit hints in his 1930–1933 lectures as to his philosophical method.[127]

Wittgenstein's occasional remarks about his new method, remarks that seem to point to what was most distinctive about his approach to philosophy without quite stating it fully, seem to challenge his audience to expressly articulate exactly what that 'new method' was. Wittgenstein did directly address 'the question of what he meant by giving hints' in the intervals between his dictation of the *Blue Book* during the 1933–1934 academic year. Alice Ambrose, who 'took down as full notes as possible', recorded the following answer to that question:

Such a remark as 'This is one of the most typical problems of philosophy' would be a hint. This remark may set you on the right track in solving a problem. But I could leave out all the hints and just treat special problems. It is only a psychological fact that people only understand what I am driving at when they begin to understand my general remarks, my hints, and cannot imagine what I am talking about when they hear me dealing with some special difficulty ... All you need to do is to observe what we do, which will be the same sort of thing each time ... Suppose someone said 'my craving is to get a general comprehensive picture of the universe. Can you satisfy this craving?' I would say 'No' ... Let us see whether doing such and such, or thinking such and such a way will, not satisfy the craving, but make you cease to have it.[128]

---

[124] Moore 1968, 33. In Flowers 1999, 1 149; 2016, 1 153. This passage is from the same paragraph as the quotations from Moore at the beginning of Section 2a.
[125] Wittgenstein 1993, 113–14.   [126] Wittgenstein 1993, 114.
[127] But see the beginning of Lecture 1, Lent 1931, Lecture 2a, Lent 1933, and Moore's summary in Wittgenstein 1993, 113.
[128] Ambrose 1972, 16. In Flowers 1999, 2 265; 2016, 2 552–553. All of the ellipses in this quotation are present in Ambrose's text.

There are clear similarities between this summary of Wittgenstein's own view about the relationship between his hints, or 'general remarks', and Moore's summary at the end of his essay. On both accounts of his philosophical practice, his discussion of particular philosophical problems aims not at solving them, but dissolving them. Instead of the traditional philosophical strategy of looking for a theory that would satisfy the 'cravings' or 'intellectual discomforts' that give rise to philosophical problems, he aimed, by means of a detailed discussion of familiar facts, to make us cease to wish for such a theory. However, Wittgenstein's remarks to Ambrose also include a clear statement that not only are the more general remarks about method dispensable ('I could leave out all the hints and just treat special problems'), but also that he considered that his method was clearly embodied in his handling of particular philosophical problems ('All you need to do is to observe what we do, which will be the same sort of thing each time'). Yet at the same time, Wittgenstein also acknowledged that those remarks about method played a crucial role in his auditors' reception of his work: 'people only understand what I am driving at when they begin to understand my general remarks, my hints'.

One natural response to the challenge of interpreting Wittgenstein's hints about his method in his lectures is to draw on Wittgenstein's other writings about the nature of philosophy in order to give a more complete account of his philosophical method, such as the 'Philosophy' chapter in *The Big Typescript*, or §§89–133 of the *Philosophical Investigations*. Indeed, many of Wittgenstein's best-known remarks about philosophy in the *Philosophical Investigations* are some of the first passages in that book that he composed, and were drafted during 1930–1931.[129] Many other striking remarks on philosophy in general, and philosophical method in particular, were composed during these years, and gathered together in the 'Philosophy' chapter of *The Big Typescript*. In their commentary on the *Philosophical Investigations,* Baker and Hacker take this to show that Wittgenstein's later philosophical method was formulated in the early 1930s, and is set out in detail in *The Big Typescript*.[130] They regard the 'Philosophy' chapter,

---

[129] *Philosophical Investigations* (Wittgenstein 1953) §§116, 119–20, 123–4, 126–9, 132; also parts of §§87, 88, 108, 111, 118, 122, and 133. For further discussion, see Stern 2004, chapter 5.2.

[130] See Baker and Hacker 1980 and 1980a; Hilmy 1987; Glock 1996; Baker, preface to Wittgenstein and Waismann 2003. For alternative approaches to the question of the relationship between Wittgenstein's discussion of his method in the early 1930s and

which includes many striking analogies and general remarks about philosophical method, as providing a much more detailed exposition of a methodology that is only briefly stated elsewhere. This approach has provided the point of departure for a great deal of subsequent discussion of Wittgenstein's method. Indeed, the issue of the nature of Wittgenstein's method, and its place in his philosophy, has taken on a particular prominence in work on Wittgenstein since the first publication of the 'Philosophy' chapter of *The Big Typescript* in 1989.[131]

However, it is clear Wittgenstein's remarks about method were intended as an aid to those who had already followed his detailed treatment of particular philosophical problems and were looking for a better sense of 'what he was driving at'. As he put it at the end of his first lecture of Michaelmas 1930, he considered his way of doing philosophy to be a skill that could only be acquired by engaging in philosophical discussion. His 'general remarks' were never intended as an accessible summary of his views about how to do philosophy that could serve as a guide to the beginner or could be detached from their larger context for expository purposes. Nevertheless, that is just how they have been used by many subsequent interpreters. Rush Rhees recognized this danger when he was considering which parts of Wittgenstein's *Nachlass* to publish. In a letter to von Wright, he explained his reasons for not publishing the 'Philosophy' chapter of *The Big Typescript*, Typescript 213 in von Wright's catalogue of the Wittgenstein papers. At the same time, he acknowledged that it would eventually be published, and would give rise to the impression that it is relatively easy to understand Wittgenstein's philosophical method without really studying what he had to say:

> You will agree that you cannot tell anyone what philosophy is, if he has never been near enough the water to get his feet wet. And it is impossible to tell anyone what Wittgenstein's conception of philosophy is, if (he) has made no long or serious study of what Wittgenstein has written. It would have been impossible for Wittgenstein himself to do this. And the remarks in that section of the Typescript 213 can have force or sense only against the Hintergrund[132] of the philosophizing which Wittgenstein does, or has done. Wittgenstein used to say something in this sense to people who wanted to come to his lectures. It is why he used (for example)

---

subsequently, see: Diamond 1991, 2004; Stern 1991, 1995, 2005, forthcoming; Schulte 2002, 2011; Pichler 2004; Kuusela 2008, 2011; Conant 2011; Engelmann 2011, 2013; Wallgren 2013.

[131] Wittgenstein 1993, chapter 9.   [132] German for 'background'.

to speak of the work of philosophy as the work of changing one's way of looking at things, <u>durch lange Übung</u>.[133] When I asked him first if I could come to his lectures, he asked if I had any idea of what went on in them. And when I said (or said something like) obviously I had only such ideas as came from discussion with those attending them, Wittgenstein said: 'Suppose you asked someone "can you play the violin?", and he said: "I don't know, but I can try."'

Of course those remarks in Typescript 213 will be published sometime, and people will quote them to show (sic) what Wittgenstein said doing philosophy was. And they will think this is all fairly easy to understand. We cannot prevent this.[134]

Ultimately, the significance of Moore's lecture notes is that they are our best record of what went on in Wittgenstein's lectures during those years, and of Wittgenstein's efforts to communicate his conception of philosophy to his students and colleagues, not by means of his hints, but through long practice.

7. Editing Moore's notes on Wittgenstein's lectures, 1930–1933

Our main objectives in editing Moore's notes were both to provide a text that makes Wittgenstein's lectures accessible and to reproduce faithfully what Moore actually wrote down. Because Moore's lecture notes are so thorough and conscientious, they deserve to be published in full, with a minimum of editorial intervention or revision. However, reproducing every mark on the notebook pages would have resulted in an inaccessible and distracting text, hindering readers from engaging with the content of the lectures. We have therefore amended the text only when the benefits of doing so outweighed the primary value of providing an exact reproduction. We have also employed a minimal editorial apparatus in this volume in order to minimize distractions from the content of the lectures. In this section we set out and explain our general editorial policies. Exceptions to these policies are set out in footnotes at the relevant points in the lectures for the sake of transparency. To help to clarify our editorial protocols, four sample pages from Moore's notebooks are reproduced at the end of this section.

---

[133] German for 'through long practice'.
[134] Letter from Rhees to von Wright, 22 January 1976. Quoted in Erbacher 2015, 184. Unlike Erbacher, we have normalized Rhees's spelling; the '(sic)' in the final paragraph is Rhees's.

a. Citations to the manuscripts of Moore's lecture notes

Moore's lecture notes are contained in a set of six notebooks which are part of his collected papers housed at Cambridge University Library. These notebooks are numbered items 4 through 9 in a series of papers relating to Wittgenstein.[135] Moore added page numbers to these notebooks in the top right corner of each double-page spread. We identify locations in the notebooks using a system of reference that incorporates the Library's volume numbers and Moore's page numbers. Thus '5:32', for example, is used to refer to volume 5, page 32. While Moore usually took notes only on the right-hand side of each double-page spread, some remarks occasionally appear in the left-hand pages, which are not numbered. We identify these left-hand pages as the back, or 'verso' of the preceding page. For example, the unnumbered left-hand page following 4:47, and facing 4:48, is referred to as 4:47v. These page references run along the margins of this volume, placed next to the line in which the page break occurs in the manuscript, in order to allow the reader to locate passages in the original notebooks easily.

The page numbers in the notebook volume 6 are unusually complicated. Moore began writing in that notebook at the start of May Term, 1931, on page 6:1. He also put some philosophical writing of his own in the first nine pages at the back of the book, which he numbered separately, starting at 1 again. However, in May 1932 he started using the tenth page from the back for his lecture notes; we refer to that page at the back of the book as 6b:10.

In the 1950s, in preparation for his articles on Wittgenstein's lectures in *Mind*, Moore wrote over a hundred tightly packed pages of 'summary notes'. These immediately follow the lecture notes in the catalogue of Moore's papers, and so are identified as item 10 in that sequence.[136] The summary notes are a collection of loose, unbound pages that are arranged in several separate sequences, each of which is numbered independently. Thus, when we quote from these notes in our footnotes we identify each page by its place in a series of facsimiles provided by Cambridge University Library. 10:76, for example, is used to refer to image 76 in this series.

---

[135] Moore, Add. 8875, 10/7/4–9. For a detailed list of the contents of the Moore archive, see Cann 1995.

[136] Moore, Add. 8875, 10/7/10.

b. Editing Moore's remarks on Wittgenstein's lectures

Moore's notebooks can be understood as consisting of three elements: (i) Wittgenstein's words as recorded in the lecture notes; (ii) Moore's contemporaneous remarks, recording his reactions to the lectures while they were being given; and (iii) comments and editorial markings added by Moore when he revisited the notes in the 1950s to prepare his series of *Mind* articles.[137] One of the central tasks in editing these notebooks was thus to differentiate these layers. Transcriptions of Wittgenstein's own words are generally written in pencil on the right-hand pages, while Moore's contemporaneous remarks usually appear in the margins or on the left-hand pages opposite the lecture notes. Comments and markings added in the 1950s are distinguished by Moore's unsteady handwriting and occasional use of black ink rather than pencil. Compare, for instance, the contemporaneous underlining in a steady hand at Sample Page B, line 11 with the later unsteady underlining in the lower portion of the same page.

In order to allow the reader to distinguish between the contributions of Wittgenstein and Moore, the main text of our edition contains only Moore's notes of Wittgenstein's lectures. Moore's comments on the lectures are reproduced in footnotes, but only when these are significant or informative. Brief responses merely indicating disagreement or confusion about Wittgenstein's intended meaning, such as a question-mark in the margin, for example, have been omitted to avoid distraction. Moore's remarks appear in <angle brackets> for easy identification. His contemporaneous comments are preceded by the phrase 'Moore added', while his remarks from the 1950s are preceded by 'Moore later added'.

Moore's later contributions from the 1950s include several features: (1) symbols indicating Moore's reactions to the lectures, such as underlining or 'X' to highlight a passage, or '?' to indicate confusion or difficulty in reading his earlier handwriting (for example, the final line of Sample Page A); (2) cross-references to other passages in the notes; (3) additional remarks on the content of the lectures (for example, the comment in Sample Page D to the right of the truth-table); and (4) attempts to interpret words that were difficult to read (for example, 'speed' at Sample Page A, line 13). We generally have not incorporated such features in this volume,

---

[137] See Section 5a for further discussion of the relationship between these three stages in the composition of Moore's lecture notes.

though we have often made use of Moore's later interpretations of words that are hard to read in our construal of the lecture notes.

We have also included a number of passages from Moore's summary notes in this volume. For the most part, the summary notes are no more than selections of key points, often in the very words that had been used in the original lecture notes. But occasionally Moore's summaries go beyond paraphrase in ways that are interesting and which make a contribution to our understanding of the notes – in which case we have included them in the footnotes. Quotations from the summary notes are preceded by the phrase 'Moore's summary notes'.

c. Editorial footnotes and appendices

In view of the extensive and wide-ranging connections between what Wittgenstein said in his lectures in the early 1930s, his manuscripts from that period, and his later work, it would have been possible to supplement our text of the lectures with numerous footnotes drawing the reader's attention to passages from Wittgenstein's writing, or others' lecture notes, where he says something strikingly similar, sets out a closely related line of argument, or can be seen as responding to views discussed in the lectures. For the most part we have not included such cross-references to Wittgenstein's writings in the footnotes, for to do so would often be a matter of substantive interpretation. Since none of the lectures were read from prepared notes, most of the connections one might draw between a remark given in the lectures and a passage written by Wittgenstein involve a step beyond the work of an editor presenting information about the text. This task is best left to the reader. However, we do occasionally provide references to some of Wittgenstein's remarks from this period when we considered them to be essential, or at least very helpful, for an understanding of particular passages in the lecture notes. Some of these references explain technical terms or a poorly drawn diagram. Others direct the reader to a more detailed exposition of particular points in the philosophy of mathematics.

While we have followed the principle of keeping editorial footnotes and appendices to a minimum, in a limited number of cases we have provided background information to aid the reader's appreciation of the lectures. For example, Wittgenstein frequently alludes to the work of other thinkers, some of whom may not be familiar to contemporary readers. We have followed the example of the editors of the fourth edition of the

Philosophical Investigations in providing information about these references whenever they have been possible to identify. We also provide translations of foreign words. Finally, we have included an appendix of short biographies of the people to whom Wittgenstein refers, except for those, such as Plato, Kant, Russell, and Frege, who are too well-known to need any introduction.

d. Transcription and editing policies

This section details the policies we have adopted in transcribing the text of the notebooks. In each case, our policies were motivated by the goal of producing an accessible text that remains faithful to Moore's notes. One significant feature of the lecture notes is that they are not in the form of a final draft. Revisions, deletions, insertions, abbreviations, and editorial symbols are ubiquitous. Providing an exact transcription of the notes in their current state would have resulted in a messy and inaccessible text. To prevent these markings from distracting the reader from the content of the lectures, we generally treat them as instructions for producing a clean copy. We silently implement these instructions in this volume and fix the occasional clear but minor errors such as misspelled words, but we have been very careful to avoid any other editorial interventions in the text. Most importantly, we have not attempted to reorganize passages or fill gaps in the text with our own conjectures.

A number of contemporaneous revisions were made to the notes by means of deletions and insertions, either to correct a mistaken transcription or to reflect Wittgenstein's revision of his own phraseology during the lecture. We treat these revisions as instructions for producing a clean copy and silently follow those instructions in this text. For example, we represent the final line of Sample Page A as 'The rules I gave you describe your understanding of the arrow.' This sentence is the result of implementing three of Moore's instructions: (1) inserting 'I gave you', (2) replacing 'the' with 'your' before 'understanding', and (3) deleting 'it' before 'the arrow'. We occasionally call the reader's attention to insertions with the use of slash-marks immediately before and after the inserted word or phrase, in those cases where silently inserting the material would make the resulting sentence ungrammatical or incoherent. This is the case, for example, with Sample Page B, line 22, where Moore writes 'dictionary' just above 'vocabulary' without crossing out the latter word. In the text, we represent this sentence as 'In the vocabulary /dictionary/, the word has no meaning.'

Similarly, we occasionally include ~~deletions~~ in the text in a strike-through font when the deleted word or phrase may be of significant interest to the reader. See, for example, the deleted sentence near the end of page 4:68.

Moore's use of punctuation can be uneven and inconsistent. If we had reproduced this punctuation exactly as it appears in the notebooks, it would have led to confusion in some cases. For example, Moore sometimes uses large spaces around a word or phrase as a mentioning device, rather than the more familiar quotation marks. On other occasions, he does not use any means of indicating that a word or phrase is being mentioned. In such cases, when additional punctuation is needed to make a sentence readily comprehensible, we have added that punctuation in a grey font, just light enough that it can be distinguished from the regular black font if one looks carefully, but dark enough that it does not unduly draw the reader's attention. This occasional use of grey font allows the reader to easily determine what aspects of the text are editorial additions without being distracted by footnotes indicating these changes. We have not, however, imposed a uniform system of punctuation throughout the text. Rather, we have used the grey font sparingly to make additions only when they are truly needed to make the text accessible to the reader and easy to follow. In a few exceptional cases, we have used grey font to add numbering, or a missing word.

Moore makes frequent use of abbreviations for certain words, for example 'wh.' for 'which' (Sample Page A, line 13), 'prop.' for 'proposition' (Sample Page B, line 7), and 'taut.' for 'tautology' (Sample Page D, last line). We treat these abbreviations as instructions for producing a clean copy and therefore replace them with the complete words in this edition. A full list of Moore's abbreviations and their corresponding expansions is found in the end matter of this volume.

Moore recalled that 'Wittgenstein always had a blackboard at both lectures and classes and made plenty of use of it.'[138] The lecture notes are usually organized into short paragraphs, which can often consist of a single sentence. However, when Moore includes material copied from the blackboard it does not always admit of a clear paragraph delineation. Moore often attempts to arrange this copied material spatially on the page in the way it appeared on the board. We have reproduced these spatial

---

[138] Wittgenstein 1993, 49.

arrangements when they are significant. See, for example, the manner in which numbers are compared to vertical strokes at 6:11.

Wittgenstein frequently used the blackboard for logical and mathematical notation. The formulas that Moore copied into the notes present an editorial challenge because in some cases they would be ambiguous or ungrammatical if reproduced exactly as written. This is particularly the case with indicators of scope. Some formulas, such as 'p. tautology = p' on Sample Page D, line 12, are potentially ambiguous as they do not include scope-indicators such as brackets. In some cases, Moore (or Wittgenstein) indicates scope with large spaces around a formula or with operators of different sizes. In order to make the notes accessible to contemporary readers, we have occasionally found it necessary to clarify the scope of operators by adding parentheses in a grey font. For example, the formula above from Sample Page D is reproduced as '(p. tautology) = p' at 5:81. As with punctuation and mentioning devices, however, we do not attempt to impose syntactical rules on all formulas, but only add parentheses in a grey font when doing so may help prevent confusion.

A variety of logical and mathematical notations appear in the notes, and Wittgenstein sometimes develops novel notations in the lectures. We generally attempt to reproduce these as they appear in the notes. The only feature of Wittgenstein's and Moore's notation that we have chosen not to follow in our volume, though, is the system of dots to indicate scope that is associated with *Principia Mathematica*. The system is not applied consistently in the notes, and in any case, few contemporary readers are familiar with this method of scope-indication. In order to make the formulas accessible to readers, we have eliminated dots used to indicate scope and instead used parentheses in a grey font. For example, the formula on the last line of Sample Page C is reproduced as '($\exists$x)(x $\in$ p . ϕx)' at 4:25. The use of dots to indicate conjunction has been retained, however.

Wittgenstein also made frequent use of the blackboard to draw diagrams, which Moore then reproduced in the notebooks. We have isolated these diagrams from digital scans of the notebook pages and edited them to produce sharp black and white images, removing the printed lines from the notebook page and other extraneous marks, such as words that are not part of the diagram. In keeping with our overall aim of minimizing editorial intervention and faithfully reproducing what Moore wrote, we have not attempted to redraw these diagrams ourselves. See, for example, the diagram at 5:76 corresponding to the arrows in Sample Page A. Nor have we attempted to clean up or fix these diagrams.[139] While we have reproduced digital images of Wittgenstein's diagrams in this volume, there is not always a clear distinction between diagrams, symbols, and formulas. Our general principle has been to produce digital images only for graphics that cannot be faithfully represented with a standard font. Sample Pages A and B illustrate this distinction. The short arrows in Sample Page B are satisfactorily represented at 6:18 with the arrows in a standard font. The arrows in Sample Page A, however, are longer and do not form regular angles. Thus, rather than reproducing these arrows with a standard font and thereby imposing an editorial interpretation on the diagram, we used digital reproductions of the arrows as Moore drew them in the notebooks.

e. Companion website

Our careful and transparent editorial policies provide the reader with much more information about the original text than any previous edition of notes from Wittgenstein's lectures. Indeed, it should provide most researchers with all the information about the source material that they need. However, as set out above, there are certain aspects of the manuscripts that we have not reproduced in order to produce an easily readable text, such as the precise placement of words on the page, many of the details of Moore's revisions, and almost all of the marginal marks he added in the 1950s. Recognizing that there will be some scholars who may be interested in using this edition in conjunction with the original notes, we have made available digital scans of Moore's six notebooks, his short paper on Wittgenstein on grammar, and his summary notes at Wittgenstein Source, www.wittgensteinsource.org, an online archive of primary texts by and about Wittgenstein maintained by the Bergen Wittgenstein Archive. The companion website also includes an updated list of any errata in this book and information on how to contact the editors.[140]

---

[139] The sole exception to this statement is the diagram at 7:70. In that case, the lines were isolated from obscuring doodles in the digital editing process.

[140] Parts of this introduction are based on Citron 2013, Stern 2013, and Stern, Citron, and Rogers 2013.

X/ If a man understands one order, he must be able to understand another.
What does "able to" mean?
It must be a description of what happens when he understands first order; & 2nd order does not enter into his understanding.
First order can only be understood as part of a system. |X

Suppose I taught you about the room by drawing arrows; I taught you a rule.

Suppose I'd also taught another language of arrows — in which arrow means move in arrow direction with speed proportional to length.

Then you may understand ⟶ as part of 2 different languages.
You can see it as part of the one system, or as part of the other system.
In system (b) "Don't go ⟶, go ↗" means nothing.
The rules describe the understanding of the arrow? |X

Sample Page A (5:76)

Sample Page B (6:18)

grammatical rules for
viz. by a kind of variable, which can be better explained as follows.

Suppose $\phi(\ ) = (\ )$ is a man in this room.
$\therefore (\exists x).\phi x$.

But suppose $(\exists x)\psi x = $ there is a colour which no one has in common

then must substitute "a man" for a colour; or "a line". |×

We can use colour then or number in the way
$(\exists x_{colour})\phi x$
or $(\exists x_{number})\psi x$.

The word for the real concept occurs outside the bracket; |×
whereas the typical word for typical concept stands inside.

I couldn't say $(\exists x_{man})\phi x$

But you must say $(\exists x_{body})\phi x$

Then you can write $(\exists t).\phi t$
but not $(\exists x).x \varepsilon t. \phi x$.

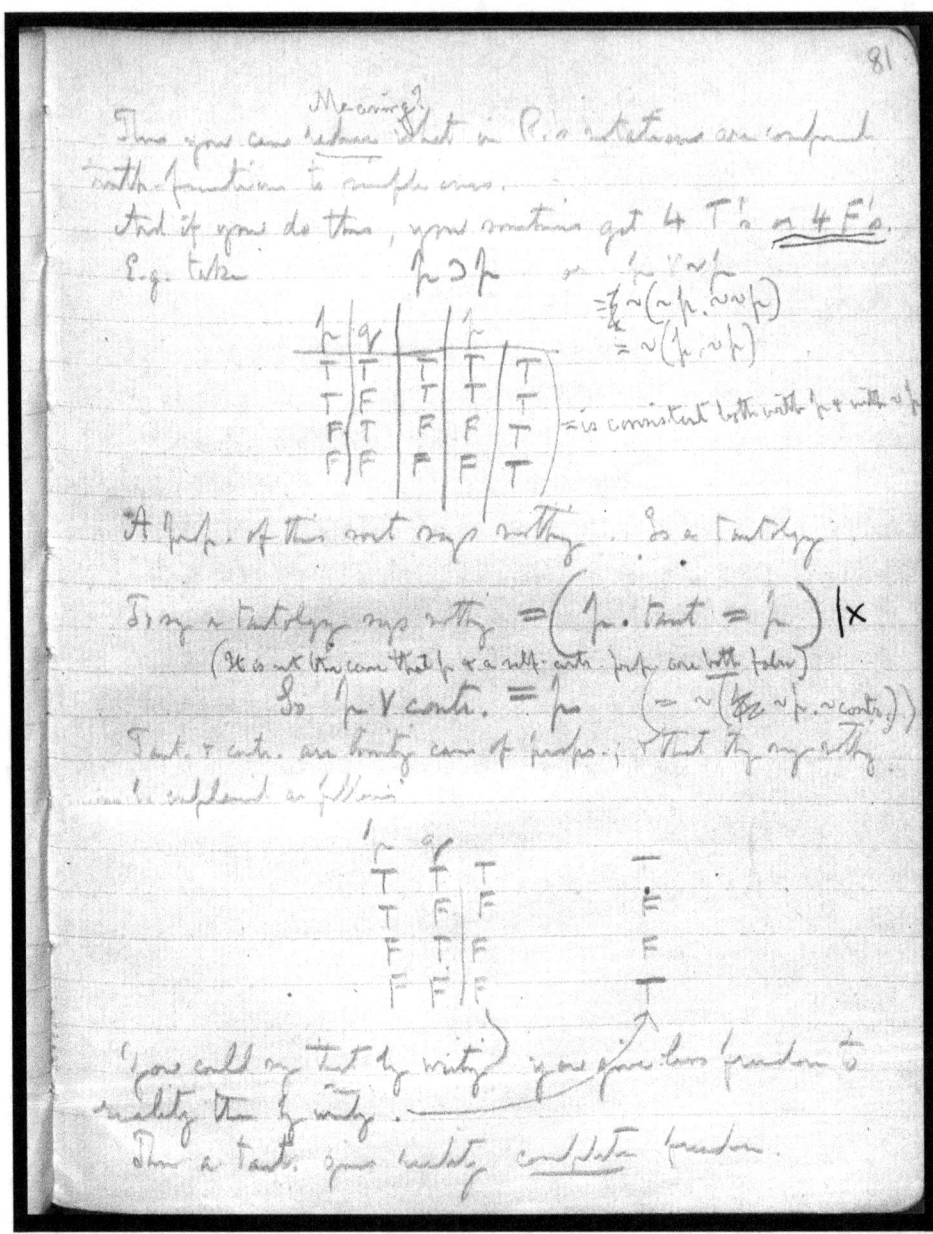

Sample Page D (5:81)

Synoptic table of contents

Lent Term, 1930

1. Puzzles about foundations of knowledge – Descriptive vs. prescriptive propositions – Propositions as pictures of reality – Word meaning – Different kinds of word .... *page* 5
2. Puzzles about foundations of knowledge – Philosophical problems derive from unclarity in our symbolism – Propositions as pictures – Understanding propositions and thinking propositions – Expectation and fulfilment – Conventions and verification – Different kinds of word and substitutability 8
3. How propositions work – Propositions, pictures, and measuring-rods – Much language requires outside help – What happens to reality must be capable of happening to language – Grammar, logic, and phenomenology vs. psychology – Grammar and axioms 13
4. No notes 19
5. Two ways that language represents the world – Proposition sense and verification – Concepts, logical concepts, and proper names – 'Thing', 'number', 'man' – Grammar and substitutability – Propositional functions vs. variables to which certain rules apply – Making classifications 20
6. Logical concepts as pseudo-concepts – Logical concepts expressed by grammatical rules for a kind of variable – The logic of colour concepts – Boundaries within language vs. boundaries of language 24
7. Colours are distinguished from sounds by rules of grammar – Linguistic conventions, rules of a game, and grammar – The connection of language to reality – The difference between concepts and pseudo-concepts – A proposition shows the possibility of its truth – The logic of 'infinite' 28
8. 'Infinite' and two senses of 'possible' – There is a proposition only when there is the possibility of truth or falsity – Infinite divisibility – No experiment ever shows anything about 33

possibility – Visual space and experiments – Geometry is the grammar of spatial objects, geometry expresses the possibilities of space

May Term, 1930

1 Different kinds of generality, and the uses of 'all', 'some', and 'every' – Russell's notations: $(x)\phi x$ and $(\exists x)\phi x$ – Frege, concepts, and possible predicates – Giving names is only possible in special cases – The different meanings of 'this' and the different meanings of pointing – Generality, logical sums, and logical products – Continuous transitions in infinite stages in both visual and physical space – Propositions, hypotheses, and verification   41

2 Expressing generality – The completeness and understandability of grammar – Sheffer's stroke and the misleadingness of talking of 'discovery' in grammar – There is no method for making mathematical discoveries – Logic and mathematics vs. hypotheses   46

3 The translatability of systems – Sheffer's discovery as the discovery of an aspect – What one is looking for must be describable beforehand – Generality, infinite possibilities, and complexity – Continuous transitions in infinite stages in both visual and physical space – Infinite possibilities in proofs and in symbols – Symbolism and translatability   48

4 Geometry and grammar give rules for the use of symbols – A sense in which grammar is autonomous, and grammar and mathematics as games – Concepts, pseudo-concepts, and logical concepts – Two kinds of generality in geometry: that of rules, and that of its application – The difficulty in defining numbers – Two sorts of proposition in mathematics: those proven by a chain of equations and those proven by induction   51

5 Equations as grammatical rules and as rules of games – Mathematical definitions, propositions, and internal relations – Proofs by induction and spiral proofs – Brouwer and the application of the Law of Excluded Middle – Three consecutive 7s in the decimal expansion of π – Rational and irrational numbers   56

6 Frege, Russell, truth-tables, and the idea that logic consists of tautologies – The value of logic – Tautologies, saying, and   60

showing – Ramsey's attempt to show that mathematical equations are tautologies – Equations are merely symbolic conventions – Calculus of numbers and calculus of tautologies – The idea that 'calculus is a game'

Michaelmas Term, 1930

1 The difference between philosophy and the sciences – Philosophy is reduced to a matter of skill – A method has now been found in philosophy   67

2 What is philosophy? – What is a proposition? – (1) Propositions as what can be said to be true or false – Relation of 'true' and 'false' to affirmation and negation – Having sense and not having sense – Propositions as things to which 'not' can be applied – Explaining the meaning of words – Ostensive definitions – Ogden and Richards and the associative theory of meaning – (2) Propositions as the expression of a thought – Thinking and operating with a plan – Understanding and translation – Science lays foundations, philosophy does not   69

3 Propositions as the expression of all kinds of thoughts – The thought lasts as long as the expression – The simile of thoughts occurring 'in the mind', and the danger of pictures – The idea that language is indirect – Teaching new facts vs. providing a synopsis – Interpreting and understanding a plan or an order – Two senses of 'can' – Propositions, meaning, signs, and symbols – Russell's theory of descriptions – Understanding the symbol does not mean going outside it – The test of understanding is use – What if I replace one symbolism by another?   74

4 The relation between a thought and its expression – A symbol is everything that is relevant to the significance of a sign – 'Not' and negation – Propositions and systems of propositions – Thought, sense, and expectation as something 'shadowy' – 'Similar to' presupposes a rule of projection – Recognition demands another test besides the recognition – Difference between a portrait and a picture – A rule of projection is only expressed in projecting   79

5 The supposition of a shadowy intermediary between symbol and fact – Confusing words with propositions – The relation   84

between an expectation and its fulfilment – Russell on wishes and their fulfilment – Comparing expectation to a mechanism –Whatever can be said can be negated – Philosophy as a synopsis of trivialities: removing intellectual discomfort

6   The idea of explaining thought or propositions – The temptation to apply scientific methods to philosophy – The only relevant description of expectation for us is its expression – The ambiguous use of 'something' – The deep-rootedness of false pictures – Confusion arising from 'in common' – Confusing the meaning of a word with certain simple propositions – Confusion regarding 'harmony between thought and reality' – Linguistic commitment: a word only has meaning in a grammatical system – The notion of a model guiding my hand in making a copy – Intention, representation, and rules – Grammar and propositions as part of a system 88

7   The expression of the harmony between thought and reality – Words, symbols, and systems of symbols – Committing to the consistent use of words – To copy is to be committed to following a rule – Words, pictures, and signals – Explaining words and understanding them – Understanding, and explanation as replacing one symbol by another 92

8   Linguistic commitment, the rigidity of language, being led by language – To be guided by a sign is to follow a rule – Seeing the general rule in special cases – Playing piano automatically, reading the score, and making mistakes – The shape of a symbol is arbitrary but once it is fixed its use is not arbitrary – There is a similarity between a score and correct playing – Rules of grammar and the limits of a symbol's possibilities of significance – Understanding and explanation 96

Lent Term, 1931

1   What is philosophy? – Differences between science and philosophy – Three vague answers to: What is a proposition? – Propositions as expressions of a thought – Thought as a symbolic process – Words having meaning by association – Ostensive definition and substitutability – 103

Understanding as a correlate of explanation, explanation as adding to the symbol – Similarity is always relative to a mode of projection – The relation between an expectation and that which is expected – No description of the world can justify the rules of grammar

2 Four answers to: What is a proposition? – Propositions must have meaning – The idea that words cannot represent but thoughts can – What is not given in my thought cannot be essential to my thought – Thought pointing outside itself and the use of symbols – Translation and being guided by symbols – Behaviourism, reading, and deriving actions from a rule – Grammar says which combination of symbols make sense and which do not – Distinguishing grammatical forms – A proposition is characterized by rules of grammar ... 107

3 What is meant by 'using language according to grammatical rules'? – Explanation and fixing the place of a word in a language – Words forming a system – What makes grammar not arbitrary is its use; but described by itself it is arbitrary – Distinguishing 'kinds' in logic – Propositions as what truth-functions apply to – Propositions as distinguished from hypotheses and mathematical propositions – Frege, truth-functions, and explaining 'true' and 'false' ... 111

4 We are not conscious of rules but we appeal to them for justification – Playing chess vs. manipulating chess pieces in accordance with the rules – Behaviouristic and introspective accounts must have the same multiplicity – The chess player sometimes <u>sees</u> something different in his move – Explaining meaning by illustration – Understanding is produced by explanation, not caused by it – T, F notation can be substituted by Russell's notation but not explained by it – Explaining 'not', the rules which apply to it – 'If p, then q' is not used in the same way as Russell's 'p $\supset$ q' – Hypotheses as rules according to which propositions are constructed ... 115

5 We use negation easily but have trouble making its rules of usage explicit – Making a chess move understanding the rules vs. doing so without understanding them – 'Not', '$\sim$', and how we know that two words mean the same – Rules, laying down rules, and following rules – Logical investigations vs. physical ... 120

	investigations – Rules determining an action and rules describing the understanding – False analogies and the paradox of ~p having meaning when it is true	
6	Whether 'not' and '~' mean the same – Understanding 'not' and seeing it differently – Geometry, logic, and defining vs. describing – Inference and the T, F symbolism – Propositions, tautologies, and contradictions – Inference, implication, following, and internal relations – Rules of inference, T, F symbolism, and seeing the internal relation that justifies inference	124
7	Inference and internal relations – Inference can only be justified by what we see – Rules of grammar can't be justified – What I say of grammar (including inference) is always <u>arbitrary</u> rules – Three-valued logic can be used, but not instead of ours – A calculus can't be true or false; nor more or less fundamental – The meaning of 'therefore' and the assertion sign	129
8	Grammatical rules are arbitrary, but their application is not arbitrary – Internal and external relations are categorially different – A gesture has to be understood as part of a system – A rule of translation never gets us any further – Grammatical bodies, grammatical rules, and the meaning of a word	133

May Term, 1931

1	Elementary propositions and molecular propositions – Every symbol essentially belongs to a system – Grammar of 'justification' and 'guided by' – The kind of investigation we are now engaged in is grammatical – 'Picture' and 'proposition' follow similar rules – Recognition is usually only a symptom	139
2	We misunderstand relation between proposition and its verification – Are words enough to convey an order? – A word carries about its meaning – What is a convention? – Interpolation between sign and fulfilment will not do away with the sign – Internal relation between order and fulfilment	144
3–5	What I call a 'picture' and what it pictures are 'similar' only with reference to a system of projection – Comparison of	147

painted pictures and memory images, imagination and spoken words – You can't describe a calculus without using it – I can only describe the inside of language – I only transcend language when I use it

6   A name represents its bearer, but is not a substitute for its meaning – The meaning of a word is its place in a grammatical system, not the thing to which I point in ostensive definition – Proposition is applied to reality like a foot-rule to a table – Complexity of a proposition – No explanation can give relation between sign and its application   151

May Term, 1932

4   Are there 5 successive 7s in decimal expansion of π? – Disjunctive and non-disjunctive senses of 'some' – Two senses of proof in mathematics – The proof of an existential theorem gives the meaning of 'existence' in that theorem – $\sim(\exists n)fn$ is usually proved by induction or recursion, while $(\exists n)fn$ is proved by finding – There is no opposite to a proof which consists of finding   157

5   Skolem's proof of the associative law by recursion – Queer assumption made in recursive proof – What I really have is a general form of proof for any number – Proving periodicity of a fraction – Grammar of the question whether there are 3 successive 7s in extension of π – Proof for all numbers cannot be the same as proof for a finite group of numbers – Analogy between bits of a series and a law for going on – Define π' as result of replacing 3 successive 7s in decimal expansion of π with 3 successive 1s – Question of whether $\pi = \pi'$ has no meaning – Criterion for whether a number has been defined is whether there is a method for comparing it to any other rational number – The proof that π is irrational shows how many digits in expansion at most can be the same   162

6   $\sqrt{2}$ is called a number because there are rules for comparing it to other numbers – π' can't be compared with every point of the number line – If a law of distribution of prime numbers were discovered, we should have different numbers – There exists no more of a calculus than we have as yet built – When a new proof is discovered, a new calculus is discovered –   169

Following mechanical rules and hitting on a proof by luck are quite different – Associative law is not a logical product, but a rule

Michaelmas Term, 1932

1–4 Senses of meaning – The definition of 'definition' – If you change your definition, you are changing your game – Rules of grammar are arbitrary – Logical laws or laws of thought – Contrast between primitive propositions in logic and experiential propositions – 'Kind' is used in different ways – Our language has a particular propositional game – It isn't possible to define 'game' – Overlapping ideas of proposition – Grammar of 'true' and 'false' is different from that of 'red' and 'green' – 'Logical proposition' is a grammatical distinction – Meaning of 'a tautology says nothing' – 'Follows' and 'implies' belong to different categories – Tautology has use only in a logical calculus, to show formal relation between propositions – Difficulties with 'atomic proposition' – Rules of inference and deduction – Rules of inference are arbitrary, neither true nor false – Presuppositions of ostensive definition 177

5 Are rules of inference like natural laws? – Senses in which rules of inference are 'arbitrary' – Rules are only responsible to other rules, not to nature – Reasons vs. causes – Rules only justified within a game – Criterion for something being a reason – Difference between reflex and voluntary action – Relation between wishing and voluntary action 194

6a Philosophical troubles are not solved by experience – Doubts can be resolved by showing that a fact is not unique – Distinguishing between 'I lifted my arm' and 'my arm went up' – Causes can be found by experiment, reasons cannot – How does a man know the reasons of his actions? – Articulate vs. inarticulate wishes – Giving a reason is going back one step in the calculus – Distinguishing different troubles of the mind – Different meanings of 'hidden contradiction' 200

6b Grammar of 'wishing' is vague – We use 'wish' in a complicated way – We can draw boundaries in trying to make language games – Verifications aren't specified exactly in 205

	ordinary language – Wishing is not an activity in same sense as letter-writing	
7a	Different meanings of 'reason' for an action – Reasons vs. causes – Different ways of using 'want' – Chain of reasons comes to an end – Rules of deduction analogous to fixing a unit of length – Rules are not responsible to facts, do not prophesy – Rule is a preparation for description – 'Length' is used in different ways	209
7b	Rules of deduction are postulates laid down before describing – Inferences involving general propositions – Relation of general propositions to logical products and logical sums – Important mistake in *Tractatus* regarding general propositions – Confusion of logical analysis with chemical analysis	214
8	Different meanings of 'and so on' – Experiment determining 'least noticeable difference' – Russell and *Tractatus* falsely supposed general propositions are logical products or logical sums – Different meanings of general propositions – Cases where Russell's notation for generality doesn't work – 'Which?' vs. 'what kind?' – Russell and Frege translated all general propositions of ordinary language into one form	219

Lent Term, 1933

1a	No notes	227
1b	Proof of mathematical theorem alters rules of grammar – Finding construction of regular pentagon – Giving a series of constructions – It makes no sense to go through all numbers – Series as law and series as extension	228
2a	Mistake of comparing huge number and 'infinite' – Mathematical discovery changes the game – Distribution of primes – Understanding the meaning of 'trisection' – Comparison with question about the meaning of 'philosophy' – Explaining the meaning of 'proof' by giving a series of proofs – Many ways of seeing agreement of special case with general explanation – Explanation of 'proof' will be inexact – Difference between explanation by means of a series and otherwise	231

2b	How can we look for trisection of angle if there is no such thing? – Explanation of a word shows what one understands by it – Explaining 'regular pentagon' without giving its construction – Not clear what's meant by Euclidean proof – Consideration of geometry which has bisection as only construction – Fallacy of not seeing where you can and can't say 'and so on' in same sense – Proving that a forced mate is possible in chess	236
3a	Consideration of geometry which has bisection as only construction – We're misled by similarity between 'constructed' and 'measured' – Possibility of a hidden contradiction – If we have no way of finding contradiction, we haven't fixed what contradiction means – Question of whether there are 5 consecutive 7s in the development of π – Confusion of what we can do with what the calculus can do	240
3b	All big mathematical problems are comparable to search for 5 consecutive 7s in development of π – Understanding a proof of one of these mathematical problems – Curious grammar of 'there are 5 consecutive 7s' – What existence means depends on sort of proof you have – Proofs of immortality of the soul – Oliver Lodge and Kierkegaard have different conceptions of soul, as shown by their proofs of its immortality – Propensity to think that where we can say 'more' or 'less', we might be able to measure	244
4a	Distinguishing atomic propositions from molecular propositions – Different senses of 'analysis' – Lack of examples of 'atomic propositions' in Russell and *Tractatus* – Can we prepare a logical structure in advance? – Discovering a game vs. discovering a fact – Criticism of Russell and *Tractatus* on logical analysis – We can't help being misled by appearance of our language	249
4b	'Atomic propositions' are not the result of a future analysis – Relation between learning a language game and understanding language – 'Truth' and 'falsehood' in language game – 'Elliptical' sentences – Do words only have meaning in propositions? – Language is not a simple game, logic ought not be built up from a definition of proposition – Vagueness	255

of 'proposition', 'language', 'sentence' – Motivations for drawing a precise line, when 'proposition' is vague

5a Language games are the clue to understanding logic – Russell's calculus is just one among others – There are no essentially philosophical words – We use our language without thinking of rules of grammar – Talk of 'direction' or 'flow' of time – We often think we are dealing with an a priori law when we're dealing with a norm we have fixed – 'Deterministic' and 'indeterministic' are properties of the system I fix arbitrarily – Memory time and information time – Circular time – Empty time – Rules governing our use of 'time' 259

5b There is no complete grammar of a word – Logical analysis can be antidote to philosophical muddles – Tooth-ache and behaviourism – Is another person's tooth-ache, tooth-ache in the same sense as mine? – Criteria for 'having tooth-ache' – Confusion of statements of fact with tautological or grammatical statements – No sense in saying tooth-ache is 'private' 266

6a Tooth-ache – Visual sensation – Visual field does not belong to any person – Idea of a sense-organ perceiving is based on particular experiences – Correlation of tactile and visual space is not necessary – Solipsism – Private sensations 270

6b Idea of a person doesn't enter into the description of primary experience – Absurdity and temptation of solipsism – 'Possible' and 'necessary' – The difference between 'I have tooth-ache' and 'he has tooth-ache' – Private language – Definition of 'game' – Purpose of identifying nonsense 274

7a What is criterion of 'making sense'? – How is 'sign' to be defined? – Can't give general definition of 'proposition' or 'game', only examples – We give rules of grammar wherever there is a philosophical difficulty – Meaning of calling something nonsense – Nonsense arises from forming symbols analogous to certain uses, where they have no use – 'Sense' is vague – It makes no sense to ask for verification, or criterion of 'I have tooth-ache' – Characterization of 'primary experiences' – What is the criterion of a certain body being 'mine'? 279

7b	Does it make sense to say 'A has tooth-ache in B's tooth'? – What is the criterion that body belongs to me? – Verification of his having tooth-ache and his behaving in a certain way – Relation between 'I' and consciousness – 'I' can be used in two utterly different ways	285
8a	My decision whether I have tooth-ache is not made by reference to a body – Grammar of ordinary language distinguishes different uses of 'I' – Talk of 'unconscious' is misleading – Freud on unconscious hatred – 'The subject' is used in two different ways – Haldane on knowing what it feels like to be a limestone mountain – Has our visual field got blurred edges?	289
8b	Fallacy of idealism and solipsism – Rules as to what is evidence of 'this happened 5 minutes ago' – Statements that cannot be refuted by experience – Giving evidence is giving grammar – Order of time in memory – Senses of 'now'	294
9	Useless statements result from being misled by an analogy – Senses of 'present experience only is real' – Russell on 'world was created 5 minutes ago' – Methods of projection – 'Thinkable' and 'imaginable' – *Tractatus* on 'proposition is a picture' – You may think you are using an expression with sense when you are not – Helmholtz on 4-dimensional space – What we are doing is to point out actual mistakes	299

May Term, 1933

1	No notes	307
2a	The connection between meaning and verification – The meaning of a symbol is its place in a calculus, the way in which it is used – Contrast between 'intuitive' and 'discursive' ways of looking at meaning – Memory as a criterion of the past – The connection between evidence for a proposition and that proposition is a complicated one – Methods of measurement – Symptoms and criteria	308
2b	Meaning of 'meaning' – Grammar, rules, and use – Vagueness of 'meaning' and 'understanding' – Verification and grammar – Is probability a priori? – Grammar of grammatical rule vs. grammar of experiential proposition	313

3a	Verification, probability, and grammar – Is 'meaning' metalogical? – Grammar, rules, and use – Relationship to a linguist's study of grammar – Grammar of 'God' – Cf. 'soul' – Idol worship – Theology and grammar – Prayer – Religion and science	316
3b	Change of meaning – Clear vs. blurred boundaries – Having something in common – Connection through gradual transitions – 'Good', 'beautiful', and 'game' – Comparison with examples in mathematics and physics – Matters of taste – Frazer's mistake regarding explanations – Criticism of Frazer on magic with an effigy	323
4a	Descriptive vs. explanatory method – Evolutionary explanations – Frazer's mistake regarding explanations – The idea that each action has one motive: to get something useful – Essence, accident, and purpose – Frazer's explanation of Beltane – Darwin's explanation of expression of emotions – 'Good', 'beautiful', and 'game' – Having something in common – How does one know whether an action or event is good? – How do I know that a face is beautiful?	327
4b	'Beautiful' means something quite different in different cases – Two senses of 'agreeable' – Questions about harmony as an example of an aesthetic question – Is *King Lear* agreeable? – The idea that one always does what gives most pleasure – The incomparability of pain and pleasure – One doesn't always choose the more pleasant alternative – One doesn't always weigh alternatives before acting – How we talk of a beautiful colour, or face, depends on what we're talking about – You were taught what 'beauty' means by being shown examples	335
5a	Close connection between 'beautiful' and 'good' – What is an actual aesthetic controversy or enquiry like? – 'Beautiful' is rarely used, but words like 'correct' and 'right' are used often – We aim at ideals, which have this status by playing a certain role in the lives of a certain people – We don't usually have an ideal before us – The ideal is the tendency of people who create such a thing – Psychology is interested in causal connections, aesthetics is not – Aesthetics is 'descriptive' – Connection with question why Beltane impresses us so much – Frazer's explanation of the Golden Bough	339

5b	Relationship between aesthetics and psychology – Questions about causes of feelings of liking can be answered experimentally – Aesthetics asks about why we like certain things – Our investigation is like solving a mathematics problem	346
6a	A reason in aesthetics is a reason for having this word in this place rather than that, this musical phrase rather than that – All that aesthetics does is to draw your attention to things – A solution must speak for itself – Aesthetic discussion is like discussion in a court of law – Same sort of reasons are given in ethics and in philosophy – Here a reason consists in drawing your attention to something which removes an uneasiness – Role of ideals in aesthetics – Relationship between aesthetics and psychology	350
6b	Freud's psychological investigation of the nature of a joke is in a sense aesthetics – It has two sides: it can satisfy us scientifically by helping us make predictions; it can satisfy us aesthetically by giving a paraphrase, a good simile – Aesthetic craving for an explanation is not satisfied by a hypothesis – In mathematics, ethics, aesthetics, philosophy, answer to a puzzle is to make a synopsis possible – Experiments on rhythm in the laboratory	356
7	Freud's view that you can find out why you laugh at a joke by psychoanalysis – In a successful analysis, the person analysed accepts the analyst's reason why – Talk of subconscious reasons is a mere picture – We've only discovered new laws, not new regions of the soul – Freud thinks a joke conceals something, and analysis brings out concealed meaning – Freud confuses reason and cause – Freud mistakenly conceives of a reason as a cause seen from inside – Is psychoanalysis psychology? – Freud's discoveries are merely striking ways of expressing certain facts, and seeing them in a system – Subconscious thoughts are hypothetical entities – Constructing language-games and putting them side by side with actual uses of a word	360

Lectures, Cambridge 1930–1933
From the Notes of G.E. Moore

Lent Term, 1930

1

I.   4:1

2 kinds of puzzle about foundations of knowledge.

(1) how on earth is this proved? e.g. infinite primes.

(2) What's reality? What is number? Are Space & Time real? What is matter? What is substance?
Can't check them.
Irrelevant to science & life.
One can't by intellect get clear about <u>use of language</u>: though we use it by instinct.

Language consists of propositions; & several different senses of "proposition".

(1) Rule out $2 \times 2 = 4$, pure mathematics "propositions". They're different instruments from
(2) There's a piece of chalk here.
Any attempt to define <u>must</u> be futile.

It <u>works</u>, by being a picture of reality.
Pictures, because we compare them with reality.
E.g. "Is there a pencil here?"
Consider them not as descriptions, but as prescriptions, according to which you can act.

      Signal must be prearranged.   4:2

How a picture?
At <u>whatever</u> time I rap once, he is to go.

Simple symbols are arbitrary; but when we combine them, obvious I've pictured order.

Signal is "that I am rapping desk now".
A spatial order can correspond to a temporal one.

There's a <u>special</u>, & <u>general</u> arrangement.

Engine-driver has to interpret condition of arm sticking out & <u>now</u>.

You have to apply general rule to special case.

Proposition must be picture in so far as it can convey something <u>now</u>.

A policeman gives a picture of what you're going to do.
His words must have same <u>multiplicity</u> as what you have to do.

Suppose I had <u>only</u> use of integers, language would not have sufficient multiplicity.

4:3 Lever with 2 positions can't regulate velocity continuously.

Putting lever midway corresponds to talking nonsense.

To prescribe, I must describe what I want done.

Since prescription, so description, must have same multiplicity as thing described.

Essence of symbol is that it can in a particular way be compared with reality: they agree or disagree with reality, but <u>only</u> in so far as they are pictures.

Has a word by itself a meaning?
Depends what you mean:
(1) It is a thing which <u>can</u> function (2) In fact it doesn't.
Need proposition express relation or predicate?

In raps no relation?

You can describe without verbs, substantives & adjectives.

Even in our language you can. There are hundreds of different kinds   4:4
of words.
This table is brown. The weather is fair. I am tired.

I can't substitute "tired" for "brown", without giving nonsense.
Hence it's misleading to call both adjectives.[1]

In Jabberwocky[2] you can say which are adjectives, substantives & verbs.

---

[1] Moore's summary notes: <Any word is of a different kind from another, if substitution yields nonsense.> (10:01)
[2] 'Jabberwocky' is a nonsense poem by Lewis Carroll, which appears at the end of the first chapter of *Through the Looking-Glass, and What Alice Found There* (Carroll 1992, 116–18).

2

4:5   II.

Puzzles about foundations of our knowledge.
Real & persistent troubles.

Thought? or language?

E.g. What is number?

"Battle of Hastings in 1066" those who <u>say</u> this, know perfectly what they mean.

When we talk about Time & Space in philosophy, we're not explaining to people what they mean.
We're not troubled about <u>thought</u>, but about clarification of thought.

= internal relations of thought; e.g. does this word mean same in this context & in that.
Only way to do this is to get hold of <u>expressions</u> of thoughts.

I can demonstrate that solution to a philosophical problem consists in finding something unclear in our symbolism.
E.g. "<u>is</u>" is used in 3 different ways.
The door is brown
I <u>am</u>
2 × 2 is 4

4:6   The solution is to discover that it's misleading to use same word in different meanings.

This doesn't make things trivial: This kind of difficulty of expression is tremendous.

Lecture 2 – January 27, 1930

Difficulty is to get one which gives a clear idea of how the word is used: an expression which prevents grammatical mistakes.

Propositions are in some sense pictures.

(1) "Picture" may mean "looks like"; & in this sense if it looked more like Wittgenstein[3] than Moore, we should say it wasn't of Moore. This is <u>not</u> my sense.

(2) Picture = is intended to be a picture. And in this case only can it be correct or incorrect picture.

<u>Prescription</u>. You want to make a man move his hand.
E.g. U, D, L, R[4]; & e.g. 3U = 3 up.

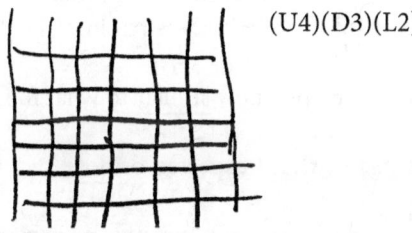

(U4)(D3)(L2)

Untrue simplifying assumption.   4:7

Suppose U4 made me mechanically go up etc..

In that case <u>language</u> would be on a level with drugs.

But did I <u>understand</u> the symbols?
Only answer would be that I reacted to them somehow.

In that case the <u>multiplicity</u> must be the same for (4 = ||||).

---

[3] In Moore's lecture notes the names appear as the abbreviations 'W.' and 'M.'.
[4] I.e. Up, Down, Left, Right.

But symbolism doesn't work in this way: I might say: I understand what you mean, but I won't do it.

(1) To understand = to think the proposition.

Relation between thought & reality is same (in important respect) as expectation, or volition or seeking to reality.

When I expect, what I expect doesn't occur in expectation.

How do we make sure that a man does understand what we mean?
Suppose a man says you didn't understand.

4:8   This would be taken as a sign that I did[5] understand.

There is always a gap between what occurs in expectation, & the expected thing, which has to be filled up by understanding.

But expectation, we feel, is somehow similar to what fulfils it (if anything).

How can I see that this is what I expected or not?

Imagine an answer to my expectation, positive or negative.

The expectation is a picture in a different sense.[6]

This is the same red as I saw yesterday ⎫
⎬ have different meanings.
This is the same red as that ⎭

We can compare reality & expectation, & compare the degree in which it resembles expectation: e.g. we can say this comes near what I expected. Just as "this isn't quite the same colour as I saw yesterday".
How can I judge the distance between things I can't put side by side?

---

[5] Sic.   [6] Moore later added: <From what? something similar to what is expected>.

That a is an expectation of b 4:9
= (1) <u>b</u> is a <u>positive</u> answer to a
  (2) <u>b</u> & <u>a</u> have same logical multiplicity.

(2) is shewn by fact that we can use same words as in
> I expect to <u>see a red patch</u>
> I <u>see a red patch</u>

The expectation & fulfilment have something in common, which is their logical multiplicity.

How do we understand?
By means of conventions. How are we taught them?

Some obviously true sentence is said, & child is left to <u>guess</u> what it represents.
We teach by <u>using</u> language.[7]

And these conventions are made by giving a <u>verification</u> of the proposition.

This establishes a connection between language & your expectations.

<u>You</u> understand: = sentence arouses in you something related to reality, in same way as expectation to reality. 4:10

Music-writing can be regarded as prescription <u>how</u> to move your fingers, or description how you moved them.

"I see the (surface of the moon)."
"I see the (moon)."

Whether 2 words are <u>really</u> of same kind, is shewn by whether substitution makes nonsense.

---

[7] Moore later added, following on from 'We teach': <(a language by using that language)>.

You can't <u>always</u> substitute "the surface" for "the moon" without nonsense: e.g. "the moon's <u>area</u> is ... square yards" but "the area of the moon's surface is ... square yards".[8]

Both expressions are all right; & express <u>same</u> thing in <u>entirely</u> different ways.

I see the moon = I see its surface.[9]

---

[8] Moore's summary notes: <"I see the moon" and "I see the surface of the moon" mean the same, but "the surface of the moon" is a different kind of expression from "the moon", because in <u>some</u> propositions to substitute "the moon" for "the surface of the moon" would make nonsense e.g. in "the area of the moon's surface is 2,000,000 square miles".> (10:01)

[9] Moore later drew an arrow connecting this line to the phrase 'Both expressions' in the previous sentence; he then added: <(Nonsense is "I see the surface of the surface of the moon".)>

3

III.   4:11

How propositions <u>work</u>.

Proposition like Measuring-rod.

And this not a simile, but an example: i.e. measuring-rod may <u>be</u> a proposition.

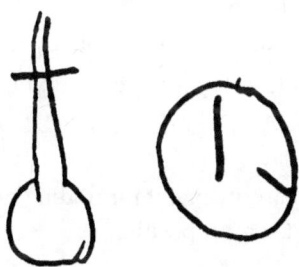

"At <u>this</u> time the mercury will stand at a certain point".

Each dash is a <u>picture</u>.

2 things are required for them to work as a picture or proposition.

(1) That possibilities for position of dashes, should be same as possibilities of position of Mercury & hand.

= must be in same space

(2) We can compare them with <u>actual</u> present position of Mercury & hand.

"O is that high."

Might express either that O is, or that Q is.

4:12 Hence (3) I must have made arrangement about <u>application</u> of measuring-rod.

You can say: Advance 2 feet, & measure what you there find
or Advance 3 feet, & measure what you there find.

(1) It must have length = be in same space.

(2) I must have made an arrangement for finding object to which it is to be applied, if it is to stand for a proposition.

"This desk is that /4 feet/ high." is a proposition; but the symbol is not <u>merely</u> the words.

E.g. you must explain "this desk" e.g. by pointing.

N.B. All the conditions that must be fulfilled in order that a proposition should be compared with reality, are rules of the application of language.

If desk is blown up: "It <u>is</u> this height" has no <u>sense</u>.

If it is <u>moved</u>, & I don't know how to find it: ~~It is also~~

"The present King of France is bald" <u>is</u> nonsensical, <u>if</u> you don't adopt Russell's analysis.[10]

<u>If</u> the existence of the King is <u>part</u> of the proposition.

---

[10] Russell 1905 is the canonical statement of Russell's analysis; there is a more accessible exposition in Russell 1919, chapter 16.

Does it <u>presuppose</u> existence of King, or not? It might do either.[11]   4:13

Describe height of O by writing "F (||||)".

Conditions of applicability are
(1) the measuring-rod: that is part of the symbol.
(2) the existence of O.

<u>Part</u> of the symbol is unessential: e.g. what wood ~~pencil~~ measuring-rod is made of.

"This is 4 pencils high" spoken, is not enough.

A great deal of language thus requires outside help.
E.g. a coordinate system is part of my language.
Suppose I want to tell a person to paint a wall a special colour: I must use a specimen, & <u>that</u> is part of my language.

Often, I eke out words with <u>memory</u>: e.g. I want to say: Paint wall that colour which you remember: here <u>his</u> memory is part of symbol.
A memory <u>image</u> is an <u>image</u> for 2 reasons.
(1) Multiplicity must be same: = they must be in same <u>space</u>.
We can understand black-board getting lighter & lighter till white.
Images can get lighter & lighter in their own way.   4:14

Part of picture is supplied by words, part by imagination.
Propositions presuppose memory & imagination: symbolise <u>via</u> imagination & memory.
~~Process called analysing propositions~~.

I can use words <u>instead</u> of imagination & memory.

---

[11] Moore's summary notes: <"The King of France is bald" <u>may</u> be nonsense, if there is no King of France; but is not nonsense if you accept Russell's meaning for it. It may be used in either way.> (10:01)

E.g. instead of "draw me an ellipse". the equation of ellipse.

This is process of analysis of proposition.

The multiplicity which language must have is supplied by rules of grammar.
= language must have same degree of freedom.

What happens to reality must be capable of happening to language.
E.g. bluish red, yellowish red; but grammar should not allow me to say "greenish-red".
Grammar fixes a certain degree of freedom.

This makes things belong to grammar, which are not supposed to.[12]

4:15 Colours are imagined placed on octahedron.[13]

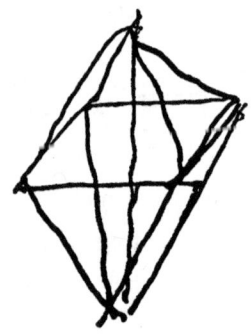

This is really a part of grammar, not of psychology.

Logic, Psychology, & Phenomenology.

---

[12] Moore's summary notes: <Grammar should not allow me to talk of "greenish red"; though of course this is saying that rules, which aren't supposed to be rules of grammar, are rules of grammar.> (10:01)

[13] The colour octahedron has one of the 'pure colours' (red, blue, green, yellow, white, and black) at each corner, with white at the top and black at the bottom. See Wittgenstein 1980, 8 and *Philosophical Remarks* (Wittgenstein 1964) §1.

"People under these circumstances have red after-images" is psychology. But "There is such a colour as a greenish-blue", is phenomenology, or <u>grammar</u>.

In grammar <u>some</u> things are arbitrary, some not.
The whole system of rules is <u>not</u> arbitrary.

Euclidian Geometry is <u>also</u> a part of grammar.[14]

Suppose our space <u>is</u> Euclidean:
then all constructions <u>could</u> be made by physical objects.
There are straight lines, & planes: e.g. edges & surfaces of rigid bodies.
The boundary between 2 colours is a line; & or points.   4:16

What this shews: "There is a straight line between any 2 points."

Euclid says there <u>can</u> be a boundary.

The proposition that a straight line goes through 2 given points has <u>sense</u>, whether true or not.

Take "3 angles of a triangle = 2 right angles".

How could we verify it, if it were a real proposition?

We must have <u>fixed</u> a method of measuring.

Suppose we get 181° by measuring.

What Euclid says is: If you get any result other than 180°, you are going to say that you've made a mistake.[15]

---

[14] Euclid's geometry is set out in his *Elements* (2006). It was written in Alexandria circa 300 BC and, in a modified form, was still widely used as a textbook at the time of these lectures.

[15] Moore's summary notes: <Euclidean Geometry is a part of grammar. E.g. the proposition that the 3 angles of a triangle are equal to 2 right angles (180 degrees) is not a proposition which can be established by measurement: what Euclid says is that if by measurement you find 181 degrees, you are to say that you've made a mistake.> (10:1,3)

We may find by measuring π = 3.140; & then we say this isn't accurate.

This is a convention of expression: If I alter one part of my grammar, I must alter another part.

4:17 ~~People~~ We say that a proposition hasn't sense, unless we can imagine it: we must be able to make some sort of image of reality.

If we can, what is expressed is <u>possible</u>; this is how possibility is expressed.

"It is possible to draw a line" = "There is a line drawn" has sense.

That a thing has been done, can't prove that it's possible <u>now</u>.

Language itself shews that it's <u>possible</u> to lift the chalk <u>now</u>.

4

IV at Priestley's.[16]

---

[16] Raymond E. Priestley, whose rooms in Clare College were the location for the weekly discussion classes. According to Desmond Lee (Wittgenstein 1980, xvi, 9), there was no lecture at the scheduled time on the fourth week of class, but there was a combined lecture and discussion later that week.

5

4:18 V.

Language represents world in 2 ways: (1) in that propositions are true or false (2) in that, whether true or false, a proposition must have something in common with world, in order to be right or wrong.

E.g. a photo may represent distribution of light & dark shades; but it must have light & dark to represent at all.

N.B. photo does not portray light & darkness; because light & dark are themselves in it.

Some features in a picture must represent features in reality, some must be the same.

Colour is both in the picture & in what is pictured.

What sort of harmony must there be between thoughts & the world?

Only that the thought must have logical form; & without this it wouldn't be a thought.

What language must have in common is contained in rules of grammar.

"p is possible" is not a real proposition.

The sense of a proposition is the way in which it's verified.

How can this be verified?

No-how; since we could only verify whether it's true or false, & in either case it must be possible.

4:19 "Internal properties & internal relations."

A red patch can be darker than a white; but can't be darker than E flat.

Logicians have talked as if being a colour was a property.

They have used words, as if there were logical concepts "thing", "number", "complex" – as if these stood for "concepts", as opposed to proper names.

This can be explained

Lecture 5 – February 17, 1930

"This is a ...": whatever makes sense here is a word for a concept, <u>not</u> a proper name.

It's important to shew that they're not on a level with "man", "book" etc.; & hence that there are no logical concepts.

If "man" is a concept, I must be able to say "A is a man"; but I can't <u>say</u> this, unless it <u>may</u> be false.

"A is a thing" tries to express something which ought really to be expressed by grammar.

Take "A stands on the floor":

grammar tells us what sort of words we can substitute – let's call whatever <u>can</u> stand on the floor a "thing".

Consider "A is a thing": if false, then, it must be <u>nonsense</u>.

So with "2 is a number", which Russell & Frege both write down. 4:20

If 2 <u>isn't</u> a number, grammar forbids to put it in the proposition at all.

How can we use such words as "number"? We <u>can</u>, but in a different way.

If $\phi(A) =_{def.}$ A is a man

then $\phi(-) = (-)$ is a man.

A concept is a propositional function.
But there is no concept ( ) is a thing
      ( ) is a number.

$(\exists x)\phi x$ = there is a <u>thing</u> which satisfies ϕ: this is <u>right</u> use of thing.
So $(\exists n)\psi n$

I.e. proper expression of "thing", "number" etc. is a <u>variable</u>, together with <s>what satisfies</s> grammatical rules.

"There's a man next door" = $(\exists x)(x$ is a man . x is next door$)$
But also $(\exists x)(x$ is a day . x is my birthday$)$.
Here rules of grammar are quite different.
In "A is a man, & B is a day"; we can't substitute B for A or vice <u>versa</u>.

4:21 What seems to be a logical concept, i.e. seems to be of same kind as "man", is not expressed by a propositional function, but by a variable to which certain rules apply.

The concept "prime number", is the variable prime number.

"There are things" is nonsense; but "There are things such that ..." is not.

We can't say: "There are prime numbers."

I can't say "There are 2 things in this room"; only "2 children" etc..

Hence not "there are $\aleph^0$ things"; i.e. there is no axiom of infinity.

$(\exists x,y)\phi x . \phi y$ = There are 2 things at least which satisfy ϕ.
There are only 2 = (this . $\sim(\exists x,y,z)\phi x . \phi y . \phi z$).
Let's write this, as a whole, short: $(Ex,y)\phi x . \phi y$.
Hence we can't say "There are 2 things".

4:22 Hence we can't talk about number of things at all, which seems paradoxical. If "There are n things" has sense, so has "There are n+1".

"A third stroke must exist" has sense, if I can describe the existence of a third stroke.
e.g. if these points were white.

Now take "There are 4 primary colours".
If this has a sense, so must "There are 5", & we must be able to describe what it would be like for there to be a fifth.

$(Exyzwv)(x$ is a primary colour . y is ...$)$

There are 4 primary colours means only that there are 4 names & no more which can be substituted, so as to give sense, in propositions which are significant about the primary colours & nothing else.[17]

---

[17] Moore's comment from summary notes: <Why not: "There are more than 4 names ...".> (10:69)

>
> 1
> (1) + 1
> ((1) + 1) + 1

The <u>possibility</u> of writing such symbols must give what I mean by number of numbers.

Russell tried to preface every proposition by $(p \supset p) \supset$ [18]   4:23
hoping thereby to secure the right kind of substitutions.
He meant: the hypothesis is only true, if you substitute a proposition.

$(4 \supset 4) \supset F(4)$, will be <u>nonsense</u>.

It is always wrong in philosophy & logic to make classifications.

To say: There are 4 kinds of etc..

This is all right, if the property is external.

There can be no definition which applies to both transfinite & finite cardinals.
They are different in form; no substitution is allowed.

---

[18] See Russell 1903 §14 and §16. Wittgenstein makes the same claim at *Tractatus* (Wittgenstein 1922) 5.5351.

6

4:24 VI.

Logical Concepts are Pseudo-concepts.

Distinguishing mark is that "This bench is a man" has sense.
But "This is a cardinal number" etc. have no sense.

"There are no logical concepts." is true.

What we try to express by "is a number", "is a body", "is a surface" is expressed by grammatical rules.

Take $(\exists x)(\phi x . \psi x)$ = There is a brown desk.
  $\phi(a)$ = a is brown.
  $\phi(\ )$ = ( ) is brown.
  $\psi(\ )$ = ( ) is a desk.

  $(\exists x,y)(\phi x . \phi y . \psi x . \psi y)$ = There are at least 2 brown desks.
I can't in the same sense write
  $(\exists x)x$ is a number.

4:25 These words <u>can</u> be used in a correct way, but it's entirely different viz. by grammatical <u>rules</u> for a kind of variable, which can be better explained as follows.

Suppose $\phi(\ )$ = ( ) is a man in this room.
  then $(\exists x)\phi x$.
But suppose $(\exists x)\psi x$ = there is a colour which so & so have in common.

  Here we can't substitute "a man" for a colour; or "a line" ...

We <u>can</u> use colour or number in this way

$(\exists x_{\text{colour}})\phi x$

or $(\exists x_{\text{number}})\psi x$.

The word for the real concept occurs outside the bracket; whereas the word for logical concept stands inside.

I couldn't say $(\exists x_{\text{man}})\phi x$

But you must say $(\exists x_{\text{body}})\phi x$.

Thus you can write $(\exists p)\phi p$

but not $(\exists x)(x \in p \, . \, \phi x)$.

Is "primary" an adjective to colour, as "black" to "gown"?   4:26

To say "blue is not primary", or "violet is primary" is nonsense. i.e. distinction between primary & not is a logical distinction.

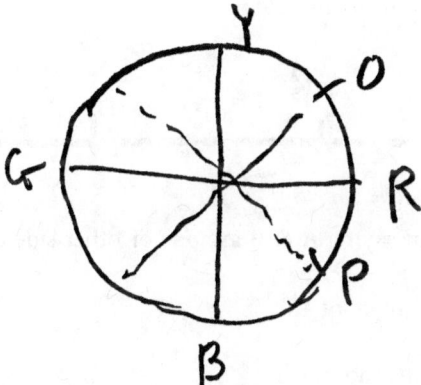

Could we not use other axes: e.g. dotted ones & say red is <u>mixture</u> of purple & orange?

If we meant by "mixture" = common element, we could.

or = lies between.

The fallacy is that there are 2 meanings of "between".

E.g. suppose I mix black pigment with red; & then blue with black. I should then get a series in which black lies between red & blue.

But <u>not</u> in the sense in which orange between yellow & red.

4:27 <u>Any</u> colour is between in some sense … so that

Red is <u>not</u> between orange & purple in proper sense.

You can't say "My wall is a mixture of yellowish red & greenish blue".

Can you say: Mixtures are allowed within 45°?

But we don't get such an angle except between <u>these</u> axes.

This is because there is no colour <u>midway</u> between blue & green.

You can say: This is <u>almost</u> green.

But take 2 <u>roughly</u> in the middle.

There's no sense in saying A & B are one or other side of middle.

I cannot halve the angle of 45.

The picture contains too much:

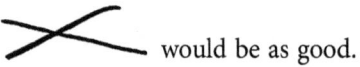 would be as good.

4:28 Therefore a square is a better picture than a circle.

Take a greenish blue; then of another that's <u>not</u> greenish, you can say that it's reddish, or that it's pure.

Take an orange & purple slip: can you mix these colours? in a sense in which green & red don't?

Purple & orange can't mix; but as you get nearer to orange, you come to a point where …

Take 2 reds you can distinguish: can you be in doubt whether they're both yellowish or both bluish?

You can arrange all colours in a line between black & white.

It's impossible that the notes C & E should be in unison: therefore it's meaningless that C^1 & C^2 are.

"I see in this picture all the primary colours" = "I see in this picture, red, yellow, green, & blue."

"Primary colour" instead of drawing a boundary within language, draws a boundary of language.

A boundary must be between 2 classes.   4:29

There's a false appearance, which arises whenever a whole space another[19].

To every boundary in my visual field corresponds one in my retina but to one in my retina, none in my visual field corresponds!

Suppose you have a dictionary of names: & draw a boundary line containing all names of people with beards.

Suppose instead I have my whole vocabulary, & also numerical words:
    & draw a line round all those that have meaning.
There can't be a proposition corresponding to this boundary.

You can't distinguish red, green, blue, yellow as having a quality which purple & orange haven't.

Certain formal rules in grammar of irrationals correspond to certain in grammar of cardinals.

---

[19] Moore later wrote a question mark over this word; it is likely that Moore mis-transcribed the sentence.

7

4:30   Lecture VII. Monday, March 3.

Colours not distinguished from sounds by fact that what's true of one is false of other.

They are represented by variables, distinguished by rules of grammar applying to them.

In $(\exists x)\phi x$, ϕ must be like "man".

But "colour" must occur in the bracket.

$$(\exists_{colour} x)\phi x.$$

In my last lecture, I was saying something about words; how they could be used.

E.g. "Red is a primary colour" = "red" can be used in this manner.

So "This colour is midway between red & blue" has no sense.

"Red is a mixture of orange & purple" is nonsense.

It was objected that I didn't give <u>mere</u> linguistic conventions: that I was talking of the <u>meaning</u> of the words, not the words themselves.

What is meant by "<u>mere</u> convention"?

That not made for fun, like the rules of a game.

4:31   Rules of a game are like grammar in a way: rules of chess <u>allow</u> certain moves, & of grammar <u>allow</u> substitutions.

You could find grammatical rules by looking at writings in a language you don't know.

And grammar isn't mere convention in this sense.

When we talk of rules of grammar, we have in mind that words are used in particular ways in significant sentences.

Language differs from a game, in its application to reality.

The value of grammar is that they're rules for a language: but the application is outside the signs.

By rules of grammar I portray a chunk of the structure of nature.

In case of a portrait, I can give reasons for what I do by means of words. In case of language we can't.

We can't ask "Do the internal properties of colour fit the rules?" because we already presuppose the grammatical rules we want to justify.

How do we describe application of language? 4:32
By "This is "Drury""; which seems to connect our language with reality, but doesn't.

E.g. "This is green" may mean 2 entirely different things.

(1) Where "This" is the substrate which is green; e.g. the skirting, or the visual sense-datum.
This is no explanation at all.
Take "I'm switching on the electric light", which might answer the question what is meant by "electric light".
The other man must then believe that I'm making a true proposition about what I'm doing. He must guess.
In this case the explanation doesn't really connect reality with the proposition.
This presupposes grammar.
(2) "This = green", – a definition.
Does this presuppose grammar? Yes.
This is no good, unless I understand what kind of word "green" is.[20]

---

[20] Moore's summary notes: <We presuppose grammar, & don't connect reality with proposition, both when we explain "electric light" by saying "I'm switching it on now", where man must believe we're saying the truth, & guess what truth. And again we presuppose grammar in giving ostensive definition of green, because I must understand that "green" is a colour-word.> (10:69–70)

Explain "A stands on the floor".

A is this, stands is this, on is this, floor is this.

I.e. these definitions presuppose that we know grammar.

4:33 These are conventions in that they don't talk <u>about</u> application, but presuppose it.

This explains what's wrong with Russell's theory of types: a theory of types is a grammar, & must not mention meanings of words.

Johnson tries to distinguish concepts from pseudo-concepts, by giving something which can be said about the one, can't be about the other.

E.g. colours are distinguished by a particular kind of difference.

There's a relation between red & green, which there isn't between red & the tone C.

	Call it ℞
He says	Red ℞ Green
	~ Red ℞ Chalk.

If so, how do you know <u>only</u> colours stand in this relation? Have you examined everything?

Johnson would say "formally certified".[21]

= by looking at it, you can see whether it's true or false.

What a proposition shews is the <u>possibility</u> of its truth, not its truth.

4:34 A priori true <u>propositions</u> = formally certified.

These aren't propositions at all: they shew something, don't say anything.

If I call some colours "primary" without giving grammatical rules which apply to one word, not to the other, I'm talking nonsense.

E.g. infinite possibility. To shew how logical distinction ought to be drawn.

---

[21] '[W]e may contrast a proposition whose truth is certified by pure thought or reason with a proposition which is certified on the ground of actual experience. Briefly we shall call these two classes "formally certified" and "experientially certified".' (Johnson 1921, 55–6)

What's meant by "There are an infinite number of shades of grey between black & white"?

Something entirely different from "I see 3 colours in this room".

To verify latter, you count colours.

You can't do this in other case; & how can you?

You might say: You <u>can</u> go on counting them forever.

The linguistic expression of "It's possible, the clock has stopped" is <u>that</u> "the clock has stopped" has sense.

But in "You <u>can</u> count them forever" this is not the case.

What's meant by "Space is infinitely divisible".

"This line can be bisected" has for its linguistic expression ""This line is   4:35
bisected" has sense".

"Infinitely divisible" is quite different.[22]

Different rules apply to "infinite" & to any numeral: it doesn't answer the question "How many?".

Suppose $f(\frac{1}{2})$ = This line is bisected

$f(\frac{1}{3})$ = This line is trisected

$f(\frac{1}{4})$ = This line is divided into 4 parts.

But there's not another $f(\frac{1}{\infty})$

Write $f\left(\frac{1}{1+1}\right)$

$f\left(\frac{1}{1+1+1}\right)$

We see a law; that an internal relation holds between 2 successive members; & that the series has no end.

---

[22] Moore's summary notes: <"This line <u>can</u> be bisected" = ""This line has been bisected" has sense". But "this line is infinitely divisible" <u>not</u> = "This line has been divided an infinite number of times" has sense.> (10:04)

Linguistic expression of infinite possibility <u>is</u> infinite possibility in language.

$(\exists x)\phi x$

$(\exists x,y)\phi x . \phi y$

$(\exists x,y,z)\phi x . \phi y . \phi z$

To assert <u>all</u> these are true = to assert there's an infinite number.

4:36 Infinity is a property of a law, not of an extension.

8

VIII. 4:37

Word "infinite" not a numeral. It occurs in connection with "possible".

I made a grammatical distinction between 2 uses of "possible".

"p is possible" is a pseudo-proposition.   =   "p" has sense.
                                                     or   "~p" has sense
                                                   or   "q ∨ p" has sense
                                                   or   "q . p" has sense

Simile. Cf. proposition with → (sense = direction)

State of affairs   ⇌
Truth = disagrees or agrees.
Possibility is represented by the arrow being what it is.

There is a proposition only where truth & falsehood is doubtful.
If sense is doubtful, not a proposition at all.

"can be divided into 2 parts" = "is divided" has sense.
       Write latter f(2)
& f(3) is divided into 3, etc. etc..
But infinitely divisible not = f(∞) has sense (it hasn't)   4:38

It means there's an infinite possibility of constructing f(2) etc. according to a law, which we see.

To finite possibility corresponds a real division.
But to infinite not.

f(2), f(3), f(4) are instances of a law: that they are = "line is infinitely divisible".

[f(1), f(ξ), f(ξ+1)] is symbol for induction
It's a symbolic rule, representing a formal series.

    f(1) = first member

    f(ξ) = any member or <u>general</u> member.

    f(ξ+1) = next to that.

We get f(1), f(1+1), f(1+1+1) ... & so on.

ξ <u>seems</u> here to denote a sort of generality comparable to the generality of x in (x)ϕx.[23]

But this is not so.

4:39 ξ has <u>no</u> meaning whatever, unless I have 1.

Though the rule has <u>some</u> sort of generality, it's not comparable to (x)ϕx, because we have to go step by step: we never get to anything general.

In what sense <u>is</u> space infinitely divisible?

Wrong reasons are given for saying it's not.

Suppose it's said there's no infinitely small part, therefore divisibility stops somewhere.

Take boundaries between colours.

Go on long enough: you'll see grey.[24]

Let n^{th} be grey: $(n-1)^{th}$ still seen as black & white.

People say the parts in (n − 1) are smallest parts.

But can you see these parts are not <u>divisible</u>?

You only see they're not <u>divided</u>.

---

[23] Moore actually wrote 'x(ϕx)', but this is surely an error, since he otherwise consistently followed the convention of putting brackets around the quantifier, as he did in his own later summary notes on this very passage (10:70).

[24] Moore's later clarification: </(i.e. go on long enough with making alternate black & white smaller & smaller)/>

While I see divisions, you see none.

People suppose the only way of making you see divisions in your visual space, is to divide.   4:40

But it might be that alcohol, should make you.

E.g. suppose you can only see millimeters as black white; & alcohol makes you see ½ millimeters.

This only means that it's last division he has seen: not that he can't see thinner ones.

No experiment ever shews anything about possibility.

This error is analogous to another.

It has been rightly said that visual space is not Euclidean.

for: a tangent does not cut a circle only in one point.

I can never see only one point, is supposed to prove this. But it doesn't.

would be as good a proof that is Euclidean.

The right reason for saying visual circle has no tangent is quite different, viz.   4:41

You don't see little bits curved.

That is proof that not Euclidean: i.e. that visual curve can be composed of visual straight. This is not an experiment.

There are 2 different sorts of lines in visual space.
One thinks: what has colour, has extension.
That one coloured stripe will do as well as another.

There's a distance at which you don't see 4 points at the corners.

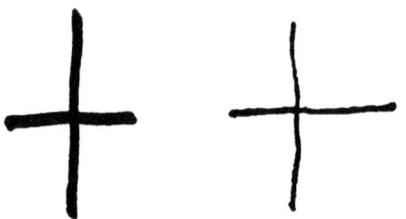

This <u>shews</u> something.

I <u>can</u> go on adding 1s for ever; & space in that sense <u>is</u> infinite.
In what sense?

Geometry in physics is so in quite a different sense, from that in which I'm using it; & space in a different sense.

4:42 Geometry is <u>grammar</u> of spatial objects, i.e. piece of chalk in physical space; & patches of colour in visual.

Every proposition of geometry expresses <u>possibilities</u> of space, not what's really the case.

Suppose axiom: A straight line <u>can</u> be drawn from any point to any point

= to describe a certain operation <u>has</u> sense.
In this sense I can't verify or falsify geometry by experiment: what geometry would say is: So & so is a possible experiment.

But in physics you can make a geometry more or less plausible.
You can't make a grammar so.

<u>No</u> experiment can tell me anything about visual or tactile space; or about space in sense in which space is a possibility.

Lecture 8 – March 10, 1930

Visual space is what we should get with eyes that can't be moved.

But what we generally think of is something combined out of this & space of movement. In which there's a sense in "behind my head".

Combined space is an order of visual impressions & those of muscular sense.

There's another order of experience connected with locomotion: & this is infinite = no step is essentially the last, no step is logically different from another. 4:43

This is the space we use in adding '|'s.

What's meant by: Infinite number of things satisfies a certain function?

Suggestion is: Let's assert all these propositions.

Instead of using dots, you can write series in form of induction.

$(\exists x_|)\phi x$

$(\exists x_|, x_{||})\phi x_| . \phi x_{||}$

$[(\exists x_|)\phi x_|, (\exists x_| - x_\xi)\phi(x_|) - \phi(x_\xi), (\exists x_| - x_\xi, x_{\xi+|})\phi x_| - \phi_{\xi+|}]$

But has it any meaning to assert logical product of all these propositions? No.

$\sum 1 + \dfrac{1}{2} + \dfrac{1}{4} \cdots$ approaches a limit. 4:44

But product of these propositions doesn't approach any limit?

May Term, 1930

1

May Term. Lecture I.   4:45

<u>Generality</u>.
    Very difficult, because many different <u>kinds</u>.

This doesn't mean a genuine concept, with species of it.

What's meant that we use expressions "all, some, every" in entirely different ways.

You can't therefore say one has one property, the other another.

But yet it's not a mere coincidence that we use the words in these ways.

They really have something in common – a structural quality.

It is like integers, & complex numbers.

In this case it is specially clear what the internal similarity consists in,

it is that the grammatical rules applying to one sort apply also in part to the other.

This is kind of similarity between space & time, brightness & pitch: e.g. that they form a series.

If we wrote a grammar of RED, BLUE, YELLOW, GREEN, & of C, $C^\#$, D, $D^\#$ we should find <u>some</u> rules in common.

(1) Kind to which Russell's notation applies.   4:46
    $(x)\phi x, (\exists x)\phi x$.
i.e. where (1) can be regarded as logical product
    (2) can be regarded as a logical sum.
Here the entities in question are what we denote by <u>proper names</u>.
These can be distinguished that in
    "ξ exists", a proper name will make nonsense.

I.e. here x must take such values, that if you substitute them in "ξ exists", you get nonsense.

This would be the sense of <u>all</u> in

>All the primary colours are in this picture.

= φa . φb . φc . φd, & <u>another</u> proposition asserting that these are all is <u>not</u> wanted.

Contrast "All the people in this room have gowns",

>here it <u>isn't</u> a logical product; because whichever you give, you must add "And there are no others".

I can't say "And there are no other primary colours".

This is comparatively rare.

(2) <u>Oftener</u> we have one which doesn't presuppose a totality.

"I met a man" <u>can't</u> = a disjunction.

"I met one of the people now alive" = a disjunction.

4:47   Take "There is a white circle in this square".

What sort of thing could be "a circle in a square", "a man in this room"?

We are regarding these as possible predicates: Frege said concepts were this.

We think of it as a substrate.

When we say "This is circular"; what is "this"? It must be something which could be recognised even, if it were <u>not</u> circular.

Giving names is only possible in very special cases.

Bring 2 pieces of chalk together; make them coalesce; & then separate them. Which is which?

If you could make 2 exactly similar chairs coalesce, you couldn't distinguish them.

"This" has ever so many different kinds of meaning, just as "pointing to" has.

I <u>do</u> the same thing, whether I point to a man or his colour; but here pointing to means something quite different.

If this were Russell's generality, there would have to be meaning in

~(∃x)~φx

= Everything is a circle in this square.

We must therefore find something which isn't <u>necessarily</u> a white circle in this square.   4:48

To find such a thing; you can take a point which is the centre of a circle: <u>that</u> need not have been.

This is a circle = Here is a circle.

There are a pair of coordinates such that they define a point which is a centre of a white circle in this square.

There is no totality of such pairs: an infinite totality isn't a totality.

In this case (∃x)φx isn't a logical sum.

And that (x)φx isn't a logical product

    is made clear by

    ~(∃x)~φx. This would mean "Every point is the centre of a circle" – which is unimaginable.[1]

Take a patch continually varying in colour from white to black.
Or take

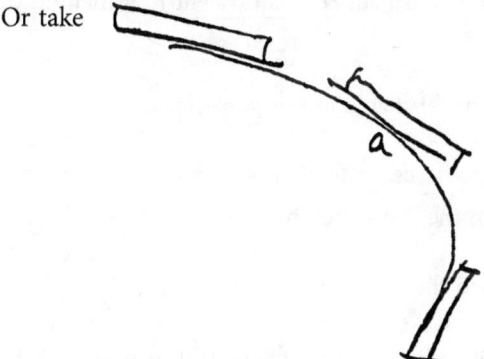

when we say, it <u>must</u> have been at a intermediately.

---

[1] Moore later added: <because there are an infinite number of points?>

4:49 The footrule rolled from here to there; & I saw it.
Does it <u>follow</u> from this that it must have been at a?

People say
"If I see a continuous transition, I must see all the infinite shades of grey".
But what is it "to see a shade of grey"?
I must mean something which occupies a <u>finite</u> part, & therefore not an infinite number.

(2) <u>Footrule</u>.
If we talk of visual place; it <u>doesn't</u> follow that it was here.
I could <u>see</u> it there, only if it was there for a finite time.

In physical sense, it perhaps never was there: it might have skipped.

There <u>is</u> a sense in which we <u>can</u> say it was at <u>all</u> intermediate places.
And that is when we're talking of <u>hypotheses</u>.

A <u>proposition</u> can be <u>verified</u> or falsified, & is <u>equivalent</u> to a method of verifying or falsifying.

4:50 Hypotheses are not verifiable or falsifiable in the same sense.

<u>Most</u> of our sentences are hypotheses.
E.g. "There is a man sitting on the last bench but one".

<u>Not</u>[2] if we take it as pointing to the future, as we do.

"This is a piece of chalk" expresses a series of expectations, which <u>essentially</u> goes on for ever.

A hypothesis is a <u>law</u> by means of which propositions are constructed.

---

[2] After '<u>Not</u>', Moore later added: <verifiable?>

I can't verify that a lark has laid this egg, if I didn't see it do so. What then do I mean by: A lark did lay it?

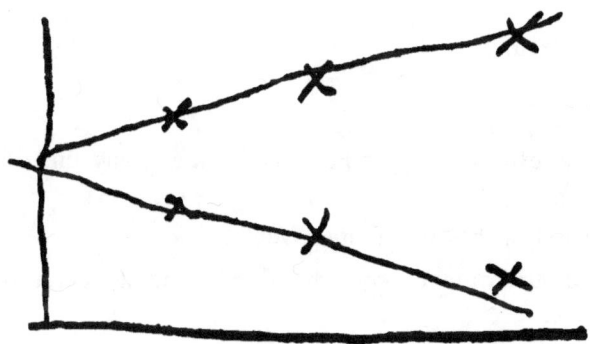

Suppose whenever we move upwards we see a spark.

What's meant by saying there was a flash, which we have never seen, & never shall?

We've abstracted from our experience, a rule pointing to the future, & <u>not</u> verifiable because it points to the future ad <u>infinitum</u>.   4:51

It's a formal rule, by means of which we construct propositions: e.g. that in <u>this case</u> I shall get 2 flashes.

2

4:52　　　May Term. II.

<u>Generality</u>. Kinds

(1) Correctly expressed by $(x)\phi x$, $(\exists x)\phi x$, where only finite number of values.

(2) Where variable has an infinite possibility.

"I will divide this distance <u>somewhere</u>" $\neq$ an infinite logical sum, either here, or there.

But this <u>isn't</u> an infinite logical sum.

Many things we can't understand; but nothing in grammar is a thing we don't understand: grammar is complete.

This seems not to be so, because there is such a thing as mathematical discovery, & therefore it looks as if what is discovered is what we didn't yet know.

But there can be no incompleteness except <u>within</u> a space; there are no gaps in grammar: it is always complete.

Sheffer's <u>discovery</u> of stroke notation is a grammatical discovery. It's misleading to call this discovery.

Discovery proper can only be made where there's a system in which we can look for something.

Sheffer had no system by which to find p | q; nor have we.

Sheffer found a new space.

People ask: is p | p really what we call ~p?

4:53　The answer is: All that is wanted is a system of a given logical multiplicity; & Sheffer found such a system.

<u>Before</u> we couldn't have said: There's a gap there; there <u>must</u> be a system with only one logical constant.

Mathematical <u>discovery</u> is always unmethodical: you have no method for making the discovery.

In logic & mathematics, it never is unimportant <u>how</u> you get there. If you get there, in a different way, you haven't got <u>there</u>.

Is every even number the sum of 2 primes?[3]
Has this sense?
(1) We <u>have</u> no method of answering this.

Therefore we can't look for the solution in the sense in which we can where we <u>have</u>.

What are mathematicians doing, when they work at it?

Suppose you'd forgotten how to multiply: would 224 × 37 have a meaning for you?

In logic & mathematics, you can't know the same thing in 2 independent ways.

Nor is there in case of sense-data.
In case of <u>hypothesis</u>, there are different evidences for same. <u>Nowhere else</u>.
What Pythagoras proved, is <u>not</u> what a man suspected from measuring triangles.[4]   4:54

Measuring a triangle is an experiment.

Euclidean Geometry does <u>not</u> prophesy about results of an experiment.

What it says is: If I measure, & get 181, then, in Euclidean way of expression, I must say "I've measured wrong".[5]

---

[3] The statement that every even integer greater than 2 can be expressed as the sum of two primes is known as 'Goldbach's Conjecture'. It remains neither proved nor disproved.
[4] Pythagoras's theorem, perhaps the most famous theorem of Euclidean geometry, states that the square of the hypotenuse of a right-angled triangle (its longest side) is equal to the sum of the squares of the two other sides.
[5] Moore's notes give the angle as 191, but this is almost certainly a mistake. Lee's notes for this part of the lecture read '181°', not '191°' (Wittgenstein 1980, 17). See also 4:16.

3

4:55   May Term, III.

Sheffer's discovery.

Are any 2 different systems of signs different "spaces"? No.

If 2 systems are translatable into one another, they are the same.

Then Sheffer's is same as Russell's.
Sheffer didn't only introduce a definition.
He does define p | q = ~p.~q.
But this isn't his discovery: Russell might have used this ~~definition~~ shorthand, without the discovery.
And Sheffer needn't have used shorthand.

His Discovery is $\left(\begin{array}{c} \sim p . \sim p = \sim p \\ \sim(\sim p . \sim q) . \sim(\sim p . q) = p \vee q \end{array} \right.$

Frege uses and & not

Sheffer's discovery = $\left\{ \begin{array}{c} \sim p . \sim p = \sim p \\ \sim(\sim p . \sim p) . \sim(\sim q . \sim q) = p . q \end{array} \right.$

Sheffer's discovery is to discover an aspect of the equations.

4:56   It's conceivable that Frege should have written everything in this way, & yet have said he had 2 primitive ideas.[6]

---

[6] Moore's summary notes: <Frege might have written everything with stroke, & yet said he had 2 primitive ideas> (10:71). In *Begriffsschrift*, Frege does have two primitive truth-functional connectives. However, they are not, as suggested above, 'and' and 'not', but rather 'not' and 'if-then'. See Frege 1879, §5–§7. Frege explicitly discusses this choice of connectives on page 20.

Perhaps to say Sheffer discovered a new "space" is misleading.

Point about impossibility of looking for space.

You can't find a connection in grammar, which is already there.

A "space" means everything of which you must be certain, in order to ask a question.
If I'm to look whether so & so is so, or not, that which I want to discover must be <u>entirely</u> describable beforehand.

You will find a ~~red~~ circle of <u>this</u> shade (shewing a colour) describes completely.

> φA contains a symbol which (∃x)φx doesn't, but the 2 descriptions are entirely alike.

Now "I'm trying to find a system with only one primitive idea" doesn't describe completely or exactly.
What makes it <u>possible</u> to describe is that description is <u>logically</u> all right.
Now you can try to find whether what is logically all right is physically so: 4:57

A generality which presupposes infinite possibilities is not therefore more <u>complex</u>.

When (∃x)φx is a logical sum, & (x)φx a logical product, the complexity of φa
$$\phi b$$
$$\phi c$$
is already contained. And a disjunction of 4 numbers is more complex than one with 3.
If p entails q, then p asserts q.

Hence if p asserted an <u>infinite</u> disjunction, it would be infinitely complex.

Does an infinity follow from: On this band there's a continuous transition from white to black?

You might think so, because you can say: This shade must be there; & so of all. But the shade occupies a finite stretch in the band.

So with a moving ball: It must have touched this end, & so an infinite number.

4:58   If we're talking of visual <u>moving</u> continuously, it never <u>was</u> anywhere: a thing only is in places where it stops.

With a hypothesis you can make up the proposition that it touched this, & that & so on ad infinitum.

In case of a figure in Euclid, the infinite possibility is represented by infinite possibility of visual space.

There's another sort of generality in logic, e.g. in

$$p \vee \sim p$$

Here's a <u>real</u> variable, & an <u>infinity</u> of special cases.

(1) This is <u>not</u> a logical product.
(2) We must have some idea of what can be substituted.
(3) No definition will help us.

The proof that angles of a triangle are 180, is a proof about <u>space</u>, not about this particular triangle.

And if it did prove about <u>this</u> triangle, it wouldn't prove about any other.

4:59   If there's an infinite possibility in your proof, this must be represented by an infinite possibility in your symbols: not by a description, nor by word "infinite".

Mathematical Induction

You seem to see: That can be done, without knowing how, in problem of "How many times must chalk be lifted to make this network?"

How is this? He has a symbolism already, but can't yet translate it into another.

4

May Term, IV.   4:60

<u>Generality</u>.

Points, lines, planes: we can replace points, by lines, & in physics take events or colours.

Geometry & grammar: gives rules which allow us to use our symbols in a certain way.

E.g. suppose we apply it to a coloured plane: ~~e.g.~~ infinite Euclidean: here lines are border lines between colours, & points are where borders intersect.

Now take "Any 2 points can be connected"

This = The proposition "they are connected" has sense.

And "<u>any</u> such proposition has sense" is grammar.

Grammar is unjustifiable by means of language.

E.g. "This combination of symbols makes sense" can't be justified by a proposition about reality & the symbols & their relations.

Why not?

Grammar is, <u>in a sense</u>, a portrait of reality; but not like a picture of a man.

Now we have an old <u>language</u> by which we try to justify our <u>new</u> language.

We have to say: What the new language forbids, is really nonsense.

But what is forbidden in the new is also nonsense in the old.

Therefore grammar is in a sense autonomous; therefore can be looked at as   4:61
a game. Whence view that Mathematics is a game.

I will try to justify this.

Consider

       "Any 2 points are connected by a straight line."

(not "all": but why not "all pairs of points"?)

Now "I have a picture in which all the primary colours are" = one in which green, blue, red & yellow are.

There is no concept "primary colour": it is a pseudo-concept, or logical concept; & its name will be an index to ($\exists$) in ($\exists x)\phi x$.

In the case of "points" & "lines", it is more difficult, because here it appears as if these were concepts & things.

"Primary colour" is like "irrational number".

"All primary colours . . ." is a finite logical product.

But there's not a finite number of points or lines.

How does grammar express that a symbol is the symbol for a point?

You might say it says: If A is a name of a point, then certain things are allowed.

E.g. It is allowed to say "Two lines meet A". But then, how about "lines"?

4:62   It would mean that the variables determine one another.[7]

The explanation is that grammar is a set of rules applying to a certain set of symbols, like chess.

This gives a hint, as to the sort of generality in "Any 2 points".

It's like that of a rule of chess: E.g. "A pawn can be moved".

It may be objected that only finite number of pawns.

But we can imagine infinite games.

We can make rule: You can play this game with as many pawns[8] as you like: we can give permission to play with any finite number, not with an infinite number.

A rule here could be: A pawn may be moved in such & such a way; where there is no definite finite number of pawns.

This rule gives the rule according to which the rules for particular-sized chess-boards vary.

---

[7] Moore's summary notes: <"Point" & "line" seem to determine one another.> (10:71)
[8] The word looks more like 'primes', but this was probably a mistake on Moore's part.

They solve a problem about the possibility of movement.
We could make use of a game of chess, as of geometry.

$\underline{2}$ kinds of generality in geometry.
(1) that of $\underline{\text{rules}}$, e.g. concerning movements of pawns; which is one in which only symbols are concerned, & is inductive[9]
(2) that of its application, which can't be expressed, because it depends on what world is like.
This latter is generality of arithmetic.

E.g. the rules $1, (1) + 1, ((1) + 1) + 1$

This is why great difficulty in defining numbers: they apply to all sorts of different "things".

There are $\underline{2}$ sorts of "propositions" in mathematics, neither of them at all like what are usually called propositions.

(1) We $\underline{\text{prove}}$ one kind by a chain of equations.
This proceeds from axioms to other equations, by means of axioms.
$$(x + y)^2 = + 2xy + y^2$$
We can start with distributive & associative laws.[10]
(2) Proof by induction.
Take the series $1, (1) + 1, ((1) + 1) + 1, \ldots$
This can be written
$$[1, \xi, \xi + 1] = \text{First number, }\underline{\text{general}}\text{ number, & its next.}$$
This has $\underline{\text{no}}$ meaning unless first number is given.

Def. $a + (b + 1) \stackrel{\text{def}}{=} (a + b) + 1$ D[11]

If b is 1, & $\underline{\text{a is a numeral}}$, we get

---

[9] Moore later added: <(mathematical induction)>
[10] Moore later added: <(He intended to discuss Distributive as well as Associative, but began with latter & never got to Distributive)>
[11] Moore later added: <= Def.> just below this 'D'.

$$a + (\underbrace{(1) + 1}) = (a + 1) + 1$$

Known to be numeral

$$a + (((1) + 1) + 1) = (a + ((1) + 1)) + 1$$

& so on.

4:63v[12]   What does this define? It defines the <u>addition</u> of any 2 numbers, <u>given</u> the meaning of + between 2 "1"s.

It is <u>not</u> a definition in the sense in which

$$(1) + 1 = 2 \text{ is so.}$$

For it only says something about a & b, not about numbers.

It works as a <u>series</u> of definitions

$$a + ((1) + 1) = (a + 1) + 1$$
$$a + (((1) + 1) + 1) = \underbrace{(a + ((1) + 1)) + 1} \text{ /by 1/}$$

& so on

4:64   Prove.[13] $a + (b + c) = (a + b) + c$ A

Assume it for c, & prove it for $c + 1$.

I.e. prove $a + (b + (c + 1)) = (a + b) + (c + 1)$

Use D & get

$a + (b + (c + 1)) = a + ((b + c) + 1) \stackrel{D}{=} (a + (b + c)) + 1$
$\stackrel{A}{=} ((a + b) + c) + 1 \stackrel{D}{=} (a + b) + (c + 1).$

<u>Shorter Form.</u>

$$a + (b + (c + 1)) \stackrel{D}{=} (a + (b + c)) + 1$$
$$\stackrel{A}{=} ((a + b) + c) + 1 \stackrel{D}{=} (a + b) + (c + 1).$$

---

[12] Usually, Moore wrote his notes on the right-hand side of each opening, leaving the left-hand side blank for later comments, clarifications, or criticism. However, 4:63v, the page facing 4:64, contains material that reads like additional lecture notes. It is written in slightly thinner pencil strokes, suggesting that it may have been written later on. We have chosen to break it into two parts and insert them at the appropriate places in 4:64.

[13] Moore later added: <Associative Law>

Lecture 4 – May 19, 1930

2 striking features.

(1) that in proving A we assume what we ought to prove

(2) that step 2[14] doesn't seem really to follow from definition,

    Since (b + c) is not a numerical symbol.

It's justified, as we know, if $c = 1$.

Therefore real proof has to begin with $c = 1$

& what we really have is a whole series of ~~proofs~~ chains of equations, or rather a law which produces them.

Why can we use A? Because, if we substitute 1 for c, then 2nd transition is allowed by D.

We then get $(a + (b + 2)) = ((a + b) + 2)$.

The proof really rests entirely on D, but it isn't simply a chain of equations.

The proof by induction means that a chain goes on, which isn't expressed by the chain.

The infinite law can't be expressed by an equation.

What relation has A to the proof?

A couldn't be the last of a chain of equations, because it is assumed as primitive.

    Point is meaning of "true for all numbers".

---

[14] Moore later added a line connecting 'step 2' to '(a + (b + c)) + 1', the second formula in the shorter form of the proof.

5

4:66[15]

$$\underset{1}{a + (b + ((1) + 1))} \overset{D}{=} \underset{2}{a + ((b + 1) + 1)} \overset{D}{=} \underset{3}{(a + (b + 1)) + 1}$$

$$\overset{D}{=} \underset{4}{((a + b) + 1) + 1} \overset{D}{=} \underset{5}{(a + b) + ((1) + 1)}{}^{16}$$

This proves that 1 = 5, which is <u>not</u> what we want.

But we <u>see</u> what we <u>do</u> want; namely that we can similarly get a proof with 2, then with 3 & so on.

<u>It</u> may be called a spiral.

How does this prove Associative Law?

It's said: We know it holds for c = 1.

      We know it holds for n + 1, if for 2.

      ∴ We know it holds <u>for all numbers</u>.

But <u>the last is wrong</u>.

We <u>haven't</u> proved it as algebraic formula; it is only a postulate as such, i.e. a rule of a game.

What we've proved is that the rule applies, if a, b & c are numbers.[17]

---

[15] The bottom half of the previous page is blank. In all the other notes for this year, a partially completed page is always followed by a new lecture, with a Roman numeral at the top. While Moore did not write a Roman numeral at the top of this page, this is most likely the point at which Lecture 5 began. However, the material after the page break is a continuation of the previous discussion, and according to King and Lee, both sets of topics were discussed on 19 May, the date of Lecture 4. See Wittgenstein 1980, xvi, 17–20.

[16] In each of the five formulas, the number '2' is written just above the first instance of '1', illustrating that the proof can be repeated for any number, not just for 1.

[17] Moore's summary notes: <As an algebraic formula, Associative Law is only a rule of a game & we haven't proved <u>this</u>; what we have proved is that it applies if a, b, c are numbers.> (10:07)

Suppose we have a chain

$$A \to B \to C \to E$$

This shews an <u>internal</u> relation between A & <u>E</u>.
If an equation is a grammatical rule, what can its importance be?
That I can replace 2 + 2 by 4, has no mathematical importance.
I could have written 2 + 2 = 5.
What gives it its importance is its demonstrability.
I.e. that, in virtue of A, $a + (b + 1) = (a + b) + 1$ D

    it can be proved from

    (1) + 1 = 2 def.

    (((1) + 1) + 1) + 1) = 4 def.

You can't question or affirm or negate the <u>definitions</u>: what is affirmable is the internal relation between 2 + 2 = 4 <u>&</u> the definitions.

The <u>definitions</u> therefore are not like propositions; what is like a proposition is the assertion of internal relation.

<u>Proofs by induction.</u>
We <u>could</u> prove in this way

$$(a + b)^2 = a^2 + 2ab + b^2$$

This would again be a spiral proof.
Thus taking

$$\begin{array}{cccc} A \to & B \to & C \to & E \\ \uparrow & \uparrow & \uparrow & \uparrow \\ \text{☉} \to & \text{☉} \to & \text{☉} \to & \text{☉} \end{array}$$

But the relation expressed by vertical arrows is quite different from that by sideways arrows.

Hence what we've really shewn is that we can substitute A for one spiral, B for another & so on.

The relation between A & its spiral is more like that between a name & its thing, then that between a conclusion & its proof.

In ordinary mathematics there is something analogous to a proof & a question.

But an induction can be neither correct nor incorrect.

The relation between A & D, is not at all the same as that between A & B.

Neither D nor A need refer to numbers; &, if not so taken, then A doesn't follow from D. There's no algebraic proof of A by D.

~~What the proof shews: is that A could be given a numerical meaning, if D already has one.~~

The spirals aren't questionable, or negatable or assertible, any more than definitions are.[18]

4:69   This is connected with:
> Does Law of Excluded Middle apply to mathematical propositions? e.g. about infinity.

Brouwer suggests it doesn't hold.[19]

That there's an alternative to being true or false; viz. undecidable.

Suppose you say

Is $\pi' = \pi$?

We can't tell.[20]

To such a case no law of logic applies.

A question is essentially something which could be answered.

It's nonsense to say there are 777's in the infinite development.

If we found them in 10 years; we should have answered the question for a 10 years' development.

---

[18] For further discussion of inductive proof, spirals, and related matters, see *Philosophical Remarks* (Wittgenstein 1964) §163 ff., *The Big Typescript* (Wittgenstein 2005) §126 ff., and 6b:14.

[19] See Brouwer 1908 and Brouwer 1923.

[20] Moore later added: <π' = the number which, if there are 3 consecutive 7's in π, has 3 consecutive 5's in the place in which π has 3 7's.>

The impossibility of developing π, is not a physical impossibility; which must be of something I can describe.

With irrationals we introduce a new mathematical world, though correlated or comparable with rationals.

= we can define a > & < between irrationals, which has same multiplicity as > & < between rationals.

There's a logical similarity between rules for rationals & irrationals.

If Smith found a proof that no 3 sevens, then he would have found a new irrational number, π′ = π.   4:70

If he only found the 3 sevens, he would have found no new irrational.

6

4:71   May Term VI.

Does Mathematics consist of Tautologies?

How did the idea of "tautology" arise? From thinking about: What is subject-matter of Logic?

Frege thought "logische Gegenstände",[21] Russell "logical constants".

Russell felt that "or" & "not" were not like ordinary names.

I was helped by Frege, who, in his first work, had <u>explained</u> (not defined) "or" etc. in terms of <u>true</u> & <u>false</u>.[22]

He gave a list something like

$$\begin{array}{cc} T & T \\ F & T \\ T & F \\ F & F \end{array}$$

What Frege said was that p . q was true, if p, & q.

This means only to give a <u>property</u> of p . q: not a complete description.

But "or" "not" etc. seem to have no other properties: this list gives the <u>essence</u> of "and" etc.: it could stand <u>as a symbol for</u> "and".

$$p \cdot q \;=\; \begin{array}{c|c|c} p & q & \\ \hline T & T & T \\ F & T & F \\ T & F & F \\ F & F & F \end{array}$$

4:72   The advantage of this symbol is that it shews <u>quantity</u> of sense: that some propositions say <u>more</u> about reality than others.

E.g. it says <u>more</u> than p or q (~(~p . ~q))

---

[21] German for 'logical objects'.   [22] See Frege 1879, §7, 17–20.

One gives more freedom, in the sense in which an infinitely long string gives complete freedom.

This symbol also shews that one combination, gives every freedom

    viz.   T
                            T
                            T
                            T

This, though obviously a particular case, is yet not a proposition at all – says nothing.

Thus it was clear Logic consists of tautologies – says nothing.

But what, then, is value of Logic?

Wittgenstein thought at first that generalised tautologies did say something: but soon saw that they say as little as the others.

The value lies in the fact that a particular combination of propositions does say nothing. Compare with a zero method of measurement: that the pointer remains at 0 shews something.

That $((p \supset q) . p) \supset q$ says nothing shews something about structure.

Mathematical propositions are not tautologies: why?

Ramsey thought he could shew that equations are tautologies.[23] His theory of identity consists of 2 parts

    (1) functions in ~~identity~~ extension

    (2) equations are tautologies.

One can talk of (2) without discussing (1).

He tried to find a function of 2 variables, such that if you substituted different values you got a contradiction, if same a tautology.

It's easy to find function doing latter;

    e.g. $\phi x \supset \phi y$.

Let's ask whether this sort of function can define $x = y$?

---

[23] See part four of Ramsey's 'The Foundations of Mathematics' (1925) (Ramsey 1990, 212–16) and the letters written by Wittgenstein and Ramsey on identity in 1927 (Wittgenstein 2012, 158–61).

No: because if you look at $\phi(\hat{x}) \supset \phi(\hat{y})$, you have no idea whether it is a tautology or not.

You can only see that it becomes one, if you already know that you have substituted <u>same</u> value. It can't help you to know whether a = b.

<u>Objection</u> to theory that a = b is a symbolic convention.

Ramsey referred to

<u>I have n pairs of shoes, & $n^2 - 2n - 3 = 0$.</u>[24]

saying that whole proposition wasn't partly about symbols.[25]

<u>Answer.</u> $(\exists n)((\hat{x}(\phi x) \in n) . (n^2 - 2n - 3 = 0))$.

Here you can replace equation by its root.

The proposition has <u>no</u> sense; unless you know solution or how to solve it.

4:74   Like "I have <u>n</u> shoes, & <u>n</u> is a number I've written on some blackboard in the world", which has no meaning.

It gives an incomplete proposition, & completes it by a symbolic rule; & says something only if you know how to use the rule.

Equations are <u>merely</u> symbolic conventions, & get significance only by being members of a calculus.[26]

What's the relation between this calculus, & a calculus of tautologies?

Take addition of cardinal numbers.

Russell wrote an addition theorem as a tautology as follows:

Use as definitions

$(\exists x,y)\phi x . \phi y \stackrel{def}{=} (\exists(1+1)x)\phi x$

$(\exists x,y)\phi x . \phi y . \sim(\exists x,y,z)\phi x . \phi y . \phi z \stackrel{def}{=} (Ex,y)\phi x . \phi y$

Then what Russell does is to say 2 + 3 = 5

$(E2x)\phi x . (E3x)\psi x . \sim(\exists x)/\text{Ind.}/\phi x . \psi x) \supset (E(2+3)x)\phi x \vee \psi x$.

---

[24] This sentence was originally 'I have x pairs of shoes, & $x^2 + 2x + 3 = 0$' but it was modified during the lecture.

[25] See Ramsey 1990, 180–3.

[26] Moore's summary notes: <Ramsey said that a = b is <u>not</u> a symbolic convention. But <u>all</u> equations are symbolic conventions, & get significance only by being members of a calculus.> (10:07)

Lecture 6 – June 2, 1930

What corresponds to theorem of addition is not this proposition, but that it is a tautology, if it is.

Take, as sample

((E1x)ϕx . (E1x)ψx . Ind.) ⊃ (Ex,y)((ϕx ∨ ψx) . (ϕy ∨ ψy)).

This is a tautology: but that it is depends entirely on number of symbols with the E's.

I use a calculus of numbers applied to calculus of tautologies.

E.g. replace 2, 3, 5 by 34, 57, 91.

The tautology can't therefore replace arithmetical calculus.

Objection to: "Calculus is a game".
    Is it a game with ink & paper? No.
But also: Subject-matter of chess isn't pieces of wood.
What's characteristic of chess is logical multiplicity of its rules.

The confusion made in this argument is that rules of chess are about bits of wood.
Suppose you looked at 2 people playing chess as a natural phenomenon.
If there were, I could use the rules as hypotheses about pieces of wood of a particular shape.
The rules of calculus, & hypotheses would be of an entirely different nature.
In the calculus I have rules for the usage of so & so; not hypotheses about so & so.
Frege inferred that mathematics deals not with symbols, but with what is symbolised: that the symbols have meaning.
What is essential to the rules is the logical multiplicity which all the different possible symbols have in common.
But the game isn't a symbol for this.

Michaelmas Term, 1930

1

I.

Object to give some firm ground, such as
"If a proposition has a meaning, its negation must have a meaning."

Enormous difference between philosophy & sciences makes difficulty.
Difficulty is that we are not accustomed to – have not been trained in – sort of thinking that is required in philosophy.
Use of 0 had once to be found out – & this one of most difficult things human mind ever did.
Those who found this out created atmosphere in which we all live.
So atmosphere of science, in which we all live, was created by Galileo & others who invented dynamics.

It's modern philosophy that one hasn't been trained in: it is a new subject.
Parts of physics very difficult, but related to easy physics as fast running to ordinary.
Philosophy requires entirely different kind of motion: different as ju-jitsu from boxing.[1]

Philosophy has reached new state now; & development is not continuous. Thus dynamics started with Galileo. Development of human thought has kinks in it: there is one now in philosophy – namely a method has been found; as when chemistry developed out of alchemy.
There have been great philosophers; but now, for the first time, there can be skilful ones.
This doesn't mean that progress has occurred; but that style of thinking has changed = nimbus of philosophy has been lost.

---

[1] Moore's summary notes: <One hasn't been trained in kind of thinking required by modern philosophy. This requires kind of thinking as different from physics as ju-jitsu from boxing.> (10:08)

Compare Architecture – what might happen to it.

Architect has a nimbus compared to Engineer.

To <u>some degree</u> a house can be determined by calculation: but calculation leaves a certain margin, which architect fills in by sense of beauty etc..

In case of bicycle or locomotive there is hardly any room for personal freedom: & so there <u>might</u> be with a house.

In that case there would be no more architects.

In some cases there is no room for expression of personality – none for nimbus.

The moment a <u>method</u> is found, one way of expressing personality is lost. And there's no reason to be sorry for this.

General tendency of this age is to take away possibilities of expression: which is characteristic of age without a culture. But a great man remains just as great.

Philosophy is reduced to matter of skill: but it's very difficult to acquire any skill.

You can't acquire it by hearing lectures: only way is to discuss.

Simile of branch planted.

5:3   It doesn't matter whether I tell you the truth or not: because the <u>method</u> is found.

2

II.

What is philosophy?

Must not be arbitrary: e.g. science of steam-engines.

Enquiry into essence of world; very general; general problems & answers, & answers must be <u>final</u> – not such that you have to wait 5 years for answer.

There is such a thing as <u>description</u> of the world. You can <u>describe</u> this lecture-room, by saying things which could be otherwise; & so the whole earth; and you can also describe psychical states. We can then look for regularities – give certain laws.

Would this be all?

No, we've missed out pure mathematics.

Also we've just begun an investigation of a different sort – something like putting in order notions as to what can be said about the world.

This is <u>part</u> of philosophy: to tidy a room, & we also get a clear idea of what <u>tidying</u> is.

We're in a muddle about things, & try to clear it up. This is all we need say.

Now descriptions, & Mathematics also, consists roughly in something called "propositions" = what's contained in a book between 2 full-stops.

We're in a haze; & what we want is that this should clear up.

We have to follow a certain instinct, which leads us to ask questions, but we <u>don't even understand what the questions mean</u>: they are the result of a vague mental uneasiness, & we have to <u>cure</u> it – e.g. either by shewing that question <u>not</u> permitted, or by answering it. It is like "Why?" by children. So is "What is so & so?" We'll ask: What is a proposition?

    1. What can be said to be true or false.

    2. Expression of a thought.

1. We could do away with "true" or "false". E.g. "that's true" = it is fine weather today.

I.e. affirmation & negation replace "true" or "false".

Whenever we say "So & so is the case" it has sense to say "So & so is not", but we don't know what "sense" is.

There's certain to be something absurd about such an answer, but also certain to be something right.

proposition = what can be true or false = whatever is affirmed or negated.

Voice of instinct is right; but has not learned to express itself correctly – clearly.

5:6   What is "having sense"?

We understand what has not sense, e.g.

   "'Twas brillig & the slithy toves."²

What's the difference?

One would say at first

   In one case the words have meaning, in the other not.

Proposition = thing to which not can be applied.

But what does "not" mean?

How can we explain words?

Many ways: e.g.

   1. "Orange" means a yellowish red.

Of course, it presupposes that you understand yellowish & red.

"Tisch"³ means table, is of same kind.

Both are obviously not final explanations.

Explaining = making you understand meaning = bringing about a psychical process.

---

² This is the first line of 'Jabberwocky', a nonsense poem by Lewis Carroll, which appears at the end of the first chapter of *Through the Looking-Glass, and What Alice Found There* (Carroll 1992, 116–18).

³ German for 'table'.

Suppose I brought this about by giving you a drug.

That is a different way from above, & from ostensive definition, e.g. by pointing out Drury.

Ostensive definition employs symbols over again: you have to say "This is Drury"; i.e. it isn't final any more than "Tisch" = table.

An ostensive definition can be misunderstood – hence there is such a thing as understanding it.

E.g. "This is white".

All we can do is to re-place one set of symbols by another.

Take "Drury is sitting on a bench in this room".

Suppose somebody doesn't understand any of these words.

You can only give a crude explanation of the words, & you can't do any better.

You can replace all the symbols e.g. by gestures: & that is a proposition.

You can replace words by their ostensive definitions.

There is a theory (Ogden & Richards)[4] that to say a word has a meaning is to say it reminds you of something by association.

Now, suppose somebody wanted to know meaning of "green"; & I said "This".

Getting to know meaning must give you something which you hadn't before, & which you carry about with you.

History of learning plays no part in the future; the essential part is what you carry about with you.

In explanation by drug, the drug drops out.

Suppose my "This is green" produces association of word "green" with a memory-image of this wall. But is the memory-image the meaning of green?

---

[4] 'In all thinking we are interpreting signs ... Our Interpretation of any sign is our psychological reaction to it, as determined by our past experience in similar situations, and by our present experience.' (Ogden and Richards 1923, 244).

It is ~~just~~ a symbol, just as the word "green" is.

To get down to reality, we must be able to compare the image with a real.

"Green" would retain its meaning, if there were no green things, & never had been.

What is essential is that you must be able to compare the meaning of "green" with any colour you see, & say this is not green.

New way to get hold of meaning.

2. Proposition is expression of a thought.[5]

Thought may be wish, or doubt, or fear.

"I hope he's going to come in" etc.

What's common to all these /expressions/ is that they can be replaced by a plan.

A command corresponds to a belief, in that obeying or disobeying corresponds to true or false.

You can always replace a proposition by a command.

5:9 Thinking = operating with a plan.

We can't say the thought is the plan, because the thought needs no interpretation, whereas the plan can be interpreted in many ways.

Can one put the interpretation into the plan?

Not even by running a film: which could mean that he's not to walk that way; it could mean a thousand different things.

You may add a rule of interpretation, but not by altering the plan.

What does understanding a plan mean?

Ask: how would a person shew that he has understood it?

Obviously obeying it, is not necessary: you can have understood, without obeying.

How do we know a man has understood?

We can only know this, if he translates it into other symbols – of which obedience is one instance.

---

[5] This is the second answer to the question, 'What is a proposition?'. See 5:5.

To shew you understand, you must translate.

The rule according to which you translate cannot be a part of the plan: it is taught by interpreting – by translating plans. The rule can only be expressed by actually following it.

In sciences, what you are doing is like building, starting from foundations, which must be firm.

In philosophy, as to-day, we are not laying foundations: you are tidying up, & for this you have to touch everything a dozen times. You can't put one thing in its place, till you've put another in.   5:10

Philosophy like an organism has neither beginning nor end.

3

5:11 III.

Proposition is expression of thought; & all <u>kinds</u> of thoughts – many different kinds of <u>mental states</u>: hope, fear etc. are all forms of it.

But a difficulty.

Suppose I expect someone to tea: is it one thought; or a sequence of thoughts; or one repeated?

Does thought take a shorter time than the expression? & is the expression only a clumsy interpretation? Or is the thought a continuous state?

I say: the thought lasts exactly as long as the expression.

Thought is <u>not</u> on a level with digestion.

There are 2 ways of looking at digestion: (1) as a process peculiar to animals (2) as the chemist does – where it interests, whether it happens in stomach or not.

Thought in sense in which <u>we're</u> concerned with it, doesn't happen in the brain: as changes in brain; it interests physiologist, but not us.

This becomes plain, if we consider what happens if we use a plan: we hear or see certain things, make certain movements, & perhaps have <u>imagery</u>.

But imagery is not "in" the mind: this simile is pernicious.

5:12 For some purposes you can compare your head to a room with someone inside it.

But when we talk of "inside the mind", we have <u>lost</u> the picture.

It is always pernicious to <u>forget</u> the picture & still use the same language.

E.g. when people use "the spirit of man", having first meant "breath".[6]

---

[6] 'Much more widespread, and still much respected, is the view which ascribes a gaseous nature to the substance of the soul. The comparison of human breath with the wind is a very old one; they were originally considered to be identical, and were both given the same name. The *anemos* and *psyche* of the Greeks, and the *anima* and *spiritus* of the Romans,

It is important to insist on the picture: as in psychoanalysis, we must make the picture conscious: <u>then</u> we can use the language without danger.

Thought, for us, is a symbolic process; & as such it's irrelevant to us <u>where</u> it happens: it doesn't matter to us whether or not it's typical for a human being.

This is connected with: Can one read thoughts directly?

What would it be like, if one could?

It <u>either</u> means that he somehow gives me symbols, which I interpret: in which case it is like reading a book, or hearing him.

<u>or</u> it means: when I hold B's hands, then I think of something & ask him whether he thought that; which isn't reading at all: it means: 2 people under certain circumstances think the same thing.⁷

The idea that language is indirect in the sense that there could be a <u>more</u> direct, is pernicious.

Everything we want lies open to inspection of everybody.

I am not trying to teach you new facts. I shall only tell you trivial things – what you all know. What's difficult is synopsis – to see them together. 5:13

We don't know which of a million keys, will open the door we want: whenever we do know, we find it quite easy to open door. It is only science which makes <u>new</u> keys.

Now I said when we replace a word by an ostensive definition, we get something like <u>a plan</u>.

Now a <u>plan</u> can always be interpreted in different ways:

Is the interpretation the mental thing we want?

What then is "understanding" a plan?

It is to be <u>able</u> to <u>act</u> in accordance with it; not so to <u>act</u>, but to be <u>able</u> to.

---

were originally all names for "a breath of wind"; they were transferred from this to the breath of man. After a time this "living breath" was identified with the "vital force," and finally it came to be regarded as the soul itself, or, in a narrower sense, as its highest manifestation, the "spirit"' (Haeckel 1900, 200). See also the discussion of Haeckel and James below (8:74–76).

⁷ Moore's summary notes: <What would it be like to read thoughts directly? Either it means (1) he gives me symbols or (2) that he has same thought as I have.> (10:09)

What is meant by saying he <u>could</u> obey an order?

Suppose I say: "I <u>can</u> lift this weight of 200 pounds". If I try, & fail, that proves I couldn't.

Suppose I feel faint now, & say I <u>could</u> then: this is a hypothesis; it is not a thing I can be <u>certain</u> of.

But there is <u>another</u> sense of "can".

In one sense: To say I <u>could</u> recite a poem, though I failed, may be something I could be mistaken about.

5:14 In another sense: I <u>can</u> may be something of which I'm certain, as regards which I <u>can't</u> be mistaken.

<u>So</u> there can't be any <u>doubt</u> as to whether I understand an order or not.

It may be true to say: "I understood that just now, but don't now".

You explain <u>sense</u> of proposition, by shewing him meaning of signs.

This means only to substitute one sign for another.

Distinguish "sign" & "symbol".

"Red" (the word) is a <u>sign</u>.

<u>N</u>ow by pointing to a red object I may have given "red" <u>a meaning</u>.

It's essential that <u>signs</u> in a proposition should have <u>meaning</u>.

Whatever is essential for so & so to have sense, is a <u>part</u> of the <u>symbol</u>.

Only when all conditions are fulfilled has a sentence sense: then what contains all of them is a "symbol", & <u>that</u> is a proposition. A "symbol" can't be nonsensical.

5:15 Russell's theory of descriptions prevents the <u>sign</u> from being nonsensical; & he might have done it in <u>another</u> way.[8]

He might have said: The king of France is part of the symbol.[9]

When <u>I</u> say "I'm tired", my mouth is <u>part</u> of the symbol.

---

[8] See the citations to Russell's theory of descriptions at 4:12.
[9] Moore later added: <But then it would be nonsense, if there was no king of France!>

Suppose you find a ~~proposition~~ sign "I'm tired now" written on blackboard: you have to ask "Who?" "when?"

All conditions necessary to make a sign significant are <u>part</u> of the symbol.
This <u>doesn't destroy</u> the essence of the symbol.
There still remains something which can be true or false.

Therefore any theory of "meaning", which says it means "recalling", won't do at all. Words <u>do</u> recall images, & images may be essential; but they are <u>part</u> of the symbol.

Hence, when we <u>explain</u> a sign, we <u>complete</u> the symbol. But <u>understanding</u> the symbol, does not mean going outside it.
Suppose we <u>forget</u> an explanation.
We need not remember <u>who</u> explained; but <u>something</u> must remain, whenever I understand "orange": e.g. an image may be.   5:16
Thus, if we can't recall an image, this <u>may</u> mean that this symbol is gone, & I don't understand "orange". I shan't be able to recognise it: "Is this orange?" will have no <u>meaning</u> to me.

Suppose someone says: "This is Mr. Smith."
(1) I may retain an image: & then I can recognise him.
(2) I may remember: "There was a Mr. Smith whom I met there."
Then Mr. Smith means something quite different. It doesn't enable me to understand "Which of them is Mr. Smith?"

I can understand "orange", even if nothing <u>is</u> orange. And therefore even if nothing was.

Suppose we explain red & yellow, by the opposites of green & blue. That is enough.

The test whether a man has understood, is <u>how</u> he uses it.

The great <u>difficulty</u> here is: –
What if I replace one symbolism by another?

What's the test for: This <u>sign</u> has same meaning as <u>that</u>?

5:17 What determines place of a symbol in my symbolism?

(1) Place is shewn by how it's used.

E.g. suppose I replace "green" by "abracadabra": then you would see what it means, by seeing how I connect it with other words.

I let you guess what word fits it.

(2) But suppose I had replaced <u>all</u> the words? How could you know what one of them means?

Every "symbol" must have one definite place in the symbolism.

Take colour octahedron.[10]

If it represented <u>whole</u> grammar, we could replace green by blue, but not blue by white. I.e. we haven't given each symbol an unambiguous place.

Take "not": or "Yes" & "No".

One way to distinguish would be

$$\begin{aligned}\sim\sim &= +\\ ++ &= +\end{aligned} \quad \text{(but } \underline{\text{not}} \; ++ = \sim\text{)}$$

Signs with different meanings <u>must</u> be different symbols.

Words with different meanings <u>must</u> occupy asymmetrical positions in grammar.

---

[10] See 4:15 and 6:8.

4

IV.

Recapitulation.
Relation between thought & its expression.
Is thought instantaneous, preceding expression; or like tooth-ache?

Some French statesman said: French has the particular merit, that in French the words come in just the order you think in.[11]
This expresses clearly an absurdity.
What underlies this is: that thinking is a series of pictures.
It's connected with: I thought of you the other day.
This leads to view that to think of a proposition is to think of its terms in some order.
This is absurd.
The mistake is that proposition is a mechanism; not a heap of parts; but words linked in a particular way.
To think of a thing = think of a proposition in which it occurs.
We think by means of the sentence: sentence isn't cause of the thinking.
What's caused by a sentence is not an expression of it.
Words are a part of the thought; whereas its cause isn't.

Sign & Symbol.
Symbol = everything essential to significance of sign.
E.g. if you use ostensive definition, you enable a man to understand the sign; i.e. you give him something essential to understand the sign = you complete the symbol (there are no insignificant symbols).

---

[11] This story is repeated in a number of places in the Wittgenstein *Nachlass* (2000). On one of those occasions Wittgenstein says that he believes the statesman in question was 'M. Brian' (MS 109, 177). This is perhaps a reference to Aristide Briand (for a fuller discussion, see Biesenbach 2014, 69–70).

I.e. the meaning of a sign is part of the symbol.

"Orange" has a different meaning, if you remember an image, & if you think of it as "the colour between yellow & red": with latter you couldn't tell whether this is orange.

Thus explaining meaning of signs = describing symbol, not transcending it.

But how about "not", "all", "any", "some"?

How can "not" express negation?

People may say it doesn't: that it's a kind of signal, saying "negate".

E.g. tap table as a signal to somebody to get up.

But a signal wants an explanation: the tapping means nothing if we haven't made an arrangement.

The railwayman has been told something by somebody – language has been used: therefore language can't be explained.

What do you mean by "negate this"?

If I can explain, I can substitute the explanation for the sign; substituting long-hand for short-hand.

"Not" is explained to a child by using it, e.g. holding a door or taking away food.

Meaning of "not" is only expressed in rules applying to its usage.

5:20 A proposition can only be understood as part of a system of propositions.

If you understand ▢ you must also understand ▨

If it merely caused the man to go, we shouldn't say he understood it.[12]

This makes symbolism appear self-satisfying; whereas essence of it seems to be that it points beyond.

It looks as if a thought foreshadowed something: contained a shadowy fulfilment.

---

[12] Moore's summary notes: <If "Go" merely caused a man to go, we shouldn't say he understood the order.> (10:09)

This shadow is what people mean by "the sense" of a proposition – or a proposition in Johnson's sense.[13]

What could this shadow be?

People would say: Something <u>similar</u> to it in a certain way.

This is <u>not</u> so.

Take expectation: coming of Smith into room is foreshadowed.

But is <u>what</u> you expect only something similar to his coming?

"Expect something similar to <u>this</u>" obviously means something different from "expect <u>this</u>".

The mistake which is made is that we don't see that "similar", presupposes   5:21
a relation which isn't there till the expected thing happens.

Similar to <u>what</u>? There is nothing till Smith comes in.

The explanation presupposes that we can tell <u>what</u> the shadow is <u>of</u> by comparing it with the <u>thing</u>.

This comes in in every case of projection.

"similar to" = "projection of", & projection presupposes a <u>rule</u> of projection.[14]

```
a | b
c | d
e | f
g | h
```

Thus ddfhb translates ccega.

Suppose I order you to translate: how can I make you understand the order?

I've given you a <u>symbol</u>, susceptible of many alternative interpretations.

The <u>way</u> in which it's used is never contained in it.

I <u>could</u> call ccega a shadow of the fulfilment ddfhb; but it's only a shadow of it <u>with reference</u> to a rule of translation.

---

[13] See Johnson 1921, chapter I, 1–17, 'The Proposition'.
[14] Moore's summary notes: <What you do in expecting is to <u>project</u>, & projection presupposes a <u>rule</u> of projecting.> (10:09)

"Similarity" won't do, because we can't explain <u>kind</u> before thing is there to which it is similar.[15]

An internal relation is there only if 2 constituents are there.

5:22 Suppose I ask: Do you know the alphabet?

Yes.

Are you sure?

How could he make sure? only by running through the alphabet in his mind.

But then he hasn't done it: he's done something like a shadow of saying it, which makes him <u>sure</u> that he can.

Let me ask: <u>How</u> does he know that what he's said is what he went through in his mind?

The 2 processes are different: why do you say they're the same?

Because of a similarity?

But what <u>sort</u> of similarity?

Only one which wasn't there till you said it.

All that's happened is that you have <u>projected</u>.

Essence of "recognition" is that there must be <u>another</u> test, besides the recognition: otherwise there's no recognition.

Is <u>this</u> what you ran through in your mind?

How can we be certain that another man sees what we see?

If there's no <u>criterion</u>, the question is nonsense.

It's absurd to ask: How do you know that this is what you expected?

5:23 All this is contained in: What's the difference between a portrait & a picture?

What makes this picture a portrait of Mr. Smith?

<u>Not</u> that it's similar; because there may be bad portraits.

---

[15] Moore's summary notes: <An expectation is supposed to be <u>similar</u> in some way to its fulfilment; but it isn't for it isn't <u>similar</u> to anything till the fulfilment happens.> (10:09)

What is exactly like Smith need not be a portrait of him.
"Exactly like" means one <u>kind</u> of similarity.

What does make the portrait a portrait?
The intention.
But how is this expressed?
Nothing could make this clear; because another interpretation is always needed.

Intending is expressed in "comparing" = internal relation only there if both things are.
Rule of <u>projection</u> only expressed in projecting.

5

5:24   V.

Last time's results not satisfactory, though can't be denied.

Every explanation of symbol can only add to symbol, hence symbol seems self-contained, which seems to contradict our notion of a symbol.

Most explanations have supposed there's something intermediate between symbol & fact – proposition (as opposed to sentence), <u>sense</u> of proposition, or thought.

What sort of thing must shadow be?

(1) People may say: must be <u>similar</u> to fulfilment.

But this won't do; because

We all know what it is to copy. But does the model tell you how to copy it? No. You can have different rules of copying.

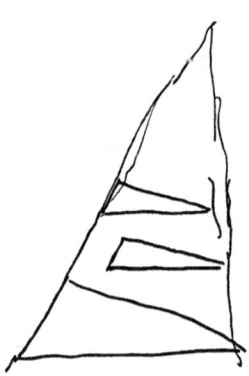

We explain translating into German, as opposed to translating into English; but not translating. We explain one rule relatively to another.

a	d		a	r
b	e		b	s
c	f		c	t

Here are 2 different rules, but both <u>given</u> by means of language.

Shadow /as similar/ can't mediate, unless one has shadow of shadow, & so on. And also because it doesn't bring us any nearer to fact. 5:25

Part of mistake we make, is that we confuse a word with a proposition.

When we say "alphabet", this does not presuppose a real alphabet; only the proposition "The alphabet is written on the board" does so.

So "tooth-ache" doesn't stand for tooth-ache: only "So & so has tooth-ache".

If they did, it would be inexplicable how we could say "There is no alphabet", "There is no tooth-ache".

What must a fact be like in order to fulfil this expectation? What must an expectation be like in order to be fulfilled by this fact?

Take latter: It makes a description.

We've already given one: It must be an expectation of Mr. Smith's coming into room, if the fact is Smith's coming.

Can anything, relevant for our purposes, be added to this?

We're not interested at all in causes of expectation, or causal working.

Nothing can be relevant, except an analysis of what we've already said, which is just another expression.

This second description may be right or wrong: if it were wrong, would the expectation of Smith's coming cease to be so? 5:26

Any description that modifies content of expectation, must modify its expression.

Only description of content is its expression.

This disposes of all explanations by means of external relations.

E.g. Russell says "We don't know what we wish for, until what we wish comes".[16]

This makes "wish" like "hunger": we don't know what will satisfy our hunger till we try.

---

[16] See Russell 1921, 32, and Lecture 3, 'Desire and Feeling', 58–76, especially 75–6.

What we wish or expect is <u>not</u> a question of <u>future</u> experience at all.

Suppose "I wish for an apple" consists in disagreeable feeling, which is removed by banana. How could I tell that this was what was wished for? Could I tell I was wrong in saying I wished for an apple?

You express content & fulfilment by same expression; & this internal similarity between expressions <u>is</u> the expression of relation between expectation & fulfilment.

Suppose you say: If something green is expected, green must be a constituent both of expectation & fulfilment.

"Green" does not presuppose something being green.

5:27 Is it a condition for the expectation being this, that green should occur in it?

That this is so is expressed by occurrence of word "green" in both expressions.

You may say it can't be the sound.

Answer to that is: No it can't; what's meant is that both expressions belong to one grammatical system.

Instead of saying expectation must be similar to fulfilment; we might say: What must expectation be <u>like</u> to <u>fit</u> the fact?

What makes a cylinder <u>fit</u> a cylindric mould?

How can you describe the necessary conditions?

By describing shape of each, e.g. by an equation.

The <u>boundary</u> must be common to both: everything else is irrelevant.

I compared expectation to a mechanism; & explanation of this is causal. Hence "working of proposition is causal" is quite true. Process of thought is a causal process like any other. But this explains nothing about logic of propositions.

E.g. What must movement of hand & needle be like, in order to make this stitch?

What must expectation be like in order to use it as we use it?

2 answers

(1) causal explanation by physical qualities.

(2) <u>logical</u> explanation of sewing. 5:28

Needle might move of itself without fingers.

But so might <u>eyes</u> without rest of needle.

Physical qualities of thread don't matter; only shape.

All that's relevant is what process of sewing has in common with thread.

Logical explanation of what sewing <u>must</u> be like to give this stitch, is already given in shape of thread.

So: What must thought be like to <u>fit</u> the world?

Only what <u>description</u> of 2 have in common.

And this is not expressed by saying anything about thought or world.

<u>Language</u> always expresses <u>one</u> fact as opposed to <u>another</u>: never expresses what could not be otherwise – never, therefore, what is <u>essential</u> to the world.

<u>For</u> whatever can be said can be negated.

Philosophy may expect to arrive at fundamental propositions. But great event to which we come is the coming to the boundary of language: to: there we can't ask anything further.

I.e. we must see we were wrong to ask questions: our intellectual discomfort must be removed. 5:29

And it can't be except by synopsis of <u>many</u> trivialities. If you leave out any, you still have feeling that something is wrong.

6

5:30   VI.

Idea of explaining thought or propositions.

To use the idea in our case is a fallacy: you can't explain them.

(1) To explain an event in physics, is to describe circumstances in which similar events take place – to give its causes & effects.

Thought is an event like any other & therefore can be explained in this sense.

(2) This doesn't interest us as philosophy.

Perhaps, what we want is an analysis.

This is just as misleading: it also is taken from science.

To analyse water is to find out something new about water: e.g. that it's compound of hydrogen & oxygen. To analyse = to do something to, such that water disappears & 2 gases appear instead.

Analysis in our sense does not mean this.

In philosophy we know all we need know at the start: we don't need to know any new facts.

What interests us in science is not the results, but the method: that the question can be asked; What is specific weight of helium?

These words tempt us to apply scientific methods to philosophy.[17]

5:31   What we're concerned with is what constitutes a thought – makes it a thought of this content.

And answer can't be a description of the process.

---

[17] Moore's summary notes: <You can't explain thought or propositions. (1) You can, of course, in physical sense: give causes. (2) Physical analysis finds out new facts about water. This is not what we want. The words "analysis" & "explanation" tempt us to apply scientific methods in philosophy.> (10:104–106)

E.g. it can't be: "In order that so & so should fulfil an expectation, it must satisfy us".

E.g. if satisfaction is a necessary condition for fulfilment, the satisfaction must be something expected.

Hence conclusion:
Only relevant description of expectation for us is the expression of it.

One confusion is due to ambiguous use of "something".
I.e. between "bananas" & "Mr. Smith" on one side, & "that Mr. Smith is coming into the room" on the other.
In consequence we think that what we expect is already on the landing, though not in the room: if it were, we could describe it beforehand.

Any kind of expression which pervades our whole language means that false picture is deeply rooted.[18]

What is common to thought & verification can't be expressed by description, but is shewn in the expression of each.
Another confusion arises from "in common". 5:32

To say that expectation & fulfilment have "red" in common, is misleading, because it would mean something entirely different.
In process of expectation there is nothing red.
We are tempted to confuse meaning of a word with certain simple propositions which contain the word: e.g. red with "This is red".

Another confusion is in "harmony between thought & reality".
There isn't a harmony, because we make mistakes.
The kind of harmony meant is one which can't be expressed by any description of both.

---

[18] Moore's summary notes: <Confusion due to "expecting Mr. Smith" = "expecting he will come", since Mr. Smith is something already existing. This false picture pervades our whole language.> (10:105)

Another way of saying it is to distinguish between having a property or quality in common, & having a constituent in common.

This is misleading, because even to say this is to ~~say~~ imply that they are on same level: whereas latter is only to make a grammatical statement – about symbols, not about things.

Now to say that similarity between expectation & fulfilment is expressed by having word in common won't do: e.g. "read" & "red".

5:33   We must ask: What justifies me in using "black", in saying "This gown is black"?

You may say: Nothing; it is arbitrary.

But, I must commit myself, if I'm making a proposition.

If I say "This gown is abracadabra", & am merely correlating a sound, that has no consequences.

The word which crops up in our minds when we look at a thing is not its name.

If having a name were merely a matter of association, language wouldn't work.

The word is unessential; I may use a new word: but I must commit myself to something. It's the way in which it's used which characterises it.

I.e. a word has only meaning in a grammatical system.

If a man understands the order, he must understand others – understand it as part of a system.

We have to understand a plan as a member of a system of plans: we have to know, how it could be altered, without altering the meaning.

If I copy a model, e.g. ⌐≤, my hand is in a sense guided by the model; & this doesn't mean that looking at the model causes me to make this.

In latter sense, if you make a slip, it has ceased to guide.

But in copying, if you make a mistake, copy has not ceased to guide.

There is a sense in which you can have an exact or inexact copy.

If we had an indicator which shewed how much rod got bent, it with figure drawn would be an exact copy.

5:34   If I make a slip, & see that I have, my seeing it, with the slip, neutralises the slip.

The intention was guided by the model.

The process of copying or representation, must have the model as a facet. The whole process of drawing & intending contains the model as a facet.

The process of representing reaches up to what it represents, & that by means of the rule.

If I intended to copy in scale 1/1, I should be guided by model in a different way from if in scale 1/2.

Result of copying does not, by itself, represent whole process.

If I draw in 1/2 intentionally, or by mistake, there's a difference in the process.

I.e. process of copying contains rule of projection; & result is not sufficient to describe it.

Take rule $2x, 4x^2 \ldots$

It can be continued by $6x^3$ or by $6x^4$.

I.e. when a man writes "$2x, 4x^2$" there's a difference, according as he writes it as a member of one series or as another: he arrives at it by a different process.

It can be understood as part of system $2n\, x^n$ or $2n\, x^{2^{(n-1)}}$.

Every proposition has to be understood as part of a system, & grammar describes system.

7

5:36   VII.

Harmony between thought & reality.

"Harmony" misleading, because it properly means a state of affairs which can be described by describing <u>both</u>.

Harmony between thought & reality can only be expressed, not by description of thought, but by expression of it.

What is here important is that what here's supposed to be fundamental is something which we can't talk about.

And this is <u>general</u>: whatever is fundamental, can't be talked about.

What philosophers mean is what makes it possible to judge rightly about the world: but this is what makes it possible to judge <u>wrongly</u>.

<u>This</u> harmony can't be <u>described</u>, & therefore is not in ordinary sense a harmony at all.

It is <u>expressed</u> by expressions /of thought & reality/ having something in common.

Having a constituent in common is not expressed by a proposition at all.

<u>Objection</u>. How should the mere having a word in common express anything?

Of course, it can't be the mere sound.

5:37 Suppose one says: That 2 expressions have a word in common can't possibly express anything.

One can answer: "Mr. Smith came into the room" <u>is</u> enough to express the fact.

The same <u>sound</u> is, of course, <u>not</u> enough.

Answer is: A propositional symbol can't be a symbol, unless it belongs to a <u>system</u> of symbols.

Lecture 7 – November 24, 1930

So & so is not a symbol, unless it's <u>understood as</u> one in a system of symbols.

If you use a symbol, you must <u>commit</u> yourself.

This is just the opposite of an arbitrary correlation between sounds & fact.

If I commit myself, that means if I use "green" in this case, I <u>have</u> to use it in others.

If I merely correlate an isolated ~~symbol~~ sound with an isolated fact, I have <u>not</u> committed myself.

If you commit yourself, there are consequences.

In the case of <u>copying</u>, to commit yourself means that you must have <u>laid down a rule</u> by which to copy.

If I can be said to have <u>copied</u> at all, I must have followed a rule. 5:38

It's not enough that there should be <u>some</u> rule which will project what I did into the model.

If I copy, my intention is <u>guided</u> by the model = I am committed, or following a rule – i.e. I can be said to be <u>right</u> or <u>wrong</u>. I must have set myself a task.

Suppose I try to follow outline of somebody with finger at end of outstretched arm: what's criterion of my doing it correctly or incorrectly?

"In accordance with" must mean "by some rule <u>stateable</u> beforehand."

Take a musical score.

We might have a rule

that these are to stand for next note to the right on the piano.

Then by doing this on piano I'm making a picture, whatever the sounds made are.

But here you suddenly meet ♯ & ♭: are these pictures of something you do on the key-board? Obviously not.

5:39 Programme is to shew that ♯ & ♭ work in exactly the same way. (Almost all our words are like this.)

I will call them signals (like railway ones).

And you can say "is a signal a picture of the train stopping?".

I said before: language doesn't consist of signals.

A signal has to be explained; which gives you something which supplements it.

Suppose I say: Putting out my arm means "stop".

Suppose I do this at 12.40; they can understand it at 12.45.

What matters is what the explanation has given them: not what happened at 12.40.

He has something, which he may lose by forgetting. He may say: Oh heavens, what does that mean? Then he's lost what made him understand.

To understand a signal, an explanation must be sufficient.

But explanation is language – using more symbols.

If there were anything in language, which couldn't be explained, it would be entirely useless: it would be magic – it would act as a drug. We could then never use language to make ourselves understood.

5:40 Now notes give a picture of motion of my hand on keyboard: ♯ & ♭ don't. But picture must have been given by explanation of them.

Suppose 2 taps are signal to get up.

This must have been explained by words, which were themselves signals.

Suppose I say "If I rap twice, get up", I'm substituting one set of signals for another.

But these words have been explained before.

Suppose I say "Paint a green patch on the board".

Here is a signal, but the <u>sound</u> "green" is not enough: you have something which you <u>might</u> lose: you <u>might</u> forget what "green" means.

You've got hold of something <u>besides</u> the sound "green".

Why won't the <u>sound</u> do to guide you to find the green paint, whereas this something else will?

Take "That's not the colour I mean: the colour I mean has no name". Then I'm <u>guided</u> by a symbol which is <u>not</u> a word.

"Red" is connected with another symbol, in another <u>language</u>.

If you understand a proposition, you've got nothing to help you but the proposition. 5:41

You say: No: I've got the explanation.

But the explanation is something of the same kind: it only adds to the symbol: the symbol must then be enough to explain itself.

An explanation of a proposition is always of the kind of a definition, i.e. replacing <u>one</u> symbol by another.

8

5:42 VIII.

How can their having a couple of words in common explain what's in common to expectation & fulfilment?

Difficulty is that word is <u>arbitrary</u>.

<u>Answer</u> that <u>in part</u> it is <u>not</u> arbitrary.

If a word is to have significance, we must <u>commit</u> ourselves.

What's the use of correlating noises to facts?
Only if we commit ourselves to using noises in a particular way again: only if the correlation has <u>consequences</u>.

But correlation has consequences only if word or proposition is part of a system: language must be to some extent <u>rigid</u>, correlation must compel me to do something else. It must be possible to be <u>led</u> by the language.

What does <u>leading</u> mean?
I am <u>led</u> by position of crotchet, only if, suppose the crotchet had been somewhere else, I should make a different movement.
But how do I know I <u>should</u>? I might die.

5:43 Yet this instructive answer must be correct in <u>some</u> way.
It <u>can't</u> mean something <u>verified</u> by experience; e.g. by the mere fact that whenever the crotchet is <u>there</u>, I put my hand <u>there</u>.
Justification must lie in what is <u>now</u> known to me; & I don't know the future.
It's a mistake to suppose that what's meant by "led" is illustrated by machinery: e.g. movement of keys by perforations in pianola roll. There's nothing in pianola itself which justifies me in saying it's gone right or wrong.
If a motor explodes, we say: Something's gone wrong; but inhabitant of Mars wouldn't say so.

We look at a machine as expression of a rule: e.g. drawing of a piston. We look on it as a <u>rule</u> of possible <u>motion</u>. The machine has not committed itself to anything. Our interpretation of it is the way it <u>ought</u> to work: what we see is the intention.

So with piano: to be guided by crotchets = to follow a general rule. The rule therefore must be contained in reading score <u>intentionally</u>. It's not contained in result, nor in result + score.

If I describe what a man plays, the score does <u>not</u> enter into this description. But description of his <u>intention</u> does contain it: I have to say: he is trying to play according to this score. <u>Trivial</u>.[19]

Thus intention <u>contains</u> both score & <u>particular</u> rule of using it.   5:44

What does "contain" mean? Does it mean it contains an <u>expression</u> of the rule?

This is obviously not the case.

E.g. if I read a book aloud, I'm <u>guided</u> by signs; but am I reporting a rule? Obviously not.

Even if I were; it would be no help.

Suppose I wanted to <u>project</u>

   1 2 3 4 5 ...
   into
   1 4 9 16 ...

If I asked you to go on, you would <u>act according to</u> model & rule of <u>projection</u>.

In order to see the law, I need not write down the rule.

This seems to contradict that 4 numbers might have been written according to another rule.

Point is that from them I am able to read one rule <u>or</u> another – able to interpret them.

---

[19] 'Trivial' is inserted before this paragraph in the lecture notes, but in the summary notes (10:106), which we have followed, it is the final sentence of the paragraph. Since Moore's comments are usually found in the margins of the page, and the summary notes suggest that this material is part of the lecture rather than Moore's own commentary, it is likely that Wittgenstein expressed this judgement.

Obviously rule is <u>contained</u> in special cases; but I can't isolate it.

Suppose we write it $\dfrac{x}{x^2}$ or $\dfrac{(\ )}{(\ )^2}$.

<u>This</u> /which is isolated/ isn't <u>contained</u> in the example.

5:45   What I isolate needs something else to shew me <u>how</u> it is to be applied.
I see the general rule <u>in</u> the special case.

Hence, when man plays piano, <u>expression</u> of rule is not isolated in his head: & if it were, it would be no use. What he needs is to <u>see</u> the rule in the score.

But: What if piano-player acts automatically? Does this mean that he doesn't read the score?

No: whether he's reading or not, depends on how he <u>judges</u> his performance; whether he says he has or hasn't made a mistake.[20]

1	2	3	4	
1	5	9	17	24
1^{+0}	4^{+1}	9^{+0}	16^{+1}	25^{-1}

General rule is a standard in terms of which he judges what he's doing.

So with accidentals: ♯ is arbitrary – doesn't give a picture of going semitone higher.

5:46   Shape of crotchet is arbitrary; but once rule is fixed, it's no longer arbitrary what we play.

Thus "if crotchet were elsewhere, we should play otherwise" is expression of a rule, <u>not</u> verified in experience, but <u>contained</u> in our intention.

There is, therefore, if a man plays correctly, a <u>similarity</u> between his playing & the score, which holds just as much in case of accidentals as of notes.

---

[20] Moore's summary notes: <Player needs to see rule in score: if isolated would be no use. And he is reading even if he acts automatically: he <u>is</u> reading, if he <u>would</u> say "I've made a mistake".> (10:106)

a↑ b↓ c← d→

(1) a a c b d

(2) ⌐¬

Are these 2 similar? First answer is: No. But there is a similarity.

This is obscured by fact that we usually confine a similarity to projection according to certain rules only.

Thus, there is a similarity between automatic signals & movements of traffic.

Red for stop is arbitrary; but once we've chosen it, there's something not arbitrary – we've committed ourselves.

A rule, once chosen, limits possibility of significance of symbolism. 5:47

If I'm guided by a score, I'm letting the crotchets guide me – leaving it undetermined what I'm to do.

If I say ♩ means nothing to me: what I mean is that rule has not provided for this possibility.

Of course, I could interpret it: but then, I am at that moment making a new rule.

Thus rules give to symbolism a certain particular degree of freedom.

Degree of freedom is expressed by what I call rules of its grammar.

Explaining how to use a symbolism, increases multiplicity of symbolism, by distinguishing different ways of interpreting: it excludes certain interpretations.

But this must come to an end: I shall not be able to distinguish any more possibilities.

"Understanding" is correlated to "explanation", not to a drug, or pushing people out.

When no more explanation is possible, understanding is achieved. 5:48

So misunderstanding = what can be removed by explanation.

Every explanation, which is an explanation, increases multiplicity of symbolism: if right one is reached, there's no more occasion for explanation.

Hence all explanation of thought is building up a symbolism = giving rules of grammar.

When this is done, every explanation has been given.

Lent Term, 1931

1

Lent Term. I.   5:49

Recapitulation.

What is philosophy? Not free to give any definition: for we have vague expectations of what sort of question

What expectation?

(1) It has to be very general. (2) Fundamental both to ordinary life & science: whatever sort of answers it gives. (3) Therefore has to be independent of special results of science – e.g. of latest experiments on cod-fish or guinea-pigs.

How about pure mathematics, which doesn't give description of world – as physics does?

In discussing its relation to science, we are doing philosophy: but we don't know whether this is all philosophy.

But we can follow track of clearing up, or tidying things: whereas scientist does something quite different – more like building a house, not tidying a room. We have to touch everything very often.

We start with being vague & hazy: & we don't mind this, provided haze will gradually clear up.

Sciences made up of a sort of unit – propositions or sentences – what comes between 2 full-stops in a book: even mathematical propositions.

We ask: what is a proposition? which question is like child's "Why?" expressing merely a vague mental discomfort.

Vague answers: 5:50

(1) Expression of a thought, or description of a fact. Come to something.

(2) Whatever is true or false.

(3) What says that such & such is the case.

All these, though very vague, have something in them.

As to (1) we're not interested in <u>thought</u> from psychological point of view – its causes and effects.

What we are interested in is thought <u>as symbolic process</u>.

Does a sentence <u>express</u> thought in same sense as <u>crying</u> tooth-ache?

Is thought momentary, or amorphous, a state of mind, like tooth-ache?

Do we have successive hallucinations of "fine", "weather", "today" when we think "It is fine today". (French so excellent, because words follow order of thoughts)[1]

Thought is <u>not</u> such a succession, nor momentary, nor amorphous.

We think by <u>means</u> of the expression.

E.g. an expectation is a thought. What is happening, when I think he is coming? Do I keep saying "He is coming", or am I in an amorphous condition of restlessness?

I call the thought only <u>what</u> is expressed: thought is as long as its expression.

5:51 Sentences have meaning; & people think that each word should remind us of something. E.g. that thinking is done by association – a series of words bringing up a series of pictures.

The idea of "meaning" is taken from a particular kind of words – viz. proper names: here the meaning is a thing.

But "and" "all" etc. have no meaning in this sense.

But where we can say "x" has a meaning, it may be transitive or intransitive.

Sometimes "<u>What</u> is the meaning?" has sense, sometimes not.

E.g. "and" has meaning, may mean something like "and" works in this sentence – it is not a mere flourish or ornament, could not be left out.

Even in transitive cases, we can talk of a person who no longer exists, or who has never existed. Perhaps some day it will be proved that Julius Caesar is a myth.

Take "red" or "green". In one sense "red" need not exist[2] in order that "I expect a red patch" should have a meaning. Need I have seen something

---

[1] See 5:18 for further discussion of this example.
[2] Moore later added: <(i.e. in sense that there need have been no red thing)>

called red before? I only need to have an idea of red. I have no proof that I've ever seen a red thing: I might have got idea by pressing eyes. Or I may have false memory.

In case of proper name you can use ostensive definition; but there you can substitute the person for the word.

The proposition doesn't merely remind us of those things to which we can point: because I could make up a sentence of the things pointed at which will still be a sentence. 5:52

And here you can't ask: what do those things mean?

Ostensive definition works exactly as does a · b = c Def.

The movement of pointing & the orange can serve instead of words "an orange": we have not replaced symbol by symbolised – proposition by fact.

Symbol is sign & all that is necessary in order that it should be significant.

E.g. man writing "I met a man" is part of symbol.

Here "understanding" = nothing more than getting hold of the symbol.

"Understanding" is correlate of "explanation": something which can be conveyed by it, not what can be conveyed by a drug.

If so every explanation adds to the symbol: by giving one, I give you more signs – more to get hold of.

Here symbol is, in some sense, self-contained.

This, in some sense, contradicts what is usually believed, because it seems essential to a symbol that it should point to something outside itself.

If I wish for an orange, this seems to foreshadow the getting of an orange: & people think there is a shadow which comes between the proposition & its verification, & which is its sense or meaning – something similar to the actual eating.

The assumption of an intermediate link does not help us; because we should need another link between it & the reality. 5:53

Similarity is always relative to a mode of projection: usually we are presupposing one of a small number of modes.[3]

E.g. picture of me in a concave mirror is "not like" me.

---

[3] Moore later added: <(i.e. using "like" = projected in this mode)>

There is a silly, but natural, objection:

How can I expect Mr. Smith to come, if he doesn't? How can I expect that which doesn't happen?

Silly answer is: I don't expect that, but something similar.

Which is obviously a misuse of language.

The bang which I expect is not a bang less loud than that which I expected.

What is true is: Expression of expectation contains description of fact which would satisfy it.

Following expression of thought = translating it according to a general rule: as in playing piano according to score.

Score doesn't <u>cause</u> us to press keys: if so there would be no right or wrong playing.

We do follow general rule, but there was difficulty about accidentals: but here also there is rule, though not picture.[4]

a a b d c c

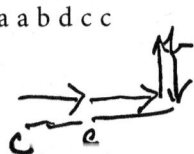

5:54   To rules of translation from language into reality correspond rules of grammar: & there is <u>no</u> possible justification for <u>these</u>: because any language by which we could try to justify would have to have a grammar itself: no description of world can justify rules of grammar.

---

[4] The use of this kind of letter and arrow diagram is first introduced at 5:46 and discussed below at 5:57.

2

II. Lent Term. 5:55

End of last incoherent.[5]

Follow instinct to clear up things in realm of <u>what can be said</u>.

Propositions <u>units</u> of what can be or is said.

We don't know what: "What <u>is</u> a proposition?" means.

(1) Expression of thought
(2) Description of fact
(3) What says: So & so is the case.
(4) What is true or false.

We feel that all these must come to same thing.

(1) Propositions must have meaning.

To say a word "has meaning" ≠ is representative.

E.g. "and".

In proper names it looks like it: but in ostensive definitions we can <u>replace</u> word by gesture & thing pointed to, & we can't <u>ostensively</u> define <u>this</u>.

But people think: Though words can't represent, yet it's peculiarity of thought, that it can represent.

This is pernicious mistake: that in the mind things can happen which can't outside.

That there is organic & inorganic part: that thinking is a sort of mental 5:56 digestion; & that chemistry of digestion is different from chemical processes in test-tubes.

If there <u>were</u> such a process, we should be able to describe it, & in the description we should be able to see nature of process.

There is <u>for us</u> no organic part of thought – only inorganic: we are only interested in what can be symbolised.

---

[5] Moore's summary notes: <Last lecture at end was incoherent.> (10:107)

Dispute can have sense only in so far as it can be written down or said.

= Thought must be autonomous.

It is thought: When we think a proposition, we are thinking of things mentioned – e.g. Townsend[6], bench, sitting; & that though <u>they</u> can't be in my mind, representatives of them are.

There's some truth in this: but if there are, it must be irrelevant, since we can't know that there's anything outside. What's not given in my thought can't be essential to my thought. It <u>may</u> be, however, that <u>both</u> the representative & what it represents are in my mind.

What is meant by: red <u>occurs</u> in my thought, or in any fact? If in "This is red" then in "This is <u>not</u> red".

Thought does not point outside itself: why we think it does, is because of how a symbol is used – i.e. because it is compared with something else. Whenever we use a symbol, we are translating it into something else = are guided by the symbol: whether we control a fact, or describe a fact, or follow an order.

5:57   Suppose I describe this room: There is given to me (1) a language (2) what I see; & I must read off the description from what I see.

E.g. there is given (1) a↑ b↓ c→ d←[7] = grammar & vocabulary

(2) a a c c c b

& I read off

I might make up my mind to describe the room in English, or in German, or in new symbols. Such choosing does go on. It doesn't matter whether I <u>collate</u>, or actually make the translation.

It may be objected:

   Understanding an order is not obeying it.

---

[6] Raymond D. Townsend was among the students attending these lectures (Klagge 2003, 342). His notes from Wittgenstein's lectures for the 1930 Michaelmas term are stored in the Wren Library, at Trinity College, Cambridge.

[7] A key to this kind of letter and arrow diagram is set out at 5:46 and 6:20.

I say: It's either adding of signs which complete the symbol or a translating into something e.g. imagery, or into movements of innervation.

Translation very often is done by a general rule.

Here's a great difficulty:

I said: If we translate into action, it is not enough that we should look at the sentence & do the action; but it's necessary we should derive the one from the other. And objection was that, from behaviouristic point of view, no-one could tell I was deriving: that this derivation is a sort of fiction. That all we mean is that the action is caused by the other.

E.g. a dog is trained to do this. Does he read the symbols? or is he just acted upon by them? 5:58

It's wrong to say behaviourism doesn't distinguish between reading & not reading: it only does it in a different way.

It must distinguish between having tooth-ache & simulating it.

Take: A man holds his tooth, & says "I have tooth-ache": another holds his tooth & says "I have not". Behaviourist distinguishes them.

So he distinguishes: between "I am looking & speaking": & "I am reading".

So with the dog.

Whether he reads or not, will be judged, from behaviouristic point of view, in this way.

He wouldn't say "he's read the bone": he would only say he reads what he's learnt: yet in both cases his action is caused by the thing seen.

Therefore essence of reading can't be that it's caused.[8]

(I'm only saying how the word "reading" is used.)

Essential thing is: If a symbolism is given sense, & I read it, then symbol for rule only adds to signs I am reading: & hence I can't prescribe use of symbolism. I can prescribe use of a particular symbol, by adding signs to it. Symbolism as a whole being complete, I can't prescribe it.

A language can be taught by Correspondence courses, but language can't.

It follows that all I can do to clear up a symbolism is to describe it; & this is 5:59
done by (vocabulary & grammar) = grammar.

Grammar says which combinations of symbols are allowed, which not = which make sense, which don't.

Can we say: Why must we follow these rules, not others?

---

[8] Moore's summary notes: <Essence of reading can't be that what I see causes action; because I only read when I've learnt to read.> (10:13)

If we could, we should have to say: Because reality is of this kind, rules of grammar must be of this. Which implies: if reality were otherwise, grammar would be otherwise.

This won't do: because if I can say that reality is otherwise, this is what grammar says I can't do.

I can't say what reality would have to be like, in order that what makes nonsense should make sense, because in order to do so I should have to use this new grammar.

A description can only be true or false.

What I can say significantly about colours, I can't say significantly about sounds – at least not everything.

Hence we can't distinguish grammatical forms by saying that one has a property, which the other hasn't; because then that it has would be false, whereas grammar says it is nonsense.

Hence sounds are not distinguished from colours by having properties which latter have not; because if the one had not them, it would be significant to say they have.

5:60 So with different kinds of numbers. Calling them all numbers, means that some rules apply to all: but we can't say that complex numbers have properties which integers have not.

Now return to: What is a proposition?

A proposition is a logical form; & therefore I can't give properties which it has & something else hasn't.

Therefore a proposition is simply characterised by rules of grammar which apply to it;

hence (4) = wherever grammar allows me to use "true" & "false"

= can be affirmed or negated.

= symbolism of negation can be applied to

= whole complex symbolism of "not" "or" "and".

Equation & proposition[9] have some grammatical rules in common, but some not: hence in one sense negation is same in both, in other different.

Suppose we ask "Is this really a king?" In one sense it is, in another not.

---

[9] Moore later added: <"Proposition" here = experiential proposition.>

3

February 2. III.

<u>Grammatical rules</u>, what combinations of words make sense & what don't: hence grammar circumscribes language, since what doesn't make sense doesn't belong to language.

What is meant by "using language according to grammatical rules"?

<u>Not</u> that the rules must run in our head: we needn't repeat them to ourselves: we need not be conscious of any <u>expression</u> of these rules.

Even if they always did, this wouldn't help us: <u>for</u>

thinking of rule takes time, though we may use a word according to it during part of the time.

Yet grammatical rules are essential to language: we must use language systematically; just as chess wouldn't be a game, if <u>all</u> moves were allowed.

When I use language, I am <u>choosing</u> my words <u>to fit the occasion</u>.

Suppose I say "Please leave the room", & someone says: Why do you choose the word "room"?

The answer must be of sort: because I've been told that "this is a room".

But this answer presupposes an understanding of language, i.e. of "this is a room".

Every explanation teaches you to understand <u>this</u> as opposed to <u>that</u> – <u>not</u> to understand. I.e. it avoids a misunderstanding, doesn't create understanding.

Therefore <u>whole</u> of language can't be misunderstood: since, if misunderstood, there must be an explanation to remove it.

Every explanation increases multiplicity, & when whole is reached there can be no further explanation or misunderstanding.

= Every word has a <u>place</u> in language; its place being determined by all the grammatical rules which apply to it = explanations which apply to it

E.g. you can substitute a piece for a king at chess – put it in king's <u>place</u> – by determining that same rules are to apply to it.

E.g. "this is "green"" (explaining meaning of word "green") is a grammatical rule = every explanation of language, previous to use of language: it fixes the place of the word "green" in language.

E.g. in a book you could explain the names of colours, by painting little squares of the required colours.

Here the colours are not arbitrary, in a sense in which the words are: they form a system, which the names in themselves don't form.

Often when we want to say a sentence is senseless, we say "You can't imagine that".

Take   p or q
           not q
           p and q

you see no system in them: but if you use Sheffer's system, you do.

$$(p \mid q) \mid (p \mid q)^{[10]}$$
$$q \mid q$$
$$(p \mid p) \mid (q \mid q)$$

The colours are like this expression in Sheffer's system: they are symbols which shew us a system.

What does it mean to choose your words to fit an occasion?

Of course, they're not spread out before you.

But a process goes on different from taking first which comes in your head; & its characteristic is that in answer to question "Why did you choose?" answer is a grammatical rule.

If words didn't form a system, they would be arbitrary: there could be no reason to choose one rather than another.

In onomatopeic words "rustle" "boom", the word in virtue of its sound belongs to a system: it is itself a picture.

We can't give reasons for grammatical rules.

A reason would have to be a description of reality: & this must be capable of truth & falsehood: & if it were false, it would have to be said in a language not using this grammar.

---

[10] Moore attempted to translate these formulas to Russellian notation in the margins of the notes, using the following schema: <p | q = ~p . ~q>

E.g. I use "sweet" in such a way that "sweeter" has meaning: but "identical" in such a way that "more identical" hasn't.

You might say that this because of a quality in reality.

But then it must be possible to say that reality hasn't got this quality, which grammar forbids.[11]

Is then grammar arbitrary?

In a sense it is, in a sense not.

It is, if you mean that we can't give reasons.

But it's not arbitrary in this sense:

To "can "hate" be used as an intransitive verb?" there are 2 answers

    (1) of course, if you use it with different grammatical rules
    (2) not, if you use it in sense in which we do.

But if you do, it would be better to use a different word, just as if you have 2 chess pieces with different rules, it would be better to give them different shapes.[12]

What makes grammar not arbitrary is its use; but described by itself it is arbitrary.[13]

When we distinguish "kinds" in logic, it means always that different rules apply; & when 2 kinds have something in common, this can only mean that some rules apply to both.

And so with Time & Space: some grammatical rules which apply to right & left, also apply to before & after.

What is a proposition?

A logical form – & hence characterised by certain grammatical rules.

---

[11] Moore's summary notes: <I use "identical" in such a way that "more identical" has no sense. If this were because of a quality in reality, it would make sense to say reality hadn't got that quality, & grammar forbids this. This is supposed to shew we can't give reasons for using "identical" in such a way that "more identical" makes nonsense (and, of course, we might use "identical" to mean "sweet"). But, if we didn't, we shouldn't be using it as we actually do.> (10:109)

[12] Moore later added: <Not necessarily: you could give them different colours.>

[13] Moore's summary notes: <It is arbitrary in sense that we can't give any reason for our rules.> (10:73)

What characterises a proposition as generally understood is that truth-functions apply to them.

= can be true or false = say "So & so is the case".

As generally understood means, so as to include what I call propositions, also hypotheses, also mathematical propositions.

If I distinguish the 3 kinds, this is a logical distinction, & it must be that there are some rules which apply to some & not to others.

But truth-function rules apply to all, & that's why all are called propositions.

"There seems to be a man here" is a proposition.

"There is a man here" is a hypothesis, & one different rule is that I can't say "There seems to seem to be a man here".

"True" & "false" are only part of a notation for truth-functions: we could do away with them, & substitute "or", "not", "and" etc..

Intricate connection between them is shewn by T F notation.

5:66 Frege explained truth-functions by explanations containing "true" & "false": e.g. he said ~p = the proposition which is false, if p true, true if p is false.[14]

But important point is not that they can be explained by "true" & "false"; but that this explanation can be substituted for the old notation – is itself a notation.[15]

$$p = \begin{array}{c|c} p & \\ \hline T & T \\ F & F \end{array} \qquad \sim p = \begin{array}{c|c} p & \\ \hline T & F \\ F & T \end{array}$$

Why Frege is misleading is because to say "p is true, if ~p is false" doesn't give an explanation, but only a relation between "not" & "true" & "false". Hence what he said would be of no interest.

---

[14] See Frege 1893, §6, 10.

[15] Moore's summary notes: <Frege was wrong in thinking that "~p is the proposition which is true if p is false" was an explanation of "not". Truth is that "p is false" can be substituted for "~p": is itself a notation.> (10:109)

4

February 9. IV.

What does it mean to use speech according to grammatical rules?

Not that we're conscious of rules or any expression of them.

But that if we need to justify our use, we appeal to a rule.

Chess is characterised by its rules: but a man who plays chess hasn't got the rules running in his head: yet he would justify a move, by appeal to a rule.

Now there's <u>some</u> difference between playing chess & manipulating pieces, as the rules <u>allow</u>: the 2 people would give different accounts.

Here & elsewhere it doesn't matter, whether we give behaviouristic or introspective account: since both must have same multiplicity.

E.g. there must be behaviouristic account of difference between real & simulated tooth-ache.

Now rules are <u>not</u> present in consciousness of man who plays chess.

Case is the same when we use language.

We might distinguish chess-player from others empirically, by looking at them, & say how person goes on: but this isn't distinction, because person would say even after one move "I'm playing chess".

Truth is chess-player <u>sees</u> something different in his move – sometimes, not always, for many are made automatically.

So when we use "and" or "not".

If we try to explain what we mean by this by a gesture, we are illustrating their meaning.

We illustrate these words by intonation (different for "not", "or", "and") & internal gestures, just as green by "pointing".

And so we illustrate negation by[16]

p	
T	F
F	T

Here's an analogy.

Same process is involved in understanding proposition as in understanding picture-story: & difference between portrait & imaginary scene, corresponds to assertion & fiction.

Now understanding a picture may mean many things:

e.g. picture of animal; have you heard of it? This not interesting.

But understanding 3-dimensionally: e.g. one part might still look like a plane. And here you understand, even if you don't know whether so & so is a stone or a lump of putty.

Now to see as a plane, & to see 3-dimensionally, is to see different things. We don't merely interpret differently. Of course the scratches on blackboard & light-rays may be the same.

E.g. we see a picture differently, having had experience of human beings of ordinary size, from a person who had only seen pygmies.

5:69 Why, if these complicated processes go on in understanding "and", "or", "not", does logic never mention them?

Understanding is what is produced by an explanation (not = caused by).

And explanation must have same multiplicity; & this is all that interests us.

Now, 2 ways of using "proposition" – wider & narrower.

In wider, explanation = "what is seen to be true or false", is quite right: it has a well-defined place in "true" & "false" game.

Now "true" & "false" are only correctly used as part of a notation for truth-functions

$\sim p, p \vee q, p \cdot q$:

hence we could do away with them.

---

[16] Moore's summary notes: <We can't get any clearer about meaning of "not". What's difficult is to make rules explicit.> (10:109)

Lecture 4 – February 9, 1931

Important point about T, F notation is that it can be <u>substituted</u> for Russell's notation, <u>not</u> that (as Russell thought) it explains it.

"~ξ" says Russell (& Frege, except he has) "is a true proposition if ξ is false, & a false if ξ is true".

This <u>doesn't</u> explain negation; <u>for</u> it might be true of other functions. But it can be used <u>instead</u> of ~ξ.

So we can use

p	
T	F
F	T

<u>instead</u> of ~p.

Now suppose I'm asked to <u>explain</u> "true" "false" "not" etc..

What sort of explanation could you want?

Not a physical, not an explanation of Russell's kind, but what's called an analysis.

Why do we want an explanation?

We feel that "not" is a kind of signal: we feel that negation is more complicated than sign of negation ~p. Yet complexity of negation is expressed in ~p – not in the scratch, but in rules which apply to it.

Usually it's said "Can you define "not" or is it indefinable?"

~p = p | p Def. is a definition, but does <u>not</u> explain ~p.

T & K are sitting here = f(C).

C = T & K

This sort of definition is just <u>one</u> of the rules of grammar about negation.

Suppose I say "I can't explain ~p: you must take it as indefinable": to say this doesn't absolve us from necessity for giving rules.

<u>One difficulty</u>.

How can it have sense to negate a proposition? For if ~p is true, nothing corresponds to p.

E.g. "The door is not open".

This is due to false analogy.

What "corresponds" to p is that ~p is the case.

Russell's "p ⊃ q"

One paradox

Russell says if p is false, you can infer q[17]

Now look at

p	q	
T	T	T
T	F	F
F	T	T
F	F	T

$\} = p \supset q$

I.e. a false proposition implies every other, & a true implies any other true.[18]

This only sounds paradoxical

(1) because we mix up implication with inference.

We can't infer every proposition from a false, nor does every true follow from any true.

(2) because he translates $p \supset q$ "if p, then q".

We never use "if p, then q" in this way.

Russell admitted this, but said we do in

$(x)(\phi x \supset \psi x)$

But we don't here either.

5:72 Where we use "if ... then" is in hypotheses.

<u>Proposition</u> has definite verification or falsification: e.g. "There seems to me to be a man here."

<u>Hypothesis</u> is like "There is a man here", where future experience may compel us to change hypothesis: & important thing is that there is no definite verification: hypothesis is a rule according to which propositions are constructed.

Suppose "Whenever there are clouds, it rains" or "All men are mortal."

---

[17] Wittgenstein here may mean that if p is false, you can infer q <u>from p</u>, i.e.: $\sim p \supset (p \supset q)$. See Whitehead and Russell 1927, vol. 1, 99, *2·21.

[18] See Whitehead and Russell 1927, vol. 1, 99, *2·02 and *2·21, where Russell interprets $q \supset (p \supset q)$ as 'a true proposition is implied by any proposition' and $\sim p \supset (p \supset q)$ as 'a false proposition implies any proposition'.

Experience bears out this hypothesis; & we can confirm it by killing people; but, if we don't succeed, this doesn't prove hypothesis wrong.[19]

Russell's formal implication is true, even if there are no x's which satisfy φ or ψ.

This isn't what we mean by "if ... then", because if we find no men that would support Russell's hypothesis, but <u>not</u> what we mean.

Take "Every cylindrical body of copper, unsupported, will fall".

We should verify it by making a piece, not by not finding one.

---

[19] Moore later added: <Also, if we do succeed, this doesn't prove it right?>

5

5:73   V.

Negation.

Important that, if someone asks you for an explanation, you have a right to say "Don't you know?" This is not so with explanation of a physical phenomenon.

We use negation easily enough; trouble arises when we try to make rules of usage explicit.

Like Augustine's "When not asked what Time is, I know; when asked, I don't know".[20]

Are we conscious of rules of grammar, when we use "not" understanding it?[21]

I.e. what's difference between making one move of chess, understanding rules, & a person who makes same move, not understanding.

He sees something in the move.

So "Jungfrau", because people saw a human figure in it.[22]

So too, seeing anger in a face: our past experience actually modifies what we see. The past experience does not enter, but something else does, caused by it.

Suppose I say "The door is not open"; & somebody asks "Is this the same "not" to which the rule "~~p = p" applies?"

---

[20] *Confessions*, XI.14: 'What *is* this time? If no one asks me, I know; if I want to explain it to a questioner, I do not know' (Augustine 1993, 219). Quoted in the original Latin in *Philosophical Investigations* (Wittgenstein 1953), §89.

[21] Moore's summary notes: <What happens when we use "not", understanding it? We are not conscious of all rules of grammar governing our use, & it's difficult to make them explicit.> (10:73)

[22] The Jungfrau is a summit in the Swiss Alps. Its name means 'young woman' or 'virgin' in German, which may have derived from the fact that the peak resembles a nun in a white habit. See Room 2005, 184.

Note question "Is it the same?"
So in: Is this the same piece of paper you wrote on & which will burn.
This is a matter of future experience.
But in case of "not", it is more like: "I see a red circle." "Is this the same as would be cut in 2 points by straight line through its centre."
This is a geometrical proposition = rule of grammar: i.e. it says we can speak, rightly or wrongly, of 2 intersections of the figure.[23]

Take the "is" in "The rose is red" is same as in "The chair is brown", but not same as 2×2 is 4: & that "is" here = "equals".
How do we know that 2 words "mean" the same?
Is it same "not" in "This door is not open" & in "This chair is not yellow"?
We ask is it the "not" to which "$\sim\sim\sim p = \sim p$" applies?
How do we know that "not" & "nicht" mean the same?
In 2 different ways
(1) Having learnt "not" as we do as children, & then being told "nicht" means the same.
(2) We may have learnt German in same way as English, & then gathered that they mean the same.
What's difference between understanding an English & not understanding a Japanese newspaper?
It is due to having learnt English, but this learning is not contained in the understanding.
You can lay down an arbitrary rule, e.g. to turn certain ways, if you see or don't see a tree: then you can read the trees.
You've taught a language to yourself.
Act of laying down rule is not contained in following it, but rule is contained.

Rules applying to negation actually describe my experience when I use "not" – i.e. describe my understanding of it; but the learning of them is not contained in that experience.

---

[23] Moore later added: <= It has sense to say "This figure is intersected in 2 points.">

If we investigate geometry of visual field, it is of same kind as an investigation of "not". In both nothing is hidden, which we want to bring to light. A logical investigation doesn't teach us anything about meaning of negation: we can't get any clearer about its meaning. What's difficult is to make rules explicit.

An investigation about nature of physical space is quite different: an experiment may make it more practical to use one kind of space – which we call shewing us something about nature of physical space.

5:76   If a man understands one order, he must be able to understand another.

What does "able to" mean?

It must be a description of what happens when he understands first order; & 2nd order does not enter into his understanding.

First order can only be understood as part of a system.

Suppose I direct you about the room by drawing arrows; having taught you a rule.

Suppose I'd also taught another language of arrows – in which arrow means move in some direction with speed proportionate to length.

Then you may understand ⟶ as part of either of 2 different languages. You can see it as part of the one system, or as part of the other system.[24]

In system (b) "Don't go ⟶, go ↗" means nothing.

The rules I gave you describe your understanding of the arrow.

5:77   The rules don't merely determine the action, in the sense that I can see by experience whether the action is in accordance with them, but actually describe the understanding.[25]

---

[24] Moore's summary notes: <You can see an arrow either as a sign of direction or as a sign of velocity.> (10:16)

[25] Moore's summary notes: <I don't learn by experience whether my action is in accordance with this rule about arrow or that one: the rules describe my understanding of

Negation.

Paradox. How can ~p have a meaning at all, for, if it's true, <u>nothing</u> corresponds to ~p?

This is characteristic logical puzzle, because it's due to wrong analogy.

It's like: How can a man wish what has happened?

We compare it with: You can't see what isn't there.

Answer is: Grammar of word "something" is different in the 2 cases.

This false analogy has led people to think that "~p" <u>means</u> that one of all the other possibilities is the case: & hence negation can be abolished.

"<u>not</u>" does mean this in some cases: e.g. this is /one of primary colours/ <u>not</u> red = this is either yellow, or blue, or green.

But "Mr. Smith is <u>not</u> in this room" is <u>not</u> same as any disjunction.

Even if you <u>could</u> substitute a disjunction, it wouldn't matter because you <u>can</u> express it by ~p.   5:78

I.e. negative proposition has <u>not</u> a different multiplicity from ~p.

Multiplicity of excluded proposition & sign "~" <u>is</u> the multiplicity of what we mean.

It's sufficient to mention thing excluded & sign of exclusion.

Feeling that negation is mysterious is always due to being misled by some wrong linguistic analogy.

We use wrong analogies, when we try to speculate about words, <u>not</u> when we use them.

the arrow. (There can be <u>no doubt</u> on my part that my action is in accordance with this rule, not that I don't learn by experience that it is in accordance.)> (10:74)

6

5:79   Lecture VI.

Negation. Applies also, mutatis mutandis, to any truth-function.

If we state "Do not shut the door": can we ask "Is this the same "not" to which the rule of double-negation applies?"

Is "~p . (~~p = p)" a proposition?

If it's to mean anything, 2nd part can only be rule of a game.

All it could do is to give first part sense; but, if it can give it sense, then first part hasn't yet got it.[26] And, without sense, ~p isn't a proposition at all, & hence couldn't be part of a logical product.

One imagines, falsely, that grammatical rule about symbolism of negation says something about negation. All that says anything about negation is e.g. ~p.[27]

Cf. Geometry. What I can say of a circle is that it's red, or blue, or there, or not there.

We said that when I understand "not", I see it in a different way; & it might be thought that therefore 2 different ways of explaining negation.

Geometry.

I can't describe the cubic shape, though I can describe a particular cube.

A cubic shape can't be described, though it can be defined e.g. parallelepiped with 4 sides equal.

Doesn't equation of circle describe a circle? Yes & No.

5:80   It's nonsense (a grammatical mistake) to say "I describe a cubical shape".

Geometry describes a circle in sense in which Logic describes negation. It gives connections which grammar allows; & this corresponds to what we mean by circle.

---

[26] Moore later added: <Why couldn't it be one of the rules constituting /determining/ meaning of "not"? It is, according to Wittgenstein; but rules about symbols.>

[27] Moore later added: <(i.e. "~~p ≡ p" says nothing about negation /if taken as expressing a grammatical rule/.)>

Lecture 6 – February 23, 1931

So negation is explained by logic.

~p = ~~~p , ~p . ~p , ~p ∨ ~p , ~p . (q ∨ ~q) , ~p ∨ (q . ~q)

These expressions are produced according to a rule, & the rule according to which I produce these expresses essence of negation – <u>characterises negation.</u>

<u>Inference.</u>

Easiest to treat this by T F symbolism.

A truth-function of <u>1</u> argument, <u>can</u> be written as a truth-function of 2.

p	p	
T	T	T
T	F	T
F	T	F
F	F	F

It's important to realise that this doesn't mention q.

Thus in "(p ∨ q) . ~q" q can be made to occur only once, namely

p	q	p ∨ q	~q	
T	T	T	F	F
T	F	T	T	T
F	T	T	F	F
F	F	F	T	F

which = p . ~q

Thus you can reduce what in Russell's notation are compound truth-functions to simple ones.

And if you do this, you sometimes get 4 T's or 4 F's.

E.g. take   p ⊃ p   or p ∨ ~p

p	q		p	
T	T	T	T	T
T	F	T	T	T
F	T	F	F	T
F	F	F	F	T

A proposition of this sort says nothing. Is a tautology.

To say a tautology says nothing = ((p . tautology) = p)[28]

So (p ∨ contradiction) = p

Tautology & contradiction are limiting cases of propositions; & that they say nothing can be explained as follows

p	q			
T	T	T		T
T	F	F		F
F	T	F		F
F	F	F		T

⟶   ⟵

You could say that by writing you give less freedom to reality than by writing. Thus a tautology gives reality <u>complete</u> freedom.

5:82   Thus an infinitely long rope is as good as none.

Thus if we say p is true, whatever q may be,[29] then connection between q & reality is broken: it looks as if there is a connection, but really there's none. Differential gear in motor-car is example.

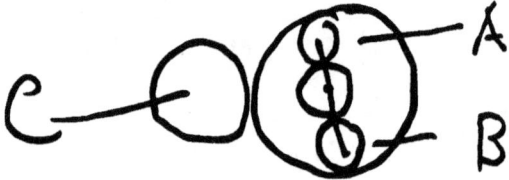

A & B engage in the middle wheel: but middle wheel is not connected with C.

---

[28] Moore later added: <But this (p . q = p) is his formula for q <u>follows from</u> p, & here q doesn't necessarily "say nothing". But p . q = p is <u>not</u> a law of logic: it does <u>not</u> say "for all values of p & q, p . q = p" which would be absurdly false: whereas "p . tautology = p" <u>does</u> say "for all values of p" & is a law of logic.>

[29] Moore later added: <whether q is true or false>

A proposition draws a line round facts which agree with it, & distinguishes them from those which don't.

Tautology draws an infinite boundary.

Contradiction draws boundary contracted to a point & leaves no room to reality.

> Now Inference.

Transition from one proposition to another, characterised by way in which we justify it – i.e. by saying that q follows from p.

This is expressed very misleadingly[30] by "If p is true, q must be", & this is supposed to give connection between implication & inference.

"Following" is called a relation, as if it were like "fatherhood". 5:83

But it is entirely determined if the 2 propositions are given: e.g. p ∨ q follows from p . q.

This is quite different from other relations.

It seems not; because you can say: If you know diameter of wire, & weight of iron, you know that wire can't support iron.

But it remains thinkable that it should.

Take "If you know nature of sulphuric acid & zinc, you know they must give zinc-sulphate."

But it's thinkable that they shouldn't.

From diameter of wire & weight of iron alone I can't know that wire will break.

I.e. "following" is an internal relation; &, roughly speaking, an internal relation holds if it's unthinkable that it should not hold between the terms.

Now a proposition works like a portrait: you can't see whether it's true or false by looking only at it.

But what about proposition: that p ∨ q follows from p . q?

---

[30] Moore later added: <because this phrase also applies to cases which are not cases of logical following>

5:84   It isn't wanted: if you don't see it by looking at them, it won't help you.

What justifies inference is an internal relation.

If I say "p ∨ q follows from p . q" everything here is useless except "p ∨ q" & "p . q".

If another proposition were needed to justify it, we should need an infinite series.

A <u>rule</u> of inference <u>never</u> justifies an inference.

What's meant by "I <u>see</u> the internal relation"?

To <u>shew</u> the internal relation on the blackboard, you'd have to write the propositions in a different way e.g. by T, F symbolism

p . q =	p	q		p ∨ q =	p	q	
	T	T	T		T	T	T
	T	F	F		T	F	T
	F	T	F		F	T	T
	F	F	F		F	F	F

and here one sees that there are possibilities which make (2) true but not (1); whereas all that make (1) do make (2).

7

Lecture VII.   5:85

<u>Inference</u>. Transition from one proposition to another, characterised by way we justify it: i.e. by saying one <u>follows</u> from other.

q follows from p seems to say there is a <u>relation</u> between them; & that it <u>justifies</u> passing from one to the other, <u>seems</u> like saying: A loves B, therefore we can't separate them.

But what makes one suspicious about this is that we perceive this relation merely by looking at the propositions concerned – that it is internal.

It is not like: That this wire will break with this weight, <u>follows</u> from weight of weight, diameter & material of wire.

When I use term "internal relation", this is misleading; but I use it because others have: = a relation which holds, if the terms are what they are, & can't therefore be imagined not to hold.

Now, with Russell's notation, it isn't obvious that

    $p \vee q$ follows from $p \cdot q$

but in Sheffer's

    $(p \mid p) \mid (q \mid q)$

obviously entails

    $(p \mid q) \mid (p \mid q)$[31]

But also it isn't obvious, with Russell's, what <u>justifies</u> the inference. A rule of inference is useless. If ι is to justify "q follows from p": then q <u>must</u>   5:86
follow from p & ι.

Hence inference can only be justified by <u>what we see</u>, <u>not</u> by a rule. <u>So</u> throughout Mathematics.

But I seem to have contradicted myself: since I've said that internal relations don't justify inference.

---

[31] Moore later added: $<p \mid q = {\sim}p \cdot {\sim}q$. Hence $(p \mid p) \mid (q \mid q) = {\sim}({\sim}p) \cdot {\sim}({\sim}q) = p \cdot q$ and $(p \mid q) \mid (p \mid q) = {\sim}({\sim}p \cdot {\sim}q) \cdot {\sim}({\sim}p \cdot {\sim}q) = {\sim}({\sim}p \cdot {\sim}q)>$

Let's use T F notation

$$p \cdot q = \begin{array}{c|c|c} p & q & \\ \hline T & T & T \\ T & F & F \\ F & T & F \\ F & F & F \end{array}$$

$$\text{while } p \vee q = \begin{array}{c|c|c} p & q & \\ \hline T & T & T \\ T & F & T \\ F & T & T \\ F & F & F \end{array}$$

Criterion is that q follows from p, if to every T in p there corresponds a T in q.

p . q <u>asserts</u> p ∨ q, but not vice versa.

Now I've here stated a rule – a rule of inference.

But this rule is simply a rule of grammar, & treats only of the symbolism.

How do you know that this justifies that? is like: How do you know that green can't be higher than red?

5:87 Rules of grammar can't be <u>justified</u>.

We can't give a <u>description</u> of reality, such that <u>if</u> it holds p ∨ q will follow from p . q, but if not, not.

This rule is a rule of a game; & its importance comes in from fact that we use it in our language.

What corresponds to a necessity in the world must be what in language seems an arbitrary rule.

I can't describe negation internally, if I mention negation in the description; because I must then know what negation means.

Once "p . q" & "p ∨ q" are used as propositions, I can't say that the one follows from the other; I can only say this of them so long as they are not used.

I can prepare language for use, before it's used: but not when I'm using it. I can give rules of language, only so long as language isn't used.

The rules prepare the game, that it may afterwards be used as a language: only when the rules are fixed, can I <u>use</u> the language.

The proposition is smallest unit in language: I can't build up a proposition of smaller units which are also units in language.

Proposition is first unit which has sense.

Now in telling rules of grammar, I'm still building: only when game is completed, have I a language.

What I say of grammar (including inference) is always arbitrary rules: they needn't be used, but if we change them, we can't use them in this way.

3-valued logic.

I can make a calculus, with certain rules, which has

    T F P.

But then the T & F are not the same as in ours.

The calculus can be used, but not instead of ours.

That we can make such a calculus is a discovery:

But (1) it's not true that we have a new logic instead of the old one; as they think.

(2) It can't be used, as they think it can.

The rules only become important, because of their application.

A calculus can't be true or false; nor more or less fundamental (as Russell & Frege believed of logical calculus: it is merely a bit of mathematics).

Tarski has added a new calculus; & made a mistake as to how it can be used.

The mistake is this:

A calculus is quite independent of what letters I use; or what words I use.

But words of a calculus are hardly ever chosen quite arbitrarily: e.g. I use T, F to remind you.

Tarski chooses P, because he thinks it corresponds to "possible", but it doesn't.

Ought any part of mathematics to be abolished?

It couldn't: as a calculus it must be perfectly all right; & only question could be e.g. whether word "infinite" suggests something wrong.

The word "therefore."[32] E.g. (p therefore p ∨ q)

---

[32] Strictly speaking, the word 'therefore' is not present in the corresponding sentence in Moore's manuscript, as he used a pair of triple-dot symbols.

People ask: Is this whole a proposition?

I seem to have denied this.

But I say: So far as it is a proposition, it is a proposition about symbols; "therefore" is like =.[33]

Russell tried to express p therefore q by writing: ⊢ p ⊃ ⊢ q.

<u>Assertion sign</u>.

The sign of a proposition must have a beginning & end. E.g. p ∨ q has no sense, unless I know that this is the whole of it.

Russell's sign marks beginning: but it's very misleading to call it "assertion sign". It just serves as a full-stop.

If it had anything to do with psychological assertion, it would have to be magic.

Asserted proposition = whole proposition:

hence ⊢ p ⊃ ⊢ q is an absurdity.

Why did Russell take ⊃ to mean something like "therefore"?

We can represent internal relation of "following" by tautologies.

Consider (p . q) ⊃ (p ∨ q)

Here we shall have   T
                                  T
                                  T
                                  T

But it doesn't <u>say</u> that p ∨ q follows from p . q: it says nothing. But fact that it is a tautology, <u>shews</u> that it follows.

Is a tautology nonsense?

"~ ⊃ p" is nonsense, because it looks like a proposition.

x is nonsense = x is not a proposition.

Hence a tautology is nonsense; since, though useful, it doesn't act as a proposition.

A tautology can occur in a proposition as a non-asserted proposition.

      p . (q ∨ ~q) is not nonsense.

---

[33] Moore later added: <In what way "like"? that "p entails q" = (p . q = p)?>

8

Lecture VIII.

Apparent contradiction. Between "This internal relation justifies inference" & no rule of inference justifies inference.

p . q entails p ∨ q

Whatever condition makes p . q true also makes p ∨ q true.

p	q	p . q	p ∨ q
T	T	T	T
T	F	F	T
F	T	F	T
F	F	F	F

I solve contradiction saying that rule is only symbolic – a grammatical rule. Grammatical rules are arbitrary, but their application is not arbitrary.

(1) that they are arbitrary: = you can't discuss whether these or other rules are the correct ones for "not" or "or", because until rules are given "not" has no meaning.

E.g. (1) ~~p = p, this is arbitrary.

If we said (2) ~~p = ~p, we couldn't ask whether this is more correct rule for "negation".

If you establish rule (1), "negation" has a different meaning from what it would have if you established (2).

"not" & "knot" are not the same word, because their grammatical rules are different.

Suppose on one page we have a description, on another the grammatical rules applying to words on that page.

Then on (1) we use the words & on (2) we have rules for a game; & what makes (2) important is that they are applied on (1), which is a description.

You can't take (1) & connect it up to reality, except by giving more signs.

Now, suppose in (1) an <u>inference</u> occurs. We shall state a proposition, & then another, perhaps with "therefore" between.

The inference is <u>allowed</u> by a rule in (2).

When we said this relation can be seen by looking at the signs, – that it was internal – we said that it wasn't like "loves".

"Internal", like <u>all</u> predicates in logic, is misleading: because internal & external relations are <u>categorially</u> of different kind.

We can do away with the word "internal", by saying: "I see a proposition with 3 T's, & a proposition with one T."

$$p \cdot q = \text{TFFF}$$
$$p \lor q = \text{TTTF}$$

5:93 I describe internal relation by saying "On top line I've written TFFF, on bottom TTTF", & here I haven't referred to a complete proposition.

I've then described the signs; & the words I used to describe could themselves be substituted for TFFF.

e.g. "<u>Here</u> I wrote TFFF, <u>there</u> I wrote TTTF."

<u>here</u> & there mean something such that it might have been otherwise; i.e. I'm describing the symbols, <u>not</u> the internal relation.

By "a description applying to them".

Suppose I say "Inference is justified by there being a TFFF on the top, & TTTF on the bottom", then I am only talking of the <u>signs</u>, <u>not</u> of a <u>symbol</u>.

A gesture has to have a kind of grammar in order to be understood; i.e. has to be understood <u>as part of a system</u>.

If an arrow makes a gesture of pointing, this can't lie in its geometrical position.

↓ may be used as opposed to ↘; or as opposed to ↓; or as opposed to ↓↓↓

5:94 Whenever we follow an arrow, we follow it in some way or other: e.g. we can say "It did not mean the direction which I was to go, but the time".

Always we can <u>subsequently</u> give a description of how it guided us, which will always refer it to a system.

"I wrote 5^2 because you wrote x^2" can have no meaning unless it refers to a way in which x^2 is related to 5^2; & this description is the grammar.

It has no sense to say "I follow the arrow", unless I act according to it in one particular way, as opposed to another.

You might say: It is not enough to give grammar of arrow, you have also to give rule of translation.

But this is not so.

    E.g. ↑

Suppose we say: This is to mean that A is to move parallel to it.

We might express this by | |

If this is expression of rule: consider ↑ | |.[34]

Do you need another rule to tell you how to translate this?

It would lead to an infinite regress = it gets you no further = you can't reach what you want, not that you would reach it by an infinite number of steps.

A rule of translation never gets us any further: all you can do with it is to tell you the grammar.

Importance is: Sign does not act by means of its suggestive power.[35]

|| is not clear in itself; only if it's clear to you that it's opposed to ⌕. If you say it's clear, you're already looking at it in a particular way.

All that's essential to the symbol, an arrow, is 2 parts which look different.

---

[34] Moore later circled this group of symbols, presumably because the arrow in the notes is slightly slanted to the right, while the previous arrow is pointing up. However, in his notes summarizing these lecture notes (10:76), the arrow points straight upward, and we have followed him in this, construing the slanted arrow in the notes as a mistake.

[35] Moore's summary notes connect this point with the discussion of meaning on the next page of the lecture notes: <Sign doesn't act by its suggestive powers. Symbol is not the sign "is", but this together with all the rules: these rules determine the meaning of the word, which is, therefore, not an object corresponding to it. Thus "The meaning of "the moon" is the moon" is misleading because it suggests "A is the father of B."> (10:19)

Suppose you write ~p, by turning p upside down: the grammar will then say: "We regarded this as this upside down".[36]

You might talk of reading off rules of grammar from a suggestive symbolism, as rules of geometry from a figure.

E.g. suppose I have a number of cubes of same shape: & say: "They're to be arranged so that sides touch – that they're side by side".

Everybody would know how they could be grouped.

A man who didn't see the original drawing as a cube could be brought to draw same lines as we; but it would be much more difficult for him.

Suppose glass-cubes, invisible except for one red side.

5:96 Suppose the rule that they're not to be broken, nor to penetrate one another.

This gives a range of possible arrangements of red squares in space.

And glass-pyramids with red squares[37] would have different possible arrangements.

So "not" or "is" are what's visible, but have different grammatical bodies behind them.

Whole symbol is not "is", but "is" with all the rules.

What grammatical rules <u>do is</u>: <u>Determine</u> the meaning of a word.

Meaning of a word is no longer for us <u>object</u> corresponding to it.

The word must carry about its meaning with it.

Thus "The meaning of "the moon" is the moon" is misleading, because it suggests "A is the father of B."

So for meaning of "red".

It doesn't carry about its grammatical rules, which describe afterward how it's used; but it does carry its meaning.

---

[36] Moore later added: <("d" as "p" upside down)>. Moore actually used a 'p' rotated by 180° for the first character, rather than a 'd'.

[37] Moore later added, after 'red squares': <as bases?>

May Term, 1931

1

Lecture I. (April 27)

Elementary propositions & their connection with truth-functions or "molecular propositions"

Here I've had to change my opinions most. Difficult & important, connected with "thing" & "name".

But first recapitulate. Should repeat important & leave out unimportant.

"Propositions" idea of, what we saw was

(1) a proposition needn't consist of words: we referred to languages consisting of gesture, drawing, painting etc..

(2) proposition needn't consist of "substantive", "verb", "adjective": nothing of the sort is essential. E.g. Russians say "This man good".

All that's wanted is correct multiplicity.

(3) Every symbol must essentially belong to a system.

e.g. a crotchet can only give information what note to play, in a system of crotchets; or an arrow must be regarded as part of a system. Same arrow can be looked at as member of many different systems.

E.g. arrow could mean direction; but could velocity, e.g. if we'd make a connection that inch = walk 2 miles an hour, 2 inches 4 miles an hour.

Now explanation of arrow is on same level as arrow itself.

E.g. suppose ‖ explains ↗: it is again a symbol.

What is there in this talk of system to which symbol must belong?

We're concerned with phenomenon of "being guided by".

Later I'll shew that our interest is of a particular kind – namely in grammar of word "guided by".

This can be replaced by "justifying, what we do, by means of the arrow". Or "controlling" what someone else has done.

To "why did you draw it this way?" you answer: Don't you see? because arrow goes this way.[1]

"Why" & "therefore" are used in ever so many different ways: it's owing to this ambiguity that causal theory of naming arises.

I must justify my statement that "why" & "therefore" have quite a different meaning, by shewing that they would give nonsense, e.g. if used with causal meaning.

If we can justify ⋯ by ↗ we feel that 1st is result of calculation.

Every justification is essentially of sort

x	3	4	6
x^2	9	16	
x^3	27	64	
x^4	81		

i.e. you can only justify 81 by pointing to x, x^2 etc.: it makes a <u>variable</u>, a general rule.

This is a <u>grammatical</u> statement about "justification".

6:3   So also "being guided by" involves the possibility of a justification by reference to a variable: e.g. by saying: I walked in direction of the arrow – when direction is a variable.

You can ask "Does that mean "go out"?"

or "Did you dislike it so much that you couldn't stand it?"

These understand <u>"Why"</u> in "why did you go out" in 2 different ways.

In what different ways can we talk of such an event as a man's leaving the room.

If to "Why did you go?" the answer is "because he pushed me", next question is "How do you know?"

But if answer is "because he told me"; then you can't ask "how do you know".[2]

In "I felt a pain, because he hit me", I may have to change my opinion. There's sense in "Are you sure?"

---

[1] See dots and arrow three sentences later. Moore's summary notes: <To "Why did you draw dots in that direction?" we answer "Don't you see? Arrow goes in that direction".> (10:76)

[2] Moore's summary notes: <What <u>caused</u> you to leave the room is a different "why" from what was your <u>reason</u> for leaving the room. You can't be sure of the cause, but you can be of the reason.> (10:20)

But there's no sense in "are you sure", if you say "because he told me to".
We're not really concerned with realm of things to which cause & effect apply.
Just as we deduce 3^4 from x^4; so in the case of the arrow:
we deduce from certain data together with a variable rule.
We substitute a particular arrow in a variable disposition of following it.
Thus you give an explanation of how to read a score, essentially containing a variable; then a particular score: & he deduces his action from both together.   6:4
Ask: Why did you do this, when I said "Put the square on the table"?
Answer would be: "Isn't this a square?", "Isn't this a table?".
I.e. it's an explanation of words: i.e. substituting for words signs.

"This is a square" is a justification. But the justification doesn't go further: you can't justify language; but only one language, by means of another.

What kind of investigation are we now engaged in?
We quote examples; & when we do this, what are we doing? We're not asking whether this does happen. The example only shews you what's possible: i.e. that it would have sense to say so & so, or that this would be an absurd answer to such & such a question. Thus we're always asking a grammatical question: Has it sense to say that?

Suppose we say "A proposition is a picture". What sort of statement is this? Is it metalogical?
No. What's the good of making it?
We're saying: the word "picture" follows similar rules with word "proposition".
It sounds paradoxical to say "Leave the room" is a picture of what he did.   6:5
They aren't in any ordinary sense.
An engineer's drawing to shew his men is in ordinary sense a picture.

    a a c c c b

& [diagram] is much more like what's ordinarily meant.[3]

---

[3] 'a' corresponds to '↑', 'b' corresponds to '↓', and 'c' corresponds to '→'. See 5:46, 5:57, and 6:20 for diagrams that include such a key. This diagram is missing a head for the arrow corresponding to the third 'c'.

But now for "leave the room": he justifies his action by the words.

I'd much rather say that "A proposition is a picture" is misleading. It just stresses a certain aspect of grammar of word "proposition".

"Recognition" usually not autonomous; in Frege's sense of autonomous. 6:6[4]

Non-autonomous[5] = I accept a means of checking; e.g. a nearer view. <u>Then</u> that I recognise is only one of the symptoms that this is the same.

It's quite different if recognition is <u>only</u> test.

E.g. how do you know that this is home?

To say it <u>is</u>, is to say that you recognise it.

That this colour <u>is</u> the same as I saw yesterday means the same as that I remember it.

I must recognise 2 goings to bed as the same in a certain respect: & then I am using a symbol – am describing.

Recognising that this is what I did is using this as a symbol for the other.

If you imagine blue, that's no more a picture of blue, than "blue" is.

In imagination you can make red pass continuously into black & white, with the word "red" you can't.

The superiority of imagination is that it has a multiplicity which the letters haven't: but that's not <u>used</u> in this case.

I can't follow language of words, in painting a thing, as I can a painted model.

<u>Both</u> are pictures, so far as you can use them at all.

---

[4] The previous manuscript page is only half filled; this page has no number, title, or date. If we were to treat this page in the same way as the previous case of such a page break (4:66), this would be the first, and only, page of notes for Lecture 2. Because the top of the following page is dated 4 May, the second Monday of the term, we treat it as the start of Lecture 2 and this page as the last page of Lecture 1. However, the date was added later, in ink, so it is possible that this is the beginning of the notes for 4 May. If so, it may be that the notes for 4 May continue on the next page, or that the following page is the start of the notes for 11 May. The next date in Moore's notes for this term is 1 June, written in pencil at the top of 6:16.

[5] Moore wrote 'Non-automatous', but this was probably a mistake.

2

6:7 Are propositions pictures? (May 4)[6]

We misunderstand relation between proposition & its verification.

Suppose we make a language of letters for colours, & use of language is to give you an order to paint these colours in the order of the letters.

Are these words <u>enough</u> to convey the order? Or in what way are they not enough?

In a sense they aren't enough: we can only understand them, if an arrangement has been made.

This process of naming is just like labelling.

What happens when I order you to draw a yellow line?

Is it essential that word "yellow" should bring an image with it?

One would say it <u>automatically</u> brings up an <u>image</u>, & this is what we go by.

Suppose this does happen: then it's just as if there were a machine such that the word caused a yellow plate to be shewn.

Can I then define "yellow" by the colour which springs up? You are at the mercy of the mechanism.[7]

Thus a bell ringing may be a <u>criterion</u> for a resistance.

But how am I to know when the bell rings?

Suppose you say: I know it rings, by getting a feel of satisfaction.

It doesn't help you to interpolate a picture: since then you still need to know whether what you do corresponds to the picture; & have you a picture of the correspondence?

6:8 Thus a memory-image can't help you.

---

[6] Moore's summary notes: <New kind of lecture, May 4> (10:77). See the Introduction, Section 3b, and the discussion of the dating of these lectures in the footnotes to 6:6.

[7] Moore later added: <(It might shew a wrong colour?)>

But our original explanations are not useless: but all they do is to give you a new language instead of the old one.

It is not useless, because the language I translate my words into has a different multiplicity.

Suppose I have a grammatical system, consisting of rules to the effect that certain words can be used in this connection & not in that.

I can't apply rules of "not" "and" etc. to colours.

Therefore I fix them to some extent: they say you can't do this. But not completely; for e.g. if I wrote blue for red etc., same rules would apply, but what was before true is now false.

If by grammatical rules you mean only those which are represented in the octahedron.[8]

There are 4 possible systems for blue, yellow, red, green. What do I do when I say which is to be used? I.e. fix the meaning of words, more than they are fixed by the grammatical rules common to all 4 possibilities.

Just as for colours, so for shapes: I can say "draw a circle" or I can say draw this.

When I explain "circle" by pointing at a circle, do I use anything which isn't a sign?

A word carries about its meaning. If you want something else to fix the meaning, you must have it; & then the word isn't a complete sign.

There's more convention about the words than about the images. Drury.

What is a convention?

Take a reading-book which has "candle" & a picture of a candle.   6:9

This is the convention.

How are we to use it?

(1) by taking out the book, & saying "yellow" with its yellow patch.

---

[8] Moore later added: <I might use "b" for "y", or for "r" or for "g"?>

This is a process of calculation like

$$\begin{array}{cccc} & 1 & 2 & 3 & 4 \\ x & & & & \\ x^2 & & & & 25 \\ x^3 & & & & \end{array}$$

Square the number 5

There <u>is</u> more convention in use of words than of colours; because using colours I could lead you to do more things than by words.

All conventions are fixing up the language once for all: when we use it, we always make a new step.

You can't give a picture which can't be misinterpreted.

No kind of interpolation between sign & fulfilment will do away with a <u>sign</u>.

I tell you to bring a yellow flower; & you bring me one. I ask why? You say: You told me to bring a yellow flower; & this is a yellow flower.

Or I might say: And this is <u>dark</u> yellow.

All justification is essentially of this sort.

You always have to repeat the order in your justification; <u>or</u> the description must be grammatically dependent on the order.

6:10 That jumping out of the window is a way of leaving a room is <u>not</u> a matter of experience, but given in the language – an internal relation.

The justification could have been put into a book of rules made once for all.

For all practical purposes a man would be colour-blind, if only when hit he sees blue & yellow, & never under ordinary circumstances.

What <u>we</u> mean by saying <u>he</u> can't distinguish between red & yellow, is that he says things are not different which we see to be different: he doesn't respond differently to these 2 things & I do.

3-5

Pictures. 6:11[9]

Similarity of picture & what it presents.

What I call a picture has, in the usual sense, no similarity.[10]

Another difficulty: –

Suppose I painted picture of us in room; & also described us in words; & then described the picture in words; & described the words in words.

What's the difference between relation of picture to us, & 2 descriptions to us?

The descriptions in words of painted picture & of us will have great similarities.

~~But description in words of us; & description of that description in words haven't.~~

But description of verbal description & of painted picture has none.

I say: there is as much & as little here as between

$$2 + 3 \qquad 5$$

The similarity here only comes out, if you've learnt whole decimal system: but then similarity is same as in

$$|| + ||| \qquad |||||$$

How can "2 + 3" be projected as "5"?

There's no connection whatever, you say.

But, if there's no connection, a boy couldn't calculate.

You say: the connection is purely arbitrary!

---

[9] The previous manuscript page is only half filled. As this page also has an underlined title at the top, it is likely that this is the first page of notes for a new lecture. The next partially blank page is on 6:18. Page 6:19 is dated 1 June, and so is the start of Lecture 6. The notes on the intervening eight pages must, therefore, be from one or more of Lectures 3–5.

[10] Moore's summary notes: <What I call a picture is not in the usual sense "similar" to what it's a picture of.> (10:20)

The boy might be quite right in saying $2 + 3 = \text{\textit{\textlbrackdbl}}^{11}$, if he went on to make the necessary connections.

6:12 There's no similarity between 2 + 3 & 5, <u>except with reference to a particular system of projection</u>: but this system of projection is in no way inferior to that in

$$|| + ||| \qquad |||||$$

The difference is (wrongly expressed) that in latter case you <u>see</u> internal relation: whereas in former you only see it when you've learnt the system.

I.e. the <u>whole system</u> to which first belongs can be projected into whole <u>system</u> to which latter belongs.

If someone is surprised that we say proposition is a picture of reality, we can say it is as much so as 2 + 3 is of 5.

Then they say it isn't.

But we answer; it <u>is</u>; only method of projection is rather queer.

Amongst the pictures we make there are some which seem to hold a quite unique place.

I've said you could use a painted picture for a memory image.

If I ask "do you understand "Leave the room"", & he says "Yes": there's a sense in which his criterion that he has understood is that he can imagine it.

When I compare painted picture to imagination, I don't mean physical object, but that which we <u>see</u>: this latter is what could be substituted for imagination.[12]

6:13 Difficulty is: that in case of images there doesn't seem to be any interpretation needed or possible.

What's true & what's false in this?

---

[11] Moore made this symbol much larger than the number 3 in the left side of the equation. Thus, while the symbol resembles a vertical line through the number 3, it is probable that Wittgenstein drew an arbitrary squiggle on the board with no prior established meaning.

[12] Moore used the abbreviation 'imag.', which is probably short for 'imagination', though in his summary notes he later interpreted it as 'image' (10:78).

When I say "I actually imagine D.[13] leaving the room", I use these <u>very same words</u> in describing the imagination, as I should in describing what it's an image of.

The image seems to be the thought, & therefore not to need or be capable of interpretation: because it's <u>signs</u> which are interpreted, not thoughts.

I say "A black patch is going to appear on the wall". Can you imagine this? You say rightly: Yes.

My point is that in "I imagine <u>a black patch</u>" & "There will be <u>a black patch</u>", the underlined words have <u>same meaning</u>.

One is inclined to think that the word "black" has a closer connection with fact that "There <u>is</u> a black patch" than to "Imagine one": but in fact it hasn't.

Your imagination is described by a sentence <u>akin to</u> that which would describe "There is a black patch".

If so, there's no <u>essential</u> difference between your imagination[14], painted picture, & spoken words.[15]

D.[16] says "You can't have an image, without knowing what it's an image of".   6:14
But how do you know that so & so is an image of the man?

If you describe language, I say you must thereby also describe what it means.

This, in one sense, is <u>not</u> correct:

namely in sense in which it's n[17]

I say: You can't describe a calculus – e.g. decimal calculus – without <u>using</u> it.

---

[13] Probably Drury, who was attending the lectures and is mentioned at 4:32, 5:6, 5:7, and 6:8.

[14] Moore used the abbreviation 'imag.'. See note above at 6:12.

[15] Moore's summary notes: <In case of images interpretation doesn't seem necessary or possible; but there's no <u>essential</u> difference between images & spoken words.> (10:20)

[16] Probably Drury.   [17] Sentence left unfinished.

If you describe it, you are using it.

You can't describe a calculation, without calculating.

Describe a sentence, <u>&</u> give rules applying to words, then you have said some of sentence again.

Grammar fixes place of a word in logical space: & place of a word in logical space <u>is</u> its meaning.

Meaning of a word must be entirely "given" (or determined) if you describe language with all its rules.

You can't say: If language is given, meaning of so & so <u>can</u> only be this.

6:15 When I explain a word /"blue"/ by ostensive definition I have not asserted or denied any of the facts which I want to assert or deny by saying "This is blue" or "not blue".

I should only have transcended language, if I did.

I can only describe the <u>inside</u> of language.

What transcends is only the <u>sentence</u>: what says "So & so is the case".

"Blue" doesn't mean there is something blue; & can be explained without saying there is.

The meaning of the words is part of the language: I only transcend language, when I use it.

Why talk of "place in logical space"?

The "place" is important; & what's in it, the scratch, is unimportant.

If the sound is unimportant, that means I can use another instead.

But how do I know I'm putting it instead? Only by knowing it has same <u>meaning</u>. I.e. meaning fixes the place.

A blue plate may be part of a sentence: but we're not transcending language because it is.

6

June 1.   6:16

Meaning of a word is <u>not</u> the bearer of the name, (if it is a name).

A name "represents" (= is a substitute for) its bearer, but a word or name is <u>not</u> a substitute for its meaning.

If we draw a map, that black patch is a substitute for London: & in the same sense "Moore" in a diary is a substitute for me – therein.

Suppose you reproduce a motor-accident by little models: the little bus is a <u>substitute</u> for a big bus, but the big bus is not its meaning.
In saying "This is Moore" pointing, we explain the meaning of "Moore", but we don't point to the meaning.
"Bus" has the same meaning in "<u>No</u> bus was present".
But how about "red"?
Is ~~there ever a substitute for~~ "red" ever a substitute?
A word can only be a substitute, if so & so is the case: its being a substitute depends upon a fact.
But the meaning of a word cannot depend on a fact.
"There is no such thing as red[18]" has only sense if "red" has meaning.
But, if it is true, "red" can't be a substitute.
Meaning is fixed inside language.   6:17

Therefore "the meaning" & "the sense" are misleading, because they sound too like "the bearer".
The meaning is the place of the word in a grammatical system.
The meaning is <u>not</u> the thing to which I point in ostensive definition.

---

[18] Moore later added: <a red thing?>

Therefore the history of how I came to understand is irrelevant to my understanding: my understanding must "omnia sua secum portare".[19]

The way in which a thought or proposition is related to reality, is the way in which a calculation is related to its result.

We could say that

$$\begin{array}{r} 25 \times 26 \\ \hline 50 \\ 150 \\ \hline \end{array}$$

has <u>sense</u>; is made true if I write 650, false, if I write 750.

Thought does not anticipate the fact, in any other sense, than this calculation anticipates 650.

The calculation does not <u>contain</u> the result; but it does in some sense determine the result.

Thus the proposition is <u>applied</u> to reality like a foot-rule to a table: it "reaches up to" reality.

6:18   I.e. there's nothing <u>between</u> the calculation & the result: the calculation is <u>immediately</u> checked by the result.

A rule for verification must be capable of being laid down <u>beforehand</u>.

<u>Complexity</u> of a proposition.

I made a mistake about this.

In a sense, a proposition needn't be complex: I can replace a proposition by a simple sign.

But the simple sign must be <u>part of a system</u>.

"Complex", as opposed to what?

What is suggestive in a symbol never matters.

E.g. → as opposed to ↘ ↑.

---

[19] Latin: '(one must) carry (or bring) everything with oneself'. This is a variant of 'Sapiens Omnia sua secum portat', a Latin proverb meaning 'A wise man takes everything he owns with himself' (i.e. intellectual assets are more valuable than material possessions).

Now it's probably wrong to call "→" complex; but there's a strong temptation to say it is.

"Ales" on a pub tells me something.

But "ales" in a vocabulary doesn't.

The proposition is complex, because what tells me is "ales" being here: = we have made ales part of a system.

In the vocabulary /dictionary/, the word has no meaning.

To call "That "ales" is here" a complex is to use a false analogy.

Compare the language for "draw a red circle". 6:19

of   (1)

(2)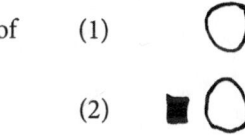

You're tempted to use "complex" for a fact i.e. for (1), because (2) really is a "complex", & means the same.

In (1) you can't talk of being red alone, & ~~being~~ a circle alone.[20]

The red circle is, however, part of a system.

---

[20] Moore's diagram was in grey pencil, without the use of any red.

6:20[21] No explanation can give relation between sign & its application: person to whom explanation is given has to make a jump.

Pattern-book:

The patterns are <u>copies</u> of the cloth; the numbers are not <u>copies</u> of the patterns.

But if you are to copy, it is not fixed how you are to copy. E.g. you might say: Copy twice as large;

One feels the copy is <u>not</u> arbitrary, while the other is.
But in what sense?
The shapes of a, b, c, d are arbitrary; I don't copy them: but the order I do copy.

$$\text{In} \quad \begin{array}{c|c} a & \rightarrow \\ b & \leftarrow \\ c & \uparrow \\ d & \downarrow \end{array} \qquad a\ c\ c\ b\ b$$

In reading aloud we don't <u>use</u> a table, as above; & if we did, it would be no use.[22]

6:21 I can order you to imagine red; hence if I order you to make a red mark, the imagining can't bridge the gulf. You can't & needn't imagine imagining red.[23]

How is explanation of a sign connected with its use?

---

[21] The previous manuscript page is only partially filled; this page has no number, title, or date. If we were to treat this page in the same way as the first such page break (4:66), this would be the start of a very short set of notes for Lecture 7. However, the notes for all but one of the other May terms end at Lecture 6, and it seems more likely that these notes are from the end of Lecture 6.

[22] Moore's summary notes: <In reading aloud we don't use a table connecting printed words with sounds; and such a table would be useless (because it doesn't itself tell us how to use or "apply" it?).> (10:79)

[23] Moore's summary notes: <In order to carry out the order "Imagine a red spot", you don't need to imagine imagining a red spot (and you <u>can't</u> do this (Why?)). Hence in order to carry out "Paint a red spot" you don't need to imagine a red spot?> (10:79)

May Term, 1932

4

May 13, 1932.[1]

Are there 5 successive 7's in development of π?

If we find them, that proves there <u>are</u>.

If we don't find them, doesn't prove there aren't.

It's something for which we've provided a test for truth, but <u>not</u> for falsehood; & this must be quite different sort of thing from where <u>both</u> are provided.

"The world will come to an end some time" has no disproof.

We <u>think</u> "some" here means the same as in "some day before next June": latter is a disjunction, former <u>not</u>, because it involves "& so on".

We can define non-disjunctive "some", by saying I'll treat each as sign that you're right, but never[2] not as a sign you're wrong, <u>& so on</u>.

But what's <u>the use</u> of such a proposition?

"Infinite" does <u>not</u> stand for a number or a quantity.

I bought a ruler with infinite radius of curvature = straight.

"I will give you <u>any</u> amount of money", <u>gives infinite freedom.</u>

How would you verify that I had fulfilled my promise?

Here <u>infinite</u> occurs in description of a reality: the <u>promise</u> really is different from any promise of a finite sum.

<u>Constant fallacy</u> of supposing "truth", "problem", "looking for", "proof" always mean the same: they mean entirely different things.

---

[1] Moore did not take notes for most of the 1931–1932 academic year, but resumed halfway through May 1932. For further discussion, see the Introduction, Section 3d.

[2] In the telegraphic wording of this sentence, 'each' and 'never' appear to be substitutes for longer phrases. Plausible expansions of these terms are 'each true instance of the variable' and 'never finding a true instance of the variable', respectively.

E.g. in mathematics 2 proofs are proofs in different senses.

(1) take proof that 25 × 25 = 625, i.e. by exhibition.

In mathematics there is a bias towards what's already proved.

To say 25 × 25 does <u>not</u> make 620, means we're talking of a general rule.

Suppose you look up logarithm-table & get one result, calculate & get another.

Can one say: There must be a mistake in one or another, but we can't tell where?

Only if they don't both belong to one system.

What if I came to different results by

    (1) multiply 25 by 26.

    (2) multiply 26 by 25.

Consider: –

    There <u>is</u> a number of digits in π which will lead to 5 7's   ($\exists$n)fn
    There <u>is</u> <u>no</u> number of digits in π which will lead to 5 7's   ~($\exists$n)fn

Proof of ($\exists$n)fn is finding one: <u>or</u> proving ~($\exists$n)fn is self-contradictory.

Finding one <u>will</u> prove it.

The other <u>proof</u> proves something else.

6b:12   ($\exists$n) <u>means</u> something different, where it's <u>possible</u> to look for it, & where it's <u>not</u> possible.

The meaning of "There is" is <u>fixed</u> by its proof.

"There is a man in the next room" may be fixed beforehand – does not depend on proof.

The proof of an existential theorem gives the <u>meaning</u> of "existence" in that theorem.[3]

---

[3] Moore's summary notes: <Meaning of "There is" is fixed by its proof, not in "There's a man next door", but in existential theorems.> (10:22)

Lecture 4 – May 13, 1932

Call "existence" finding a number
& "proof of existence" what gives me the means of finding.

$$x^2 + 2x + 1 = 0$$

Proof of existence of root is finding one.

Suppose a man says he's given a proof that there is a root, & his proof doesn't provide a method of approximation.

People believe they've made a connection which they haven't; but their calculus is always all right.

What do we take to be a proof of $\sim(\exists n)fn$?
Usually the kind of proof given is by induction or recursion.
E.g. $\sim(\exists n)((n > 2) . (n \times 3 = 5))$

<u>Proof</u> $3 \times 2 = 5 + 1$
    $3 \times a = 5 + b$

I'll then <u>prove</u> that $3 \times (a + 1) = 5 + (b + 3)$
I shall never get to a number which multiplied by $3 = 5 + 1$.   6b:13

(α) $3 \times 2 = 5 + 1$

$3 \times (a + 1) = (3 \times a) + 3 = (5 + b) + 3 = 5 + (b + 3)$

This proof proves "There is no number which, multiplied by 3,[4] gives 5."

(α) gives an example of a number which, multiplied by 3, does <u>not</u> give 5.

If I make a mistake in this proof, to correct it <u>wouldn't</u> give you a number which does.

---

[4] Moore mistakenly wrote 'multiplied by 2' on this line and the next.

By looking at a proof you can see what it proves; therefore you must also be able to see what the opposite of what it proves is.

6b:12v[5] $3 \times (2 + 1) = (3 \times 2) + 3 = (5 + 1) + 3 = 5 + (1 + 3)$ /etc./

could be quite well be taken as a proof of the same thing.
I can look at it & see formal properties in it, or not see them.
By underlining you can make things seen not seen before.
or combining you can make it into an algebraic calculus.

With ~~these we~~ can say that this is a proof
      that $3 \times 51 \neq 5$
Recursive use of algebra, can be entirely done in this way.

These are regarded as proving
      $\sim(\exists n)fn$
Whereas $(\exists n)fn$ is proved by finding.
But proof shews that this $(\exists n)fn$ is not the opposite; for opposite is what you could get by making a mistake.

6b:13 I can't give you an example of a proof that
      $25 \times 25 \neq 625,$
but I can give other examples in same system – a proof of other inequalities.

There is no opposite to proof which consists in finding one.

It is often asked how does a proof which proves something for one triangle, give a result for all triangles?

---

[5] Usually, Moore wrote his notes on the right-hand side of each opening, leaving the left-hand side blank for later comments, clarifications, or criticism. However, 6b:12v, the page facing 6b:13, contains material that reads like additional lecture notes, providing further explanation of equation (α), and so we have inserted them here. This discussion probably took place after the last notes for this day on 6b:14, which end with the phrase: 'Recursive proof'. For further discussion of this topic, see *The Big Typescript* (Wittgenstein 2005) §128 (or *Philosophical Grammar* (Wittgenstein 1969) II, §31).

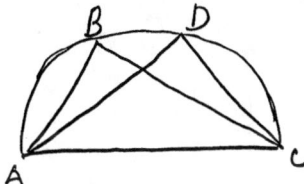

In proving ABC is a right angle, you can say your construction also proves ADC to be so.

6b:14

You have to be sure that ADC is analogous in relevant respects; but what's the test whether it is or not?

That ADC is analogous is proved by fact that it is an angle in same semi-circle.

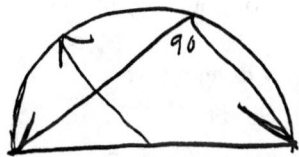

Recursive proof.

5

May 20.

What are we doing in talking so long about simple mathematical proofs?

We are doing <u>infantile</u> mathematics: in sense that it's problems which occur to mathematician about 10 years old; they thus occur & are not solved & are "repressed".

Mathematician's disgust is due to his having been told it's not proper.

Take proof of associative law $a + (b + c) = (a + b) + c$.

Skolem's proof.[6]

First, how <u>he</u> put it. He says he'd prove this Law. And this makes one expect he would prove it from other formulae.

But it begins in an <u>entirely</u> different way.

6b:15   It begins with recursive definition.

$$a + (b + 1) = (a + b) + 1 \text{ def.} \quad (D)$$

$$a + (\underbrace{(1) + 1}_{b}) = (a + (1)) + 1$$

You use for numbers the notation, (1), $(1) + 1$, $((1) + 1) + 1$ etc..

$$a + (\underbrace{((1) + 1) + 1}_{3}) = (a + \underbrace{((1) + 1)}_{2}) + 1$$

Law (P) is <u>assumed</u> for a number c; & then it is shewn that, if it holds for c, it holds for c + 1.

That it holds for 1, follows from definition.

Queer thing is to <u>assume</u>, even if only temporarily, what I have to prove.

---

[6] See Skolem 1923, 'The Foundations of Elementary Arithmetic Established by means of the Recursive Mode of Thought, Without the use of Apparent Variables Ranging Over Infinite Domains'. For further discussion of Skolem's proof, see *The Big Typescript* (Wittgenstein 2005) §§127–30.

Lecture 5 – May 20, 1932

He proves that
$$a + (b + (c + 1)) = (a + b) + (c + 1).$$

i.e. that $\underline{if}$ associative law is true for c, it is true for (c + 1).

$$\underline{a + (b + (c + 1))} \stackrel{D}{=} a + ((b + c) + 1) \stackrel{D}{=} (a + (b + c)) + 1$$
$$\stackrel{P}{=} ((a + b) + c) + 1 \stackrel{D}{=} \underline{(a + b) + (c + 1)}$$

Therefore says Skolem, P holds; but it only comes in as a means of proving something else.

Transitions made by D, are natural enough; queer transition is made by P. What's the justification?

He says: It has been proved for 1.

Real fact is you don't use P: you don't $\underline{assume}$ P.

What I really have in the proof, is a $\underline{general}$ form of proof for $\underline{any}$ number.

    Now I'll write proof in my own way.

(1) $a + (b + 1) = (a + b) + 1$ def.
(2) $a + (b + (c + 1)) = (a + (b + c)) + 1$ proved by def.
(3) $(a + b) + (c + 1) = ((a + b) + c) + 1$ proved by def.

If I put c = 1 in (2), then (2) & (3) become identical.[7]

$$\therefore \quad a + (b + 2) = (a + b) + 2.$$

Now what have we proved?

We have proved (2) & (3) by means of (1).

Discursive proof consists of (1), (2), (3).

---

[7] Moore later added:
(2) becomes $a + \{b + (1 + 1)\} = \{a + (b + 1)\} + 1$ Are these identical?
(3) becomes $(a + b) + (1 + 1) = \{(a + b) + 1\} + 1$
In virtue of definition, $\{a + (b + 1)\} + 1 = \{(a + b) + 1\} + 1 = (a + b) + (1 + 1)$

Now write (1) in form $\phi 1 = \psi 1$
           (2) in form $\phi(c + 1) = F(\phi c)$
           (3) in form $\psi(c + 1) = F(\psi c)$

F here = the adding of +1 at the end.

By (1) $F(\phi c) = F(\psi c)$
∴ $\phi 2 = \psi 2$

This is general form of inductive proof.

And it's said to prove associative law for <u>all</u> numbers.

What does <u>all</u> mean?

What is proved is (2) & (3): i.e. to prove $\phi c = \psi c$ for <u>all</u> numbers <u>is</u> to prove (2) & (3).

6b:17 It seems therefore to prove for <u>all</u> numbers. How could you get hold of them?

Now take $1 \div^8 3 = 0.\dot{3}$.

How can one get 3 ad infinitum?

This <u>means</u> nothing but that $1 \div 3 = 0.\dot{3}$, & 1 is remainder, i.e. dividend is remainder.[9]

But it will be said: It doesn't <u>mean</u> this; it's only a <u>symptom</u> for it.

Here it is meaningless to say for <u>all</u> divisions (as it is not meaningless for a doctor to say man's stomach is in such & such a state).

Why should we say such a queer thing: as 3's in infinites will come?

---

[8] Moore here, and throughout this passage, wrote down a colon, i.e. ':', the sign Wittgenstein used for division; he later added: <divided by>. Following Luckhardt and Aue's practice in their edition of the *Big Typescript* (Wittgenstein 2005), we have replaced these instances of ':' by '÷'.

[9] Wittgenstein indicates the periodicity of a fraction by writing the remainder (1, in this case) under the divisor (3, in this case) and underlining both the dividend and remainder. See instances of this on the next page. Rhees provides the following explanation of Wittgenstein's notation: 'The dash underneath emphasizes that the remainder is equal to the dividend. So the expression becomes the symbol for periodic division' (Wittgenstein 1969, 398).

For further discussion of the periodicity of a fraction, see *The Big Typescript* (Wittgenstein 2005) §§127–8 and §§132–3, or *Philosophical Grammar* (Wittgenstein 1969), II, §§30–1 and §§35–6.

If a man asks "will you get 0.333", we could say: Yes, on ground of $\frac{1 \div 3}{1}$.
If a man asks "will you get 0.3333" we could say: Yes on same ground.
Proof that you will get 0.333 is just $\left(\frac{1 \div 3 = 0.3}{1} \right)$ + 0.333.
& $1 \div 3 = 0.\dot{3}$ is just a general form of all these proofs.

$$\begin{array}{c|c} 1 \div 3 = 0.33 & 1 \div 4 = 0.25 \\ \underline{1} & 0 \end{array}$$

What corresponds to $1 \div 3 = 0.\dot{3}$ is fact that <u>same</u> result is got each time. A man might go on dividing, without it striking him that 1 is remainder each time.

Just so 1, 2, 3, 4, 5 may be <u>all</u> the numbers: it is a complete arithmetic.   6b:18

So there might be an arithmetic in which there is <u>division</u>, but no recurrence – no periodic division.

I'm going to call $1 \overset{3}{\div} 3 = 0.333$

$$1 \overset{4}{\div} 3 = 0.3333$$

$$1 \overset{2}{\div} 4 = 0.25$$

In primitive arithmetic, without periodic division

the proof of $1 \overset{4}{\div} 3 = 0.3333$

looks like $1 \div 3$
                    1
                       1
                         1

In ours it looks like $\underline{1} \overset{4}{\div} 3$
                            $\underline{1}$

Now go back to: Is it true that (1) (n)f(n)
                          or (2) (∃n)∼f(n)?

We have no method of verifying (2), unless we happen to find one.

E.g. Is there in extension of π, 3 sevens one after another.

Is there a number of digits of π such that after that there will be 3 sevens.

If you find one you have proof that there is; but you can't prove that there's not.[10] This gives the grammar of the question.

6b:19 But you can get things which can only be proved in a general way.

E.g. we say we have proved

$$(n)(\phi n = \psi n)$$

(1), (2) & (3) can't be called the proof of this.

They don't prove that one or other of $(n)f(n)$ or $(\exists n)\sim f(n)$ is true.

We imagined this was like going through a finite series, & seeing whether it's true for all, or there's one for which it isn't.

Fact that this proof proves what we're asking shews we're not dealing with an extension at all.

One talks of a finite part of $2, 2^2, 2^3, 2^4$ & the whole.

But one should talk of a bit of the series, & the law which generates it

i.e. 2^n

this is the expression which corresponds to the series.

Isn't it queer, if in order to write 3 digits, we have to write 3; or to write 4, to write 4; but to write an infinity, I only need to write $0.\dot{3}$.

So to prove associative law for all numbers, can't be same thing as proving it say for 3: for then you'd have to give it separately for each of 3.

6b:20 There is an analogy between bits of a series, & the law; but we don't see where it arises.

E.g. $\frac{1}{1^1}, \frac{1}{2^1}, \frac{1}{3^1}$

expresses a law: we all know how to go on.

Now consider question: shall we get 3 sevens in development of π?

---

[10] Moore later added: <(i.e. ~(∃n)fn)?>

We seem to be able to define π′ as the number which differs from π (only) in that where /if/ 3 777s occur in π, 3 one's occur in π′ in same place.[11]

And then it seems we can say π either is same as π′ or not.

Is π′ a number?

It's a prescription leading us to put down digits quite unmistakable.

But there's no way of finding out whether it = π or not: therefore this question whether they are or not has no meaning.

If I find out tomorrow, I have 2 numbers which I can compare; but I haven't 2 now.

Suppose you have a number axis: π is a point on the number axis, but π′ is not: it doesn't define a point on the number axis.

If you call it a number, it's a queer sort: it's not comparable with other numbers. π = π′ is meaningless.

Say I'm going to talk of the number got by writing 1 when a penny comes heads, & 0 when it comes tails.[12]

Does this define a number? It has been said it is an infinite decimal fraction.

Let's say: number = what corresponds to a point on the number axis. 6b:21

Now suppose by throwing heads or tails, I try to determine a point as follows.

Heads, I halve right side; tails I halve left.

Am I getting nearer to a point?

My choice seems to get smaller & smaller; but there are just as many possibilities in an inch as in a yard.

I don't approach any point: there are always & will remain 2 points.

---

[11] On page 499 of *The Big Typescript* (Wittgenstein 2005) Wittgenstein defines this number as the result of replacing three sevens with three *zeros*. For further discussion of the question whether 3 sevens occur in the development of π, and of π′, see *The Big Typescript*, §139, 'Kinds of Irrational Numbers'.

[12] For further discussion of this example and the line-dividing scenario discussed below, see *The Big Typescript* (Wittgenstein 2005), §140, 'Irregular Infinite Decimals'.

But isn't this so with π or $\sqrt{2}$?

No: because there is a construction for these.

What's criterion for: Does π define a point?

Whether you have a method for deciding whether $>$ or $<$ than any rational number you choose to take. And you have.[13]

Suppose you'd thrown $0.11010000\ldots = T$

Then ask: Is $T = 0.1101$, you can't tell till you find a 1.

However far you go, there's always new rational number with which you can't compare it.

The proof that π is irrational, shews how many digits at most can be the same: it will change not later than some given number.

6b:22   Define P as follows

Go through cardinals, & for any prime put a 1, for any non-prime a 0.[14]

Now, since there's proof that there's infinite number of primes, we know that it won't stop; & shews also that there can't at most be more noughts than so many.[15]

For it says if 7 is prime the next prime must come before 7 factorial + 1.

But it might be that it isn't prime ordinal, & therefore incomparable with rationals.

---

[13] Moore's summary notes: <π' is not a number on the number axis: it's not comparable with other numbers. Same true of the number got by writing 1 when a penny comes heads, 0 when it comes tails. This can't define a point; but π can, because you have a method for deciding whether it's $>$ or $<$ than any rational number you choose to take.> (10:22)

[14] For further discussion of this topic and related matters, including many of the topics discussed in the following lecture, see *The Big Typescript* (Wittgenstein 2005), §139, 'Kinds of Irrational Numbers. (π', p, f)'.

[15] Moore later added: <before you come to another prime>

6

May 27.

Suppose we produce a decimal by a prescription (1's + 0's in order of primes & composites)

e.g. P = 0.11101...

<u>Is</u> this a real number?

If you choose you can <u>call</u> it so; but you must distinguish it from those obtained by <u>other</u> sorts of prescriptions, such as enable us to compare them with rationals as > or less.

$\sqrt{2}$ is not less "fundamental" (though less simple) than cardinals.

It is <u>the</u> number which there are <u>then</u> rules for comparing with rationals.

"greater" & "less" are defined by rules.

$\sqrt{2}$ is called a number because of rules of > & <.

$n > \sqrt{2} = n^2 > 2$.

This rule makes $\sqrt{2}$ similar to a rational.

Thus P can't be compared with a rational, & hence is not like $\sqrt{2}$. 6b:23

Take π' = number made out of π by 0 instead of 3 sevens.

π' can't be compared with every point of number line; e.g. not with π.

E.g. with π you know after how many digits a recurrence must come.

If you hadn't you couldn't tell whether

$\pi - 3.1\dot{4}$ is positive or negative.[16]

---

[16] There is a more detailed exposition of this point in the last paragraph of page 501 of *The Big Typescript* (Wittgenstein 2005): 'If I state a rule ρ for the formation of extensions, but in such a way that my calculus knows no way of predicting what is the maximum number of times an apparently real recurring period of the extension can be repeated, then ρ differs from a real number in so far as in certain cases I can't compare ρ − a with a rational number, so that the expression ρ − a = b becomes nonsensical. If for instance the expansion of ρ so far known to me were 3.14 followed by an unlimited series of ones (3.1411111...), it wouldn't be possible to say of the difference ρ − 3.14$\dot{1}$ that it was greater or less than 0; so in this sense it can't be compared with 0, i.e. a point on the number axis; and it and ρ can't be called numbers in the same sense as one of these points.'

What was the case before we had the theorem which tells us this of π?

Then it was not determined in our calculus whether it's a number or not.

If a law of distribution of prime numbers were discovered, we should have different numbers.

Not that 7 would be altered.

We have 2 things: (1) the law
                  (2) many extensions

    not an infinite extension.

We now have a different law for generating prime numbers, hence a new meaning of prime number.

Prime number is not a description, such that another description might have same extension.

A proof that all numbers which satisfy 1 concept satisfy the other, can't be controlled[17] by seeing whether a whole set do.[18]

That they generate same series is what's meant by a formal relation between 2 concepts.

6b:24   Thus a man who uses an endless series of numbers uses a different calculus, person who uses say only 5.

$\sqrt{2}$

Suppose we'd taught a man the algorithm of producing decimals.

$\sqrt{2}$, as thus defined, would not be what we mean, because it would not be connected with other calculuses with which ours is connected.

There exists no more of a calculus than we have as yet built.

It's not true that when North Pole was discovered, there was a new earth one with & one without.

But positive numbers are complete by themselves, without negations.

---

[17] Moore later added: <tested>

[18] Moore's summary notes: <Prime number is not a description such that another description might have same extension: we can't test whether they do, by seeing whether all numbers which have one have other.> (10:22)

A figure in trigonometry is not like an illustration to a book; it's part of the calculus.

(1) 314 × 668 is provided for in my rules already, in the calculus I already possess

(2) suppose S has made a mathematical discovery. Here no rule has been provided for in my calculus.
But why do we admit that it's right?
What happens when to a man who was looking for the construction of the pentagon it is proved that there isn't?   6b:25
He says "That's what I really meant".
His idea has shifted, on a rail on which he's ready to shift it.

When a new proof is discovered, a new calculus is discovered; & we need not, though we do, go on using same name.

Suppose we sought in our calculus proof that $\sqrt{2}$ is irrational?
There can't be a contradiction: the proof creates the statement.
The statement "π − 3.14 is greater or smaller than 0" simply didn't exist; it was <u>incomparable</u>.

Following mechanical rules, & hitting on a proof by luck are quite different.

    (1)   a + (b + 1) = (a + b) + 1   given as rule
    (2)
    (3)

This is called proof of associative law for <u>all</u> cardinals.
Where does generality come in? In (1)
(1) could have been written in form of series

    1 + (1 + 1) = (1 + 1) + 1   1 + (2 + 1) = (1 + 2) + 1
    2 + (1 + 1) = (2 + 1) + 1
    & so on

6b:26 Is there here an opposite! There are <u>some</u> which don't?
No.

Give the rule

$$a + (1 + 1) = (a + 1) + 1 \quad p_1$$
$$a + (2 + 1) = (a + 2) + 1 \quad p_2$$
$$a + (3 + 1) = (a + 3) + 1 \quad p_3$$
& so on

Here we can use "all"

we can say: for all x $a + (x + 1) = (a + x) + 1$.

What's the opposite of this last?
Suppose it is

$(\exists x) \sim fx$

We have likened p_1, p_2, p_3 etc. to an infinite logical product.
Then opposite is

$\sim p_1 \vee \sim p_2 \vee \sim p_3$ etc..

Now first rule allows us to write down any number of these; & the supposed opposite does not forbid it.[19]

In fact, rule is <u>not</u> a logical product; the examples are only there to explain the rule.[20]

6b:27 A logical product says <u>more</u> than a part of it

p_1, p_2, p_3 says more than p_1

We can't compare a rule to a logical product.

---

[19] Moore later added: <(Why not? because, however many you write, you don't exhaust the possibilities?)>

[20] Moore's summary notes: <The rule $a + (b + 1) = (a + b) + 1$ is not a logical product, but a rule; the examples only explain the rule.> (10:22)

The opposite of a rule like this is not an infinite disjunction, but any finite one which contradicts a finite set.

> e.g. $6 + (7 + 1) = (6 + 5) + 1$ contradicts our rule, but there's none of form $(\exists x)\sim fx$.

The proof is not something internal to probatum[21], but gives actual multiplicity of your statement.

$$a_n x^n + a_{n-1} x^{n-1} + \ldots = 0$$

Suppose I say: "There is a proof that <u>all</u> such equations have a solution."
We should say we all know what this means.
But what do we understand?
We understand "equation".
But "solution"? We understand, by examples.
But can we inquire what the proof would be like?   6b:28

---

[21] Latinate English: 'thing proved'.

Michaelmas Term, 1932

1-4

Senses of Meaning. 6b:29[1]

People use word "meaning" in following ways. Whole idea is to avoid confusions.

(1) They use it as a name for a process accompanying use of word, or hearing of word.

(2) An entirely different thing is meaning as defined by grammatical rules which apply to word.

Difficulty: You say: What $\underline{is}$ the meaning?

General difficulty to understand: What $\underline{is}$ so & so?

One sense of question is: What is water? where answer is: is H_2O, giving proportions.

But: What is water? $\underline{might}$ be asking for a definition, e.g. if you had been talking of all sorts of chemical compounds, & were asked which is water: you might write "water = H_2O", meaning I shall from now on use "water" where I have used H_2O.

    E.g. OH = hydroxyl group.

That "water" was already known to you makes it difficult to look on it in same way.

In "water is H_2O" he's $\underline{not}$ saying anything about the word, because "water" already belongs to his language: i.e. you're saying what it yields when you analyse it, & it's either true or false.

"H_3O = water" is not a wrong definition, though it may be misleading: you $\underline{can}$ use water = H_3O.

---

[1] While the page break and the name of the term at the head of the page clearly mark the start of Lecture 1, there are no partially completed pages, dates, or other clear indications of breaks between sets of lecture notes for the next 22 manuscript pages. The notes on the intervening pages are much too long for it to be plausible that they are all from Lecture 1. Our title only indicates that these notes were taken during some, or all, of Lectures 1–4.

6b:30　If you ask "How have you used "water"?" the answer is not a definition: it is about me.

So too "I will use "water" so & so" is not a definition, but contains a definition.

You can call a definition a radical of ever so many different statements.

What sort of an entity is a definition?

is of form "What is x".

Now answer is here, not of form what properties has it.

We are asking, what is the definition of "definition".

Suppose you'd used A for a person; & somebody had asked "Who is A".

You can point; but the person you point to won't be the meaning of A. That person may be ill; but the meaning of A can't be ill. The person is bearer of the name.

A red patch is not the bearer of name "red" in same sense.

The words "bearer of "Moore"" & "meaning of "Moore"" have quite a different grammar.

You give a rule for use of "red"; & the rule may be to use the red patch as a synonym for the word, but often not.

6b:31　The answer to what is x, is: x is so & so, where this is one among many grammatical rules.

It is wrong to suppose that definition is the explanation of a word.

You can give an explanation, by giving rules.

You can explain anything by giving rules of its use.

If 2 words mean² each a person, & both mean Moore, then I'm going to say they have same meaning. Is one rule.

What is a rule?

---

² Moore later added: <= are names of?>

Of course, this is: How is "rule" used?
And answer is: In many ways.

I'm comparing <u>use</u> of words, with moving a chess-man according to rules.
I.e. there's some similarity between 2.

Consider "Napoleon won battle of Austerlitz".
I could define "Napoleon" in different ways.
But suppose you say this: & I ask, what definition are you using?
Take Moses. Whom do you mean?
You might say: man found by Pharaoh's daughter in a basket.
I say there <u>was</u> no such person. Then you might say it doesn't matter. Say person who led Israelites across Red Sea.   6b:32
If you change your definition, you are changing your game.

If there are confusions as to use of "meaning", it is convenient to have a few tables of rules ready.
We want to tabulate a few rules about "definition", & about "meaning".
This is all I do.

Suppose you're teaching a child language, by saying "Fetch me a stick", "Fetch me a book" etc..

Suppose one asks "What is the number 1?"
I answer: let's not answer.
Let's give several <u>games</u>, which we can compare with people's actual uses.

Suppose one wanted to ask: What properties has 1?
One answer would be "There is only one window in this room".

$$\sim(\sim p) = p$$

People think this <u>follows</u> from <u>meaning</u> of $\sim$: i.e. that some statement of meaning of $\sim$ can be given from which these all follow.
But this idea is due to false analogy.
In a language which we know, a word creates a certain "impression".

6b:33 How can this rule <u>agree</u> with a <u>feeling</u> we have when we hear "not"?
Perhaps there's a causal connection between the rule & this feeling.

I will distinguish between these 2 meanings of "meaning": I'm going to talk of the sense of meaning, in which the rules <u>define</u> or <u>constitute</u> the meaning.

I can give any rules I like.

Rules of grammar are arbitrary.

E.g. take rule about = or identity, & give rule: It's transitive.

You'll say: This isn't arbitrary: if you meant something intransitive it wouldn't be identity.

<u>Of course not</u>. The rules would then no longer agree with the rules with which we use the English or German word: the rules of this word are the paradigm which we apply to a suggested rule.

Now take a cube.

We say we know: You can put another alongside of it.

This means: You're accustomed to one particular use of this figure.

But the figure does not contain the rules of geometry. It is only a common constituent of them all.

You can't have a game of chess in one lump.

The rule you give by pointing and saying "This is blue" is only <u>one</u> of the rules. You can alter them; but if you do, it won't be the English word "blue".

6b:34 You may say: then rules aren't arbitrary in at least one respect: they mustn't contradict one another.

But here you're only giving the grammar of the word "rule".

People say you mustn't admit contradiction, because if you did, it would make havoc of our thoughts.

But why not? There's no harm in not knowing what to do.

But "Leave the room & don't leave it" is <u>not</u> an order. You could say "Nonsense".

If the sense of a proposition has to <u>expression</u> relation like that of written music to performance: e.g. slots in reel of pianola might be expression, &

the sounds the sense. Then you can say of slots in some arrangement that they produce a senseless noise, & others music.

p . ~p may produce a discord. But, if process of thought consists in calculation by means of passing from symbol to symbol, this is irrelevant.

The contradiction is characterised not by anything psychological, but by a certain calculus.

You might say: "Come in & don't" isn't an order because you can't follow it. But why can't you? You can if rules are provided for following it: e.g. if you say it means, Come in & then stand straight.

Logical Laws or Laws of Thought

What about $p \supset p$?

Russell begins with primitive propositions & deduces others by rules. 6b:35

This procedure is used in physics and geometry. And this fact should disturb you, if you suppose Logic is somehow unique.

In case of physics. You might say: Deductions are all right, but how did you get your premises? Answer would be: Known to us by some very general experience.

But can you say same with Logic?

Frege & Russell said primitive propositions were self-evident.

What's peculiarity?

(1) They are never used. And that's not because we know them so well, that they're not worth saying.

Consider: You'll get wet, if you stand in the rain. I know this so well, that it's not worth saying; but yet I can try it, can see whether it will happen, – can tell what it would be like if it didn't.

But contrast: If it rains, it rains.

You can't try whether this is so.

We don't use it, if at all, as we use experiential propositions.

People say "You can't think it".[3] But how queer! Can you try whether you can or not?

---

[3] Moore later added: <that it's false>

Truth is we don't use it, or allow others to. We should say: He knows nothing about meteorology.

6b:36 You can say: They aren't propositions at all: if you mean by a proposition a set of symbols to which certain rules apply.[4]

You may say: They're a different kind of proposition. All right: but you mustn't suppose "kind" is here used as in "kind" of apple.

"Kind" is used in 2 entirely different ways:

(1) you distinguish kinds by their qualities; by different things being true of them. E.g. people by colour of hair.

Here it's essential that

if a & b are of different kinds

then some proposition is true of a & not of b, i.e. F(a) & ~F(b).

This presupposes that it has sense to say of the sour apple that it's sweet. It has sense to say F(b) & ~F(a).

(2) Suppose you say "red" & "tall" are qualities, but different "kinds" of quality. Does this mean that they have different qualities?

No they have different grammars.

Thus of rational 1, & cardinal 1.

rational in "I'm 1 foot tall"; cardinal in "There's one man in the room".

What's sense in the one case, is nonsense in the other: e.g. "he's 2 feet tall", "he's 2 feet red."

And this is like distinction between king & knight in chess.

6b:37 To distinguish between "formal" & "experiential" is like saying that 2 pawns are distinguished in spite of having same rules. We must shew a grammatical rule which applies to one & not to the other.

We have to shew that calculus dealing with $p \supset p$ is different from that dealing with what I call "experiential" propositions; if we want to distinguish these "kinds".

I can define, circumscribe, what I mean by "proposition", as I please, & very narrowly.

---

[4] Moore later added: <(rules of experiential propositions?)>

E.g. I'm going to call it something of the form "This chair is 3 yards from that wall, & 4 from this."

In order to describe a game of Logic, I <u>could</u> begin by giving such a <u>very</u> narrow meaning to proposition: different propositions differing only by difference in numbers.

We seem to have a general idea of "proposition" which needs to be made clearer.

But: No. It's like saying: We all know what a number is. But I could bring you one, with regard to which you have to make a new decision.

Trouble about "propositions" is:

Our language has a particular propositional game. There is subject predicate copula: a certain kind of jingle.

Now degrees of different games can be played with same jingle: e.g.

"$2 + 2 = 4$" & "That sun is red" have same jingle.

If you <u>do</u> try to look at rules of game, I can shew you border-line cases, where <u>you</u> won't know whether it is a proposition or not – where you have to be arbitrary.

6b:38

But then: Why not <u>begin</u> by being arbitrary?

There <u>isn't</u> any sharp line; any more than there is between a <u>game</u> & not a game.

It <u>isn't</u> possible to define "game"!

"Game" "rule" so & so haven't got <u>one</u> border-line already drawn.

You have a clear idea as to what you are going to call "cardinal number", but not as to what you're going to call "number".

  Concept of "language", concept of "kind".

"Kind" used in 2 different ways (probably in many others), (1) distinguished by some proposition being true of one & false of other.

In this case, it has <u>sense</u> to say of a thing of one kind, that it is of another: it's simply <u>false</u>.

But this is not as simple as it seems: e.g. of A, who is tall, it has sense to say A is short; but <u>not</u> if part of my definition of A is being tall. This leads to constant confusions.

(2) The other is: several kinds of number; or kinds of object – including e.g. bodies & surfaces. I.e. "body" & "surface" are not predicates in the sense in which "tall" etc. are. You could call these <u>logical</u> predicates; but then you'll be apt to think that there are 2 <u>kinds</u> of predicates.

Cf. surface of moon is yellow, & moon is yellow, might be held to shew that grammar of surface & moon is same. But you can't talk of surface of surface, but you can of surface of moon: it isn't simply that moon's surface hasn't got a surface.

In case of visual field there is no proposition "This place has a colour", because there is never "This place has no colour".

      Idea of language or of proposition.

There are many overlapping ideas of proposition, <u>none</u> having sharp boundaries.

<u>'Twas</u>   <u>and the</u>
    <u>did</u>   <u>in the</u>

If Carroll[5] had left them out, it would not have had the appearance of a proposition: what he <u>had</u> to leave in, gives you jingle of a sentence.

If you read a sentence backwards, it has no resemblance to a sentence, yet of course it has everything necessary to the calculus & can easily be translated.

If we want to define a particular sense of proposition for ourselves, we've <u>got</u> to define it by a calculus; just as we do cardinal number from rational number.

Now <u>one</u> definition is of this kind, by rules applying: viz. proposition is what <u>can</u> be true or false.

"True" & "false" are extraordinarily misleading because they are adjectives, & make us think it is like apples being green or red.

Now we can do away with "true" & "false" by saying

    p is true $= p$

    p is false $= \sim p$

(So of "agrees with reality").

This shews how utterly different grammar is from that of "red" or "green".

---

[5] Lewis Carroll's poem 'Jabberwocky' begins: "Twas brillig, and the slithy toves / Did gyre and gimble in the wabe' (Carroll 1992, 116).

"This is green" can't = this.

This seems to distinguish propositions by a quality – that of being "either true or false", whereas e.g. chairs are "neither true nor false."

Now we could distinguish a group of things which either stand on 4 feet or hang from ceiling.

But "true or false" is quite different, because it means what I shall call true or false; & we could say "can be negated".

Whole point is to define proposition as part of a system which I describe.

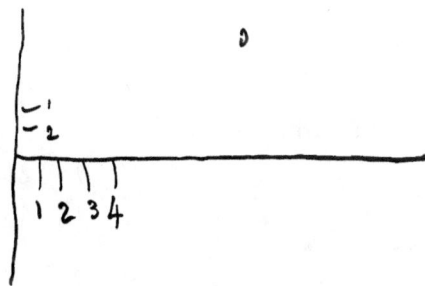

You can say: I'm going to mean by proposition "red 3, 5".

Or you could take 3, 5; meaning I would meet a point; which, if I don't meet, it's false.

By saying "anything which is either true or false", I give one characterisation of a calculus.

So "board-game" gives one characterisation of a number of games.

E.g. if I use this as my definition, then I must call 2 + 2 = 4 a proposition.

Hence whether you say 2 + 2 = 4 is a proposition or not, depends on how you define proposition.

If you say it's not, you mean that certain rules which do apply to experiential don't apply to it.

So "logical" propositions is a grammatical distinction.[6]

---

[6] Moore's summary notes: <"Logical proposition" is a grammatical distinction, because it means propositions to which some rules do apply, others don't.> (10:80)

We notice some differences about p ⊃ p; e.g. we shouldn't say anyone knew anything at all, if he only knew if it rains, it rains.

Some people say: it is self-evident; but this <u>must</u> be something psychological, & therefore doesn't interest us.

Now it is easy to shew a formal difference between the game played with

$$\begin{matrix} p \supset q \\ p \vee q \end{matrix} \quad \& \quad \begin{matrix} p \supset p \\ p \vee \sim p \end{matrix}$$

Simplest way is to introduce a symbolism (which however is so misleading that it's worse than useless).

p	
T	F
F	T

= ~p

p	
T	T
F	F

= p

Now suppose I wanted to write

p ∨ ~p

If instead of q in p, q, I write ~p.

I could write p in form

p	p
T	T
T	F
F	T
F	F

with symbolic rule that 2 & 3 are to help out.

Suppose /if/ you have a

p	q
T	T
T	F
F	T
F	F

you could write T against <u>every</u> pair getting a tautology.

When we then say "All propositions of logic are tautologies", what does this say?

It gives a common formal property of Russell's propositions, <u>both</u> primitive <u>&</u> derived:

i.e. that if you write them this way, you get T, T, T, T.

"A tautology says nothing" I said. 6b:43

What does this mean?

That p . (q ⊃ q) = p

e.g. It's raining, & I've either got grey hair or I've not = It rains.

We could also say

> A tautology follows from every proposition.
> Absurdity of

"Every proposition follows from a false proposition."

There's here a confusion between "follows" & "implies"; which belong to different categories.

Write p ⊃ q in T, F notation

p	q	
T	T	T
T	F	F
F	T	T
F	F	T

Whether one proposition follows from another or not, can't depend at all on its truth or falsehood, but only on an internal or grammatical relation between them.

> ((p ⊃ q) . p) entails q
> ∴ ((p ⊃ q) . p) ⊃ q is a tautology.

> (~p ⊃ (p ⊃ q)) is a tautology 6b:44
> ∴ p ⊃ q follows from ~p.

> (q ⊃ (p ⊃ q)) is a tautology
> ∴ p ⊃ q follows from q.

Something follows from proposition that p is false, but not from p, in the case in which it is false.

What have "follows" & "⊃" to do with one another? (Don't talk of the "distinction" between them, anymore than of that between a railway-guard & a railway-accident).

Symbolic expression of
> p follows from q is
> (p . q) = q

In <u>my</u> calculus I'm going to use these to mean the same.
Then you ask: Does this agree with our ordinary use of "follow"?
I shew it does; but I haven't truly justified it.

Where (p . q) = q
it may be either a derived or primitive rule.

> ((p ⊃ q) . p) entails q
> ((p ⊃ q) . p) . q = (p ⊃ q) . p

6b:45 First is already said /<u>thought</u>/ when you've said /<u>thought</u>/ last: means only: by rules of my calculus this equation holds.

p	q	p ⊃ q	p	(p ⊃ q) . p	q	((p ⊃ q) . p) . q
T	T	T	T	T	T	T
T	F	F	T	F	F	F
F	T	T	F	F	T	F
F	F	T	F	F	F	F

Whenever it's true that, wherever one column has a T another has one but not vice versa, then we say latter follows from former.

Here I was only applying my notation of following to Russell's calculus & shewing that it gives ((p . q) = q) = p follows from q.

"A tautology says nothing" means "it adds nothing to any other proposition", means "the product of it with any other gives the first proposition".[7]

What's the use of a tautology, as it says nothing?
Not much use.

---

[7] Moore later added: <won't do, because same holds of propositions which do say something; but will do, if you attend to <u>any</u> proposition.>

It has use only in a logical calculus.

p . q	p ∨ q	(p . q) ⊃ (p ∨ q)
T	T	T
F	T	T
F	T	T
F	F	T

Suppose I have a p & a q which are truth-functions of same arguments,   6b:46

((p ⊃ q) = Tautology) = p entails q.

The <u>use</u> of tautologies is that, if I combine certain propositions in such a way as to give a tautology, this shews a formal relation between them.

"follows" & "is implied".

Does p ⊃ q require a formal relation?

As defined by Russell, No.[8]

If p is an axiom, & q a mathematical proposition which follows from it, you have a temptation to say: Surely p implies q only because there is an internal relation? but you are only saying p entails q.

((p ⊃ q) = tautology) = q follows from p.

q follows from p . q

= (p . q) ⊃ q is a tautology = tells us nothing.

That (p . q) ⊃ q tells us nothing = q follows from p . q.

Tautology plays a similar rôle to 0 in Arithmetic.

When I say "tells nothing" I am comparing it to its arguments.

Take "atomic proposition" = no such signs as "or" "not" etc. occurs, e.g. "It is raining" "I'm too hot", i.e. propositions in which either logical sums or logical products occur.

<u>Atomic propositions. 2 difficulties.</u>   6b:47

Suppose <u>prima facie</u> there are no "and", "not", "or": mayn't there prove on <u>analysis</u>, to have them? This is an important question, but <u>not</u> for my purpose.

---

[8] Moore's summary notes: <p ⊃ q may be true, without any formal relation between p & q.> (10:81)

I'm going to mean prima facie not molecular nor general.

E.g.   3 . 5 tells you there is a patch on the blackboard in one place.
      2 . 5 gives you there is a patch on the blackboard in another place.
But (3 . 5) or not (3 . 5) tells you nothing.

If (6 . 6) . k = 6 . 6, then k says nothing.[9]
> Now take Laws of Logic (all propositions in *Principia Mathematica* before generality, that are <u>not</u> expressed in words).

E.g. $\sim(p . \sim p)$
This is a tautology, & says nothing.
Let atomic propositions be arguments: e.g. 4 . 6
Then $\sim((4 . 6) . \sim(4 . 6))$ tells you nothing as to whether there is a patch with coordinates 4 . 6 or not.
So too 4 . 6 $\supset$ 4 . 6 gives you no information: they all give you the same information, i.e. none whatever.
They leave <u>entire</u> freedom to the facts.
But I <u>can</u> treat it as a true proposition.
I <u>can</u> exclude these entirely from my language, as no use; but I <u>can</u> say
p . tautology = p, & then am treating it as <u>true</u>.

6b:48 $\sim(p . \sim p)$ gives us no information about things about which the atomic arguments give us some.
How then did it become famous?
We say one proposition follows from another <u>in virtue of</u> such a logical law.
E.g. we could deduce $\sim(\sim p)$ from p, in virtue of law of contradiction.
> You can't have both p & $\sim$p
> ∴ if you have p, you haven't $\sim$p.

Could you say $\sim p \supset \sim(p)$.

---

[9] Moore later added: <Surely not? k may be something which <u>follows</u> from 6 . 6. "p . q = p" means "q follows from p", & q may quite well say something>

If ~p is the case, then p is not the case.[10]

What does it mean to say p follows from q, <u>in virtue of</u> r? or that r <u>allows</u> the inference from p to q?[11]

If you give a law of inference you give it for future use, not for <u>one case</u> only.

If I need a law at all, I must need another law to allow me by the use of the first to infer Q from P: e.g. ~~Q from Q.

The other day I expressed a <u>rule</u> of inference by

$$((p \lor q) \cdot p) = p$$

i.e. I said this was a rule of inference; viz. (p ∨ q) follows from p.

You may ask what's the difference between this & ~(p . ~p)?

Difference is that equation is a <u>rule</u> of grammar: = I allow you to write p instead of p . (p ∨ q). 6b:49

So 2 + 2 = 4 allows us to put 4 instead of 2 + 2.

We could write 2 + 2 = 5, allowing you to replace 2 + 2 by 5.

Difference is that we have a <u>system</u>:[12]

    e.g. we start with <u>arbitrary</u> equations

    1 + 1 = 2 Def.

& then having fixed them, other things follow.

We can treat 2 + 2 = 4 either as a primitive or a derived equation.

Russell thought "= Def." meant something different from "=".

I say: No.

We give some as primitive, then rules of inference,[13]

Suppose I write 13 × 41 = 533

---

[10] Moore later added: <this is playing with language>
[11] Moore later added: <Is it a law /rule/ of inference?>
[12] Moore's summary notes: <Why we can't say 2 + 2 = 5, is because we have a <u>system</u> ...> (10:82)
[13] Sentence left unfinished.

I calculate by fixed rules: i.e. I've made up my mind to recognise as a rule of substitution, any which follows from certain arbitrary given ones, by <u>rules</u> of inference[14] – which are rules of a different sort.

$$(p \vee q) \cdot p = p$$

<u>might</u> be <u>either</u> primitive <u>or</u> deduced; in one system primitive, in other deduced.

Primitives build up my system before I begin to operate with it.

6b:50 You can say 1 + 1 = 2 def. <u>gives</u> meaning to 2; whereas (1 + 1) + 1 = 3 <u>presupposes</u> the meaning.[15]

$(p \vee q) \cdot p = p$ <u>presupposes</u> meaning of "or" & "not" means that it <u>follows</u> from other rules.

From $(p \supset q)$ & p Russell wants to infer q.

The rule, in this case is, $((p \supset q) \cdot p) \cdot q = (p \supset q) \cdot p$

In Russell's sense of <u>laws</u> of inference, there aren't any.

But I've now given you <u>rules</u> of inference.

Can one say that rules are correct or incorrect? If one could they would be <u>laws</u>.

I say there's no such thing as "truth" and "falsehood" in my rules: they are quite arbitrary & <u>fix</u> the meaning of symbols that occur in them.[16]

Take "If a thing's red, it isn't blue."

This could serve in same way as Law of Contradiction.

$$\sim(B(x) \cdot R(x))$$

I say it tells us nothing about red & blue, but is a rule of grammar about the <u>words</u>: & also an <u>arbitrary</u> rule.

---

[14] Moore later added: <Is ~(p . ~p) a rule of inference? one which "says nothing" whereas equations say something about symbols? But he has said: "(p . q) = p" <u>is</u> a rule of inference?>

[15] Moore's summary notes: <(1 + 1) + 1 = 3 <u>presupposes</u> meaning of 2.> (10:82)

[16] Moore later added: <But they are the rules we actually use>. This remark is connected with a line to the words 'B & R <u>mean</u> something different' appearing further down the page.

You could adopt another rule; which would be saying that B & R mean something different.

But now, suppose you define B & R ostensively: one will say "Now you can't say B(x) . R(x)." 6b:51

But does the ostensive definition fix what the other rules are to be, or is it only one of them? Do they follow from it?

You only understand an ostensive definition if you can ask which colour is red, which colour is blue.

I.e. your question already was grammatical rules applying to red & blue: i.e. presupposes[17] all the rules about colour,[18] except the one the ostensive definition is an answer to.

Could there be a hidden contradiction?

---

[17] Moore later added: <presupposes p = follows from other rules>
[18] Moore later added: <Doesn't it fix rules about colour?>

5

7:1[19] Are rules of inference responsible to some sort of reality? = are they in some way like natural laws? are they <u>justified</u> by experience in sense in which Law of Gravitation is?

Such rules have form

$$(p \cdot (p \vee q)) = p,$$

& I said such a rule is "arbitrary" in senses:

(1) it is an equation: = you can put this for that

(2) it may be primary – a rule with which I start

(3) it may be derived – I got it by means of a rule of inference, which I have to give you.

(4) in sense in which "$\sim(\sim p) = p$ is arbitrary" which determines meaning of $\sim$: but I might have used "$\sim$" = otherwise, only then it would not have same meaning as "not".

Take sign "=" & rule $(a = b) \cdot (b = c) \supset (a = c)$.

Is this arbitrary? Yes, in sense that <u>it</u> fixes meaning of "="[20]

It is not the case that the paradigm for the rules is a "heap" out of which they can be drawn, but the paradigm is a set of rules. We are deceived if we think we can compare rules spread out with one body.

7:2 Suppose we say: All properties of chalk are contained in this object – holding up a lump.

So we say: These rules "follow from" the meaning.

We're misled by such simple similes as taking things out of a box.

---

[19] The previous manuscript page is only half filled; this page, at the start of a new notebook, has no number, title, or date. It is likely that this marks the beginning of a new lecture. The little over nine pages of writing that follow are only slightly longer than the average for the dated lectures that follow, so it seems likely that they form a single set. The possibility that these are actually notes for both Lectures 4 and 5 cannot be ruled out, however.

[20] Moore's summary notes: <If I'd not had this rule, "=" would not have meant what it does.> (10:82)

So in Plato: 2 beautiful things, & αὐτὸ τὸ καλόν,[21] like brandy & whisky & pure alcohol.

The mere fact that we have the expression "the meaning" of a word, must lead us wrong.

Thus we're led to think the rules are responsible to something <u>not</u> a rule, whereas they're only responsible to rules.

Suppose we say "rules about red are guided by <u>nature</u> of this colour we see."

But what's meant by "nature"?

We can say: It's nature of chalk to act in such & such a way.

Do we say that rules about red agree or not, with experiments?[22]

The sense of "red" can't depend on truth or falsehood of proposition in which "red" occurs.

So you say length of Greenwich foot is arbitrary.[23] 7:3

Remember about how meaning of "brown" is given by pointing: that pointing can't answer your question, unless you know it's a colour you're to look for.

Does <u>one</u> rule determine <u>any</u> others?

People might think it excludes all that <u>contradict</u> it.

Can we give reasons for thinking as we do – drawing inferences as we do? e.g. according to logical laws.

Suppose I look in my diary, & find Smith down to come to tea on Monday.

What reason have I for thinking he will come?

What reason has anyone for thinking fire will burn?

---

[21] Greek: 'Auto to kalon', i.e. 'the beautiful (or: fine, noble) itself'. See Plato, *Republic*, trans. G.M.A. Grube, revised by C.D.C. Reeve. Plato 1997, 1102–1103 [476a–b].

[22] Moore's summary notes: <Rules about "red" are not guided by colour we see; it's "<u>nature</u>" of chalk to act in certain ways is discovered by experiments; but we don't discover rules about red, by seeing whether they agree or not with experiments.> (10:82)

[23] Moore's summary notes: <Rules of grammar are arbitrary in same sense in which length of Greenwich foot is arbitrary.> (10:83)

Anyone who doesn't think so won't have made a mistake, won't have calculated wrongly.

Why do people calculate strength of boiler-plates?

Ask for <u>reason</u> of a move in chess.

You may give a rule of the game as a reason.

7:4 When you pick up a coin, because you want it, how does your "reason" act?

To "why?" you might answer: "Because it was mine".

This may or may not describe anything that happened when you did so.

With our definition of "for this reason", e.g. I <u>said</u> at the time "This is mine", it won't be true you did for that reason unless you did say the words.

Suppose "my reason" = the calculation I actually made.

Every "reason" is a reason only within a game.

"Nobody ever does anything without a reason."

In what sense?

What is your reason for objecting to my sticking a knife in you?

Did you <u>actually</u> make a calculation? In any case, if you did, it would come back to "So & so <u>always</u> has happened". You can't give a reason <u>why</u> so & so <u>is</u> a reason.

You mustn't mix up <u>reason</u> with <u>cause</u>.

7:5 Within a calculation there will be right & wrong according to certain rules; but if you ask <u>why</u> these rules? only answer is: There the game stops.

Does a "cause" supply place of a "reason"?

Yes, in sense that it may set your mind at rest.

Does the question "what reason had you?" lead to an infinite regress?

If this means: <u>Can</u> you extend calculus indefinitely?

Of course, you can.

Suppose we use table,

> red
> blue

in such a way, that if I say "Fetch me a red thing", man compares 2 colours, & fetches like one.

We can ask: Why did you fetch this one?

He may answer, <u>because</u> it's left of "red".

You may ask: Why was it's being left of "red" a reason?

So on <u>ad infinitum</u>.

A reason is always <u>possible</u>; but it is not always <u>necessary</u>, in order to get validity.

Why did you shut the window?

Because it was draughty.

What reason had you for supposing shutting the window would stop the draught?

It always has done. ("& is therefore probable", is a mere flourish)

Is that a reason?

That's just what we mean by a reason.

Question is: Is such & such a word a part of my calculus? does it lead me on to anything? "It is probable" doesn't do this: it is like the Creator – you stop there, but you might have stopped before.

<u>Compare</u> (1) "Why did your mouth water?"

(2) "Why did you run to the door?"

and (3)[24] Because I've always got food by doing so, when the bell rings.

Now I say: "Do you mean that the bell was the cause of your running? Here you give a <u>cause</u>, got at experimentally.[25]

---

[24] Moore wrote '(2)', perhaps because what follows is a reply to the second question.

[25] Moore's summary notes: <If you say "I ran to the door, because I've always got food by doing so when the bell rings" does <u>not</u> mean "The bell caused me to run". That it caused could only be got at experimentally.> (10:83)

What is <u>criterion</u> for so & so being a reason?

<u>Perhaps</u> (1) that you actually calculated from that.

(2) that that's what you say when asked.

Difference between <u>reflex</u> & <u>voluntary</u> action.

If he says: I had <u>this</u> reason for making my mouth water; you would ask: <u>Can</u> you make your mouth water?

In the end we shall get to: Does it mean anything to want to want?

When you raise your arm voluntarily: what's connection between your <u>wish</u> to raise it, & the raising of the arm?

Suppose S wishes from 5 to 5.30 that Smith should come into the room, what did he do from 5 to 5.30?

We know what's meant by saying, he whistled from 5-5.30.

Suppose: We take "I wish to drink water"; & I ask "what does wishing mean".

7:8 Now I understand "I wish to drink <u>x</u>": <u>this</u> needs to be explained.

And to explain it you must give me a process, such that if I saw you doing it, I could tell <u>both</u> that you wished for something <u>and</u> what you wished for.

E.g. suppose to wish to drink water = to turn a tap with "water", to wish to drink wine = to turn a tap with "wine": <u>this</u> would explain.

If you <u>wish</u> to drink ⅝ water ⅜ wine: any explanation must make it clear what it would be to wish ¾ & ¼.

Any explanation must give some process having same <u>multiplicity</u>: e.g. said that he wanted.

Any suggested explanation <u>either</u>

(1) correlates to wishing for water, e.g. crying which can't tell me what wishing for wine would be.

Then you haven't defined "wish", but only "wishing for water", which only accidentally has anything in common with "wishing for wine".

It's the difference between <u>index</u> & function.

A_1 = water, A_2 = red, A_3 = Frege

then I haven't defined <u>A</u>.

(2) There must be a <u>system</u> of wishes corresponding to system of expressions of wishes.

7:9

This is difference between defining a function by a <u>list</u> or by a <u>law</u>.

If you ask what's connection between wishing to raise arm & arm raising? I answer, <u>either</u>

(1) it's of <u>sort</u> that wishing belongs to articulate group – having same multiplicity as expression

or (2) it's of other sort.

Q. Why did you lift your arm?

A. To protect myself.

This <u>must</u> mean an <u>articulate</u> process.

Now I might have wanted to protect myself, & yet arm not gone up.

"Try to attract this piece of chalk."

Can you try? can you try to try?

Movement is dependent on your act of volition; but is act of volition dependent on you?

7:10

Voluntary lifting consists of arm raising & something else.

You can be reduced to: I <u>can't</u> wish that.

Try to draw a square & its diagonals by looking into a mirror. You <u>can't</u> do it; but it's a quite different phenomenon from the <u>can't</u> because someone is holding your hand, where you try & you can't.

In the case of the mirror you <u>can't try</u>: your hand doesn't do, what you'd like it to.

6a

7:11   Monday, November 14.

Cause – reason – motive.

Voluntary & involuntary action.

Important thing is to shew that this subject has nothing to do with ours.

We have nothing to do with questions decided by experience.

Why won't I deal with them? Because troubles called philosophical are not questions solved by experience.

A problem which seems "philosophical", if it can be split up into one part which can be answered by experience, this part has a different smell: e.g. problem "how many people can wiggle their ears" has different taste.

Where we can say "Everybody knows", that's a sign it's <u>not</u> philosophy.

Psychology alone seems to have something to do with philosophy: it makes you fall into traps. Sometimes a philosopher makes a psychological remark – & it seems queer. E.g. self-evidence is a psychological matter.

I never have to tell you facts: you can always do with those you know.

But <u>sometimes</u> facts are useful, especially in one particular case.[26]

7:12   Philosophical trouble is essentially this: You seem to see a system, yet facts don't seem to fit it; & you don't know which to give up. Near it looks like a stump, then like a man; then again.

This is how this happens:

Influence of words so strong. E.g. "number" makes you think it must be cardinal. You first remember rules then forget them. The system seems embodied in language; yet when you look nearer at the rules, you see it isn't.

Now you can be quieted sometimes by being told a fact. Suppose you regard a fact as unique. In a way this satisfies, in a way is irritating.

---

[26] Moore's summary notes: <Facts may be useful by shewing you that so-and-so is not unique.> (10:84)

Lecture 6a – November 14, 1932

You can resolve doubts by shewing so & so is not unique: reminding people of facts they know then has a sedative effect – of facts similar to a unique-seeming fact.

It shews you that that fact has nothing to do with system of world.

All I do is to distinguish: e.g.

(1) I lifted my arm

(2) My arm went up.

In both cases, arm goes up; but in first something else happens as well.

(1) You can give an answer, if asked which you do.

(2) You may have lifted it against opposition. 7:13

One might say: My will doesn't act on my finger, but on the muscle. That when muscle moves, finger moves is dependent on mechanical laws. But can I move my muscle? People might say: No you can only affect electric current in nerves.

We can't find anything subject to will directly, as opposed to indirectly.[27]

What's meant by: "muscle moves"? What is verification? Not an experience of willing, but visual experience: & your visual muscle can't be dependent on

A voluntary act is an experience like an involuntary, but a different one.

Question was: In which cases is answer to "why" a reason, or a cause?

If you ask what a cause is characterised by, we refer to experiments.

But if you ask for "reason"; could any experiment shew you?

In saying this, I am merely (1) reminding you of way in which word "cause" is used, & (2) of way in which you use "reason".

When I say "reason can't be found by experiment", I'm saying: It has no sense to say: Reason is found by experiment.

How does a man know reason why he did a thing? 7:14

A man may try to remember. But what do you try to remember?

Let's say: If he remembers motive, & expresses it.

Why did you leave room?

---

[27] Moore's summary notes: <e.g. not muscles as opposed to finger; nor nerves as opposed to muscles.> (10:28)

Because I wanted to bring in a chair from landing.

But how do you know?

We use "because" in 2 quite different ways; just as we do "want" or "appetite"

(1) You may mean: My stomach wants food; & of this you can't be certain. You may verify it, by giving food, & finding he hums.

Here wanting: is a hypothesis.

(2) Something which can't be verified or falsified by subsequent experience. E.g. something which is not disproved, by finding that you get a stomach-ache.

Suppose I call "wishing for an apple" "saying that he wants an apple". Then it's quite clear we should have case (2), not (1).

7:15 Call (1) inarticulate (2) articulate; & one mark of articulate wish is that you wish in a language.

Some phenomena are a language; some not.

If by wishing is meant something which could be refuted by experience, then that I wish is an hypothesis.

Suppose you see a man making efforts: & say: He wants to open window. Here: it's clear you may possibly be wrong: here it's a hypothesis.

But suppose you ask him?

2 cases

(1) where, by looking at a hope, you can see what it is a hope for.

(2) where by looking at a hope, you can't.

If you so use "wish", that to wish for ⅔ wine & ⅓ water is to be different from ½ wine & ½ water, then[28]

7:16 Suppose S says: Putting 2 cups is expecting 2 people, putting 3 cups is expecting 3 people.

---

[28] Sentence left unfinished.

When you express your expectation in words: is it a case of <u>translation</u> from one language into another? or is it <u>not</u> a case of translation, but only of a conclusion (invariable concomitance)?

Test we apply to shew a man's not lying:
A says "I expect 3 people". 3 people come, & you then say "A was not lying".

We came to this from Laws of Inference. Why do we think as we do think?
Now to: Why do you think there's no-one in the room?
<u>Within</u> a game, there are reasons.
E.g. table of colours, <u>provides</u> a reason.
Reasons for your reasons are not in your mind.
Do you want a reason, why so & so should be a reason?
Giving a reason is going back one step in the calculus.

Is it depressing that our chains of reasons should come to an end?
Difficult to distinguish different <u>troubles of the mind.</u>   7:17

Some troubles are relieved by a <u>reason</u>: you therefore think <u>all</u> will: but this is not so.
What is wrong with us is not (as we think) that we haven't had enough reasons.

Scientific way of thinking consists in scientific solution to scientific problem: always – going a step further in a certain direction.
<u>Hertz</u>. People ask about "essence" of electricity; not about "essence" of gold. When contradiction has been cleared up question hasn't been answered; but mind ceases to ask it.[29]

---

[29] Wittgenstein is alluding to a passage in the preface of Hertz's *The Principles of Mechanics Presented in a New Form*: 'When these painful contradictions are removed, the question as to the nature of force will not have been answered; but our minds, no longer vexed, will cease to ask illegitimate questions.' (Hertz 1899, 8). He later considered using it as a motto for the *Philosophical Investigations* (Wittgenstein 1953).

Aren't rules about red determined by nature of red?

Other rules would not be compatible with <u>meaning</u> of red because meaning is determined by these among others.

Suppose I have a rule <u>p</u>, & certain rules of inference which from p lead to ~p.

7:18 Incompatibility is defined as a particular event in a calculus, & you can define it as you please.

<u>Suppose</u> we define it as: proposition of form <u>p</u> is incompatible with ~p.

Suppose we have a game, where rules are fixed: then we can find whether there's a contradiction, by going through them pair by pair.

"Hidden contradiction" may mean 2 different things: in a calculus which <u>does</u> give you a way of finding one, & in one which doesn't.

Hidden where there is a way of finding, & where there isn't.

With p, ~p as type of incompatibility.

Take rule

(a is red) . (a is not blue) = a is red. (which is a rule of the English language)

Then from this & <u>other</u> rules, I can deduce

(a is red) . (a is blue) is a contradiction.

Here's a case where you can <u>try</u>;[30] as in case of question: Is 7 a factor of this number?

---

[30] Moore's summary notes: <Here you can <u>try</u> whether it's a contradiction or not.> (10:28)

6b

November 18.   7:19

Believing, wishing, expecting, thinking <u>that</u> so & so was or will be case.

Draw attention to one fact:

<u>Wrote letters</u> from 5 to 5½[31], can be described more or less exactly.

You can say: if he did this, he was writing, e.g. describe movements of his hands.

But difficulty in describing: He wished to drink water from 5 to 5½.

What is characterisation of this?

What this <u>means</u> is that the grammar of "wishing" is in a way more <u>vague</u> than that of "writing".

You can describe bodily actions, such as going to the tap; but these could happen <u>without</u> his wishing, & so with lots of other things, having images etc..

Hence you may be tempted to say: the wishing is a sort of feeling & the others are accompaniments.

Thus we know what <u>writing</u> is, & there are lots of other things which may or may not accompany it.

Thus we use "wish" in a very complicated way.

How did we learn to use "wish"?   7:20

It is a collective word, meaning all sorts of things. Have they anything in common? Perhaps, but you can't draw boundary.

We describe a calculus. But does anyone <u>use</u> this calculus, when he uses "wish"?

All we can do is to contrast a very simple calculus, & say this is something like wishing.

We could say wishing to drink water = imagining drinking water & having a feeling of thirst.

---

[31] This is a telegraphic way of writing '5.30'; see page 7:7 above.

If you say "This isn't how we use it"; I say: Yes, it isn't <u>confined</u> to this, but no lines are already drawn.

Take "a leaf"; with many things we should say this is a leaf; but in other cases we shouldn't know.

But you haven't fixed the boundaries of the concept.

This is old question of "heap of sand".

Suppose I say "Make the <u>smallest thing which</u> is a heap of sand".

You have to say: This means nothing.

Government might define "heap of sand" = not smaller than a cubic foot.

7:21 Then government is drawing <u>new</u> boundary. The 2 concepts; new one <u>with</u> boundary, & old without still coincide.

With "wishing" it's characteristic that no boundary is drawn.

But we can, in trying to make language games, draw boundaries.

Suppose you have 2 squares

& are asked to draw <u>definite</u> boundaries <u>like</u> these.

You can get <u>nearer</u> to one than the other.

<u>Why</u> try to draw these pictures?

They are absolutely unnecessary, <u>except</u> when people prepare to tell us: so & so are the rules.

Say: Wish to do so & so = imagining yourself doing so & having a certain feeling.

Having a feeling of thirst, won't do for wishing to go for a walk.

But if you say "I want to drink water", do you describe your state by these words? Do you describe an activity, as if you said "I am writing"?

In fact, the use of the words may be part of the <u>behaviour</u> which constitutes wishing: e.g. you might say: Wishing to drink water is to be thirsty & to say "I want to drink water" or an equivalent phrase.

I.e. in this case the language doesn't <u>describe</u> your behaviour, but is part of the behaviour.

Thus behaviour constitutes one sense of "A expects Smith".

But it doesn't constitute "I expect Smith".

"I wish x" <u>may</u> mean: "x will satisfy me". (Rarely!)[32]

or it may mean something that was true, although it didn't satisfy me.

It has sense to say: My wish has been fulfilled, but I'm not satisfied.

We are not accustomed to place calculuses side by side with ordinary language: if we do, queer things happen.

E.g. I have tooth-ache, he has tooth-ache.

<u>New start.</u>

If we want to know what a man <u>wants</u>, one way is to <u>ask</u> him, another to observe him.

Here are 2 different verifications for: S wants so & so.

For "There's a desk in my room", there are all sorts of verifications.

We should say: Here we learn <u>same</u> fact in different ways.

<u>I</u> should say: Here we have <u>different</u> facts in different ways.

In physics: If I measure a length in a different way, what I mean by <u>length</u> is different. Sometimes it means result of one measurement, sometimes of another, sometimes of a disjunction.

Suppose we say there are different senses of "There's a desk in the room": (1) a blind man's tactual experience (2) a visual experience.

Or, as in ordinary language, where no boundary is drawn.

Take the proposition "There is on this mantelpiece a thing of cylindrical shape".

---

[32] Though Moore often puts his own responses within the lecture notes in parentheses, this comment is unusual in that it is hard to be sure whether Wittgenstein or Moore was the author.

Verification: (1) look on the mantelpiece
          (2) measure diameter with pair of compasses
          (3) walk round & compare different views of it
          (4) photograph it from different positions

Do these verify <u>same</u> proposition or different ones?

You can say what you please.

You <u>can</u> define by (4), which is independent of others.

7:24   These all give different meanings of "There's a cylinder here".

And we <u>could</u> give: satisfies <u>one or other</u>
         or satisfies <u>both</u> or all.

What do we mean by "2 minutes to 6"?

You can say: by Trinity clock.

But how do you compare your watch with Trinity Clock?

We <u>haven't</u> got <u>exact</u> idea of what it means; & we can't make it <u>more</u> exact: we <u>alter</u> it, e.g. if we add Greenwich time.

Now, in ordinary life, we don't specify our verification.

Since "writing" can be verified in different ways; we can say it's <u>different</u> facts.

In <u>some</u> cases to say "I wish S would come" & to have a queer feeling is <u>all</u> that is meant by wishing.

There are 100 things which may be called wishing, none of which is actually what is so-called.

7:25   The only use of this is against philosophers. E.g. against the person who thinks wishing is an <u>activity</u> in same sense as letter-writing.

Does your calculus leave the possibility of a lie? And, if so, have you decided how a <u>lie</u> is to be verified?

"I looked at Jones" is comparatively definite: "I meant Jones" much more indefinite: there are many different ways of using "meaning Jones".

To intend may mean: If somebody had asked me, I should have <u>said</u> I intend to see Smith.

So too, there are 100 things that may be meant by "knowing" a fact.

7a

November 21. 7:26

We got to "expecting" etc. from idea of "reason"; as distinguished from "cause".

Why do you come in to this room? Because there's a lecture going on there.

In <u>what</u> sense is this his reason? Had he it in his mind?

Someone may say: How do you know it is his reason? & then that will shew what is meant by saying it is.

Now we could give many <u>tests</u> for "There's a cylindrical object here", & therefore many <u>meanings</u>.

The tests may not coincide; & I may settle on one, or on a disjunction, or conjunction.

I'm not going to describe 100 games but only a few.

(1) A man does so & so for a reason = He does it as a result of a calculation.

Here reason = way he arrived at it.

E.g. if act is writing down 325 & reason of writing it down was arriving at it by multiplying 25×13 on blackboard.

"In order to attend my lecture." <u>might</u> mean:

Goes through days of week & hours in diary, & sees "Wittgenstein" there, & sees in a book Wittgenstein Whewell's Court K10.[33]

In this sense "reason" is involved in the act, in a way in which the cause isn't. 7:27

If I describe whole process, I'm saying nothing about cause & effect.

We may compare "reason" to a <u>way</u>. <u>How</u> did you get to Grantchester?[34]

Suppose we ask: Why are you frightened? This may mean: What are you frightened at? or What's cause of your fear? These are 2 absolutely different things.

---

[33] This was Wittgenstein's address at the time, and the location of the lectures.
[34] Moore's summary notes: <"Reason" may here be compared to "way" in "Which way did you go to Grantchester".> (10:86)

"I shiver because X came in", if causal statement, is an hypothesis, & we can only find out if it's true by series of experiments.

But "What are you frightened at?" hasn't got hypothetical answer.

What is cause of your being frightened at X, does not ask: What is cause of his causing fear in you.

Similarly: I'm portraying M, does not mean, M is cause.

There is no question; Are you really portraying him?

But we can't say, you aren't allowed to use "X is frightened at Y". X is frightened because Y has come in.

Just as (1) wish x means something which involves x

    (2) wish x means shall be satisfied by x.

7:28 Suppose you say "I want a coloured print by so & so here".

Someone may say: Is that really what you want?

And you may admit: No, it isn't.

This is a 3rd way of using "want".

Thus "really meant" often means something which is true, when you had not got the thing in question in mind.

Suppose in Mathematics you convince someone by a certain process.

E.g. proof that you can't trisect angle. You gradually change your idea of trisection.

We can say "Did you mean so & so" & he may say "Yes", though he hadn't known the thing in question.

We talked about "reason", because we raised the question whether we thought as we did for certain reasons.

E.g. why do we adopt laws of deduction?

Now chain of reasons comes to an end: & yet they're no less reasons.

There is pernicious idea that if you don't give a reason, there must be something wrong. But when a reason has been given for something, we could ask: What reason was there for this reason, but you needn't.

7:29 The superstition of saying "This is rational" is deeply rooted.

Lecture 7a – November 21, 1932

Induction

That it always has happened, is a reason for saying will.

Now go right back to Deduction.

"Rules of inference are not true or false" is apt to give uncomfortable feeling.

Compare measuring a length, & fixing what is to be taken as unit of length.

These 2 are totally different. Reasons (if any) for fixing unit of length do not make it not arbitrary; in sense in which statement that so & so is length of this, is not arbitrary.

Rules of deduction are analogous to fixing of a unit.

Metre is to be so & so related to diameter of earth: it looks as if you must have another standard behind.

But standard is only method or apparatus described: e.g. you might use pendulum which swings in a second as unit of length.

But you don't measure time in same sense in which you measure space.

Measuring time is such & such a process & has only a very remote analogy to measuring a rod.   7:30

Rules of deduction are rules of measurement, not statements of length.

E.g. $2 + 2 = 4$.

Suppose I have 2 foot measuring rod; apply it to blackboard trim, & say it's 4 feet long: because $2 + 2 = 4$.

Is "it's 4 feet long" the same as "I got   "?[35]

But don't take rationals, take cardinals.

Is "I've put 6 apples on mantelpiece" same as "I've put 3, & put 3"?

One experience: is counting up to 3.

Another: is counting up to 3 again

3rd: is counting up to 6, i.e. arriving at number 6 by counting all.

Does $3 + 3 = 6$ prophesy, that I shall have 3rd, if I have other two?

Suppose someone says: $3 + 3 = 6$ is purely arbitrary.

---

[35] Moore seems to have intentionally left this space blank.

And you answer, surely not: because putting 3 + 3 means there being 6.

7:31 But you can imagine putting 2 groups of 3 there, & then getting only 5.

And to say "one <u>must</u> have vanished" means only, if you keep arithmetical rule 3 + 3 = 6, you have to say so.

Take a whole set (of which number can't be seen at a glance)

Suppose you add one; & then count again, & find the same number, or one fewer.

You say: One <u>must</u> have vanished!

That is only grammatical way of completing description of what has occurred.

Call "some" an indefinite numeral, & give the rule

    Some + some = some.

Use of "some" <u>is</u> analogous to use of 2, 3 etc. in some respects, but <u>not</u> in this.

3 + 3 = 6 is not responsible to facts, because it doesn't prophesy.

It's a rule as to the way we're going to talk about apples.

It is pre-description; a preparation for a description, just as fixing a unit of length is a preparation for measuring.

7:32 "Length" is used in 2 different ways.

(1) "The length of this rod is my unit of length."

= In order to get at length of something else, take this & carry out this operation with it.

(2) "The <u>length</u> of this rod" may be opposed to "the breadth".

Measuring b by a, we may get 3; c by b get 4; & then c by a we <u>might</u> get 10.

With our rule 3 × 4 = 12, we should say: There must be some mistake.
But we could change our arithmetic & say 3 × 4 = 10; only then 3 would not mean the same as it does now.

The length of this rod is 4 feet is one usage.
The length of this rod is my unit of length is quite different.

7b

7:33 November 25.

Rules of deduction are <u>not</u> something like laws of nature – aren't reducible to any reality – don't say anything about nature; but are postulates – arrangements laid down <u>before</u> describing – method of description.

$2 + 2 = 4$ is rule of deduction.

This can be put in another way.

Take $p \cdot (p \supset q)$ entails q.

This could be written as equation

$$((p \supset q) \cdot p) \cdot q = (p \supset q) \cdot p.$$

If I say this is arbitrary, first objection is that it can be deduced, e.g. by T, F schema.

(2nd) If you say it <u>depends</u> on meaning of "and" & "$\supset$": I say it <u>constitutes</u> the meaning.

Compare confusion between these laws & laws of nature with confusion between fixing a standard of length, & making statements <u>about</u> length of things.

Fixing a standard is a rule of grammar; & <u>sense</u> of statements about length of things will depend upon how we fixed it.

7:34 We talked of difference between $\supset$ & entails; & said, if we give Russell's meaning to $\supset$

$$(p \supset q) \neq q \text{ follows from } p$$

but that

$$((p \supset q) = \text{tautology}) = q \text{ follows from } p$$
$$= ((q \cdot p) = p)$$

Now let's talk of <u>following</u>, not as here from <u>molecular</u> propositions, but from or to <u>general</u> propositions.

Take $(x)fx$ entails fa

E.g. If <u>anybody</u> is here he has a hat

entails If Smith is here he has a hat.

Or take
> fa entails $(\exists x)fx$.

Now there's a temptation, to which I yielded in *Tractatus*, to say that
> $(x)fx$ = logical product fa . fb . fc . . . .[36]
> $(\exists x)fx$ = logical sum, fa ∨ fb ∨ fc . . .

This is wrong, but not as absurd as it looks.

Suppose we say that: Everybody in this room has a hat 7:35
> = Ursell has a hat . Richards has a hat etc..

This is obviously false, because you have to add
> & a, b, c . . . are the only people in the room.

This I knew & said in *Tractatus*.[37]

But now, suppose we talk of "individuals" in Russell's sense, e.g. atoms or colours; & give these names,

then there would be <u>no</u> proposition analogous to "And a, b, c . . . are the only people in room".

The <u>class</u> of things would <u>not</u> be determined by a <u>proposition</u>, but by our dictionary.

Let's give an example of such a case.

Take 4 primary colours.

Consider "In this picture there are 3 primary colours."

This = there are either blue, green, red <u>or</u> red, green, yellow etc..

Or "in this square there is <u>one</u>" = this is either yellow <u>or</u> red or blue etc..

Why is this different from case of hats?

<u>There</u> there is a proposition such as Moore is in this room etc..

But there is no <u>proposition</u> "red is a primary colour". 7:36

So too "he whistled 3 notes of the octave C to C" this is a logical sum, because the octave C to C = C, D, E, F, etc..

---

[36] Moore later added: <(of <u>all</u> propositions of form fx)>
[37] Moore later added: <(4.52?)>

Now in our dictionary looking under "colour", we should find names of colours.

i.e. this is a class defined by <u>grammar</u>, not by qualities; & is therefore equivalent to a list.

Now <u>where</u> (x)fx <u>is</u> a logical product, business of deduction is quite straightforward: it is same as in molecular propositions.

~~There's an important mistake in *Tractatus*.~~

Consider "In all the circles in this square there is a cross."

Call them A, B, C etc., laying down rules for identity.

7:37 Let S(A, B, C ...) = A, B & C are in the square.

†(A, B, C ...) = There's a cross in A, in B, in C.

$$(x)(Sx \supset \dagger x)$$

does <u>not</u> say S(A, B, C ...) & †(A, B, C ...)

but from S(A, B, C ...) & †(A, B, C ...) together with there are none other in the square.

$$(x)(Sx \supset \dagger x) \underline{\text{ follows}}.$$

There's a most important mistake in *Tractatus*.

Let's use T, F, F, F as short for p <u>and</u> q; & similarly <u>all</u> molecular propositions.

Now, if <u>all</u> general propositions were identical with logical products or logical sums (as would be only if given in grammar).

Now take Sheffer's

p | q = ~p . ~q

~p = p | p

p ∨ q = (p | q) | (p | q)

I extended this, & said

Write ~p, ~q   F, F, F, T   7:38

& similarly

~p, ~q, ~r, ~s ...   F, F, F, F, F, F, F, ... T

I said

let negation of p, q, r, s ...

be written [- - - - - - - T]

and then any <u>general</u> proposition could be written in this way,

$\quad\quad (\widehat{\xi})$ [- - - - - - T]   Proposition

suppose $(\widehat{\xi})$ = x is in this room

Then Proposition = negation of all propositions that are values of ξ.

The fallacy here is one that is common in Mathematics.

I pretended that Proposition was a logical product; but it <u>isn't</u>, because "..." don't give you a logical product.

It is fallacy of thinking

$\quad\quad 1 + 1 + 1 + ...$ is a sum.

It is muddling up a sum with the limit of a sum.

$\quad\quad \frac{dx}{dy}$ is not a quotient, but the limit of a quotient.

it doesn't obey <u>all</u> rules that $\frac{x^2}{x}$ obeys.

Suppose $(\exists x)fx = fa \lor fb \lor fc$ ...   7:39

(I couldn't here write "& so on", unless it were the "& so on" of laziness: A, B, C, D & so on (for alphabet), <u>is</u> of laziness, because it <u>could</u> be replaced by an enumeration.)

In my book I supposed that

$\quad\quad (\exists x)fx = fa \lor fb \lor fc$ <u>& so on</u>

was of laziness, when it wasn't.

There was a deeper mistake – confusing logical analysis, with chemical analysis.

I thought: "$(\exists x)fx$ <u>is</u> a definite logical sum, only I can't at the moment tell you which".

Now difficulty arises: How can special case follow from general proposition? or general proposition from special?

"Follow" must mean something different.

Solution is $((\exists x)fx) . fa = fa$ is <u>deduced</u> in case of molecular propositions; but <u>here</u> is taken as primary proposition.[38]

---

[38] Moore later added: <& similarly $((x)fx . fa = (x)fx?)$>

8

November 28, 1932. 7:40

(x)fx <u>entails</u> fa; fa <u>entails</u> (∃x)fx.

Difficulty was that, if (x)fx has nothing to do with logical product, nor (∃x)fx with logical sum, then "entails" seems to mean something utterly different: & why call both "entails"?

This doesn't seem to be a difficulty, if logic & mathematics are taken as a sort of natural science.

But realise that "entails" stands for an operation in calculus; not merely for writing one down, then ∴, & then the other. <u>Then</u>, why use same word?

What is in common?

The rule "p entails q = ((p . q) = p)"

In *Tractatus* I said (x)fx & (∃x)fx were truth-functions, – first a logical product, 2nd a logical sum.

My mistake was to think the product, though we couldn't find it now, was contained in it.

My <u>good</u> point was that I did make <u>one</u> calculus.

Now in <u>some</u> cases, if (∃x)fx is a translation of "There is", & (x)fx of "all", first <u>is</u> a logical sum, & 2nd logical product; but not generally. 7:41

Now I was misled by fact that

(x)fx can be replaced by fa, fb ... which is <u>not</u> a logical product.

Now <u>dots</u> mean several different things.

(1) dots of laziness: A, B, C, D ... & so on.

(2) Cardinal numbers are 1, 2, 3, 4 <u>& so on</u>, is not of laziness.

(3) "This is a table, this, this, this ... & so on". This again is <u>quite different</u>.

What do you mean by "a circle in a square"? This ⌞°⌟, this ⌞◦⌟, this ⌞o⌟ & so on.

If one asks: How <u>many</u> different positions are possible? Question has no meaning.

Someone might say: Couldn't you settle by experiment how many?

E.g. suppose I had a disc, that can be moved by a screw with fine thread, as in micrometer. I may turn, without seeing difference of position. You can then find out how many different positions you can distinguish.

But what has happened? Visual disc admittedly didn't move. So all you've got is 20 positions of micrometer in physical space, for which you can distinguish positions in visual space.

The movement that occurs when you see no difference of position, is, of course, not visual movement.

So, if I have a magnifying glass, & you not, in my visual space it may move, & in yours not.

As micrometer turns, you will say: I see no difference of position; I see no difference of position: and then: I do see a difference.

This experiment determines "least noticeable difference".

These 20 positions are not determined by geometry of visual space; they're not characteristic of visual space, but of co-ordination of visual with another.[39]

On an egg there are 2 points ausgezeichnet[40] by geometry of egg; in a sense in which on sphere there are none.

Suppose you'd had a particular drug, perhaps you would have found 40!

Experiment only shews that 20 are to be got in this way.

When rain is falling, & you see many drops: if I ask, how many did you see? There is no answer. There is an experience, seeing 3 drops; & seeing 4 drops; & a quite different one seeing many: Here you can say, e.g., all the drops were grey. – & this is not a logical product.

I & Russell falsely supposed this. If we'd been right, there would have been an experiment which told us something about logic.

$$(p \vee q) . p) = p \quad (p \text{ entails } p \vee q)$$

This could in Russell's algorithm, or in mine, be derived from primary propositions

$$((\exists x)fx . fa) = fa \quad (fa \text{ entails } (\exists x)fx)$$

---

[39] Moore's summary notes: <... coordination between visual & physical.> (10:32)
[40] German for 'distinguished' or 'picked out'.

Now, at time of *Tractatus*, I should have asked. How <u>can</u> latter be true, unless $(\exists x)fx$ is a logical sum?

But <u>real</u> connection between this & logical sum is

$(\exists x)fx \,.\, fa \lor fb \lor fc \ldots = fa \lor fb \lor fc \ldots$

It's often useful to write $(\exists x)fx$, by $fa \lor fb \lor fc \ldots$, because this stresses analogy with a logical sum: <u>only</u> you must remember <u>it isn't one</u>.

If you fix your rules for the dots (don't use them as a sloppy sign), they are as good a sign as any other.   7:44

     Problem of generality.

Different meanings of $(\exists x)fx$

We've pointed out 2

(1) In this tune, the composer uses <u>all</u> the notes in the octave.[41]

In this picture, I see 3 of the primary colours.

Both are logical sums.

[42]So too: In <u>all</u> the circles in the square there are crosses, this <u>might</u> = logical product.[43]

Represent this by $(x)fx$

Then $\sim(x)fx$ has sense;

& also $(x)\sim fx$ has sense,

therefore $\sim(x)\sim fx$ has sense

But now suppose we want to say: There are circles in the square.

     $(\exists \xi)\phi\xi.$

But can you give meaning to: All things are circles in the square?[44]

Or to: Nothing is a circle in the square? Or to All circles are in the square?   7:45

---

[41] Moore added: <Logical product?>

[42] Moore crossed out '(2)' here and was probably correct to do so; he may have confused hearing the word 'too' with the number 2. However, the result of this deletion is that '(2)' doesn't actually appear in the text. The second topic has to do with those cases where we can't list the members of the domain, which is taken up shortly afterward.

[43] Moore added: <(How about "And there are no others?"?)>

[44] Moore later added: <Yes!>

"One of the patches on this wall is a circle"

has a good meaning, & so have all the different negatives, if we take "patch on the wall" = x

$\qquad$ (x)fx.

If "circular" is adjective, we can regard "patches" as substrates in which it inheres.

But what is the substrate for the property of being a patch?

"There are patches on the wall" has meaning; but "All patches are on the wall" has none.

Russell's notation won't work in cases where you thus can have: "There are 3 patches on the wall", but no proposition "All patches are on the wall."

"All things are on this island" is nonsense.

Russell & Frege translated ordinary language into a symbolism.

The whole muddle can be reduced to muddling up the questions: Which circle? what kind of circle?

7:46 One of them may make sense, where other makes none.⁴⁵

Which man was in the room? has a sense.

But which circle is in the square? may have no meaning.

"There are patches on the wall". "Which patches?" is meaningless.

Which? is answered by giving a proper name.

Take "There are 3 men on the island".

It may have meaning to ask: Which? or it may have no ~~sense~~ meaning.

If there could be ever so many doubles of me, we should perhaps give the name to the common character.

We give names, because there is nobody else exactly like.

You can make 2 shadows on a screen coincide, & separate; & then it has no sense to ask which is which.

---

⁴⁵ Moore's summary notes: <Russell & Frege were guilty of muddle between questions: Which circle? & What kind of circle? 2ⁿᵈ may make sense, where first makes none.> (10:88)

But in this case in which there can be no proper names, we could quite well have "There are 3 patches".

That we can ask "Which man", depends on a particular use of proper names; which is quite independent of their being men.   7:47

"There are men on the island" may make sense, where "Which man" has no sense.

There are in English general propositions

e.g. "There are 3 patches on the wall", "I met 2 people in the King's Parade", "Nobody came to my lecture".

Russell tried to reduce them all to the form: There is a thing such that: there being always in his head, a thing such that you could ask: Which thing?

In fact we need not have any name-notation – not merely need not have given one.

Pointing at a man will answer[46]

---

[46] Sentence left unfinished.

Lent Term, 1933

1a

One lecture omitted. Had bad cold.[1] 7:47v

---

[1] Since Moore writes 'One lecture omitted' on 7:47v, to the immediate left of the 20 January lecture, this suggests that the missing lecture is from the Lent term, since the left-hand page is usually used to comment on material on the right-hand page. This is precisely how Moore treats the missed lecture at the beginning of the next term. However it is possible that Moore is referring to the final lecture of the previous term.

1b

7:48   January 20.

Proof of mathematical theorem alters rules of grammar.

What does "hidden contradiction" mean?

If we have no method of looking for it, what we mean by "contradiction" is not defined.

"Looking for" means different things

(1) Essential thing about it in ordinary sense, – e.g. finding North Pole – is that it is <u>thinkable</u> that we could describe beforehand accurately & exactly all that happens in finding. But to give this description is <u>not</u> to have found the North Pole.

(2) But in mathematics, if you look for a proof, & have described it, you have <u>found</u> it.

<u>Finding construction of regular pentagon.</u>

What does finding it supply? In what sense can we look for it? What <u>is</u> looking for it – for construction by rule & compass?

How does teacher explain <u>idea</u> of regular pentagon?

Suppose he draws a circle & by good luck gets exactly right length of compasses to divide into 5.

7:49   He has then given an <u>idea</u> of regular pentagon.

But is it <u>what</u> he has asked them to construct?

No: so it is an idea they don't need at all.

Or else he might have <u>defined</u> it as figure with 5 sides all equal.

But if he had <u>given</u> them the construction?

That is quite different.

There is a regular <u>series of constructions</u> up to 6, each of which corresponds to a cardinal number.

And here it's clear (1) how each is correlated to its cardinal number (2) & that it's done by rule & compass only.

The teacher has given you (1) 5 & (2) the idea of construction by ruler & compasses.

To shew latter you have to shew one or make one.

But he has failed to give connection between this & the number 5: which can only be done by doing it.

What is "giving the series of constructions"? It may be: examples, + a law.

And suppose that of them pentagon was not one of the examples.

Compare this.

How did we learn to multiply?

We weren't taught all possible multiplications.

We were given examples, & a rule: & the rules did not contain examples not given.

All this throws a light on what's meant by: He gave you the series of all constructions.

One meaning is just: Gave you the law; & you mustn't suppose it means any more. That is, there's no reason for surprise that having given all in this sense, he hasn't given this one.

"We were taught to do any multiplication sum."

Then I suppose you were taught to do this one.

Yes.

Take "He has given you all your garments".

Where to go through them all has a sense.

And contrast: a proposition about all numbers, one among them, where to go through them all has no sense.

When we hear "all", we naturally think (1) that there is sense in saying "go through them all" & (2) but that sometimes owing to human weakness we can't.

It's difficult to realise that with all numbers, it makes no sense to go through them all.

We are, more than we think, influenced by symbolism we are used to: e.g. 10 means a round number, because we have decimal system.

Now he may have given you <u>all</u> constructions, & yet no means of finding construction of pentagon.

Suppose we are to look for a cardinal number with a particular property, e.g. that of being next prime number after 7.

And the teacher has given us what is meant by <u>next</u>, & also what's meant by <u>prime</u>.

Suppose he'd given you the rule: prime is always between a & factorial a.

7:52   He <u>seems</u> to have given you a description, like all the people in Cambridge with grey flannel trousers: i.e. one thinks as if there were 2 series, the actual people & the descriptions of them.

But $1 + 1$ is <u>not</u> a description, in the sense that we can enumerate the things which it describes.

E.g. "<u>the</u> cardinal numbers". Does this mean those which have been written down? If <u>not</u>, it means the law, & there is <u>no</u> infinite extension as described.

Suppose you give series of consecutive intervals in which you can find prime numbers.

Suppose I'd given 2 descriptions common & peculiar to those in this room. Then whichever description you give <u>finding</u> <u>which</u> has the blue hat, is the same.

Teacher has <u>not</u> defined problem by telling you what a pentagon is, & what construction by rule & compasses is.

And the series of constructions is <u>not</u> a law <u>within</u> which you can find it. Though there may be <u>another</u> within which you can.

2a

January 23, 1933.   7:53

Last lecture turned on difference between <u>series</u> as law & <u>series</u> as extension.

E.g. series of constructions with ruler & compasses, & series of cardinal numbers.

Series of cardinal numbers is not <u>very long</u>: all that is true is that any length can be generated by that law.

Why are we tempted to think of it as <u>very long</u>? What tempts us to do so will be our justification for doing so.

In some ways grammar of a huge number & grammar of "infinite" are <u>similar</u>.

And this "similar" brings in the mistake; for it is sense in which grammar of complex & cardinal numbers are similar: but this is not like "these 2 people are similar": there is a <u>radical, categorial</u> difference – they are not <u>comparable</u>.

Try to bring this out.

We know prime numbers, but don't know the <u>law of their distribution</u>: but there must be such a law, though not yet <u>known</u>.   7:54

This is a natural thing to say: it suggests that it's through our clumsiness that we don't know the law.

The question: "What is the distribution of prime numbers?" seems clear, only the answer not known: it seems here's a problem which we can try to answer.

Now I said a mathematical <u>discovery</u> changes the game, in a sense in which working out a multiplication sum doesn't.

We are mistaken, because we are thinking of distributions of primes among a finite series: we have no idea as to what could be meant by distribution of primes in an infinite series.

In writing down 1, 2, 3 <u>& so on</u> we are <u>not</u> giving a <u>law</u>.

Distribution of odd & even is given by a law.

What do you mean by <u>distribution</u>?

He would /both (1)/ give examples, e.g. by distributions
(1)   1 + 1 + 1
(2)   + 1 1 + 1
(3)   1 + 1 + 1

Distribution of crosses is different in (1) & (2), same in (1) & (3).

7:55 (2) in case of infinite series (e.g. even numbers), he would give (a)² a formula or law, & then (b) giving a finite bit.

1 <u>2</u> 3 <u>4</u> 5 <u>6</u> ...

Now if you'd <u>understood</u>, you'd be able to answer: "What's the <u>next</u> even number?"

Now about distribution of primes

1, <u>2</u>, <u>3</u>, 4, <u>5</u>, 6, <u>7</u>, ...

(Ursell says 1 is not called prime.)

<u>This</u> could not tell him whether there are infinite number of primes or not.

Consider question: <u>Is</u> there another prime, following 7? This <u>seems</u> clear; but what is your method of <u>answering</u>? You think of it as <u>similar</u> to: "Is there a prime between these 2, "m & n""; but it isn't.

Do we feel sure we <u>should</u> – requiring an answer to the question?

Ursell says we do.

Now:

> Consider regular pentagon.
>
> Everybody knows <u>in a sense</u> what that means: can tell that so & so isn't.

7:56 But if our test was measuring by means of a machine which changed its distances that might be more like ⌐⎯⎯⌐ than ◁.

Suppose we define a construction, we shall be glad to admit that it is of regular pentagon if it leads to a figure so & so, rather than so & so: but <u>only</u> if sides are of <u>same</u> length.

---

² Here we follow Moore's summary notes. There is a '(1)' at this point in the lecture notes, but there is no subsequent '(2)'; (10:35) replaces the (1) by an '(a)' and then puts a missing '(b)' in front of 'a finite bit'.

Cf. trisecting of angle.

If we prove that this is impossible, we change his idea of what is meant by trisecting.

Yet we should recognise that what has been proved impossible is the very thing we are trying to do: because we are willingly led in this case to identify 2 different things.

Compare.

Why do you call what I'm doing "philosophy"? Is it the same thing as Plato or Berkeley did?

I should say "No": but some of you may be willingly led to say "That's what I really wanted."

E.g. Metaphysics (in Whitehead) seems like a kind of science; & yet there is no appeal to experience.

And then I say "You ought to clarify ideas". You may feel that this takes the place of the other, though the other is really a different thing. 7:57

Suppose a man has spent his life trying to trisect an angle with rule and compasses.

~~You ask him what it means to trisect?~~

He would say: If you understand both what's meant by trisecting; & what's meant by bisecting by rule & compasses; you must understand trisecting by rule & compasses.

I say: No. Can you imagine trisecting by rule & compasses?

He would have to say: There's a gap in my imagination.

And there would be no such meaning gap in his imagination of division into 8.[3]

Or rather:

Let's suppose he can imagine it. And gives us circles & actual trisection.

We should then tell him: This is wrong: it isn't a construction at all.

But we may not be able to make him admit this. 7:58

---

[3] Moore's summary notes: <But you can't imagine "trisecting by rule & compasses". There's a gap in your imagination which there isn't in imagining dividing into 8 equal angles.> (10:90)

Skinner says: Couldn't we ask him: How do you prove it?

We should have to ask, how do you know what is a proof?

We can answer:

You've explained what you mean by "proof"; but make it more exact, by giving a series of proofs. He gives the series. But then we still don't understand what's meant by proving this is a trisection.

Suppose you point to 7 chairs, & say they are chairs; & then a person asks you whether another is a chair. You would call him a fool.

But there was nothing in what I did to shew it was a chair; whereas there was in case of multiplication business.

Now, if I ask what a proof is, you shew me different proofs; & this explanation will explain what would be meant by giving a proof of some things, but not of others.

Suppose I was to say: He made the sort of movements, a man makes in trisecting an angle with rule and compasses. You would have to say I was talking nonsense.

7:59 What is meant by saying of anyone A, when you give him a proof, that he recognises it as a proof?

How can he see that it agrees with his previous idea of a proof?

There are many ways of seeing that it does.

It may agree in many different ways.

The agreement of the special case with the general explanation, means different things in different cases.

We have a wrong view as to this.

We have to consider relation between explanation given & result wanted (without bothering whether a person would be a fool, if with that explanation he can't get the result).

He might take rule expressed by first 3 rows, that what last row said is that you must take number of steps having next prime number to last.

So an explanation of "proof" will be <u>inexact</u>.

Whereas explanation of cardinal number can be <u>exactly</u> given by a law.

E.g. an explanation of "number", by saying: Oh, it is cardinal numbers, rationals etc.; would be called inexact.

Suppose you were beginning mathematics; & we had a few odd proofs, e.g. one that bisection can be done by rule & compasses, one about numbers & so: anybody might fail to see what was meant by a proof.

There's a great difference between <u>following</u> one of Euclid's proofs, & <u>inventing</u> it.

This is all connected with: How far is what we're engaged on entirely futile?

It's futile, unless it puts right definite errors.

Does Wittgenstein pretend to put things on a different basis, or give a complete analysis of things? so as not only to give rules about <u>some</u> words, but to give rules about "rule", & so <u>ad infinitum</u>?[4]

With a Time-Table, if a man asks, how did you know train was 6.40? you may point out to him. But he may ask: Why did you interpret this way rather than another?

Now because you <u>can</u>, without end, give an explanation of each explanation, it doesn't follow that the first isn't an explanation.

It is: if it's needed, it is. All explanations are futile, but what are needed.

In the case of a particular muddle, I can draw attention to a distinction – give you a particular rule: & that is all I need do, & is worth doing.

Look at the difference between <u>explanation</u> by means of a series & otherwise.

Don't ignore difference between construction of pentagon, & multiplication.

You tend to make mistake of thinking of construction by rule & compasses as an <u>extension</u>, whereas what is given is only the <u>rule</u>.

These distinctions become all-important, only where all-important muddles are cleared by them.

There are a <u>few big</u> blunders made by philosophers of mathematics; whereas I seem to give ever so many distinctions, which nobody confuses.

---

[4] Moore's summary notes: <I don't pretend to give a complete analysis of things, nor to do more than give rules about <u>some</u> words.> (10:36)

2b

7:62   January 27, 1933.

Good way of making clear about construction of pentagon: –

How can we look for trisection of angle by rule & compasses if there <u>is</u> no such thing?

At first sight, it looks as if the answer is: Just as one can look for a unicorn, though there is none.

But, no.

For compare: (1)⁵ There is an animal with a regular pentagon on its forehead which is exactly like "There is a unicorn".

(2) There is an animal with construction shewing trisection of angle on its forehead.

These are not same: (2) = can't be an animal with this = (2) is nonsense.

(2) is like saying: There is an animal with 3 horns & at the same time only 1.

In (2) there is no description of an animal at all.

<u>Now</u>

If we give man construction of regular pentagon we give him new idea of what we mean by regular pentagon.

I take <u>explanation</u> of a word as shewing what a man understands by it.

7:63   E.g. idea of 1 /+1/ gives idea of cardinal number.

<u>How</u> could I explain "regular pentagon", without construction?

We could give series of <u>figures</u> themselves, which don't contain construction.

We could give /2 series of normal regular polygons/ series of constructions.

(1) triangle, hexagon etc.

(2) square, octagon etc..

---

[5] Here we follow Moore's summary notes. Moore retroactively numbers this sentence as '(1)', and the following sentence as '(2)', thus clarifying the references to '(2)' in the discussion that follows (10:36).

Does this give construction of regular pentagon?

You can say: You've got to do something <u>analogous</u> to them.

But "analogous" here means something quite different from construction 16-sided polygon analogously to octagon.

But how is it that when we're shewn the construction, we say: That's what we were looking for.

Now Ursell said: We know what we mean by a Euclidean proof.

What we <u>do</u> know is what it looks like.

But this isn't a concept which we should use in Mathematics.

Euclidean proof = proof with rule & compasses.

Let us now restrict its meaning by definition enormously more.

Suppose there was a people which had only one construction – namely bisection.

A geometry which <u>only</u> allows this is just as good as one which allows more.

E.g. you could have an arithmetic of the odd numbers, which is a closed system, not essentially a part of a larger system.

You e.g. might have an instrument that allowed you to bisect & nothing more.

Then in <u>this</u> geometry, the trisection of straight line is <u>impossible</u>.

However it isn't <u>clear</u> what's meant by Euclidean proof: it may be quite difficult to see whether a given figure <u>is</u> a construction in that geometry or not.

~~Suppose now I introduce a construction which does allow trisection.~~

Consider how you would <u>explain</u> to a person who had learnt only this, that you wanted him to trisect angles.

You might give several different ideas of trisection.

Suppose I shewed him bisection, quadri-section etc., & then said: you've got to trisect <u>analogously</u>.

He would find that "analogously" here meant nothing.

Compare a person who discovers ultra-violet rays; with a person who discovers a new proof.

He changes our idea of colour, in a way in which we're all ready to go!

A fallacy constantly occurring in philosophy of science, is not seeing where you can & can't say "and so on" in same sense.

Thus you can't go on with series of colours in rainbow <u>in same way</u>.

So you can't get 4th dimension, by going on <u>in same way</u> as you got 3rd.

E.g. define numbers by regular figures beginning with equilateral triangle & proceeding by bisection:

i.e. 3, 6, 12 & so on.

In <u>this</u> system there is no 5; in same sense as among cardinals there is no ½.

In <u>this</u> arithmetic, you can't tell anybody to produce 5.

7:66 You might found a system on combinations:

a b   a b c
1
3
6

In this system there is no 5: hence a person who asks must be asking in cardinal arithmetic.

Is 5 a combination number? is <u>not</u> a sum in combination arithmetic.

In the bisection geometry, the question: Is there trisection of a line? leads outside our system.

Chess Problem.

If a man finds that he can force a mate from a certain position, has he altered game of chess?

He would have found a rule which founder hadn't provided.

You might have rule that move is to be decided by throw of a dice.

7:67 We should say: We know that this position leads to a forced mate.

Suppose you then say: There's no hope for you!

He may say: Why?

You might then (1) shew him, i.e. finish the game, or (2) refer to a proof, which you remember, which may be in a drawer.[6]

---

[6] Moore's summary notes: <A man wouldn't have altered game by finding that from a certain position he can force a mate; but game would be altered by rule that move is to be

If you remember certain scratches on piece of paper that isn't remembering that $25 \times 25 = 625$.[7]

One way of finding that a mate can be forced is to do it. But there's another.

There might be a general rule for shewing that it's possible to force a mate in less than 50 moves.

This would be a rule not belonging to geometry invented by founder of chess.

What proves I <u>could</u> mate you with king & queen?

Is it the same game

(1) to play to mate

(2) to play to a certain point, & then refer to a game played yesterday. 7:68

> settled by throw of die. In case (1) we should say: we know that this position leads to forced mate; & if man says "Why?" we may either (1) finish game (2) refer to proof in a drawer.> (10:92)

[7] The notes incorrectly have '725' as the product, rather than '625'.

3a

7:69   January 30.

It's useful to simplify problem like: "Angle can't be trisected by rule & compasses", by considering geometry which has for only construction bisection of a line.

Such a geometry is not incomplete: not a part of Euclidean.

In such a geometry, you <u>couldn't</u> trisect a line.

We have talked as to how an arithmetical /vague/ <u>task</u> can be explained.

In order to explain "Construct regular pentagon" we should have to give analogies.

You would give series – but they would never reach the point we wanted.

In a sense <u>result</u> wanted is clear, but <u>means of getting at</u> it is not:

but in another <u>result</u> isn't clear: for "constructed pentagon" is <u>not</u> the same as "measured pentagon". That same figure will be both, depends on physics.

We're misled by similarity between constructed & measured.

But the constructed <u>might</u> look quite different: e.g. if we look at it in some queer mirror which distorts it all.

7:70 Why we <u>call</u> the construction that of pentagon, is because of properties of our compasses etc. – physical properties.

Cf. trisection in a geometry (where bisection only construction)[8]

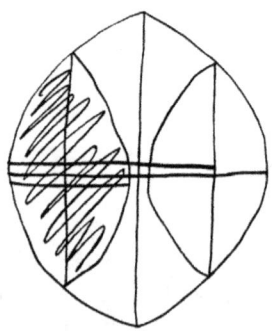

[8] For further discussion of this example, see *The Big Typescript* (Wittgenstein 2005), §124, 'The Trisection of an Angle'.

There's an analogy between shaded & whole.

There's no analogy between part of figure corresponding to middle line & whole figure.

Imagine series of bisection, quadrisection, 8-section … you can <u>see</u> they form a series.

Look at construction, not as a result, but as one picture.

Result of trisection might look like ⊢———⊣ or ⊢—⊣—⊣.

We <u>seem</u> to determine what construction we're asking for by <u>result</u>.

The real result is sort of end-surface of the proper construction.

An algebraic proof <u>is</u> a geometrical construction.

We're given 1, ½, ¼   7:71

And the meaning ½, ¼ = ¾

But we've <u>not</u> given him 3 in denominator.

We can't point out the result of a construction, without the construction; since such a thing as ⊢—⊣—⊣ is only <u>externally</u> related to it by our physics.

<u>Possibility of a hidden contradiction.</u>

In a peculiar way our grammatical rules are arbitrary.

Suppose someone says: Surely those of negation aren't! You couldn't have "~~p = ~p"!

Then, I should say: What do you mean by negation? Part of the rule that gives meaning to negation is not (not p) = p.

Rule is not arbitrary = it's responsible to the meaning = it's responsible to the rules.

Meaning is not something from which rules follow.

Then it is said: Rules mustn't contradict – are so far not arbitrary.

I should say: This means that if they contradicted, they wouldn't be rules.   7:72

Frege said: If we didn't use law of identity, it would confuse our thinking.

Now in a set of rules we have <u>open</u> contradiction, if ~~one~~ says p, & another ~p.

Now a hidden contradiction in such a set might be such as: rules which contain q & $\sim^n$q,⁹ where n was such that you couldn't easily see whether it's odd or even: here it would be a contradiction if n was odd, not if it was even.

But there must be a way of finding whether it is a contradiction or not.

What applies to hidden contradiction, applies to hidden dependence: when you say set of axioms seem mutually independent.

If we have no <u>way</u> of finding contradiction, we have not yet fixed what contradiction <u>means</u>.

E.g. it is said: If ever you got to "a $\neq$ a" it would upset everything.

7:73   I know certain algebraic constructions which <u>yield</u> this: but what's meant by <u>yield</u>? Not simply that they lead to this meaningless sign.

Grammar of p, ~p depends on what we are allowed to do with them.

What idea have I given you of <u>p</u>?

I can only give examples; & they aren't examples, if there's a hidden contradiction in them.

Suppose we fix rules of transformation, & give a series in which every possible transformation comes somewhere.

Now if series was finite, we have means of finding whether any one is contradictory.

But if infinite, the <u>law</u> ~~says that it can't come~~ & examples don't contain a series: & we think we might hit on one.

But "all transformations are contained in this series", means this law is what I mean by transformation.

Suppose in first 100 members you find a contradiction: this shews it had sense to ask.¹⁰

Are there 5 consecutive 7's in development of π? The calculus contains no means of deciding this.

7:74   Our concept of π is a law of construction, & this has no connection with being 5 consecutive 7's.

---

⁹ '$\sim^n$q' represents the result of prefixing 'q' with n instances of '~'.
¹⁰ Moore's summary notes: <If you find a contradiction in first 100 numbers, that shews it has sense to ask if there is one.> (10:93)

Now I say: (1) It is sense to say: There are 5 consecutive 7's in first 1000 digits.

(2) It makes no sense to say: There are somewhere in the development.

It means: (P) There are in first 1000 → (Q) There are somewhere.

But what is the explanation of Q?

Q ≠ there are in first 1000

Q ≠ there are either in first 1000, or 999, or 998 etc.

You suggest:

Q = either in first 1000 or 1001 or ...

You can't say: "Of course it makes sense, to say somewhere, because it follows from: there are in first 1000".[11]

What, then, of a proof that there are, but gives no idea where?

That proves that "there are" here means something quite different.[12]

We confuse: What can we do; with what can the calculus do.

---

[11] Moore later added: <Why not? (Because it's compatible with these not being in any you give? or because you might have a proof that doesn't prove where?)>. Moore's summary notes: <That "There are somewhere" follows from "There are in first 1000", does not entitle us to say that "There are somewhere" has sense.> (10:38)

[12] Moore's summary notes: <If you could have a proof of Q which gives no idea where, that would prove that "there are" means something quite different in Q from what it does in P.> (10:93)

3b

7:75   February 3 / 1933.

In an important sense, if you haven't fixed a method for finding a contradiction, you haven't fixed the meaning of "contradiction".

You think you have because you've specified sort of result you would be looking for, if you looked for one: but in fact contradiction would be a construction of which result would be as it were end-surface.

All big mathematical problems are of nature: Are there 5 consecutive 7's in development of π?

They are therefore quite different from multiplication sums, & not comparable in respect of difficulty; as are e.g. 2 gymnastic feats.

E.g. take: Prove that these laws lead to no contradiction.

Now suppose I read in news that a man has solved one of these problems: should I understand what was meant or not? There are many different cases:

E.g. (1) A man has found 5 7's somewhere in development of π.

(2) Mr Smith has proved that there are 5 7's somewhere in development of π.

"There are 5 7's somewhere" is compatible with there being none in any series you give me.

7:76   Now, if asked, Do you understand notion in *Times*?[13] You're inclined to say: Yes.

Then ask: Explain. And you might say: Perhaps in this series; perhaps in that; & so on.

Suppose you had paper-money, with equations on it which you can't solve but bank-clerk can, then you wouldn't know whether you could buy anything with it or not.

If you have a dog on a line, that gives him a restricted freedom.

---

[13] I.e. in *The Times* newspaper. Moore's summary notes: <Now if asked: Do you understand statement that a man has found there are? you're inclined to say: Yes.> (10:38)

But suppose you had an infinite line; i.e. you had a bit of string fastened to your hand, & another fastened to a dog. Then dog is quite free.

Now it is like this with a proposition & its verification.

If you say p is true, if & only if q, you are restricting reality, it may be rather narrowly.

Now a tautology in this sense gives reality infinite freedom.

Now "There are 5 7's somewhere" in one way gives no restriction; but "it has whatever use its grammar allows", means a restriction.

Now, as a rule of a game, "Write down a development of π" has a clear sense.

Now that "There are 5 7's in development" is compatible with there not being in any you can give, gives this a very curious grammar: but you oughtn't to say: It has no sense.

In the sense we have given, the only criterion for truth of "There are 5 7's" is "There are in the digits up to 10,000" or so on: & each different criterion makes it a different proposition.

If you measure with a yard rod that will contract to any extent, but not expand beyond a certain, then your result can only be of form: This can't be more than 5 yards. And it's not natural to call this measurement.

(2). Suppose you ask: What would the proof be like? You couldn't say.

Suppose the news was "Mr. Smith opened a passage from one room to another", then you could imagine many ways in which it might have been done.

"We know that a sequence has a limit, though we don't know what it is". I should say: Shew me your proof; I can then understand what it proves, & therefore what you mean.

What existence means depends on what sort of proof you have.

Result of a proof is not isolated, but is end-surface of it.

Consider: Proofs of immortality of soul.

This is one of cases where a word is used in two entirely different senses without people realising it.

This question has meant a lot to many people, & these the greatest. Hence not mere bosh.[14]

---

[14] Moore's summary notes: <"Immortality of soul" has meant a lot to many great people, & is therefore not a mere mistake.> (10:94)

But yet, when you hear of proofs of it, something will smile inside you.

Now one might think: These people have just made a scientific mistake.

But a mere mistake never means so much to anyone.

This question, & many others, have always been treated in 2 ways, a hot, & a cold: & that when treated cold, an absurdity results, does not prove that when hot they're absurd.

Once I was woken from profound sleep by a severe cramp, & for 2 hours I felt as if my soul had not quite come back. I was in great state of excitement.

The feeling that there was something not quite coincident with me, was irresistible to me; though I don't habitually think in terms of body & soul, etc..

Or, in case of person dying, one feels that he has gone very far away.

7:79   Suppose you have developed a theory: & talked about measuring distance between soul & body, there bosh would begin.

Certain analogies may be irresistible, & yet only hold in a very restricted field.

Read Oliver Lodge[15], you'll find pseudo-experiments, & bosh – false scientific statements.

But, I read in Kierkegaard, about duty, that his father when he was a boy, gave him a task to do, & he felt that even death could not rid him of the duty: & then he said: this was a proof of immortality.[16]

This struck me as giving one meaning of immortality which made it important.

That ~~my~~ Ursell's voice should be heard after death would be a very extraordinary phenomenon; but about the last theory I should adopt is that he was still there: but, whatever conclusion I draw, what significance would it have? I should say: I wish you were dead: you seem to be occupied with very trivial things.

---

[15] See Lodge 1930, 10–11, and 1929, 35–6.

[16] Judge William tells this story of his childhood in Kierkegaard's *Either/Or*. See Kierkegaard 1987, 266–70. Wittgenstein learned Danish in order to be able to read Kierkegaard and described Kierkegaard as 'by far the most profound thinker' of the nineteenth century (see Lee 1979, 218, in Flowers 1999, 2 195; 2016, 2 483, and Drury 1984a, 87, in Flowers 1999, 3 180; 2016, 2 767).

Now: If you want to know what a proof proves, look at the proof: shews that Lodge & Kierkegaard don't mean the same by "immortality of soul".

This has to do with everything that has been said about Ethics. 7:80

That we use "good", "ought", "right" is the case.

But who, except a philosopher, who ever talked about a best possible universe?

So we do use "better".

But if we go on to use "best" or to talk about <u>measuring</u>, this is only rubbish.

It has often happened that a common word is taken up by some sort of science, & then talk of meaning.[17]

People think that then science means the same, only more exact. But this is a mistake. E.g. This gives more light than that.

So with probability: We constantly talk of one thing being more likely than another.

Then there is another sense, where you can measure it.

And people then think that when we say: It's extremely unlikely an eagle will come in here: they think this must be <u>capable</u> of being measured: which is bosh.[18]

We all know that we prefer one pleasure to another, or will sacrifice a certain amount for a pleasure.

Then people say: therefore a pleasure-pain calculus is possible. 7:81

A butcher weighs meat, in order to settle how much to charge, & does so only because there's a certain regularity in the result.

Thus it would only be worth while to make pleasure-pain calculus, if there were a regularity, which there isn't.

---

[17] This word in the text is unclear; Moore later wrote 'measuring?', but the original word looks more like the way he usually writes 'meaning'. On the other hand, 'measuring' fits better with the subsequent discussion.

[18] Moore's summary notes: <A common word is often taken up by a science & then people think it means the same in the science, only is more exact. E.g. we constantly talk of one thing being more probable than another, & since there is another sense of "probable" in which it can be measured, people think that it must be <u>possible</u> to measure how unlikely it is that an eagle should come into this room now.> (10:39)

There's a <u>very</u> dangerous propensity to think that where we can say "more" or "less", there we might measure.

There are many cases where a use, which may seem in accordance with grammar, is absurd.

E.g. Austrian general's: "I will think of you in next world, <u>if possible</u>".

This makes it ridiculous, because it shews he's ~~trying to talk~~ thinking he's talking scientifically.

4a

February 6.

Part of point of "hidden contradiction" discussion was to make it possible to talk about "atomic" propositions, as opposed to "molecular" & "general".

<u>Distinction</u>. You might say it was impossible.

There <u>are</u> propositions containing "and", "or", "not"; & idea is that they consist of others <u>not</u> containing them; & these are atomic.

<u>First objection</u>. That p can be written "$\sim\sim p$", or "$p \cdot p$".

This is easily answered: you say that by "molecular" you mean occurrences of "and" & "not", where it cannot be eliminated, as in this it can.

2nd objection. Take "It's raining, & it is cold".

Is it possible that analysis may shew that after all "it's raining" is a logical product? = that there is a "hidden logical constant".

This could be put: Is there a method of analysis? If so, apply it, & we shall see.

Suppose we say of 25×25: Perhaps there's a hidden 6 in it. We have a method here of finding whether there is or is not.

Now in <u>some</u> cases we may have a method of analysing a proposition: e.g. if we had defined "rotten weather" = "cold & damp"; then "it's rotten weather" would be a logical product; & our method of analysis might be to look up in the table of definitions.

Get clear as to <u>analysis</u> of a notion or concept –

(1) It's quite clear that we are free to fix grammar of a word as we please.

But this doesn't answer the question: Is the word <u>actually used</u> according to these rules.

Suppose I've laid down a notation, for e.g. defining "mental" or "mind".

If we have a table of such, we can analyse by substituting out of the table. This would be like analysing a proposition in *Principia Mathematica*, by means of a rule which will shew whether it's a tautology or not. We may want to see what a proposition looks like, when the definition is substituted.

E.g. we might "analyse": S walked $\sqrt{47}$ miles an hour; by finding square root of 47.

This is analysing by using a previous definition. In this sense we move inside a calculus.

7:84 (2) But <u>analysis</u>, where it means giving a grammar that corresponds to people's usage, is <u>something quite different</u>.

Here there may be no exactness; you can give something similar.

We are <u>taught</u> the use of words; & the explanations given to us of any word were probably all slightly different.

It is one thing to <u>draw</u> an outline; & another thing to portray another thing by means of an <u>outline</u>.

Our words haven't an outline, & therefore it's not a weakness that we can't draw an exact outline.

This applies to "table" etc..

Now what's meant by "hidden logical constant"?

In sense (1) nothing is hidden, but what I have hidden: i.e. there's a method of finding.

In sense (2) we have a quite different question, which doesn't belong to logic.

Hence we can say: what looks "atomic" <u>is</u> "atomic."

If you look at Russell & at *Tractatus*, you may notice something very queer – i.e. lack of examples.

7:85 They talk of "individuals" & "atomic propositions", but give no examples. Both of us, in different ways, push question of examples on one side.

Now there's <u>something wrong</u> here: but it's very difficult to say why. I thought at first I'd solved the problems.

I & Russell went wrong in different ways.

Russell & Ramsey thought that, in some way or other, you could prepare your logic for possible existence of certain notations.

E.g. Russell in *Principia Mathematica* talked of "functions" & "propositions"; & meant by "propositions" what we do mean; & thought that in talking of foundations of Mathematics he had to arrange for application of arithmetic.

Now arithmetic applies to functions: Smith comes in, 2 come in, 3 come in.

Now either (1) it doesn't matter a hang what it applies to, & mathematics is always so taught.

I.e. pure mathematics doesn't need application.

or (2) it does need it, as Russell & Frege thought. I.e. they thought you can't talk of 3 independently of what it applies to; & you need to begin by classifying your functions.

Frege (roughly) said a number is a property of a property e.g. being a man in this room has property 6. Russell does the same.

If so, we seem to need some classification of functions.

Why?

(1) "man in this room" & "flowers in Fellows' garden" were functions to which same calculus applied. So Russell didn't need to talk of each separately; but of types of functions.

Now right way to teach arithmetic is by abacus: this gives us a calculus; & we can apply it afterwards.

It's not true that we must begin by *Principia Mathematica*.

Calculus of propositions & functions, is not needed; before we give calculus of numerals.

Suppose we've made a hierarchy of types of functions: and I ask for examples:

Of 2-termed he will give me "love".

Of 3-termed he will give me "jealousy".

But if I ask him: Is there 37-termed? he could not give one, but would say he has prepared a notation for them.

Now were the 3-termed relations bound up with the examples? Were the examples essential?

Could we construct logic without the world?

Can we prepare a logical structure in advance; as we prepare tea in advance?

In latter case I'm preparing for something to be the case, which may not be the case.

But in former I'm preparing for: what?

If I write R(x,y,z,w) can I say <u>what</u> I'm expecting? I couldn't describe it, because description would have to contain a 4-term relation.

What does a man find, when he finds an example of a 2-termed relation? E.g. "A loves B".

I've not found a fact: only a <u>proposition</u>, which is a case.

Now when I introduce "a R b" you are inclined to think this is empty, & that an example gives it content.

But I <u>don't</u> discover something to which this <u>applies</u>.

7:88   Could you find a two-term relation in a new country?

No: because you <u>could</u> have described beforehand, whatever you found.

"In this country, they have a way of discussing in which 5 people stand in the angles of a regular pentagon."

Finding an example does <u>not</u> consist in discovering a phenomenon.

Thus "a R b" isn't first empty, & then meaning given to it.

What we discover is <u>only</u> that we have <u>in our language</u> a word which obeys certain rules; but if there hadn't been we could have introduced one.

Discovering a game is quite different from discovering a fact.

I say in *Tractatus* that you can't say anything about structure of atomic propositions. my idea being the wrong one, that <u>logical analysis</u> would reveal what it would reveal. I only referred to prophecy, but otherwise had same idea as Russell.

I should have said "7-term relation" has no meaning, except in connection with an example.

7:89   My idea was: Suppose this book contains all my language. I can't increase the vocabulary, by adding new words. Suppose I take all the relation terms, & then analyse them, I should find e.g. that "love" has "a R b" structure, jealousy has "R(a,b,c)" etc.: but that I might or might not find R(x,y,z,w).

I thought we <u>might</u> find e.g. that <u>all</u> relations are 4-termed & that then we couldn't <u>talk</u> of 2-termed.

Suppose you talk of "molecular logic" & "atomic logic".

Now I said: "molecular logic" forms a system, independent of experience, which I can just write down. But "atomic logic" <u>may</u> shew you that "2-term relation" has a meaning, but "4-term" none.

Suppose English grammar = grammar which no-one could write except a person who had completely analysed our language. And then ask: Will this grammar contain 2-term relation? The answer must be: wait till analysis is complete. (This is what I said.)

Russell & I agreed in waiting for analysis; but I said we can't tell what analysis will yield; but Russell said it must yield this or that.

I was right in one way; Russell in another.

I was right, in thinking you can't prepare for a word to have meaning.

Russell & I both were unclear about "analysis", thinking that further work at logic would shew us the elements.

I was right in thinking there can't be hypotheses in logic: you can't say: "If a word had meaning", (when it hasn't). You can't construct an ideal Logic: one not "covered" by meaning.

I thought Russell had no right to say that the result of analysis would be 2 term, 3 term relations etc..

It's quite right to say "Socrates is a man" is subject-predicate, "Socrates loved Plato" is 2-term & so on.

I was wrong in supposing that it had any sense to talk of result of final analysis.

Whereas I did say: We don't know what the result of it will be.

He & I both took our notion of "analysis" from what he & Frege had done – e.g. analysis of cardinal numbers; or of $\supset$ in terms of $\vee$ & $\sim$.

What then has become of "atomic" or "elementary" propositions? I say those which on the face of them don't contain "and" or "or". Not those which wouldn't, when we had revealed hidden constants.

Russell's view of structure of propositions was far too simple. Grammar of different kinds of words is much more different than you would expect.

We can't help being misled by appearance of our language. Words are made of 26 letters & look much alike.

If you're in cab of an engine, you see lots of handles, which have roughly same shape – determined by size & shape of human hand. But what you do with them differs immensely.

So what we do with our words in different cases has no similarity at all.

Suppose a man said: There are 3 kinds of handles (1) wheels (2) ⌒ (3) ～. I said this is a bad classification because all 3 can be used in same way.

Thus classifying into substantives, adjectives & verbs is like this: though they may generally differ in use.

4b

February 10 (Friday).

Main point about "atomic propositions" is that they're not result of some analysis which has yet to be made: we use them, if at all, to mean propositions which don't, on the face, contain "and" "or" etc., or else don't contain by some exact definition that has been given.

One mistake I made was this: That you could enumerate entities in the world, & therefore all possible atomic propositions: I thought you could; though I couldn't.

Note vagueness of "proposition".

E.g. (1) define "proposition" as symbol one could make oneself understood by: but then what is it to make yourself understood? When you teach a child a language, part of what you do is to teach him a language-game: e.g. names of colours, or "up", "down", right", "left".

But where does use of a proposition start?

You train a child as you train a dog: but, if that is all, would you say the child understands?

I think you'd have to say: Don't know.

Suppose you'd taught child to touch objects, when you said "red", "yellow", "blue" etc..

Would you say, you'd taught the child to understand sentences?

Suppose we propose to talk of "propositions", only when use of truth-functions comes in: e.g. "not red", "but blue", "red & blue".

(1) There is an ambiguity in use of "language" & "proposition"; which of course you can remove by making definitions: e.g. by saying "proposition" is to be used only when truth-functions come in.

This isn't a bad way: but though you can draw a line round a concept, you can't pretend that it exactly represents the concept.

(2) The language-game is not fundamentally different from use of propositions as defined. You might think they only prepare for language: & he knows language only when some sudden waking up occurs, which might be called "understanding". There is no fundamental difference when "not" etc. are understood.

Looking at language-games is awfully helpful to understand <u>language</u> & <u>logic</u>.

There can be many games: e.g. (1) nothing but orders (2) nothing but questions & answers (3) nothing but questions & Yes or No. And each will in a sense be <u>complete</u>: nothing is lacking, any more than if I walk & don't jump.

What happens to "truth" & "falsehood", if we look at it from point of view of language-game?

There's a pitfall here.

Suppose I say "The book, please", & you bring one; & you want to draw a distinction between this & what happens to the child, you would say the man knows it means "Bring me the book", but the child doesn't.

But is "bring me the book" any more complete?

Of course, "The book" is <u>not</u> what we call a sentence. We might call it an "elliptical" sentence; but <u>this</u> misleads us into thinking that something <u>more</u> must be in man's mind: that a language which says "he healthy", is missing something.

The translation into a complete sentence is not <u>essential</u> to understanding, though it would be essential (necessary) to a man who had only learnt them.

What happens to "<u>truth</u>" & "<u>falsehood</u>" or "agreement with reality" or "disagreement"?

In the "up" "down" game, neither word "true" nor any equivalent comes in, nor need come in.

Suppose the game is question: "How many chairs?"

Here "true" <u>may</u> come in, since the child may be taught to say "Three chairs agrees with reality".

(3) Another kind of game is one in which <u>false</u> propositions could come in. E.g. suppose we'd taught child to shout red, green or yellow, as signal exposes light: & then he shouted "red" when green came. We should say it had <u>not</u> played the game, in sense in which a move in chess, against the rules, is not playing the game. But when we make a <u>mistake</u>, we are not going against the rules.[19]

---

[19] Moore's summary notes: <We should say he's not playing the game, just as if in chess he made knight's move with pawn. But when we <u>make a mistake</u>, we <u>are</u> playing the game.> (10:96)

It has been said: Words, except in propositions, have no meaning. This is true or false, as you understand it.

In language-game it has meaning, by itself; & may in our ordinary language, if we've provided one.

The meaning of "red" in language-game, is different from what it is in "I like his red blazer" (because latter isn't a mere order): different rules apply. But yet there's something in common; which is shewn by fact that latter game, may be derived from old one. What's in common is mostly of this sort. Suppose before children were taught chess, they were taught a simpler game something like it – but yet such that no move in old game was retained in new.

Suppose we define proposition by use of truth-functions; it's still possible to play many entirely different games: e.g. arithmetic, & propositions which describe sense experience.

"Twice 2 are not 5" is a proposition, if you're going to define by use of truth-functions; but that doesn't make it a proposition in same sense as others, nor game the same.

This is meant to drive at: Language is not a simple game; I oughtn't to start from a definition of proposition, & then build up logic from that.

You might say "Book" gives the information "I wish you to bring me the book". Is this so or not? If so, you might say that child doesn't understand it, but does it mechanically, until he so interprets it.

Now, if you only play the game "Book", "chair", etc.; then "I wish you to bring" doesn't belong to that game, but are parts of a larger game.

In the coloured bits game "Red", "Bring me red", "I wish you to bring me red", mean exactly the same. For the point of different words is only when different substitutions are possible.

"Red" is not really a description of a state of mind, unless it's part of a game which contains descriptions of states of minds.

Suppose a king in chess were made of 2 bits, but we never took them apart in our game; then this multiplicity would be irrelevant. But if we had a game in which it meant something to replace the head by a knight's head, then the multiplicity would have meaning.

Sum up: Vagueness of "proposition" "language" "sentence". E.g. consider use of diagram in proposition "A unicorn looks like this". Is the diagram a part of the proposition? You can say whichever you please. If you include the diagram it is more like "A unicorn looks like a horse with a horn."

I want to go on with "logical or philosophical analysis", & to see what it can do. Can it fit all possible uses? or make you understand words better? It can only remove particular difficulties, <u>when</u> they crop up.

I said this for following reason: I talked about <u>analysis</u> in connection with "hidden contradiction" or "hidden truth function". It isn't a process in which we can be surprised by the results: we can only use rules we have laid down. I can't give you <u>one</u> game, & say: <u>This</u> is language. There are all sorts of different ones.

7:98 If outline of "proposition" is so vague, what's object of drawing a precise line? (1) I may want to shew what it's like to someone else (2) I may want to get clearer myself – But (3) main use is that I use one outline to kill another – to shew it isn't the only one, or to shew it misleads you: to shew in which way others are (1) arbitrary (2) won't fit.

5a

February 13.

Pointed out: –

How <u>vague</u> (in particular sense) notion of "proposition" & "language".

& did this by reference to <u>language-games</u> – which are the clue to understanding of Logic.

Since it is more or less arbitrary what we call "proposition", therefore Logic plays a part different from what I, Russell & Frege supposed it to play.

I said at Wednesday lectures[20] something that could not be understood: When Frege tried to develop Mathematics from Logic, his idea (roughly expressed) was that the calculus of Logic was <u>the</u> calculus: that hence whatever followed from it was correct Mathematics – what didn't couldn't be correct Mathematics.

This idea belongs to same <u>class</u> of ideas, as that all Mathematics could be deduced from arithmetic.

The idea is that Mathematics is one building, built on Logic.

<u>Now</u> I should say: Russell's calculus is just <u>one</u> among others, one bit of Mathematics, & a bit that doesn't deal with numbers.

This idea of <u>one</u> calculus is connected with consequence: that certain <u>words</u> are on a different level from others: e.g. "proposition", "world", "word", "grammar", "Logic".

I had the idea this was so: that certain words were <u>essentially</u> philosophical words. As opposed to "chairs" & "tables".

We are talking about language, & therefore it's natural we should use words "language" & "grammar":

---

[20] This is a reference to a set of Wednesday lectures that Wittgenstein gave under the title 'Philosophy for Mathematicians', which Moore did not attend.

[21] Moore numbered this page as '99a'. It is likely that he accidentally skipped this page when adding page numbers to the notebook and decided to label the page between 99 and 100 as 99a rather than renumber all the subsequent pages.

but it's not the case that those words have a different position from the others.

E.g. I could now just as well start *Tractatus* with a sentence in which "lamp" occurs, instead of "world".

One could ask: How is it that in this investigation certain words come up again & again? Is it because you ascribe to them a greater importance? Or merely because they happen to represent your subject-matter, as animals are of Zoology?

I should answer: because I'm concerned with language; with troubles arising in our thought from a particular use of language.

Characteristic trouble we are dealing with is this: We use our language without thinking of rules of grammar. And propositions we make arise from practical situations.

But we're sometimes tempted to utter a sentence in a different way: namely when we look at language, & make up a sentence, which we say "sounds English" "ought to have sense", with no practical object.

7:100 E.g. when we talk of "direction" or "sense" of Time.

We all understand direction of an arrow, of a train, of a river.

And since we talk of "flow" of Time & river, it's natural also to talk of direction of Time.

Why do we say "flow of Time"?

Suppose we have logs floating down a river: We could say: When log 150 arrives here, Smith will come; when 60 was here, I had dinner.

We could measure time in this way.

But, apart from that, there is this: Suppose every log when it passed me, made a noise.

When we recognise usual noises coming at equal intervals; this is a quite different meaning of "equality" from that of a clock. Only we've made our clocks so that what is equal on the clock, will roughly seem equal.

Also: we have sense of time passing quickly or slowly.

When we hear a rhythm, we may immediately tell it goes quicker or slower.

But if a bang came only every 5 minutes, we should have no sense of rhythm at all.

Yet we can say "The time between these 2 passed much quicker than between those". This is a quite new experience, different from other meaning of "quicker".

In ordinary life, we sometimes refer to one, sometimes to others, by same word.

Now suppose we measured time by the river with logs of wood at equal distances (equal meaning "seems equal").

Then we have an experience of velocity of river: meaning velocity which looks to be the same (though a clock might give that it isn't). Let's say it is uniform in this sense.

We could still say: Yet the time passed quicker between 120 & 130, than between 130 & 140.

But nothing literally "passes" except the logs!

We are imagining something "flowing quicker", as a river may.

Suppose you ask: What would happen if direction of time were reversed? You become giddy.

Why there's the problem, is because we have this simile of flowing rooted in our language, & we think if there's a flow, there must be a direction.

Where people talk of "sense" of Time, they take one event going in a certain direction, & talk about reversal, if it goes in the opposite.

E.g. suppose everybody always walked in direction of his nose, we might say time was reversed, if somebody walked backward.

E.g. if one talks of direction of time as fixed by change in entropy, & talks of Universe getting from more orderly to more disorderly state: you can talk as if Time would travel backwards, if you could unshuffle cards.

The idea that Universe becomes more & more disorganised is supposed to be a priori, & not on same level as: Everyone walks in direction of his nose (if true).

A priori laws: –

It is experiences which make us think that world becomes more & more disorganised:

(1) experience is that you can disarrange cards in so many ways, arrange them in only one.

(2) Motoring²² chocolate, with raisins & nuts.

Cadbury want to produce a more or less equal distribution of the nuts & raisins. And that a simple mechanism <u>does</u> do this is simply a matter of experience: it <u>might</u> quite well not have been so!

People have queer idea that this <u>must</u> happen.

I should say: What if it didn't happen?

7:103   You say: If it didn't, there <u>must</u> be some explanation.

I say: What "must" is this?

Do you mean that it's the same thing?

We often think that we are dealing with an <u>a priori</u> law, when we're dealing with a norm (of expression) which we ourselves have fixed.

People say "Cause is always proportional to effect".

Then suppose I make huge explosion by pulling a trigger.

People say: Real cause <u>must</u> be something else.

But we're forced to say this:

If we <u>find</u> another, we say: There you are: if you don't, we say, I haven't found it yet.²³

Suppose we find a planet not moving according to calculation: we should say "There <u>must</u> be <u>another</u> planet to account for it".

To fix on a hypothesis, is to fix a certain way of expressing the thing.

E.g. Hertz proposed to explain by "invisible masses".²⁴

---

[22] The 'Motoring' chocolate bar, containing nuts and raisins, was introduced by Rowntree's in 1925; in the early 1930s, it was competing with Cadbury's 'Fruit and Nut' bar (Fitzgerald 2007, 86, 315). 'Motoring was marketed as a filling bar suitable for long journeys. Its name was purposely linked to the popular interest in motor cars, and it was thereby associated with a highly desirable life-style.' (Fitzgerald 2007, 166)

[23] Moore's summary notes: <If I make a huge explosion by pulling a trigger; people say <u>real</u> cause can't be mere pulling of trigger: But this is a thing we've <u>fixed</u> to say. If we don't find another cause, we say "I haven't found it yet".> (10:43)

[24] 'If we try to understand the motions of bodies around us, and to refer them to simple and clear rules, paying attention only to what can be directly observed, our attempt will in general fail ... If we wish to obtain an image of the universe which shall be well-rounded, complete, and conformable to law, we have to presuppose, behind the things which we see, other, invisible things – to imagine confederates concealed beyond the limits of our senses ... We are free to assume that this hidden something is nought else than motion

Suppose I saw a thing rolling down a surface, I could make my laws of mechanics such that they explained some cases, & in the others we can say there are invisible masses.

There is the idea of a norm of explanation – a norm of description, which can't be either right or wrong, but may be practical or unpractical.

Suppose all events in nature were patches on a surface, changing their shapes & moving about.

We could then describe what happened by a network or lattice.

The shape of the lattice is a priori: it's the norm we use. But of nothing that we describe by its use can we say: It must be the case.

I may have a mechanism which provides an explanation independently of any experience:

i.e. it may lay down beforehand[25] what I am to say, if certain things happen, without saying that they will happen.

What you're going to observe, I don't say; but for any possible case, I fix an explanation: i.e. an answer to the question why.

Thus, in this system, there is a system of causes.

But you might have a system in which there was not – an indeterministic system.

Suppose I put weights on one scale, till pointer points at 0; & then say: It weighs so & so.

But if I want to be accurate, I say: take the average of 10 experiments.

And I might say that in my physics: I'm not going to account for the variations.

I could then say: In this system there is no cause of the variations. But it would be stupid to suppose that this was a new discovery about Nature.

---

and mass again, – motion and mass which differ from the visible ones not in themselves but in relation to us and to our usual means of perception. Now this mode of conception is just our hypothesis. We assume that it is possible to conjoin with the visible masses of the universe other masses obeying the same laws, and of such a kind that the whole thereby becomes intelligible and conformable to law' (Hertz 1899, 25-6). See also the discussion of invisible masses below at 9:38.

[25] Moore later added: <(a priori)>

"Deterministic" & "indeterministic", in this sense, are properties of the system I fix arbitrarily.

Whether my system can describe all possibilities is a mathematical question, not of observation: it is a question of grammar – of the adopted norm of explanation.

Has time a beginning?

Imagine Ursell asked me to describe what I did yesterday; & I dictate a description from memory, saying I had lunch with A, tea with B. Suppose he enquires of A & B & finds it hasn't happened. Suppose he always found this, but that always what I had said happened yesterday, always did happen the day after.

Would you say I had remembered the future? or that I had the past? or neither?

This can certainly be described & is a possible phenomenon.

7:106 You could say: He has remembered the future in one sense.

We have 2 independent orders of events: (1) in my memory & several orders here: e.g. I entered door, walked to mantel–piece etc.. This is an order of events in my memory, which I will call memory-time. (2) There's an order in the information-time.

In (1) with respect to one particular event will be past & future & in (2) with respect to any particular day.

In memory-time there is no sense to talk either of remembering the past or of remembering the future: there is only earlier & later, not past & future.

It's sensible to say: I remember that which in information-time is future.

The mere internal description of my memory won't shew any difference between mine & other people's; the only difference will be relative to observation-time.

Supposing that at certain intervals situations repeated themselves; & people said this shewed time is circular: that after 100 years, here was February 13, 1933 over again.

Is this right or wrong?[26]

---

[26] Moore later added: <I suppose he meant "Neither"; but I should say "Wrong".>

If we talk of "flow" of Time, this is a picture which has an enormously strong hold on us.

Suppose one asked: What's its length?

We could say: It doesn't go <u>straight</u> past us; it comes back, only things slightly change.

This wouldn't say anything about real world other than we do: they would only describe things otherwise.

Suppose they said: There will be 100 more logs & that will be the end?

Could we say: This is a matter of experience?

What could be meant by: Time hasn't ceased yet?

<u>Empty time</u> – going on when events have ceased.

What is criterion for time ceasing, or going on?

Suppose you had a time-river: you might then perhaps have no such substantive as "Time": you might talk only of logs, "100 logs ago", "in another 100 logs". Then they might say "Logs have come to an end".

Suppose there were no events earlier than 100 years ago: would there have been no time before that?

We've got to make the rules, before we can play a game. And we can alter the rules. We have to notice how we use "Time".

People say: Has Time been created? or was the world created in time?

But what would be meant by "making" Time?

Has "before" been created? means nothing at all.

Personification of Time wouldn't have occurred if there'd only been "before" & "after".

This is a case of extending language, by only looking at language, instead of using practically.

5b

7:109   February 17.

I wanted to destroy view that logical analysis helps us to understand our propositions better: my view is that it's always an antidote to a poison - some kind of philosophical error.

Idea might be that complete logical analysis gives us complete grammar of a word.

I say there is no complete grammar.

But there is use in making a rule, if someone else has made a rule we don't wish followed.

There's no sense in which a person, who didn't know the rule, didn't understand the word as well as we do.

But philosophers may make a muddle:

E.g. think time could be reversed; then it's useful to clear up rules about Time, & shew that things are just as trivial as they seemed before.

I want to take as example of logical analysis: question connected with Behaviourism.

When we say: He feels tooth-ache; is it correct to say this tooth-ache is only his behaviour?

And when I talk about my tooth-ache, am I talking about something else?

7:110   People say: I can never know he has tooth-ache, I can only know that he behaves so & so.

Now consider "having".

What about a tooth-ache which nobody had? which was unemployed?

This shews that "had" doesn't mean "owned" in sense in which a book is owned.[27]

Grammar of "having" in 2 cases is different.

---

[27] Moore later added: <A book can be owned by nobody, a tooth-ache can't.>

(1) Compare "have" in sense of "hold in hand": he holds in his hand, I in mine.

Here experiences which make us say each, are similar.

We might have an experience in which it wasn't clear to whom a hand belonged.

I might see my hand in a mirror, but not know whether it was mine: settling by moving it.

(2) Consider "this tooth has tooth-ache".

What is criterion? Does it forbid my having tooth-ache in Ursell's tooth?

There are several criteria.

I am aiming at: Experience of my having tooth-ache is the same, in whoever's mouth the tooth which has it is.

You might say: "My tooth-ache must be in my mouth."

How is my mouth distinguished from another person's?

Can't it be imagined that I lived all my life opposite a mirror, & saw faces in it, without knowing which was mine?

Suppose I saw 4 bodies. It is describable that I should change my body.

When one moved its arm, I should have a certain feeling; & when another did, I should have same feeling: this would describe "having changed my body".

We started with "Is tooth-ache of another person, tooth-ache in same sense as mine?"

If there could be "my having tooth-ache in someone else's tooth", then it's clear this is something quite different from "he has tooth-ache".

It is clear, & admitted that what verifies /is criterion for/ "I have tooth-ache" is quite different from what verifies /criterion for/ "He has tooth-ache".

And then, if I say criterion is what it means, it follows that it means mostly different.

But this is not to say "he hasn't got it, but only behaves as if he had it".

If you pity a man for having tooth-ache, do you pity him for putting his hand to his cheek?

Tooth-ache doesn't only mean a particular kind of behaviour, but it could mean that.

Young asks: How can you tell whether a person <u>has</u> or is only pretending? & answers: "Dentist has told me he can't have it" may be my reason for saying he is pretending.

I seem to people to deny that another person ever really has what I have: if I <u>did</u> that, I should be talking nonsense.

And I seem <u>also not</u> to deny that something is true of him, but to deny that I can know this.

What is the criterion for his having tooth-ache?

Can it be that in <u>my</u> case I know directly that I have tooth-ache, in his case indirectly? as I might know directly that I have money in my pocket, indirectly that he has?

No: because I couldn't <u>feel his</u> tooth-ache.

We have to conclude: I feel <u>my</u> tooth-ache; is incorrect grammar.

7:113 "His tooth-ache was worse than mine" is quite correct.

But "I feel my tooth-ache" is not.

People say "2 people <u>can</u> never see exactly same thing"

"2 people can never have exactly same sense-datum".

It is a statement of fact, that 2 people never see a thing from quite same angle; but this might be otherwise, if person had a transparent head.

And there's great danger of mixing up statements of this sort: e.g. 2 people never have exactly same hands.[28]

With, such as:

2 people never see through the same pair of eyes.

Now in my mirror-case, it would be quite possible for 2 people to have tooth-ache in <u>same</u> tooth: 2 people cry out.

Question is: What can we describe? What would make sense?

That 2 people can't make their eyes coincide, is a statement of fact.

But these are confused with tautological or grammatical statements.

[28] Moore later added: <statement of fact – empirical>

What is criterion for "not seeing the same thing"? or for knowing whether they do?

People say: It's clear sense-data are private & add (1) We know they are not the same (2) but we don't know whether they are alike or not.

I ask: What is meant by saying tooth-ache is "private"?

People would say: Nobody else can feel it.

I say: there's no sense in saying it is private.

How does "I" come in, in these cases? ~~We could make up a language where "I" could be left out.~~

In our language we have "I have tooth-ache" & "He has tooth-ache" which we know have quite different criteria, but we confuse this with "I have money" & "He has money".

We might avoid this confusion, by inventing a language in which we didn't use "I have tooth-ache" & "He has": e.g. for first said "There is tooth-ache here", & "He is behaving so & so".

6a

8:1   February 20 / 1933.

<u>Tooth-ache.</u>

Extraordinarily difficult: that difficulty lies, not in fact – but in that whole field is filled with misleading notations. So with "infinite": notation is so misleading that we think of it as remote.

Difficulty is shewn by fact that it is question between Realists, Idealists, & Solipsists.

We said that, if we talk of <u>having</u> tooth-ache – different verification is <u>provided</u> for "I have tooth-ache", "He has tooth-ache": hence <u>meanings</u> must be different.

Then people say: Surely you are saying that he hasn't got what you have got?

Now, if this question had <u>meaning</u>, I should be making a statement of fact.

I admit that other people do have tooth-ache – this having the meaning which we've given it.

Difficulty lies in "having", & this applies to <u>me</u> "having" it as well as to another.

Main point is that it's <u>absurd</u> to say: Tooth-ache isn't disagreeable, but is only disagreeable, if somebody has it.

8:2   Let's take visual sensation.

"I see a red patch" I know directly; whether another does I only know from what he tells me & his behaviour.

You can therefore say "Smith sees a red patch" has a different meaning from "I see a red patch".

Question is: How does <u>a person</u> come in to sensation at all?

If I describe the visual field, no person comes necessarily into it at all.

I do see something I call my body; but I needn't.

Suppose I were transparent, I could still describe visual field.

There is no organ of vision essential: no physical eye is necessary.

None is required in description of visual field.

But visual field has certain internal properties, such that you can describe motion of a ring as motion towards the <u>eye</u> (<u>not</u> physical eye).

Is it essential to describe visual field as <u>mine</u>? Will there be mine & another's?

I should say: Visual field is nothing that belongs to any person.

<u>Enormous difficulty</u> in thinking about such things as 8:3

e.g. Is it <u>necessary</u> that eye which sees visual field should be above mouth which speaks?

Imagine yourself in front of mirror, so that all bodies you see are on a level: we do this, in order to get rid of difference between <u>my</u> body & other bodies.

Another difficulty is: I hear my voice coming from somewhere near my eyes; & we think this <u>necessary</u>. But it <u>isn't</u>, though it always happens. Don't be prejudiced by anything, which <u>is</u> a fact, but which <u>might</u> be otherwise.

I might quite well hear my voice coming from somewhere else – e.g. out of a loud-speaker.

So, in case of mirror: it might be arranged that voice should seem to come now from one mirror-image, now from another.

In such a case, the idea of an <u>ego</u> seeing & hearing would become utterly different.

We are inclined to think of visual field as a sort of box in a bit of Euclidean space, fastened to our eyes.

That a person is thought to enter into visual field, is due to mere matter of 8:4 fact that a particular body always has a unique position in it. But it needn't.

We could abolish whole idea of <u>a sense-organ perceiving</u>. This idea is based on particular <u>experiences</u>; not on essential nature of visual field.

I have to eliminate our peculiar correlation between tactile & visual experiences: & imagining case of mirror does this.

There <u>is</u> an eye in visual-field: i.e. a particular property of visual field – that of ring approaching.

I could see without a physical eye: but having a body which would always be pretty near the eye of visual field.

Suppose you had a tube fixed to your eye, giving on a mirror. Then you might see hand moving in mirror.

Visual field does not essentially, in any way, belong to an organ of sight, or to a human body. But we can establish connections between it & a human body, utterly different from what we are accustomed to.

I can: (1) separate visual field from an organ of sight: e.g. by supposing my body transparent

(2) establish connections between it & bodies quite different: e.g. I might transfer <u>my</u> voice to any one of several mouths.

8:5 <u>My</u> voice = a voice connected with certain tactile experiences. But my mouth would not be under my eye; nor my body near <u>it</u>.

Should I in this case be inclined to use "I" "my" at all?

If I say "I have pains in my hand", this can be verified in different ways.

(1) If I didn't see my hand, had been long blindfolded. I should still say "He's pricking my hand".

(2) But this experience has been long associated with a visual one.

We have a feeling that tactile & visual space are <u>one</u>; but mirror-experience shews that this correlation is not necessary.

In "I have a pain in <u>my hand</u>" what's meant by <u>my hand</u>?

If my hand was transparent & was pricked, you might think that even if I have no organ of vision, yet the pain is somewhere near the eye of the visual field:

8:6 A sensation is not essentially the property of someone. Our use of "I have tooth-ache" is due to certain correlations, between pains & other kinds of experience.

<u>Correlation</u>. (1) There is an experience of temporal coincidence between pains, & visual experiences.

& (2)[29]

---

[29] This line was not filled in.

Solipsism.

Solipsists say: Only my experience is real. Which, as statement of fact, is absurd.

But truth is: No person necessarily enters into a sensory experience at all.

Description of a sensation does not contain description of a sense-organ, nor therefore of a person.

Private sensations.

People say: No 2 people can have same sensation.

But what is meant by same sensation?

Is there a difference, intrinsic to tooth-ache, called belonging to so & so?

We talk of 2 chairs looking exactly like; but we can't talk of 2 colours looking exactly alike.

8:7

6b

8:8   February 24.

Most important point:

Is there such a thing as subject & object, in the description of primary experience?

In ordinary language we do use "I have tooth-ache", "he has" etc..

I tried to shew, that if we described an experience such as having tooth-ache or seeing a red patch, the idea of a person doesn't enter into the description just as an eye doesn't enter into description of what's seen.

It is an experiential proposition that an eye sees things: we can in geometry of visual space speak of an "eye", but this wouldn't involve a physical body, nor is it a matter of experience; we can talk of motions away from & towards the eye – meaning by this something on same level as curved & straight.

In "the white patch moves towards the blue patch", "towards" would have a different meaning from in "the white patch moves towards the eye". The eye is not a visual object at all.

We mentioned Solipsism – saying: Only real thing is my experience; & can distinguish 2 forms: (1) inconsiderate: nothing is real but what I experience; (2) considerate: nothing is real <u>for</u> anybody, but what he experiences.

8:9   Both are absurd; but there's something which tempts towards both.

(1) "No pains are real but what I feel."

First question: How do you know? which means: Is it a matter of experience that you have pains, & others not?

Nobody would say that it is.

But: e.g. If you did feel pains, how could I know?

If Solipsist says "Only real pains are mine" & other person says "Surely not; mine are", Solipsist sees at once that other person has not answered him[30]: just as Dr. Johnson didn't answer Berkeley.[31]

---

[30] Moore later added: \<hasn't he?\>
[31] 'After we came out of the church, we stood talking for some time together of Bishop Berkeley's ingenious sophistry to prove the non-existence of matter, and that every thing

Realist who says "Surely this is real", is answering question "Is this made of stone, or a mirror-image, or a mirage?" correctly: e.g. Johnson's kicking shewed that it was a stone & not a painted one. But Idealist would say: That wasn't what I meant; &, if fairly clear would agree with Realist.

But they still <u>seem</u> to disagree; & here I think both, in a particular sense, are talking nonsense – nonsense in this way.

Way in which nonsense is produced is by trying to express something in propositions of language, which <u>ought</u> to be embodied in the grammar.

8:10

Prototype of this is what we do with "possible" & "necessary".

These express part of grammar by a simile taken from physical events. We all understand "Nobody can lift Whewell's Court,"[32] "I can't play chess": i.e. "to be able to" is familiar to us; & then we use it for logical possibility, e.g. "I can't feel his tooth-ache", where doesn't it mean "I feel his tooth-ache" has no sense? So that it doesn't express a fact.

Whenever logical "can't" is used, you can also say "can't even try to".

When we hear "you can't", we cut this out of our language; & where we hear "you must", same thing happens.

All arguments for Solipsism or Idealism are all of form "you can't" or "you must".

No Solipsist maintains that his doctrine is proved by experience: if it were, a future experience might refute him.

If he gives as argument "I can't feel his tooth-ache", we have to ask "what would it be like to feel his tooth-ache?"

Suppose a man says "I feel your tooth-ache", what am I to answer? If it makes <u>sense</u>, I am already refuted: I must say "That's impossible", &, if asked <u>why</u>, must say "If you feel it, it isn't mine" – a matter of grammar.

8:11

The difference between "<u>I have</u> it" & "he has it" is not like that between "it is in <u>this</u> place" & "is in <u>that</u> place".

---

in the universe is merely ideal. I observed, that though we are satisfied his doctrine is not true, it is impossible to refute it. I never shall forget the alacrity with which Johnson answered, striking his foot with mighty force against a large stone, till he rebounded from it, "I refute it *thus*.'" (Boswell et al. 1846, 262-3)

[32] This was the part of Trinity College where Wittgenstein lived, and gave this lecture.

Could you imagine that I & another had a tooth in common? E.g my nerves & another's were joined to same tooth. We might both say: "I have tooth-ache in this tooth."

This would shew clearly that <u>locality</u> of tooth-ache has nothing to do with person who has it.

Pains can travel, but they can't travel from you to me.

How do you verify who is possessor of tooth-ache?

We have to say: In one case, "I feel it"; in the other, "he says so". And hence the propositions verified must have different meanings.

But really "verification" is used differently in (1).

How do you know that you have it? Because I feel it.

Is this like: How do you know there is a table here? Because I see it.[33]

  I have T

  & You have T,

I want to say these are not values of a single function "x has T".

8:12 To shew that they're not: take

  (1) I don't know if I have tooth-ache

  & (2) I don't know if you have tooth-ache:

(1) is absurd, (2) not.

Could we say here: This is so for you, but not for me? Is there a private language, which I understand & you don't?

What's meant by "I <u>can't</u> understand, what you mean" or "I <u>can't</u> have your thoughts"?

This can only mean: It is to be excluded from your language.

All this I haven't put correctly: to put it straight, I must plunge into something terrible.[34]

What's meant by decision that a sentence makes, or doesn't make, sense?

In my jargon you would answer: One constructed according to rules of grammar makes sense; one not so constructed doesn't.

---

[33] Moore later added: <There might have been a table here without my seeing it; but I couldn't have had tooth-ache without feeling it.>

[34] Moore's summary notes: <<u>Something terrible</u>, because what said hitherto not put correctly. What's meant by does or doesn't "make sense"?> (10:100)

But could one say: ~~Must rules be of a certain~~ Why not let it make sense, by just altering your grammar?

This is same as to ask: What is a proposition?

Suppose I said: There's a propositional game; what's a proposition is shewn by the rules.

Can one ask: <u>What</u> rules must a thing follow to be a proposition?   8:13

To answer, one would have to give rules of grammar of propositions, & I said before that proposition is ambiguous (vague).

I talked of language-games; & proposed to say any thing with truth-functions is a proposition.

But if you asked me for <u>further</u> characteristics: I couldn't give any.

So, if you'd asked me: What's a game?

I could begin by making rough distinctions, e.g. tennis, chess, card; & say "These & similar are games."

Same thing happens with propositions: I give many examples, & then you might think, with such a rough definition, it must be very difficult to exclude anything & say it doesn't make sense.

But it works this way.

Take chess: Suppose a piece of chalk were lying on the board; & someone said: What's this? & I might answer either "It's not part of the game at all", or "It is".

Or suppose a third King is on one of the squares.

"A game with 3 Kings" doesn't define any particular game. You would have to give rules for a 3rd king, & this would make game utterly different.   8:14
You've got to shew e.g. whether there's to be a 3rd player, or one player is to have more pieces than another.

We often think that when we use an expression, it is not necessary to give rules, when in fact it is.

I say <u>neither</u> "I feel his tooth-ache" nor "I feel <u>my</u> tooth-ache" makes any sense.

How am I to persuade anyone of this?

And suppose he says: I will make a rule that it has sense.

Then he has to answer all sorts of questions about the rules.

E.g. does it make sense to say: I have tooth-ache, but don't feel it?

And, if he says: Yes, then,

<u>How does one know</u> whether you have or not?

What am I trying to do by this question?

(1) To discover how he plays his game (2) To discover how to <u>use</u> it.

Suppose somebody said "A canvas on a chair has a colour which nobody sees",

what I want to find out is how one can tell – what is the use of it. And, if there's none, I should say it's not a proposition.

8:15 If I say "So & so makes no sense", I can only get you to agree, if I can shew you that you'd said it thoughtlessly, thinking that you'd made rules for it, when you hadn't, & will therefore give it up as useless.

If you say "It makes sense to me", I can only say I can't make any use of it. I can't do anything with it.

Suppose you said "Chair follows red", you would be inclined to accept this as nonsense.

but not "This chair has a colour which nobody sees" because this seems to be constructed in accordance with English grammar: it sounds like a proposition which could be applied.

7a

February 27. 8:16

"I have tooth-ache" is different from "He has tooth-ache", because "I seem to have" makes no sense, "He seems to have" has sense.

""I seem to have" makes no sense" = "There <u>can</u> be no doubt about it"[35]

& here "can" does not = however hard I try, I don't succeed.

"There can be no doubt" = It has no sense to talk about doubt.

What should I answer to: What is criterion of "making sense"?

First answer: p makes sense, if it is constructed according to rules of grammar.

But, if rules of grammar, are arbitrary: A person can always say: I make rules according to which it has.

Now "sense" is misleading: has misled me: just as "meaning" is.

We talk not about propositions in general, but about <u>special examples</u> e.g. about special language-games.

I could put my point of view: If "sense" is correlative to "proposition", & if proposition is not sharply bounded, so also with "sense."

Take such as "There seems to be a table here", i.e. propositions such that 8:17
you can't add "<u>seems</u>" again, as opposed to those like "There is a chair" to which you can,

& mathematical propositions

& propositions like "This comet will travel in a parabola".[36]

---

[35] Moore's summary notes: <It makes no sense to say "I doubt if I've a pain".> (10:100)

[36] Moore later wrote above this sentence: <="There <u>is</u> a table here"?> On the facing page he first wrote: <How different from "There's a chair here"?> He later added: <4 kinds? No: only 3.>

Presumably, the three kinds are the ones set out in the previous sentence, namely: (1) experiential propositions to which 'seems' can't be added; (2) experiential propositions to which 'seems' can be added; (3) mathematical propositions. In these comments, Moore is wondering whether Wittgenstein regards propositions of science as a fourth kind, or as belonging to (2).

All these have something in common – namely[37] that they are within a system of truth-functions, i.e. we can use disjunction, conjunction, negation etc. with all: negation be defined by certain rules e.g. $\sim\sim p = p$.

There are cases where negation is identical with a disjunction: e.g. This chair is not yellow = This chair is either p or ... or (5 other primary colours).[38]

But "There is no white patch here" is not identical with any disjunction.

People are tempted to treat all cases as if they were uniform.

Suppose I say "We'll use proposition for any sign that is part of a system of truth-functions": but this is necessarily vague: how is "sign" to be defined?

8:18 I can give examples of "signs" e.g. in language-game "red", & you ask me are these propositions? I can say: No, because we've not yet got "not red" or "red or green".

You might have a game, where you had to form expressions in the language (analogous to telling a story): & you might do this in the infinitive.

An important distinction between signs is "those used by themselves" & "those not used by themselves".

Proposition = sign used by itself, within a system of logical constants.[39]

(This applies to "Do come" & "Don't come".)

But if you say this isn't enough to define proposition, I agree & I can't give you a general definition of "proposition" any more than of "game": I can only give examples.

Is this inexact?

I should say: Any line I could draw would be arbitrary, in the sense that nobody would have decided whether to call so & so a game or not.

We are quite right to use the word "game", so long as we don't pretend to have drawn a definite outline.

8:19 I said "Sense of a proposition is its use" – & this, of course is vague; so also is "If you want to know sense, ask for verification", which applies to propositions about positions & movements of physical bodies.

---

[37] Moore later added: <(this is only one thing.)>
[38] Moore's summary notes: <Sometimes negation is identical with disjunction: e.g. this chair is not yellow = either red, or green, or blue, or black or white.> (10:48)
[39] Moore's summary notes: <Proposition = sign used by itself within a system of truth-functions.> (10:49)

When we do philosophy, we give rules of grammar wherever there is a philosophical difficulty.

With $1 \div 3$, we can ask: Is there a period?[40] & what is the period? 2 different questions.

We can have a method of calculation which answers both; & if this were your only method, 2 questions would mean the same.

Suppose you have no method of finding a period, but you know one when you see it.

$7 \div 13$ doesn't give you a method of finding, because you don't know where in infinite development it will come.

We could ask: Have you found a period? & What period have you found? & these are different questions. A man could answer (1) without answering (2), but not vice versa.

Grammar of question "Is there a period?" will be different when we have a method of finding one, & have none.

Answer in second case will be: "Yes" or "I haven't found one", but can't be "No".

We can talk about (1) particular propositions (2) classes of propositions.   8:20

E.g. we could begin with a narrowly defined class: e.g. proposition which determines position of a rigid body within this room, by coordinates from wall;

or. e.g. determines positions of circles on blackboard: "There is a circle 2 inches from top, 5 from left hand."

Now in what case should we say: This makes no sense?

Suppose (2,5) meant the above; & someone wrote (2,5,7), we could say: This makes nonsense in this game.

Why do we call it nonsense? what does it mean to call it so?

You might justify the 7, by explaining that you were playing another game.

You might say, through stupidity you wrote 3 numbers instead of 2.

Point is: 7 is no use, unless you make it so, by inventing a new game in which it comes in.

---

[40] If dividing x by y results in a repeating decimal, then the period of $x \div y$ is the number of digits in the repeating sequence. So the period of $1 \div 3$ is 1, as $1 \div 3 = 0.333333\ldots$

"Goodness is red" is nonsense, though it's an English sentence.

But if I whistle a phrase, nobody would call that nonsense.

When we call this sentence nonsense, it is because of some similarity with things which have sense.

8:21 If we'd made a code with chairs, certain positions of the chairs would be nonsense.

"Mr. Stevenson has come to today's redness" is already nonsense, & no change would make it more so; but certain changes could make it <u>less</u> like a sensible sentence.

Therefore if I point out that so & so makes no sense; you could always theoretically answer that it does.

But then (1) I might ask you: What use do you make of it?

E.g. with (2,5,7): does 7 represent a distance?

In general, problem of what is sense need not arise, because we know that nonsense always arises from forming symbols analogous to certain uses, where they have no use.

E.g. 3 numbers might have use in one game, not in another: we could say "Don't you see we have only 2 distances in this game?"

"Making sense" has to be explained in particular cases, & will have different senses in different cases.

The word is useful, just as "game", "winning", "losing" are: but it alters its meaning as we go from proposition to proposition; just as "losing" & "winning" mean something different in patience & chess & golf.

We <u>can</u> use the words, in spite of not having clear definitions.

8:22 Just as "sense" is vague, so must be "grammar", "grammatical rule", "syntax".

Now go back: –

"I have tooth-ache"; "He has tooth-ache".

<u>Verifications</u> are different, but in different senses of "verification".

In case (1) we might say "because I feel it": but I feel it = I have it.

(2) we might say by "inspection"

Inspection = <u>looking</u>, as distinct from seeing. E.g. by concentrating attention on a finger, you might <u>get</u> a pain, & therefore find a pain.

But it makes no sense to <u>look</u> if you have a tooth-ache: to say "I'll see", "I'll find out".

<u>Here</u> therefore it makes no <u>sense</u> to ask for a verification, or criterion: to ask "How do you know?"

This places "I have tooth-ache" on a different level in grammar from "He has tooth-ache".

Now I said "I" in "I have" does not refer to a person: & this can be explained as follows.

At first sight "I" & "Jones" are arguments to "<u>x</u> has tooth-ache".

With "Wittgenstein has", "Stevenson has", I could talk of the possessor varying.

But from "Wittgenstein has" I can't substitute "I" without altering whole business: it is no longer same function <u>just</u> with different arguments.

But this doesn't <u>always</u> apply to "I": e.g. in "I've got a matchbox" "Wittgenstein has a matchbox", it is a case of 2 different values of same propositional function; in both cases it is a "possessor".

so with "I have a bad tooth"; "Skinner has a bad tooth".

Here we're giving what characterises "primary experiences", i.e. that in this case "I" does not denote a possessor.

Just as there is no "eye" in seeing, so there is no "Ego" in thinking or in having tooth-ache.

We are dealing here with one particular department of grammar – in dealing with direct experience.

I call a certain human body "my body"; & the body to which my nose is attached, could be called its possessor.

Suppose I saw human bodies only in a mirror, & gave them names A, B, C, D, I could talk of "A's nose" etc.; & so if I called one of them "me", I could talk of "my nose".

But it would be utterly different if I said "This is my body": I'm not mentioning a possessor of it, as of the nose.

What's the criterion of a certain body being "mine"?

I might say: If <u>I</u> have a certain feeling, body which moves its arm will be mine; & here <u>I</u> does not denote a possessor, any more than in "I have tooth-ache".

You <u>could</u> have a notation in which these sentences would be written in a different form.

Solipsism is right, if it merely says: "I have tooth-ache" is on quite a different level from "He has tooth-ache".[41]

If he says that he has something which the other has not; he is absurd & is making the very mistake of putting the 2 on the same <u>level</u>.[42]

If I ask "What is so & so like?" this is a vague question, but any answer to it will be a development of its grammar, giving me relation between e.g. it & another language, or it & a picture.

I expect you to give me connections: such as: What follows from this? From what does it follow? Has it a verification or none?

People sometimes think certain questions irrelevant: e.g. Is "How does one know so & so?" to "What does so & so mean?" But they're wrong: For here no cause is being asked for, but a reason – i.e. the answer to it is a grammatical answer.

8:25

Consider "You <u>can't</u> know so & so", here the "can't" is grammatical.

Present day discussions in Physics – e.g. essential part of Theory of Relativity – are of this grammatical nature – applying "How does one know?".

---

[41] Moore later added: <They are not values of same function "x has tooth-ache"?>

[42] Moore later added: <This would be to say "He has tooth-ache" is value of same function as "I have", but is false?>

7b

March 3.

If we have a function "x has tooth-ache", then by substituting "I" or "he" we don't get a value of the same function.

That this is so is shewn by "I don't know whether I have tooth-ache" is nonsense. "I don't know whether he has tooth-ache" is not.

Put it another way:

In "I have tooth-ache in his tooth", 2 people seem to enter.

You might ask: Whose mouth says this?

Does it also make sense to say "A has tooth-ache in B's tooth"?

Ask: What's the criterion? And we might answer: He says so. But could we also say: He says so with B's mouth?

The criterion for A's saying it, is its being said with that mouth – i.e. the mouth of that body.

Suppose "Ursell says "I am Stevenson"."

Let's go on in a different way.

I call a certain body "my body". This body is seen in a different way from others; but this could be done away with – in supposition of looking-glass.

By "So-and-so's voice" I mean the voice that comes from that body.

Now what's criterion of my body being mine? That this arm is mine means it belongs to this body.

You are tempted to suppose that this means "The body which belongs to my soul", or "belongs to me".

In that case: What is criterion that it belongs to me?

Suppose we saw all the bodies in a mirror:

We might say: it's the body whose arm moves, when I have the feeling of moving an arm.

Could we similarly say: Jones's body = the body whose arm moves when Jones has the feeling of moving an arm?

But what's criterion of: Jones has the feeling?

If A says "I have tooth-ache in B's tooth"; then to: Who has tooth-ache in who's tooth? answer is: first <u>who</u> is the body who says it, second, who is the body whose tooth it is?

I.e. ownership is here verified by reference to a body.

If there is an ownership such that <u>I</u> possess a body, this isn't verified in same way.

If "I" is replaceable by "this body", then there's no difference between "I" & "he".

8:28 But if <u>not</u> replaceable by "this body", it isn't replaceable by a proper name either.[43]

Suppose I talked in such a way that the voice came from a microphone in the wall: to question "Who's Wittgenstein?" I should have to answer by pointing at my body. But as it is – my voice coming from my mouth – I can answer "I".

The answer to "Who has?" is pointing to a body.

When a person says "I have tooth-ache", do we take it that the body has it?

"He feels, when he has tooth-ache, what I feel, when I have it."

In "His eyes are yellow; therefore there's something wrong with his gall-bladder", there is an argument by analogy.

How about: "If I behave like that, I feel certain things, therefore since he behaves like that, he feels certain things". This is quite legitimate.

You conclude that he has tooth-ache from his behaviour.

There might be a jaundice without yellow eye-balls; either might be without the other.

"But how <u>can</u> I know that S has tooth-ache?" is a grammatical question. And if it's <u>like</u> jaundice & yellow eyes: then the answer to this grammatical question, must be different from behaving.

8:29 What are the <u>2</u> verifications (1) for his having tooth-ache (2) for his behaving in this way?

In <u>my</u> case there is a verification for my having, quite different from that for my behaviour.

---

[43] Moore later added: <But children <u>do</u> use proper name, for "I". This, however, shews that <u>we</u> don't.>

In "he feels, what I feel" there is an analogy; but is it external, or does it go deep into the grammar?

In "A has glasses & B has glasses" the analogy goes deep into the grammar – i.e. all the grammar of the 2 statements is the same.

Lichtenberg said: "For "I think" we ought to say "It thinks"." ("Es blitzt".)[44]

What could be the answer to "Who?" except to point at the body?

You might distinguish people by their voices.

If it makes sense to ask "Which of these bodies is mine?", (let's leave out question what would happen if 2 bodies looked alike) could it similarly make sense to ask "Which of these bodies is Ursell's?"

The answer has to consist in a correlation of 2 things.

If I drilled in A's tooth, B might cry: & that would be a criterion for "B feels tooth-ache in A's tooth".

There must be a relation, which there isn't in "This is my body".

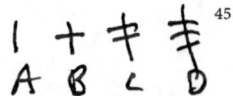[45]

How do we decide "Which body is mine?"?   8:30

If you called my voice Wittgenstein, we could ask which body belongs to Wittgenstein, but then we couldn't ask which voice belongs to Wittgenstein.

Final thing:

It has been asked: Does Psychology deal only with what we're conscious of or with other things too? E.g. Freud says: There is an unconscious part of the mind.

Now "I" & "conscious" are equivalent in one sense – not in another.

Compare magic-lantern[46] & pictures on screen. The picture in the lantern has neighbours; but the one on the screen has none.

---

[44] German for 'there's lightning' (translated as 'it lightens' in the following translation of the aphorism alluded to by Wittgenstein). 'We should say *it thinks* [es denkt], just as we say *it lightens* [es blitzt]. To say *cogito* is to say too much as soon as we translate it *I think*. To assume, to postulate the *I*, is a practical requirement.' (Lichtenberg 2000, 190, K:18; 1971, Sudelbuch K 76, 412)

[45] This may be a diagram of the 'bodies' of A, B, C, & D.

[46] A magic lantern was an early type of image projector.

I could call one picture in lantern "I" & the rest "he" etc., & then they would be all on the same level. But I <u>could</u> use it to refer to picture <u>on</u> screen, & here it would be unnecessary.

We could say the picture which is projected is conscious: then it is pictures on the film that are conscious or unconscious. But the word can't be applied to the picture on the screen.

So my body has a neighbour; but Ursell's tooth-ache is not a neighbour to my tooth-ache.

8:31 "I" as opposed to others can be used in 2 utterly different ways: one in which it's on a level with others; in the others it is a characterisation of being on the screen, as opposed to being on the film.

8a

March 6.

2 kinds of use "I" – or any word denoting "subject".

What I said came to this: –

If it's a question of who, of a number of people, has tooth-ache, the criterion is connected with human bodies: it will always apply to one body & not to others, or a pair of bodies (as in case where one person should have tooth-ache in another's tooth) as opposed to another pair.

But my decision whether I have tooth-ache or not is not made by reference to any body; I might have tooth-ache, even if there were no body – if my body was destroyed.

If in answer to "Who sees? who has pity?" etc. the answer refers to one or more human bodies, then you can say that in all these cases where we talk of subject & object, the "he" will have to be defined by reference to some human body – (or, e.g. a voice, differentiated either by position from which it came, or only by its quality). E.g. "Who has tooth-ache?" might come to "Which voice says "I have tooth-ache"?".

But if I call one voice "my voice" (not used as a proper name, but = "the voice belonging to me"), the decision is not made by reference to a body or a voice, but is of an utterly different kind.

Suppose someone says: Do you mean to say that your tooth-ache is of a different kind from mine?

Answer is: No; because "of a different kind", in our language, = different as a sharp pang differs from a long dull pain. And in this sense my tooth-ache may, of course, be either of a different or of the same kind as anyone else's.

When people wanted to make clear the particular difference between "I" as my body, & "I" where there is no question of a body, they have always made statements about tooth-ache, instead of statements about the grammar of our ordinary language.

This could be made clearer.

E.g. talk of "space", in which we move about:

(1) physical space,[47]

Now let's talk of "conscious" and "unconscious".

Freud talked as if he'd found out that there is in the human mind unconscious hatreds, volitions etc..

He has found out phenomena & connections not previously known.

But the talk of "unconscious" is very misleading; because we always, whether consciously or not, interpret it by the picture of the difference between a chair which we are seeing, & one which is in another room e.g. a closed room, which we don't see.

In some ways this is useful: but what's extremely misleading is this.

Suppose the chair in the other room were separated by a wall of glass, without any door, so that though I could see it, I could not get at it.

We <u>could</u> talk of unconscious tooth-ache.

Freud talks of unconscious hatred, when a person suddenly behaves as he hated B, & on psycho-analysis remembers e.g. that B trod on his toes in childhood.

Now suppose I said "unconscious hatred is of an utterly different kind from conscious". First answer would be: Of course.

But are you quite sure what the use of "hatred" with the 2 different adjectives means?

We think of it like "seen bit of chalk" & "unseen bit of chalk".

But it is <u>not</u>.

The grammar of "felt" & "unfelt" hatred is quite different from that of seen & unseen chair.

Similarly "artificial flowers" means something quite different from "blue flowers": the adjective means something different. The former aren't a class of real flowers (though we might use "flowers" in a sense in which they were).

Now we might talk of "sub-conscious tooth-ache"; if a person had an urge to put his hand to his tooth, & the tooth was bad.

---

[47] Moore added: <(Couldn't go on)> after the separating line below. This appears to be Moore's comment on why the notes break abruptly.

If this were so, subconscious tooth-ache would be bound up with a human body: I couldn't have it, if my body were destroyed. But I could have conscious tooth-ache, without any body or any tooth.

So: the human eye is not pre-supposed in visual space; but on the other hand there is something in visual space which might be called "the eye", but has nothing to do with a body: e.g. in a dream a ring may move towards my eye, though none is moving towards my bodily eye.

We could say "the subject" is used in 2 different ways: (1) for the whole or a part of the human body (2) for something different.

~~E.g. moving of a voice from behind to in front, or from right ear to left, is something which~~

Change of pitch, or intensity, does not require any "auditory ear".

For movement of sounds what is needed is a "system of co-ordinates" which might be called "auditory ear".

"This sound moves round my head clockwise" has meaning independently of the physical head.

2nd use of "subject" always refers to a particular property of some space, auditory, visual, or space of tooth-ache.

8:36

Tooth-ache can move; or be in 2 teeth simultaneously – quite independently of human body.

People say "My tooth-ache I know from the inside, other people's only from the outside".

Or "I know my body from inside, others don't".

Or "If I saw his brain I should be seeing from outside his thoughts which he knows from inside".

"Points of View: J.B.S. Haldane"[48]: –

---

[48] This is a reference to a passage in a talk of Haldane's, first broadcast by the BBC in October 1929. 'When I look at a limestone mountain I realise that, grim and lifeless as it appears, it was made by countless billions of my microscopic fellow-creatures. What is more surprising, I think that I can even have some very dim inkling of what it feels like to be limestone. We know material bodies in general from the outside. We know our own bodies from the inside. Just as everyone knows what it feels like to be hot, so I know from my own personal experience what it feels like to consist of an abnormally large or small amount of calcium carbonate, of which the limestone mountain is built. In this concrete

"~~I now turn to visible world.~~ "We know natural things from outside; we know our own bodies from inside."

Can I have an inkling of what it would be like to see with 1000 eyes (like a fly)?

Not unless I have of what it would be like to see with 3.

It would be nonsense to say: "I could perfectly imagine that there was no eye in visual space": this would alter geometry of visual space.

A fiction must be described in our language.

J.B.S. Haldane says "I know what it feels like to be a limestone mountain".

8:37 This would have meaning if it meant: I know what feeling you have, when you get more & more calcium carbonate in your body.

Intimately connected. "All that is real is the experience of the present moment.": "All that is certain is the experience of the present moment."

Why is there a temptation to say this? I myself have been often tempted to say it.

"The present thought is the only thinker."

Is there "a head" involved in thinking, as there is an "eye" involved in visual space?

Thinking may take place nowhere in physical space.

Intimately connected again. "Our visual field is blurred at the edges". Very queer statement; true in a way, false in another.

Suppose you ask a person to fixate a point, & then draw what he sees.

He will draw something with blurred edges.

But has our visual field got blurred edges?

(1) Do we ever notice it?

(2) Could we say what it would be like if it were otherwise?

8:38 If you draw your visual field in a sense you are bound to draw edges blurred, but you must also admit that this isn't quite like what you see.

and detailed way I feel my relationship to the world around me.' (Haldane 1929, 602. In Dickinson et al. 1939, 78)

A picture of a cloud has a blurred outline, & a picture of it will be like what you see when you see the cloud.

But the visual field has no outline.

What's at the edge of visual field <u>may</u> be blurred in sense that it can't be recognised.

This experience couldn't be reproduced in a drawing by a blurred outline.

The 2 senses of "blurred" are quite different; just as blueness in a film picture is quite different from the characteristic of a dream.

In one sense what is blurred <u>could be imagined</u> with a sharp outline; but I can't imagine my visual field with a sharp outline.

The visual field has no boundary: it has no sense to say that the visual field has one.

"Blurred round the edges" of visual field, is either (1) nonsense or (2) describes a particular experience, which you needn't always have.

"Present experience alone is real." 8:39

One might ask: "present", as opposed to what?

In my memory there is a direction from more remote to nearer, which I might call direction <u>towards the present</u> – which I might call "memory-present" analogous to eye in visual field.

Obviously "memory-present" can't be only real.

In "I remember now", "now" is not a point in memory time.

8b

8:40   March 10 / 1933.

"Only reality is the present experience."

"Only reality is my present experience."

One isn't more absurd than the other; but idea expressed in this way is of enormous importance – as some fallacies are. In what sense is it a fallacy?

Anyone who has any temptation to hold Idealism or Solipsism knows the temptation to say this.

Russell "Outline": "Remembering which occurs <u>now</u> can't possibly prove that what is remembered occurred at some other time, because world might have sprung into being 5 minutes ago, full of acts of remembering which were entirely misleading."[49]

This is precise fallacy of "Idealism".

Apply question: What is verification of "world sprung into existence 5 minutes ago"?

If you admit <u>no</u> criterion, the sentence is useless wheel in your mechanism.

What difference would it make, if world began 5 minutes ago?

If we give it such a grammar that there is no evidence for or against it, we have made it a useless one.

8:41   Take "Mr. Smith came in 5 minutes ago". This gets its sense from system to which it belongs. E.g. How do you know? I looked at my watch.

Answer to "How <u>can</u> you know?" is a rule of grammar, because it is decided independently of any facts.

I lay down what is to be taken as evidence: it is a game which I construct.

---

[49] Moore refers to chapter 1 of Russell's *Outline of Philosophy* (1927) as the source of this citation and discusses it at some length (Wittgenstein 1993, 110). On page 7 of that book, Russell wrote that 'apart from arguments as to the proved fallibility of memory, there is one awkward consideration which the sceptic may urge. Remembering, which occurs now, cannot possibly – he may say – prove that what is remembered occurred at some other time, because the world might have sprung into being five minutes ago, exactly as it then was, full of acts of remembering which were entirely misleading.'

"What is evidence for ...?" <u>may</u> be one of grammar, & <u>may</u> be one of psychology.

E.g. it may mean "What <u>will</u> convince you?" which is announced by conjecture, on ground of past experience, & of course may be found wrong.

But if someone says "This happened 5 minutes ago" & says he measures it by his watch this is a rule which he lays down.

So if I say "Room is 9 feet long", I may give a method of measuring, e.g. by theodolite: & this gives a <u>meaning</u>, whether method is ever carried out or not.

Now the trouble is:

We don't, as a rule, lay down explicit rules. There are no rules to be found as to what is evidence for or against, or what is or isn't relevant to "He came here 5 minutes ago".

But though no rules have been laid down, we are <u>following</u> some rule, & should accept so & so as evidence for or against it.

8:42

Russell is refusing to admit as evidence for having existed more than 5 minutes ago, what we all accept as such evidence; & is therefore making it meaningless.

There may be a wheel in a watch which is "leer-laufend",[50] "otiose", but which doesn't look as if it were "otiose".

So Russell's "World didn't exist 5 minutes ago" looks as if it were like "I wasn't here 5 minutes ago", but <u>isn't</u>, if he refuses to take evidence for it.

Compare this with other statements which look as if they "meshed" with reality, but don't.

"This chair isn't still here when I close my eyes."

For "it is still here" I can take as evidence that <u>you</u> tell me you see it; or that a thing is still there, unless it has been destroyed.

I <u>could</u> assume that it doesn't, but this would make you wrong, or would compel me to complicated set of assumptions.

Suppose I say "If no-one sees it, it doesn't exist"; then I've made my sentence have a meaning such that all possible experience would agree with it.

---

[50] German for 'free-running', i.e. not connected to any other part of the mechanism. See the use of this term at 8:50.

8:43 "There's a white rabbit between A & B, whenever nobody is looking." This can't be refuted by experience, but is therefore meaningless.

It only appears to mean anything different from "There's no rabbit between A & B", because in some cases "There is a rabbit …" means something different from "There is no rabbit …": whereas in this case it really has none.

Suppose I used a picture-language – a picture of a rabbit.

We can imagine the world beginning 5 minutes ago, so long as we admit a means of checking it: we could make a picture of it. This would remain a picture, though it was an otiose element in our symbolism.

Suppose I see a white rod, which has a certain length; & I may see this because it has a measuring rod alongside. And I only see it because it emits light, & is therefore moving.

One criterion of motion is that we see it; & in this sense the rod isn't moving.

But if you say particles are moving, you must hold that it is essentially impossible to see their movement: & this must mean that "moving" means something different.

8:44 In all these cases we are asking for evidence, & pointing out that giving evidence is giving grammar.

Now in Russell's statement "5 minutes" is arbitrary; he could have said "2 minutes", or "½ minute"; & hence could have said "World began now".

Russell says "This isn't logically refutable." = "Only reality is experience of present moment."

If his statement has meaning, is there also a meaning in: World came to an end 5 minutes ago?

Could one say: Only reality is what happened 5 minutes ago?

When Russell says "Remembering now", what does "now" mean?

Not "at such & such a time by my watch".

"Now" here has a meaning similar to "I" when not used = a proper name.

There's an order in memory: e.g. Stevenson came first, then Ursell, then Moore. I describe content of memory by means of an order, in which there is a later & an earlier.

Now suppose Ursell had written events of day. <u>In</u> his manuscript there would be an order: he would use "before" & "after", & grammar would be that if A before B, B before C, then A before C. There would be a transitive order, as in my memory. Or there might be an order of films.   8:45

These <u>orders</u> we may call times: "memory-time", "narrative-time", "film-time".

In "memory-time" there is a point which all these events approach. It will have no <u>sense</u> to say: B occurred <u>after</u> the present in memory-time.

What I[51] ought to have said is:

"World might have been created now"

In <u>what</u> time is this "now" a point?

Answer might be: at 6 o'clock on March 10. What would this mean?

Suppose I had lantern with a long film, so that events on screen went on for years. There would be a sense in saying: First picture on the screen was one with picture of a room with clock pointing to 6 & calendar shewing March 10. We should have to give a similar meaning to "World began ...".

"Now" should be a point in an order. In <u>what</u> order? Not in memory-order.[52] He[53] doesn't give us a time in which it is a point.

Hence "5 minutes ago" has no meaning, because he hasn't said what the time is measured by.   8:46

So "World began <u>now</u>" would mean nothing, because I've not said in what order "now" is a point.

What is criterion for "is taking place now"?

There are at least 2

(1) Suppose I say "Clock is striking now". Then "now" is <u>present</u> in our memory-time. "now" as opposed to "some time ago" in memory.

(2) Suppose I say "Mr. Smith's lecture is ending now", because I have been told it is to end at 6.7, & I look at my watch & find 6.7.

"It's 6.10 <u>now</u>" has sense: therefore "now" not = "at 6.10".

---

[51] Moore later deleted 'I' and replaced it by: <Russell>.
[52] Moore later added: <(according to Russell)>.
[53] Moore later deleted 'He' and replaced it by: <Russell>.

But the order in which "now" is a point, is not the order of this hand reaching different points, because here there is no essential "now." "Now" wouldn't come in, in "reaches 1 before 2, & 2 before 3".

If anyone says "5 minutes ago": you can ask "what by?" And any answer to this question alters the meaning.

"5 minutes ago by the clock" will make "world began 5 minutes ago" nonsense, because "10 minutes ago by clock" has sense.

8:47 What tempts us to say this?

A difference of opinion which can't be removed, isn't a difference of opinion.

Compare case of dream where bang on door wakes him: a dream so long that it takes ½ an hour to tell; though banging only lasted ½ minute.

Has he dreamt it since we began to bang or not?

What is criterion?

9

March 13 / 1933. 8:48

Present experience only reality.

Natural answer: Surely past is too; do you mean to say you didn't get out of bed this morning?

But this common-sense objection doesn't really meet the point, though true enough.

Our man will answer: Past is real no longer, future isn't real yet, which are useless statements.

And this means that he has the image of something moving before his eyes. Whenever a man makes this kind of useless statement, he's always misled by some analogy; & we have to find out what it is. So with man who says boundaries of visual field are blurred.

Such a man tries to draw a picture of reality, that is right as opposed to wrong:

If we ask how people are distributed in this room: we can draw a picture, which is one of a system, some of which will be wrong & one right.

So "blurred" as opposed to "sharp edges": only present experience real, as opposed to past & future real too. 8:49

But can you imagine these alternatives? What would they be like?

Now I am at cross-roads: 2 subjects

(1) Thinkable & imaginable.

(2) "Present experience only is real" is not meant to be a mere fact of experience. They would say they couldn't imagine it otherwise.

And about this I would say: Then it has no sense. Nothing can really characterise reality, except as opposed to something else which is not the case.

(3) "Present experience only is real" arises from imagery which imagines events to pass before us like film in a lantern.

It would be all right, in case of lantern, if pointing to one picture of the film – we say "this is the only one which is in the lantern now": and we could call this "real".

But if he pointed to screen & said "this is only real picture" he would talk nonsense, because it has no neighbours.

It is same mistake as supposing we "see" things in visual space: what we see is "chairs".

8:50 We can say: This among tactual pictures is the only one I see.

We could say of screen-picture: This is only one projected; if we meant e.g. This has a blue patch in it; when we know of film-pictures that one projects a blue patch, other a red.

To say "Surely future is not yet here" means nothing unless it means "Future is future".

Both he who asserts & he who denies is talking nonsense.

Russell's statement.

I said: This isn't strictly an hypothesis at all, because he'd made such arrangements for it, that whatever our experience were it would be in harmony with it: it is "leer-laufend"[54]; therefore it means nothing.

But you might say: Surely it means something?

Does it mean anything to say: World was created 5 minutes ago?

Michelangelo's picture[55] has something to do with what we mean by creation of world.

Suppose we had 2 parallel planes, & that I described figures on 1 by describing figures on 2: e.g. "There is a circle on 1" is to mean "There is

8:51 a figure on 2 which is orthogonally projected from 1".

Next let the projection not be orthogonal, but could vary within + & − 2°.

Then: there could be an infinity of possible figures on 2, more or less circular.

Suppose I said, let there be no limit to method of projection: then to say "There's a circle on 2" would be meaningless.[56]

---

[54] German for 'free-running', i.e. not connected to any other part of the mechanism. See the use of this term at 8:42.

[55] Probably a reference to Michelangelo's Sistine Chapel frescos of the first six days of creation.

[56] Above the '2' in this sentence Moore later wrote <1?>, and this change is reflected in his summary notes which are as follows: <Suppose I had 2 parallel planes, & described figures on 1 so that e.g. "Circle on 1" = "There's figure on 2 orthogonally projected on 1". If I said "There's to be no limit to method of projection", then "There's a circle on 1" would be meaningless.> (10:54)

So with Russell: "was created 5 minutes ago" is a well-accredited term, like "a white rabbit" & therefore seems to mean something; but he has made arrangements for them which render them useless.

That a white rabbit is on <u>one</u> plane, doesn't mean that there's a white rabbit on another: we must first know method of projection.

Suppose an equation of oscillation were given (1) for visible oscillation of a rod (2) for essentially invisible oscillation of particles.

Suppose I arranged that a sine curve is to be projected in one mode, & the superimposed sine curve is to be projected in a totally different one: e.g. the superimposed were projected on a cylinder, not on the plane.

We naturally think of the oscillation of particles as being finer than that of rod as being coarser: but really the sense of "oscillation" is quite different.   8:52

Suppose we had theory that ends of rod oscillate & produce light and on a screen there appears a sine-curve; & I as scientist say that this corresponds to sining[57] of particles at end of rod.

Suppose sine-curve on screen shewed me amplitude, but didn't shew <u>place</u> of small sine-curve relatively to big one.

My experience at first could have been represented by a sine-curve.

The drawing has to be understood <u>quite</u> differently from if it said that the rod has 2 movements, a coarse one & a fine.

We are used to pictures being used in a certain way: but if this familiar usage is departed from, we no longer know what it means or whether it means anything.

When I say "That means nothing" I mean that you have altered your method of projection.

"Thinkable & "imaginable".   8:53

Everybody uses these words to mean the same: Could we imagine it?

Not quite correct: Imaginable is only a special case of thinkable, connected with *Tractatus* "Proposition is a picture"[58].

---

[57] 'Sining' is presumably Wittgenstein's neologism for the movements of the particles that generate the appearance of a sine-shaped curve.

[58] See *Tractatus* (Wittgenstein 1922) 4.01 ff.

First note: (what I hadn't then noticed) that idea of "picture" is vague: e.g. score is "picture" of music.

Is it imaginable that everyone in this room should be standing on his head? Answer is: Yes; but this doesn't say anything about our psychology.

In the case of things in this room, any description can be translated into a painted picture, & vice versa.

(Billiard balls can be substituted for complicated objects, for which there is no suitable language.)

 & A(5,7) come to the same thing.

It seems to me useful to say "A proposition is a picture, or something like it", which doesn't really give away my point.

8:54 I extend "picture", just as I did when I talked of projecting sine-curve (1) into sine-curve (2) into colour.

Suppose I had limited myself to propositions about billiard balls in this room, in such a way that I could replace any by a picture.

Then proposition that Ursell is whistling would have no picture corresponding: it could only be represented by picture, if mode of projection were different.

Call "imaginable" = "paintable": then we might say proposition was ~~unthinkable~~ nonsense, if not paintable.

Now suppose I picture his whistling by ⊂≡≡⊃.

I've introduced a new way of picturing: & now I can imagine more.

Thus I could introduce way of picturing strength of notes: & I can then imagine more.

If I thus extend notion of "picturing", how can I be right in saying "This makes no sense"?

You can make a new system; but you're apt to think you've made such a system, when you haven't.

8:55 What would prove that I am right in saying metaphysical propositions are meaningless? Only if you say to yourself: Oh yes, this is what I meant.

I said: You can't say "This picture is only one on screen".[59]

If a person says so, I can only ask: What do you mean? meaning "What is grammar of your statement?".

And then there are 2 possibilities: He may admit he has been misled; or he may shew me a new grammar he is using.

You <u>could</u> say "Everything is thinkable", because for everything you <u>could</u> make a method of projection.

I say "That isn't thinkable", meaning: With common method of projection, it means nothing.

Does it make sense to say "I threw this ~~chalk~~ right-hand glove out of 3-dimensional space into 4-dimensional"?

You'd say: No: because who says this will be thinking of it on analogy of throwing from one room to another.

But, if I meant "My right-hand glove has disappeared, & a left-hand appeared instead", then it would make sense.

Any expression <u>may</u> make sense: but you may think you are using it with sense, when you're not.

Helmholtz said that in happy moments he could imagine 4-dimensional space.[60]   8:56

Mustn't he have been talking nonsense?

I.e. isn't it true it makes no sense <u>in</u> the system he was using?

---

[59] Moore later added: <2 or more pictures might be shewn on a screen.>

[60] According to Hans Biesenbach, commenting on a parallel remark in Wittgenstein's *Nachlass* (2000) about Helmholtz on the imaginability of four dimensional space (MS 162b, 38v), no such statement can be found in Helmholtz's writings (Biesenbach 2014, 255). Indeed, Biesenbach quotes a representative passage from Helmholtz's famous lecture 'On the Origin and Significance of Geometrical Axioms', an exploration of the question whether non-Euclidean geometries can be visualized, where he defends the view that it is absolutely impossible for us to imagine a fourth dimension: 'As all our means of sense-perception extend only to space of three dimensions, and a fourth is not merely a modification of what we have, but something perfectly new, we find ourselves by reason of our bodily organisation quite unable to represent a fourth dimension.' (Helmholtz 1881, 64)

"I threw the chalk into 4-dimensional space" may quite well mean "It first disappeared, & then appeared again".

Is "Leave the room, & don't leave it" nonsense?
If you can <u>do</u> anything with it, use it in a language game, then it's not.

"It's human weakness that we can't write down <u>all</u> cardinal numbers" I called meaningless, on presupposition that anyone who said it was using "human weakness" as in "It's human weakness that we can't write down a billion".

"I see 5 fingers" has sense, where "I see a billion" has none. But even if a man <u>had</u> given a meaning to latter, he wouldn't have given one to "I see an infinite number".

8:57 In Mathematics if a man introduces $\sqrt{-1}$, he knows he has to explain what system this belongs to.

Gauss first said what it means.[61]

What we are doing is to point out <u>actual</u> mistakes. If no-one was inclined to make them, all I say would be quite useless.

---

[61] The sentence is followed by a question mark, and enclosed in parentheses in Moore's notes; these are probably later additions by Moore. Gauss introduced mathematicians to the 'Gaussian plane' and the idea of a complex number as a point in the complex plane, and coined the term 'complex number'. Gauss worked out these ideas in 1796, but only published them in April 1831. Consequently, historians of mathematics give priority to Caspar Wessel as the discoverer of complex numbers, as Wessel's paper on the topic, 'On the Analytical Representation of Direction', was published in 1799, setting out the result of work he had done in the 1780s. However, because Wessel published in Danish, his paper received no attention until it was rediscovered in 1895. See Nahim 1998, chapter 3.

May Term, 1933

1

Missed one April 21. (T's party)[1]

[1] This was the first class meeting of the May term; the term began on 19 April.

2a

8:58   April 24.

Meaning of proposition <u>is</u> way of verification?

or You can <u>determine</u> meaning by asking how verified?

This is necessarily mere rule of thumb, because "verification" means different things, & because in <u>some</u> cases question makes no sense – e.g. in "I have tooth-ache".

Roughly speaking rule comes to same as: "What do you do with this proposition?" or "How do you apply this proposition?"

This question is a <u>reaction</u> against way of looking at things, which treats such questions as irrelevant.

It can be roughly expressed: If you hear a proposition, which you understand, we all of us have more or less characteristic experiences connected with proposition & even with particular words. If I said a Chinese word, e.g. "bo", there would be no other characteristic experience except just the sound. Naturally we can't hear "table" as a mere noise (not that this fact interests us very much). A footstep on the stairs stands out from other noises I can hear. So "but" "and" & so on produce a particular feeling in us, because we know the language. There's again a difference between hearing Japanese & hearing a dog bark – we feel that former is a language.

8:59   When you've learnt meaning of a symbol, you have a particular feeling while you use it; <u>but</u> I don't call this "meaning".

If by meaning of a sentence you mean a series of such experiences; then to say that you must ask for verification sounds absurd. Verification has nothing to do with meaning in this sense.

What I mean by "meaning" is place of symbol in a calculus – the way in which it is used.

It's, of course, true that if it were used differently, your feeling would be different: but this doesn't interest me.

I stress the point of view which says: to know meaning is to know use.

"Discursive" & "intuitive".

"Intuitive" refers to seeing the same thing for a time – 2 minutes, 3 minutes, or a second: = taking something in as a whole at a glance; & if you can take it in in a moment, so for an hour.

But a melody I must run through: I can't take it in as a whole at a time.

"Discursive" way of looking at meaning is to call meaning use: e.g. to teach meaning of $\int$ is to teach the calculus.[2]

"State" of a physical body is different from tooth-ache as a state. What is criterion for physical body being in a state – e.g. exercising pressure? "Knowing how to play chess" is a state of my mind, in sense in which being elastic or exercising pressure is: but you are then using it for a hypothetical state, quite different from a conscious state. It's not like a state of a thing, part of which you perceive, part not.

Suppose we talk of "unconscious tooth-ache", this easily leads to a confusion.

If people say "tooth-ache is a rotten tooth seen from within"; then they could say a man has it all the time, but perceives it during part of the time, during part not. With us it has no meaning[3] to say he perceives it: he's got it.

Memory as a criterion of the past.

Memory is only verification in case of a dream.

In this case "I remember this happened" means the same as "This happened".

If I say "Cambridge has won the boat-race", & you remember my rule about verification, question arises: Does that Cambridge did win, mean that I read it in the newspaper? And of course I don't mean to say it does; but it has something to do with it.

Connection between them is clear from the way in which anyone would explain the meaning of "winning a boat-race".

---

[2] '$\int$' is the sign for integration; together with differentiation, its inverse, it is one of the two basic operations of calculus.
[3] Moore originally wrote 'meaning' but later changed this to 'no meaning'.

8:61 Connection between "I saw Cambridge win" & "Cambridge did win", is not (1) that the 2 mean the same nor (2) that Cambridge won = either I saw or – or –. It is a much more complicated one.

I was accused of Idealism for saying this.

If idealist says "A chair is a visual picture of a chair", this is obviously bosh. So to say "A chair is a class of visual pictures".

Mistake about all this is that you want to explain one thing by means of another thing. (should have been said by): "chair" & "visual picture of a chair" have utterly different grammars.

It is mistake which led Russell to define number 3: to ask "What is the number 3?"[4]

But though a chair ≠ visual picture of a chair, the 2 are not related as is a chair & a photo of it. We can only explain what we mean by chair, because we have visual pictures. That you can see a chair is essential to meaning of "chair".

I could be said to point at a visual picture of a chair, if I pointed to a mirror.

I could explain what chair is by reference to wooden bars. But a chair isn't composed of visual pictures in sense in which it might be of bars.

8:62 I can't explain what "chair" means without explaining what "visual picture of a chair" means.

Suppose S. asks: "What does "chair" mean?" and I shew him view in a stereoscope. He would understand what "chair" means, because he has seen views of a chair; because he would understand use of the word.

There is no further question: What is it?

If a man saw a boat-race, after you'd described what a boat-race is, & didn't know it was, we should say he hadn't understood description.

In recent times people have seen that time is mirrored /measured/ by a clock.

But time is independent of way in which we measure it. We measure it in different ways, & therefore "an hour" means different things.

If I say "This room is 6 yards long", I haven't decided on any particular way of measurement.

---

[4] See Russell 1919, chapter 2, 'Definition of Number', especially 11 and 18.

If you understand the particular misunderstanding which is due to forgetting <u>how</u> I explain what's meant by "a yard long", viz. by shewing the <u>measure</u>: the misunderstanding which consists in supposing that being a yard long is something independent of the way in which it is measured.

"At half past 4 precisely." Could I make this more precise? No: it's essential to its meaning, that it should <u>not</u> have been fixed whether he's only to have been said to be <u>precisely</u> at <u>4</u>.30, if he touches the handle at moment of middle of Trinity clock's last stroke.

8:63

In certain cases of <u>scientific</u> experiment we <u>do</u> lay down precise method of measurement: & yet there is something analogous here to what I mean by "6 yards long".

Compare "These 2 chairs have same colour". I shall know what I mean, if I know verification. There may be many: e.g. (1) I don't know which is which, when I mix them up (2) I can't see a transition between them when laid side by side. In ordinary life, I haven't fixed on any.

I said idea expressed by "This distance is six yards, quite independently of how we measure it" forgets that to explain what is meant by "6 yards" we must shew a man how we measure it.

So to explain "boat-race" we must shew a man what a boat-race looks like, by shewing one, or a picture of it, or by giving a description. But you couldn't explain by shewing him notice in newspaper. Therefore not <u>any</u> verification of boat-race being won will explain meaning. You wouldn't say a man understood meaning of "boat-race", unless he would recognise a boat-race when he saw one.

8:64

We have boat-races, conversations about them, & what newspapers write about them.

Now consider the pure writing about them. Couldn't it be done as a game in itself?[5]

Cf. Time. There is memory-time; but there is also what might be called written time – i.e. the order established by the words "before" & "after". An order could be established, without knowing what it was about. We might call it "grammatical" time.

---

[5] Moore later added: <e.g. on Mars ...>

Suppose we received wireless messages, which we knew weren't sent from anywhere, but were merely due to electric discharges, but which said "Cambridge has won the boat-race" & "Oxford has won the boat-race", we might adopt the language & mean only the messages.

There could be 2 kinds of meteorites, one of which gave lines similar to Roman letters, the other to Greek, & then we might call the one kind Roman the other Greek – not meaning, of course, what we do now mean.

8:65 On the one hand (1) /we don't actually use them to explain/ we don't explain what a boat-race is by same things which we should say were verifications of Cambridge having won; although in some cases we might.

(E.g. there are 2 Chinese, one of whom has killed the other, & a European judge has to do something about it, & knows that they quarrelled about some news[6], without knowing what the news was – i.e. understanding the word. Suppose the word means a particular kind of dress, which may only be worn by a priest. He needn't know what kind of dress; but needs to find out whether A did wear it or not. The judge would use the word in a different way.)

It would upset our whole grammar if we excluded something as a symptom which always admittedly accompanied the meaning. i.e. if by a rule we said "this is not to be used as a symptom of raining".[7] (This does happen in theology. E.g. nobody has ever said what would be the criterion of Transubstantiation; which shews that such a proposition is not a scientific one, & can't so be used.)

---

[6] This word, which as written appears to be 'news', may be the transliteration of a Chinese term for an article of clothing, or Wittgenstein may have made up the word entirely. Moore later circled this word in the notes, likely indicating his own uncertainty on this question.

[7] Moore's summary notes: <It would upset all our grammar if we refused to admit x as symptom of y, if x always accompanied y: if we said "x is not to be used as a symptom of y".> (10:103)

2b

April 28 / 1933.

Meaning of "meaning".

If I say meaning of a word is <u>determined</u> by its grammar – by rules, I've been asked do I mean that the meaning is a list of rules.

Of course, not. You wouldn't be so tempted to ask the question whether I do, unless you supposed that when you have a substantive "the meaning" you have to look out for something at which you can point & say "this" is the meaning.

Talking of the use of money, you can say the use is to buy things. But you can buy things you can't point to e.g. permission to sit in a seat at a theatre, or your life.

Just as you can sometimes buy a cow to which you can point, sometimes a permission to which you can't; so sometimes you can point to a thing which a name stands for, sometimes you can't.

I said that, without much change, we could talk of the meaning of a chessman – though there is nothing it stands for.

What we call the sense of a proposition is much more similar than one would think to the meaning of a melody or theme. People say a theme has a meaning for them, & if you ask them what it means they can't tell you. You can say e.g. that a tune is like a question or answer.

All that this shews is that the way we use "meaning" or "sense" is floating.

Of course, "ask for verification" isn't applicable to a musical phrase; but neither is it to an exclamation like "Damn!".

You can construct sentences with regard to which it is not clear, if you look at them, whether they have meaning or not.

E.g. I have x pence, & $x^2 + 3x - 2 = 0$.

Unless one can see at once what the root is, one can't see whether it has sense or not.

Suppose $x = 0$: did my statement have same sense as "I have no pence"?

The sentence has no sense <u>at all</u> unless I know how to solve the equation.

This is rather a good example to shew in what way the meaning of a phrase has nothing to do with the momentary impression it produces on us.

Vagueness of "meaning" & "understanding" is shewn by this:

Also by, suppose one opens a novel & sees "After he'd said this, he left the room": do you understand this or not? You might say you do, because it's English; but also you don't, because you don't know who "he" was, nor what he said.

Sum up:

8:68 Ideas of "meaning" & "sense" are in a way obsolete; unless we use them in such phrases as "this means the same as that", or in "this has no sense".

I said "p is a reason for q" <u>can</u> be given in the grammar.

I meant that whether p is a reason for q is <u>not</u> a question of experience.

This was directed against the statement: ""How can you know?" is not the point; but "What does it mean?"."

Does "that the pavement is wet" which verifies "it has rained", fix the meaning of "it has rained"?

"That the pavement is wet" is a symptom.

Verification determines meaning, only <u>where</u> verification gives the grammar; & in this case it gives very little of grammar.

In theory of probability, it is often asked: Is this <u>a priori</u>, or not?[8]

Are you talking of a calculation /mathematical question/, or of a question of experience?

Take 2nd law of thermodynamics, shuffling cards, or mixing nuts & raisins.

People say 2nd law of thermodynamics seems to have some sort of "apriority" about it.

Is it a matter of experience that nuts & raisins become more mixed as you turn the mixing machine?

8:69 Can't you imagine that when put in mixed, they should become separated?

You can. But then people will say: In that case there <u>must</u> be a difference in weight.

You may mean: You're going to assume some other force, even if you can't verify it.

---

[8] Moore's summary notes: <Is probability <u>a priori</u> or not?> (10:56)

To decide between grammar of grammatical rule, & grammar of experiential proposition,

"When it rains, wall gets pink" will hardly give any explanation of what's meant by "rains"; but it does explain just the little bit of grammar as to whether you are dealing with a grammatical rule or experiential proposition, when you say "it has rained".

"If only you throw often <u>enough</u>, it will come heads & tails equally frequently."

When people say "Laws of physics give only certain frequencies: physics doesn't say "Kettle on fire will boil", but only that it does so in a certain proportion of all cases" /"that if you take sufficiently long series, cases where it doesn't will be negligible compared to those where it does"/. I say "In that case, physics says nothing", for it will allow that every time for 100 years it freezes.

How does giving a symptom (experientially connected) give you grammar? Suppose a person says "My symptom for having tooth-ache is that I'm swollen", this would shew that he did not mean by tooth-ache a feeling.

8:70

3a

May 1.

Example of case where bit of grammar that needs to be illustrated is where we say that verification of so & so is some symptom.

How far is giving verification of a proposition a grammatical statement about it?

E.g. how far does: The wall has turned pink (if a symptom) give the grammar of "It has been raining"?

That when it rains, wall turns pink, is <u>not</u> a proposition of grammar at all.

But that we can here talk of a <u>symptom</u>, <u>is</u> a matter of grammar.[9]

In case of probability we do have problems, where people aren't clear whether a given proposition is a bit of mathematics <u>or</u> a bit of physics.

E.g. Law of Thermodynamics – Here it is worth asking: What is your criterion that shuffling of cards make arrangement more irregular? Are you simply saying how you're going to use words? E.g. a man might say: Somewhere else cards have been unshuffled; & it <u>must</u> be the case: which shews it's a law you've taken to regulate your mode of expression.

Suppose you say: Everybody is really going to Paris; most don't get there; but everybody would, if he lived long enough.

This can't be an experiential proposition. But it may serve in this way. You may be determined to describe every human being's life-path as a way to Paris with deviations.

So of a thing going nearly in a circle, you could say it moves in a circle, with a correction for deviations.

Then: Everything moves in a circle with deviations; is <u>grammatical</u> not experiential.

When we talk about "meaning" & "sense" & "grammar", there's this problem connected with it:

---

[9] Moore's summary notes: <"When it rains, wall turns pink" is <u>not</u> grammar at all. but "Pinkness of wall is <u>symptom</u> that it has rained" is matter of grammar.> (10:103)

Does, that we talk about it so much, mean that these are subject-matter of philosophy? Are these more important than chairs, tables etc.? Is "meaning of meaning" central question of philosophy?

Is "meaning" metalogical?

First answer is: No; because there are problems concerned with meaning not of "meaning", but e.g. of "Time".

The words "meaning", "proposition", "world" have no special place in our investigations. What gives "meaning" a special place, is that our investigations are about language, & about puzzles that arise from use of language. Hence we shall use these words more frequently; but our investigations won't be all of meaning of "meaning".

Is meaning of "meaning" different, in "meaning of "book"" & "meaning of "and""?

When I <u>buy</u> a seat in theatre, or a book, are they both "my money's <u>worth</u>" in same sense? In "I <u>got</u> a seat" & "I <u>got</u> a book", "got" means something different.

$r(1,2) \vee b(3,4)$

A <u>red</u> circular patch has coordinates 1 & 2, a <u>blue</u> has 3 & 4.

We use "meaning" to say that r & b have different meanings.

or that $r(1,2) \vee b(3,4)$ <u>means</u> the same as $b(3,4) \vee r(1,2)$

or that "(" has no meaning.

We might say meaning of word is its place in grammar, just as meaning of a chessman is its place in system of rules.

Grammar = any explanation of use of language. An English grammar does not contain <u>all</u> the rules. But we can't say that what's left out is the essential or philosophical part.

"This is white" /pointing, saying "This is what I mean by white",/ is a rule of grammar.

That "is" can sometimes be explained by "=", sometimes not, is a rule of grammar.

Russell's theory of definite descriptions is a rule of grammar.

What is relation between that study of grammar which a linguist makes, & that which we are making?

(1) Linguist is concerned with history, we aren't.

(2) We are interested in "There is an individual such that" (Russell) which isn't good English.

(3) Our object is to get rid of certain puzzles, in which the grammarian isn't interested at all: e.g. "Time flows".

<u>Is</u> what we say about "Time flows" grammar at all?

English grammar would allow "Space flows" just as well.

I say in "Time flows" & "Water flows", "flows" is used differently.

To ~~shew~~ explain what "flows" means, I ~~should~~ might point at a river.

Now we shouldn't naturally call this /the doing of this the giving of/ a rule of grammar.

8:74   The grammarian looks merely at "This is red", whereas we should say this has no meaning without another sign – e.g. pointing.

We are interested in puzzles which grammarian isn't, & for which he is partly responsible.

Partly we are pulling ordinary grammar to bits.

I have always wanted to say something about grammar of ethical expressions, or e.g. of "God".

One great trouble our language gets us into is that we take a <u>substantive</u> to stand for a <u>thing</u> or <u>substance</u>.

Ordinary grammar doesn't forbid us to use substantives in this way: the origin of all use of substantives & verbs is in fact a simile for physical bodies moving.

Genders shew that things must have been compared with male & female.

Now: use of such a word as "God".

It has been used in many different ways: e.g. sometimes for something very like a human being – a physical body.

Cf. "soul" which has sometimes been described as something "gaseous".[10]

But others haven't meant by "soul" anything like this.

I've often said: How misleading is the question: What <u>is</u> the number 3?

8:75   "Concrete" & "abstract" never shed proper light because they suggest something like "solid" & "gaseous" – which are comparable. We want

---

[10] See Haeckel 1900, 200, quoted above at 5:12.

something not comparable like "chair" & "permission to sit in a chair"; "railway" & "railway accident".

If I restricted use of "soul" to such phrases as "His soul is at rest" or "His soul is easily stirred", you might say I'm denying that there is any soul: but you may mean by "Men have souls" simply that such propositions are true.

Fact that "I hope to God" is used by a man, may mean that he does believe in God in a sense.[11]

When a man worships idols

(1) One possibility is that he believes idol is alive & will help him. Then man must have forgotten that he made it: but this <u>can</u> happen.

(2) In millions of cases, this will not happen, but e.g.

(a) God <u>dwells</u> in the statue:

But what does "<u>dwells</u>" mean?

By asking what he would say, & what he wouldn't, you can get at how he uses the word.

Haeckel said "God is a gaseous vertebrate",[12] meaning that that's what people meant.

This is like saying "Soul is a gaseous human being"; & answer is <u>sometimes</u> people so use this word, but sometimes not at all.

James on "breath" & relation to soul.[13]

Being a substantive people try to find a substance for "soul"; e.g. it's really the brain, it's really the breath.

---

[11] It is likely that Wittgenstein had in mind Dorothea Schönfund, a character in Gottfried Keller's novel *Green Henry*. See Wittgenstein TS 219, 6, and Keller 1985, part IV, chapter 11, 631.

[12] 'In the higher and more abstract forms of religion this idea of bodily appearance is entirely abandoned, and God is adored as a "pure spirit" without a body. "God is a spirit, and they who worship him must worship him in spirit and in truth." Nevertheless, the psychic activity of this "pure spirit" remains just the same as that of the anthropomorphic God. In reality, even this immaterial spirit is not conceived to be incorporeal, but merely invisible, gaseous. We thus arrive at the paradoxical conception of God as a *gaseous vertebrate*.' (Haeckel 1900, 288)

[13] 'The "I think" which Kant said must be able to accompany all my objects, is the "I breathe" which actually does accompany them ... breath, which was ever the original of "spirit," breath moving outwards, between the glottis and the nostrils, is, I am persuaded, the essence out of which philosophers have constructed the entity known to them as consciousness.' (James 1904, 491; 1912, 37)

A. "Soul is really only activities of body". B. "Can't you see that soul can't be body".

If you have given up pointing, you still think that you must explain a substantive by some other substantive such as "activities".[14]

Thus: "3 is not the figure 3" is quite true – meaning that we don't use "3" & "the figure 3" in the same way: but those who say this try to say "3 is a class of classes".[15]

Are rules of chess propositions about wood? No, we shouldn't naturally say so.

No-one ever maintained that a chair was the word "chair". Why then did anyone say that 3 is the figure 3? Because he wanted something to point to.

When I get a title, the title is not a scratch on a piece of paper, or a sound; but to say he has the title is to say something about a word. So about "Ding an Sich"[16]: we only have views of the chair: people want the chair itself to be on a level with a view of a chair.

Luther said: "Theology is Grammar of word of[17] God".[18]

---

[14] Moore's summary notes: <If you give this up, you still think that you must explain a substantive by some other substantive – e.g. say that soul is the activities of a body.> (10:58)

[15] 'Accordingly we set up the following definition: – *The number of a class is the class of all those classes that are similar to it.* Thus the number of a couple will be the class of all couples. In fact, the class of all couples will *be* the number 2, according to our definition.' (Russell 1919, 18)

[16] 'Ding an sich', a German phrase usually translated as 'thing in itself': an expression introduced by Kant for a thing as it is independent of our representation (or view) of it, as contrasted with the thing as it is in our representation (or view) of it.

[17] Moore later circled this word and put a question mark by it, possibly indicating his belief that Wittgenstein's intended meaning was more likely 'Theology is Grammar of word God'. Indeed, this is how Alice Ambrose's edition of her notes of these lectures presents this remark: 'Luther said that theology is the grammar of the word "God"' (Wittgenstein 1979, 32). However, in his 1937 diary Wittgenstein wrote 'I read somewhere, Luther had written that theology is the "grammar of the word of God," of the holy scripture' (Wittgenstein 2003, 211), indicating that Moore's initial transcription may well have been accurate.

[18] A possible source for this attribution to Luther could have been Johann Georg Hamann's letter to his brother of 19 February 1760. There Hamann quotes Johann Albrech Bengel's report that Luther said that 'The science of Theology is nothing else, but Grammar, exercised on the words of the Holy Spirit' (Hamann 1956, 10; Bengel 1858, 44). Wittgenstein was familiar with some of Hamann's writings (Biesenbach 2014, 244, 558, 677).

This might mean: An investigation of idea of God is a grammatical one.

Now (a) suppose "god" means something like a human being; then "he has 2 arms" & "he has 4 arms" are not grammatical propositions but (b) suppose someone says: You can't talk of god having arms, this is grammatical.

Austrian general: "I will remember you after death, if this is possible".

That so & so is ridiculous (as this is), or blasphemous, shews grammar.[19]

This is ridiculous, because "remember after death" is really metaphorical. (You might say "Adding 3 to 3" is metaphorical from "Adding 3 more apples to a heap of apples".)

That "The Lord is my shepherd" is metaphorical, means that the words have a certain grammar: e.g. it doesn't follow that I am a sheep.

There are many controversies about meaning of "God", which could be settled by saying "I'm not using the word in such a sense as that you can say ..."

If parents believe that they have an answer to prayer, then in a sense they have an answer from God.

If we get a psychological explanation of how the idea came into their head, this doesn't prove it didn't "come from God" – that they were mistaken.

The son of these parents began to have doubts as follows. He wanted to go to a theatre. Parents told him to pray. He prayed & got "Yes"; they prayed & got "No". He was wrong to doubt on this ground: or rather his religion was merely scientific.[20]

If you interpret your experience on this basis, it is possible that different people should get different answers.

Wittgenstein may also have been led to this notion by reading Mauthner. In *Tractatus* (Wittgenstein 1922) 4.0013, he refers to Fritz Mauthner's 'critique of language'. The epigraphs to the first section of Mauthner's *Contributions to a Critique of Language* include a related passage from Hamann's correspondence: 'Do you understand now my principle that reason is linguistic and that with Luther I turn philosophy entirely into grammar?' (translated from Mauthner 1923, xx). For further discussion, see Hamann 2007, 22, note 5; Biesenbach 2014, 345-6.

[19] See Wittgenstein 1966, 53.

[20] Moore's summary notes: <If one man gets "Yes" in answer to prayer to know whether so & so is right, and another gets "No", this doesn't prove God doesn't answer prayers. If you think it does you are taking religion scientifically?> (10:58)

Such difficulties <u>can</u> be solved by "We didn't pray in the right way". Disagreement of 2 answers can quite properly produce a <u>religious</u> conflict; but this <u>need</u> not be religion of that kind which takes religious statements <u>scientifically</u> (as the son did).

It <u>seems</u> at first sight as if there were 2 ways of using such words as "God", either the <u>real</u> or the metaphorical. But different religions treat something as making sense, which others treat as <u>nonsense</u>: they don't merely one deny a proposition which other affirms.

8:79   Different religions are as man says <u>beforehand</u>

if "Yes" does lead to bad plays, I shall give up praying; but it never does.

if it does, it must be sent me by God for some particular purpose.

3b

May 5 / 1933.

<u>Certain class of topics connected with Ethics.</u>

I've talked about way in which one explains meaning of a word.

But I haven't talked about one problem:

I've said that, though I compare use of words with a calculus, grammar with a game, yet we don't generally think of the rules according to which the words we use are used, & we change our rules as we go along. E.g. if we speak of "Moses" & someone says "Who was Moses?" & we say "The man who led Israel through the desert", & someone says "But he didn't, someone else did", then I may say "The man who performed the 9 plagues in Egypt". Everyone would agree that definition of a word determines its meaning; but here we have different definitions, therefore a change of meaning. We should say "We meant something"; but what this points to is that the meaning isn't anything that's <u>present</u> when you say the word; & it also points to this: that, when people play with a ball, they follow certain rules, & it's useful to compare this with usage of language, because in this way we can get rid of certain difficulties which arise when we <u>believe</u> that we are following a certain rule – falsely.

Now people can say "Meanings of words are vague". This may mean that we haven't fixed certain rules: e.g. whether if very tall & with very small top, we shall call it a table. If we compare a concept like "table" with a boundary, we can say the boundaries of actual usage are blurred. But we may, for certain purposes, draw a clear boundary & compare it with the blurred one.

You <u>can't</u> draw a <u>precise</u> boundary <u>identical with</u> the <u>blurred</u> one; only one <u>like</u> it in certain respects.

There are harmless cases in which one can say: This word is used in so many distinct ways, & give them.

But there seem difficult cases. E.g. "What is a "game"?", you might say: let's see what's in common to all games, e.g. patience & football. But, if they have something in common, does it follow that we mean this, when we call so & so a game? Not at all. To explain "game" we might say "Like hockey, football & similar things".

Suppose there are gradual transitions of shape, having shewn a table, similarity will extend by gradual transitions indefinitely. But as in colours, you can use a word for red & its surroundings, another for blue & its, & then there will be nothing in common; but also you can use a word to cover all of them.

If we wanted to lay down rules for "good" or "beautiful"[21] or "game"; we should in different cases have to compare different games with that particular use. And if we ask why the same word is used in all these ways, the reason need not be that there's anything in common, but that there's a gradual transition. The thing you say in the end may not be what you meant in the beginning, though it has a connection through gradual transitions.

9:3

So in Mathematics: people thought of trisecting angle; then it was shewn that this was impossible. If I shew a man who has been trying to trisect, the proof of impossibility: in what sense could he say, That was what I really wanted? He could only say: you've led me to substitute one meaning for another – a meaning which takes the other's place, in one or other of usual senses. One investigation may for lots of good reasons be the natural one to take the place of a completely different one.

We sometimes use a word, & then give a definition. E.g. "force" was always used: but in physics a definition was given. Here a new concept replaced, for good reasons, the old one.

This is connected with: We can't find out meaning of "good", by looking for what all cases have in common: even if there is something in common, we may never use "good" for that.[22]

---

[21] In his discussion of 'good' and 'beautiful' Wittgenstein probably had in mind two symposia which took place at the Joint Session of the Aristotelian Society and the Mind Association in July 1932. The first consisted of three papers on 'Is Goodness a Quality?' (Moore, Joseph, and Taylor, 1932); the second comprised three papers on 'The Limits of Psychology in Aesthetics' (Reid, Knight, and Joad, 1932). In the subsequent discussion of these topics, Wittgenstein may be referring to Knight's paper (9:28), and alluding to some of the others.

[22] 'It will be admitted, I think, that the actions to which, in prospect or after performance, we apply the epithet "right," are very various; and that if one were asked what they have in common, in virtue of which we call them right, we should find it difficult to answer: so much so, that Prof. Prichard, while holding that each right action is made right by being

You could name 4 activities, & then say: I'm going to call any activity except these 4, a "game".

What I'm driving at is: It's not the case that (1) if we use a word for a whole range of things, it must be because they have something in common, nor (2) that we can say, the word = either this, or that, or that.

There may be nothing in common between the 2 ends of the series.

The way in which you use "good" in particular case is partly defined by the topic you're talking of.

Each way in which A can convince B that x is good, fixes a meaning in which "good" is used – fixes the grammar of the discussion.

9:4

When people say "This is a matter of taste".

Supposing I discussed with someone "What kind of flower will be the nicest in this window-box?",

the difference of taste needn't be as simple as "I like this", "You like that".

there can be discussion of all sorts of kind, & then in the end you may come to something which might be called a difference of taste: e.g. Yes, you always prefer slightly stronger contrasts, I always prefer slightly weaker.

One could say:

Nothing would be more astonishing than if "good" had the same meaning always, considering the way we learn it.

So it may be very difficult to find anything in common between 2 uses of "good", but there will be gradual transitions from one to the other, which take the place of something in common.

In the *Golden Bough*,[23] Frazer constantly makes one particular kind of mistake in explanation.

There have been 3 accounts of punishment (1) to deter (2) to improve (3) to take vengeance.

---

of some definite sort – payment of a debt, maintenance of a parent, or what not – contends that we can say no more than this of it to justify our calling any action right. To me it seems that this makes of our obligations an ununified heap. I should like to find something common to the reasons why I ought to do this *and* that *and* that.' (Joseph, in Moore, Joseph, and Taylor 1932, 132)

[23] Sir James George Frazer, *The Golden Bough: A Study in Magic and Religion* (1922). For a discussion of which edition Wittgenstein may have used, see the notes to page 9:7 below.

But if you ask "Why does a father punish his son?" there may be none of them, or all 3, or something between 2 of them.

In case of a community, <u>Why</u> is that crime punished? <u>Who</u> wants to improve?

9:5

Why do people go deer-stalking?

In the case of <u>one</u> person, there may be many reasons & not necessarily one predominating.

One main reason for preferring playing one instrument to another, may be the posture you take up in playing it.

There's a way of explanation, e.g. of why do people hunt, which says "<u>This</u> one thing is the reason", & then, if you say "Not consciously" answers "Then unconsciously".

Frazer talks of Magic performed with an effigy, & says primitive people believe that by stabbing effigy they have hurt the model.

I say: Only in some cases do they thus entertain a false scientific belief.

It <u>may</u> be that it expresses your wish to hurt.

Or it <u>may</u> be not even this: It may be that you have an impulse to do it, as when in anger you hit a table; which doesn't mean that you believe you hurt it, nor need it be a survival from prehuman ancestors.

Hitting has many sides.

Frazer also talks of festivals in which effigy of a human being is killed; & explains <u>all</u> as due to fact that once this was done to a man.

This <u>may</u> be so; but it's not true that it <u>must</u>.

The experience of making an effigy & throwing in water[24] has a peculiarity which may be satisfactory for its own sake: like tearing a photograph of an enemy.

---

[24] See Frazer 1922, 311 ff., and chapter 32, 'The Death of Adonis', 335–41.

4a

May 9.[25]

Connection between Logic & what I was talking about.

What I was trying to talk about last time was a propaganda for a descriptive method, rather than an explanatory. (When it's said that Sciences don't <u>explain</u>, of course, one thing they do is to <u>explain</u> in some sense.)

I was talking of a tendency, ~~characteristic of~~ /which came along with/ European science, to give an evolutionary explanation: "This developed out of this"; & to add "This <u>really</u> is this".

E.g. Frazer's explanation of dressing up a stick, and drowning it, as a vestige of the custom of really drowning a man.[26]

It's important to see that this needn't be so, for one particular reason. The idea underlying this sort of explanation, that in the case of each action there is a motive which is <u>the</u> motive. I eat <u>not only</u> to nourish myself, but also because I get an agreeable taste or because ... etc. etc..

E.g. there are lots of aspects of deer-stalking: not only the getting of food.

Frazer says: Surely an effigy wouldn't have been burnt, if there hadn't been a man burnt. And goes on to explain: You kill the god of fertility, in connection with the annual death of vegetation. Essence is: People at a certain stage thought it useful to kill a person in order to get good crops, & from this developed habit of pretending to kill a puppet.

The idea is: Action can only be explained, as having as its motive to get something useful.

But in fact: We <u>don't</u> do everything, even in any degree, to get food etc..

---

[25] This set of notes is dated Tuesday, 9 May, instead of the usual day of the week, Monday, 8 May. The Monday was the date of the last of a series of pairs of lectures by Sir James Frazer at Trinity College. It is very likely that Wittgenstein moved his lecture so that he could attend Frazer's lectures, published in Frazer 1934, 97–138, lectures 5 and 6. This information is taken from Rothhaupt 2016, which includes a detailed discussion of this history. The first references to Frazer are in the notes for the previous lecture; there are extensive discussions of Frazer's *Golden Bough* in the notes for this week.

[26] See Frazer 1922, 339–40.

If a man says we do, that is a mere rule of grammar.

This view is very old, & is embodied in "essence" & "accident". It's the essence of so & so to be a table. And this is embodied in our language: e.g. to question "What is this?" we always answer: "It's a book", "it's a pair of scissors", "it's a match".

It's a queer thing that there's one purpose of a thing so dominant, that we call it by the corresponding name; but this is not a logical necessity, & in some cases we don't. E.g. we call so & so "A lump of sulphur"; but we don't call a table "a piece of wood".

We say "The essence of this is to be a table": it belongs essentially to class "tables" & only accidentally to others.

So: there are theories of play, each giving one answer only to question: Why do children play?

The tendency to do this is enormously strong.

Return to Frazer:

Surely, he says, one wouldn't think of burning an effigy, unless one believed it was a human being, or unless one's ancestors had burnt a human being.

Chapter on Fire Festivals in Europe. Beltane Fires (May-day in the Highlands)[27]

> In the Central Highlands of Scotland bonfires, known as the Beltane fires, were formerly kindled with great ceremony on the first of May, and the traces of human sacrifices at them were particularly clear and unequivocal. The custom of lighting the bonfires lasted in various places far into the

---

[27] At this point in the lecture Wittgenstein read aloud a passage from Frazer's *The Golden Bough*. A second passage from *The Golden Bough* was read out during the next week's lecture (Lecture 5a; see note at page 9:24). Moore provides only very condensed summaries of these passages in his notes. The boxed sections contain the passages from *The Golden Bough* that Moore probably heard during the lectures. Wittgenstein most likely read from the one-volume abridged edition of *The Golden Bough* (Frazer 1922), rather than the complete twelve-volume third edition (Frazer 1911). While the differences between the abridged and third editions are very small in the case of this first passage, the passage that was read out in the following week's lecture is so much longer in the third edition that it probably could not have been read out in full in the time available. See Rothhaupt 2016 for a detailed discussion of the textual evidence that Wittgenstein did not use the first or second editions.

eighteenth century, and the descriptions of the ceremony by writers of that period present such a curious and interesting picture of ancient heathendom surviving in our own country that I will reproduce them in the words of their authors. The fullest of the descriptions is the one bequeathed to us by John Ramsay, laird of Ochtertyre, near Crieff, the patron of Burns and the friend of Sir Walter Scott. He says: "But the most considerable of the Druidical festivals is that of Beltane, or May-day, which was lately observed in some parts of the Highlands with extraordinary ceremonies. . . . Like the other public worship of the Druids, the Beltane feast seems to have been performed on hills or eminences. They thought it degrading to him whose temple is the universe, to suppose that he would dwell in any house made with hands. Their sacrifices were therefore offered in the open air, frequently upon the tops of hills, where they were presented with the grandest views of nature, and were nearest the seat of warmth and order. And, according to tradition, such was the manner of celebrating this festival in the Highlands within the last hundred years. But since the decline of superstition, it has been celebrated by the people of each hamlet on some hill or rising ground around which their cattle were pasturing. Thither the young folks repaired in the morning, and cut a trench, on the summit of which a seat of turf was formed for the company. And in the middle a pile of wood or other fuel was placed, which of old they kindled with *tein-eigin*—i.e., forced-fire or *need-fire*. Although, for many years past, they have been contented with common fire, yet we shall now describe the process, because it will hereafter appear that recourse is still had to the *tein-eigin* upon extraordinary emergencies.

"The night before, all the fires in the country were carefully extinguished, and next morning the materials for exciting this sacred fire were prepared. The most primitive method seems to be that which was used in the islands of Skye, Mull, and Tiree. A well-seasoned plank of oak was procured, in the midst of which a hole was bored. A wimble of the same timber was then applied, the end of which they fitted to the hole. But in some parts of the mainland the machinery was different. They used a frame of green wood, of a square form, in the centre of which was an axle-tree. In some places three times three persons, in others three times nine, were required for turning round by turns the axle-tree or wimble. If any of them had been guilty of murder, adultery, theft, or other atrocious crime, it was imagined either that the fire would not kindle, or that it would be devoid of its usual virtue. So soon as any sparks were emitted by means of the violent friction, they applied a species of agaric which grows on old birch-trees, and is very combustible. This fire had the appearance of being immediately derived from heaven, and manifold were the virtues ascribed to it. They esteemed it a preservative against witchcraft, and a sovereign remedy against malignant diseases, both

> in the human species and in cattle; and by it the strongest poisons were supposed to have their nature changed.
>
> "After kindling the bonfire with the *tein-eigin* the company prepared their victuals. And as soon as they had finished their meal, they amused themselves a while in singing and dancing round the fire. Towards the close of the entertainment, the person who officiated as master of the feast produced a large cake baked with eggs and scalloped round the edge, called *am bonnach beal-tine*—i.e., the Beltane cake. It was divided into a number of pieces, and distributed in great form to the company. There was one particular piece which whoever got was called *cailleach beal-tine*—i.e., the Beltane *carline*, a term of great reproach. Upon his being known, part of the company laid hold of him and made a show of putting him into the fire; but the majority interposing, he was rescued. And in some places they laid him flat on the ground, making as if they would quarter him. Afterwards, he was pelted with egg-shells, and retained the odious appellation during the whole year. And while the feast was fresh in people's memory, they affected to speak of the *cailleach beal-tine* as dead."[28]

9:8 "The most considerable Druidical festival is Beltane. On hills, because degrading to suppose god in a house, & near the sun. Cut a trench, build a pyre, & used to use forced fire (tein-eigin), & still do sometimes. All fires extinguished night before. For sacred fire wood wimbles & board. 3 × 3 or 3 × 9 persons. People guilty of adultery or murder were supposed to prevent it kindling or to prevent it having its usual virtue. After kindling, they prepared food, danced round fire; master produced large cake (Beltane cake), which was distributed; & there was one piece, such that anyone who got it was called "Beltane carline": & some tried to put him in fire, but he was rescued by others. Sometimes people pretended to quarter him."

Frazer thinks this is a remnant of a feast in which a human being was burnt.[29]

But to say this fails to explain why the story makes an impression independently of its origin. It is queer that people should pretend to burn a man.

It's also queer that one particular piece of a cake should have this significance.

---

[28] Frazer 1922, chapter 62, section 4, 617–18. Cf. Frazer 1915, volume 1, chapter 4, section 3, 146–8.

[29] See Frazer 1922, chapter 64, section 2, 652 ff. 'The Burning of Men and Animals in the Fires'.

The people who do it don't believe that once a man was burnt. Hence it follows that pretending to burn is something which has its own feeling & its own seriousness. And, that in other cases a real human being was burnt, only shews that all sorts of different things exist side by side.

So the alternative of 3 × 3, or 3 × 9, only shews what varieties there are.

Cf. Darwin's explanation of expression of emotions: Why do we shew our teeth when angry? because our ancestors wanted to bite.[30] Why does our hair stand up when frightened? because our ancestors, like other animals, frightened their enemy by looking bigger.[31] Why do lacrimal glands produce tears, when we're in grief?[32]

You can find out what nerves act on glands, & what makes nerves act.   9:9

But to give a reason why it was useful to cry, is something quite different: e.g. that there was a custom to throw sand, & tears were useful to wash it away.

And what makes one want an explanation of this sort? Why does Darwin think that without it what we do would be unintelligible?

Suppose one said, it's unintelligible that tables should be combustible. But it may be intelligible that they should be made of wood, & it just be an accident that wood is.

Now Darwin wouldn't have thought an explanation of this sort required for every detail about our bodies. He thinks expressions of emotion need it, because he finds expressions are very important, & then thinks they can be important only if useful.

The charm of the argument is that it reduces something that's important to utility. (Important in sense that it impresses us.)

What has this to do with methods of philosophising?

If I could talk about Ethics, connection would be clearer.

I was recommending "descriptive method" = method which tells you various things in right order = order which impresses you, without pretending to thread them on historical thread.

The word "good".

---

[30] See Darwin 1998, 238–41, 245–9.   [31] See Darwin 1998, 295, 298, 309.
[32] See Darwin 1998, 175, 193–4.

I was talking about way in which meaning changes.

9:10 One way of looking at Ethics is to say that meaning of "good" must be what is common to all things we call "good". So with "game":

I said this was far too simple.

And also that, though this is wrong, it doesn't follow that right thing to say is that it has several different meanings: for there may be a connection, though not that of having anything in common.

The idea that there must be one element which all games have in common, is an old one; & e.g. underlies Plato's question "What is knowledge?"[33] or "τί ἐστι τὸ ὅσιον?"[34].

I have said "football, cricket & similar things" is a good answer to "What is a game", whereas Socrates says "No".

This view of something common is connected with view, that a quality like καλόν[35] is an ingredient in beautiful things: & could be sort of caught in a bottle by itself, like an essence. (This is "essence" in medieval philosophy.) Pure goodness, like pure sugar.

Compare confusion between "mixture of pigments" & "mixture of colours": what's meant by a "mixed colour"?

"good" & "beautiful".

Supposing you say "good is a quality of human actions & events, & one can't explain further what sort of quality".

Then ask: How does one know whether an action or event has it?

(I don't despise this question: it is connected with meaning, & way in which we learnt meaning.)

9:11 Answer might be: Study the action, & you'll find out; just as you might study a thing to find out whether it's steel or not.

Now can I know the action in all its details, & not know whether it's good or not? Is that it's good one particular experience, like that it's hard?

---

[33] See Plato, *Theatetus*, trans. M.J. Levett and Myles F. Burnyeat, in Plato 1997, 162–3 [145e–146a].

[34] Greek: 'Ti esti to hosion?', i.e. 'What is piety (or: righteousness, holiness, godliness)?'. See Plato, *Euthyphro*, trans. G.M.A. Grube, in Plato 1997, 5–6 [5d–6e].

[35] Greek: 'Kalon', i.e. 'beautiful (or: fine, noble)'. See Plato, *Republic*, trans. G.M.A. Grube, revised by C.D.C. Reeve. Plato 1997, 1102–3 [476a–b].

Suppose I studied all the movements involved in a murder, & also all the emotions. Is there a ~~particular experience which is that it's good?~~ separate investigation, having studied the whole action, whether it's good or not?

Take "elasticity".

If I want to find how elastic a rod is, I can imagine 2 ways: –

(1) With a microscope I can see the structure, & can say it is elastic.

But do I mean this structure by "elastic"? I might.

But (2) I might investigate by pulling the rod, & seeing what happens.

This might be what I mean, & the structure only a symptom.

So with "good".

We might mean by "good" simply "action of this sort": & if we say this is merely a symptom, then there must be some other way of finding out whether it has the character of which that is a symptom.

How do I know that a face is beautiful? a visual impression of a face?

If all the shapes & colours are determined, is it determined that it is beautiful? Is there, when I know what the shapes & colours are like, another investigation as to whether it is beautiful? 9:12

If it must be beautiful, then there's a great confusion in calling beauty a quality – an indefinable quality.

A table has the quality "brown", only if it might have been "red" instead.

Suppose τις[36] says

"No arrangement of colours is in itself either ugly or beautiful".

The beauty of a face is a particular thing, different from the beauty of a chair; though of course there are similarities, e.g. that both are agreeable.

In different cases e.g. beauty of a face, of a flower, you are playing quite different games; & this is shewn by the way in which you can discuss whether the face is beautiful or not.

If you want to know how "beautiful" is used: ask what sort of discussion you could have as to whether a thing is so.

---

[36] Greek: 'Tis', i.e. 'someone'.

A says. "These eyebrows are specially beautiful". B says "Aren't they too far apart?" A replies "They might be too far apart, if the mouth had been so & so". This shews they're not talking about their feelings.

But of course you <u>sometimes</u> are talking about feelings.

4b

May 12 / 1933.

Beauty.

It's not true that "beautiful" means what's common to all the things we call so: we use it in a hundred different games.

If you want to construct a grammatical game roughly parallel to use of word, you have to look at what sort of discussion you could have about the beauty of an object.

To shew ambiguity (& more than this), suppose

(1) you are calling a smell beautiful; & can say no more than "I like the smell of lilac", "I don't care particularly about it"

(2) you are talking about arrangement of flowers in a bed: here you can say much more.

This shews that "beautiful" means something quite different in 2 cases.

Whether you mean "agreeable" or not will be shewn by kind of discussion that's possible.

But "agreeable" itself gives rise to a confusion.

Do you mean (1) it causes a pleasant sensation.

Then it's a question of experience whether it does cause the sensation or not: you can't feel that it causes. Suppose you say a tooth-ache you feel is due to the dentist drilling; & he says No: it's due to that draught. And this can be tested by seeing whether if he stops drilling the pain goes on; & if he stops the draught, its stops.

Do you mean (2) that you enjoy a shape, in the sense in which the shape enters into the enjoyment. Similarly to say you're afraid of a thing, is not to say it causes your fear; your fear may be caused by overwork which you don't fear.

By "Lust-betont"[37] of a sensation, I think was meant to distinguish from merely "accompanied by pleasure"; and there is such a thing to be distinguished.

---

[37] 'Lustbetont' is German for 'accompanied or characterized by a very pleasant feeling'; it is considerably stronger than 'angenehm', the usual German word for 'pleasant'. Moore's wording is telegraphic here; it is probable that Wittgenstein said something like 'By saying "Lust-betont" of a sensation, I meant to distinguish it from merely "accompanied

One could say "Smelling a flower, looking at a flower, hearing a piece of music, all put one in the same frame of mind – e.g. make one exhilarated". In this case the feeling of exhilaration is one same thing caused by all 3. In that case it doesn't tone the experiences.

Suppose one says that finding a face terrible is similar to tracing an outline of it with a shaking hand: the outline is contained in the shaky outline; & so finding it terrible is performing an activity directed by the face. This is a good comparison.

One example of an aesthetic question is question about harmony. In a book on harmony you find no trace of psychology. It says: you mustn't make this transition etc..

One might suggest that this is just elliptical for a psychological proposition: e.g. people don't like such sequences; It's more pleasant to hear this than that. And in a sense this is true. And it might be argued this must be so, because e.g. the Chinese haven't got these rules.

9:15 It has something to do with what human beings like. But let's see what Psychology can do about it.

Suppose you say it says: Sequences of fifths are disagreeable. How do I know they are disagreeable? Similarly what harmony allows isn't always agreeable: sometimes it's terrific, sometimes boring etc..

Suppose I ask: Is *King Lear* agreeable? You may say: Of course it is, because I go to it.

Many people have said: One always does what gives most pleasure; one always chooses the less disagreeable of 2 alternatives.

Something queer happens here.

In physics we know that you could do away with hot & cold, & give only degrees: hotter = less cold. But in the case of sensation, cold is quite a different sensation from heat: not merely different in degree:

In the same sense "pain" & "pleasure" are not on the same scale. Hence, if I jump out of window, I'm not choosing a greater pleasure: I'm choosing

> by pleasure"'. Rather than drawing a distinction between two different degrees of pleasure, Wittgenstein seems to be contrasting those cases in which the experience is accompanied by pleasure, or causes pleasure, on the one hand, and those cases in which the pleasure enters into the experience, or 'tones' it, on the other.

a less pain. Sometimes you do choose an alternative because more pleasant; but very often you don't.

So when I jump into water to rescue someone, though very afraid of getting drowned, I don't weigh any alternatives at all. If you say a body always moves from a place of higher potential to one of lower, you must have an independent way of measuring potential, unless it is a mere definition.

What "choice" does happen, if there is one, when you jump in to save someone? Not a choice between pleasures, nor yet between pains. There will be pros & cons, & then something will happen. But there is nothing which I compare, in the sense in which I compare 2 pieces of chalk to find which is longest.

9:16

So to say *King Lear* is "agreeable" is like saying a chair has a smell. *King Lear* is a very complex experience, & this is about the least important thing you could say about it.

But now you might say: Surely people who have said that the beautiful is the agreeable, can't have been such absolute asses as to overlook this? There must be some truth in it.

Suppose one talks of a beautiful colour. To say this has 100 meanings, & which way we use it depends on what we're talking about. If I say of a flower "Isn't this a marvellous colour?" I mean something quite different from if I shew a painted pattern, where it may mean "is good for a wall-paper".

One might ask: Which colour would you like to look at for an hour?

And suppose I shewed various shades of green: we shouldn't say one looks "prouder"[38] than the other, as one might of 2 colours of 2 leaves.

Discussions about the design of a door don't mention "beautiful". They say such things as "It's top-heavy". And it isn't true, if you choose one design, that you choose it because it's agreeable.

One thing more.

You often use in discussing a door the same sort of expressions as you do of a human face or body. But you can't say of a human face the same sort of thing as you can of the binding of a book. So what you mean by "beauty" in the case of a human face, is bound up with mouth, nose & eyes.

---

[38] Uncertain word. Moore marked it with a question mark, indicating that he was unsure of its reading.

9:17 Consider how you were taught what "beauty" means. Not by being told it means appropriateness; but by being shewn examples. But you don't see suddenly a quality which an ugly face has in common with Whewell's Court.[39] The game you learnt when you learnt the application to human faces, was not the same as in the case of flowers: though it has some similarity. A "stupid-looking" hand means something quite different from a "stupid looking" face: & if I said this piece of coke looks stupid: you might fairly ask me: Do you mean in the sense in which a hand does, or that in which a face does?

Suppose I say "A face is stupid".

We don't usually mean (though we might): This is the kind of face stupid people usually have.

We mean: A particular expression of a face.

And this looks as if I were saying: "stupidity" was <u>quality</u> of a distribution of colours in visual space.

But in what sense "quality"?

---

[39] Wittgenstein's lectures at this time took place in his rooms in Whewell's Court, Trinity College.

5a

May 15 / 1933.   9:18

<u>Concept of an Ideal.</u>

Practically everything I say of "beautiful" applies in a slightly different way to "good".

What does it mean to say there's an indefinable quality which a thing possesses?

(1) What is specific criterion for it possessing the quality?

If you ask: Is this flower beautiful or not? What test is there for right answer?

Let us be calling a certain arrangement of colours in space, a flower. How then do we know that it is beautiful?

Are the specific colours & arrangement merely <u>symptoms</u> that it is beautiful?

This is not, of course, what we mean.

But if we <u>meant</u> by "beautiful" "giving me stomach-ache /pleasure/", then it would be merely a symptom: experience would tell us whether it does or not.

People sometimes say that we always choose course which gives least pain or most pleasure: but they don't really here mean that it is a question of experience: they mean that it <u>must</u> be so, i.e. that it is a tautology, & yet think that it has some meaning.

If we have a certain arrangement of colours & say it is beautiful, & you suggest that what this means is that it gives us pleasure.   9:19

I ask: Why should we use so many different means to get pleasure?

Answer isn't merely that you can't get asparagus in winter; but obviously that what you want is not merely pleasure but a certain <u>kind</u> of pleasure.

And if you want a certain <u>kind</u> of pleasure, e.g. tulips admired with pleasure; why shouldn't you want the tulips without the pleasure?

Obviously the ideal of a tulip, & the ideal of a face, haven't something in common called "ideality"; nor do both produce in you the same sensation.

We have to ask several questions:

(1) What is an actual aesthetic controversy or enquiry like? not what philosophers think it is like; but how e.g. musicians use "beautiful", if they use it at all, in a discussion.

(2) Are these enquiries, psychological enquiries? Why do they look so very different?

(3) How is it that the ideal of a face changes with time, & yet each time we should say: "This is the ideal"?

(1) In aesthetic controversy "beautiful" & "more or less beautiful" are hardly ever used; whereas words like "correct" "right" are: e.g. that doesn't look quite right yet.

9:20 Suppose your problem is to write an accompaniment to a song. You say of one you find: No, that won't do, it isn't right.

You use beautiful in: "Look how marvellous".

But you don't say "This isn't beautiful enough".

& so you don't in Ethics "This action isn't good enough".

Cf. writing a good accompaniment; designing a good door; choosing a suitable wall-paper.

Suppose you find a bass too heavy – that it moves too much; you aren't saying: If it moves less, it will be more agreeable to me. That is should be quieter is an end in itself, not a means to end.

You might say: If so, why should we say that making a door less pompous, also brings it nearer to an ideal?

I say, it's not that in both cases we wish to produce some effect – e.g. an agreeable feeling.

Take the ideal Greek profile of a face. What makes one say that it was the ideal?

I say: a certain rôle which it played in the lives of a certain people.

That that profile was the ideal means a lot of things: That it was used in sculpture; that people were taught by reference to it; that it was used at height of Greek sculpture.

But what does "height" mean, e.g. when you say "height" of German music was about 1800?

Obviously "height" & "decadence" are words like "ideal".

In "The ideal of a Greek face" & "the ideal of roast-beef" ideal means something different.

9:21

When you talk e.g. of "decay of German music", you can't understand what's meant by this, unless e.g. I tell you: After Beethoven there was a difficulty in writing last movement of a Symphony. And that you can't understand, unless e.g. you see there was something too lengthy about it.

But decay of German music, decay of Greek sculpture, decay of English poetry, mean each something quite different – though no doubt there is some analogy.

(2) In what sense, when we discuss whether a bass will do, are we discussing a psychological question?

We're not trying what gives us the most pleasant effect.

Psychology is no more involved than it is in Physics; in both it is in a way, because we are human beings.

One might say that what we're trying to do is to bring the accompaniment nearer to an ideal.

But we haven't got an ideal before us, that we are trying to copy. You may say: Where is your ideal?

I might shew you a different tune: & say: See, this is correct.

If I teach you what colour it is we call "lilac", you can then recognise that colour when you see it, & people suppose that this is done by having an image. But this happens rarely. You don't, when told to pick a red flower, call up a memory-image & then compare it with the flower.

9:22

Suppose I say I can paint you the colour of our house-door at Vienna. Is this like copying a sample? No; you haven't an image before you: You can say: This isn't dark enough; without having an image which is darker.

So, if you say: "This bass ought to be quieter" means you have an ideal: this is like saying in the other case; You have a memory image.

When I say "This isn't the colour I mean; it's too cold", I don't hallucinate the colour I mean.

To find what ideal we're directed to, you must look at what we do: the ideal is the tendency of people who create such a thing.

Can one call the activity of trying to get an accompaniment correct an investigation? You're not trying to discover a truth.

Is it a matter of Psychology, to say the German people felt so & so about a certain piece of music, at a certain time?

Merely to describe a person's state of mind isn't psychology, which requires such statements as "Whenever so & so happened, so & so happened".

You can say "It's a matter of psychic history".

In Aesthetic investigations the one thing we're not interested in is causal connections; whereas the one thing we are interested in Psychology is causal connections.

9:23

I.e. Aesthetics is "descriptive" in sense I said.

We were in a state in which we thought that whenever we were puzzled, what we wanted was a cause: we thought "why" always meant: What is the cause of this?

Now we do ask: Why is this poem beautiful? What is beautiful about it?

And people thought this was asking for causal explanation.

Somebody who suffered from ill-temper, thought that if someone could tell her for certain what it was due to, she would be satisfied.

What is the answer to the puzzle we feel when we ask, What makes this beautiful?

I say answer is the same as to question: What's wrong with this accompaniment?

And answer is not a causal one; but such as "This is too loud", "This bass moves too much, should be quieter" "These 2 voices shouldn't be in unison".

"Why is the smell of roses so pleasant?"

What sort of an answer do you expect?

(1) All the smells which tickle your nose in this way are pleasant. This would be interesting to some people; & could satisfy a person who meant to ask that question.

(2) This answer would not remove our aesthetic puzzlement.

I can answer the question "What is beauty?" by shewing you what the ideal of Greek sculpture was. 9:24

But if you say: "Surely other things are beautiful; I want to know what's common to them all."

I should say: If you want to know what's common to 2, compare them; but how to find what's common to all, I don't know.

This won't supply you with the meaning of a word which you didn't know before.

We do know things, & yet can't answer the question what knowledge is. /(Plato said we can't)/

We can play chess, without being able to answer the question what a game is.

Beltane Festival.

In this case you can observe the same thing being puzzling, as in an aesthetic question. You ask: Why does this thing impress us so much?

Frazer thinks he answers this by: This festival has developed from one in which a real man was burnt.

I say, This doesn't do justice to what we feel.

It does impress us, because it has a relation to burning a human being, but not necessarily the relation of having developed therefrom. What impresses us is seeing this event along with other similar events.

Frazer, Chapter I, King of the Wood.[40]

> Who does not know Turner's picture of the Golden Bough? The scene, suffused with the golden glow of imagination in which the divine mind of Turner steeped and transfigured even the fairest natural landscape, is a dream-like vision of the little woodland lake of Nemi— "Diana's Mirror," as it was called by the ancients. No one who has seen that calm water, lapped in a green hollow of the Alban hills, can ever forget it. The two characteristic

---

[40] The boxed section contains the text that Moore probably heard. See note at page 9:7 for discussion of which edition Wittgenstein used. The two paragraphs after the boxed section are Moore's summary of the first few pages of the first chapter of the book, entitled 'The King of the Wood'.

Italian villages which slumber on its banks, and the equally Italian palace whose terraced gardens descend steeply to the lake, hardly break the stillness and even the solitariness of the scene. Diana herself might still linger by this lonely shore, still haunt these woodlands wild.

In antiquity this sylvan landscape was the scene of a strange and recurring tragedy. On the northern shore of the lake, right under the precipitous cliffs on which the modern village of Nemi is perched, stood the sacred grove and sanctuary of Diana Nemorensis, or Diana of the Wood. The lake and the grove were sometimes known as the lake and grove of Aricia. But the town of Aricia (the modern La Riccia) was situated about three miles off, at the foot of the Alban Mount, and separated by a steep descent from the lake, which lies in a small crater-like hollow on the mountain side. In this sacred grove there grew a certain tree round which at any time of the day, and probably far into the night, a grim figure might be seen to prowl. In his hand he carried a drawn sword, and he kept peering warily about him as if at every instant he expected to be set upon by an enemy. He was a priest and a murderer; and the man for whom he looked was sooner or later to murder him and hold the priesthood in his stead. Such was the rule of the sanctuary. A candidate for the priesthood could only succeed to office by slaying the priest, and having slain him, he retained office till he was himself slain by a stronger or a craftier.

The post which he held by this precarious tenure carried with it the title of king; but surely no crowned head ever lay uneasier, or was visited by more evil dreams, than his. For year in, year out, in summer and winter, in fair weather and in foul, he had to keep his lonely watch, and whenever he snatched a troubled slumber it was at the peril of his life. The least relaxation of his vigilance, the smallest abatement of his strength of limb or skill of fence, put him in jeopardy; grey hairs might seal his death-warrant. To gentle and pious pilgrims at the shrine the sight of him might well seem to darken the fair landscape, as when a cloud suddenly blots the sun on a bright day. The dreamy blue of Italian skies, the dappled shade of summer woods, and the sparkle of waves in the sun, can have accorded but ill with that stern and sinister figure. Rather we picture to ourselves the scene as it may have been witnessed by a belated wayfarer on one of those wild autumn nights when the dead leaves are falling thick, and the winds seem to sing the dirge of the dying year. It is a sombre picture, set to melancholy music—the background of forest showing black and jagged against a lowering and stormy sky, the sighing of the wind in the branches, the rustle of the withered leaves under foot, the lapping of the cold water on the shore, and in the foreground, pacing to and fro, now in twilight and now in gloom, a dark figure with a glitter of steel at the shoulder whenever the pale moon, riding clear of the cloud-rack, peers down at him through the matted boughs.

Lecture 5a – May 15, 1933 345

> The strange rule of this priesthood has no parallel in classical antiquity, and cannot be explained from it. To find an explanation we must go farther afield. No one will probably deny that such a custom savours of a barbarous age, and, surviving into imperial times, stands out in striking isolation from the polished Italian society of the day, like a primaeval rock rising from a smooth-shaven lawn. It is the very rudeness and barbarity of the custom which allow us a hope of explaining it. For recent researches into the early history of man have revealed the essential similarity with which, under many superficial differences, the human mind has elaborated its first crude philosophy of life. Accordingly, if we can show that a barbarous custom, like that of the priesthood of Nemi, has existed elsewhere; if we can detect the motives which led to its institution; if we can prove that these motives have operated widely, perhaps universally, in human society, producing in varied circumstances a variety of institutions specifically different but generically alike; if we can show, lastly, that these very motives, with some of their derivative institutions, were actually at work in classical antiquity; then we may fairly infer that at a remoter age the same motives gave birth to the priesthood of Nemi. Such an inference, in default of direct evidence as to how the priesthood did actually arise, can never amount to demonstration. But it will be more or less probable according to the degree of completeness with which it fulfils the conditions I have indicated. The object of this book is, by meeting these conditions, to offer a fairly probable explanation of the priesthood of Nemi.[41]

"Turner's picture of Golden Bough. Picture of lake of Nemi. In antiquity scene of recurrent tragedy. Called Lake & grove of Aricia (but 3 miles off). In grove a certain tree, round which a grim figure was prowling. Rule of sanctuary that no-one could succeed to priesthood, except by slaying. He had title of "King". To gentle pilgrims sight of him might seem to darken landscape. 9:25

Rule of this priesthood has no parallel in classical antiquity. Obviously barbarous, though surviving to Empire. Let's detect motives which led to similar institutions elsewhere, & led also to other classical institutions: we may fairly conclude they led to this."

Now you are puzzled by this story. And you're puzzled less, if you have similar stories.

But story can't be made to seem natural, by giving <u>causes</u> how it arose.

---

[41] Frazer 1922, chapter I, section 1, 1–2. Cf. Frazer 1911, chapter I, section 1, 1–10.

5b

9:26   May 19 / 1933.

"Beautiful" ≠ "agreeable", I said: but I omitted to say: Man might answer: Surely it is agreeable, or you wouldn't go to hear it? But you <u>can</u> say: I'm not going~~, not because it isn't agreeable, but~~ because I can't stand its greatness: i.e. if anything, it is disagreeable.

Also, every one knows how varied experiences are in face of a work of art. E.g. in music, one can often say: This is charming; but in 50 years it won't be: this other is not so charming, but it will last. What I should prefer to hear may be just nothing compared to another piece to which I prefer it.

Ursell says: You can only decide whether A is beautiful or not, by <u>seeing</u> it: hence: has something to do with Psychology.

You <u>can</u> find out what people like a given smell or not, & whether almost all people do. This is a psychological experiment. But is it Aesthetics? It has only a very far off connection.

Suppose you try the experiment: Alter this piece of music: Does it sound better now? or <u>now</u>? or <u>now</u>? This provides you with causal connection between set of notes & feelings of liking. Not necessarily.

If this were all, Aesthetics would be a matter of taste.

"Which part did you like best in this piece?" is <u>not</u> a causal question.

9:27   Let's make an assumption about nature of "liking" <u>it</u>. Suppose we meant that A followed a certain part with movements of the larynx, & had a pleasurable sensation.

Then I might find out, by experiment, that he had followed <u>these</u> bars with these movements.

And I might by further experiments make generalisation (causal) to the effect: Tiny bits are followed by Ursell with his larynx.

But this isn't Aesthetics.

The question of Aesthetics is not: Do you like it? But, if you do, <u>why</u> do you?

Is "This bass moves too much" a psychological statement? Is it about human beings?

If ever we come to: I like this; I don't, there is an end of Aesthetics; & then comes psychology.

"Is it this note or that note that makes it sound so heavy?" Is this a psychological question? It would be, if we were asking: Is it this note or that that causes our displeasure? But what we do, is much more like a piece of mathematics.

In what way? Don't the rules of harmony, though they don't <u>mention</u> our feelings, always presuppose that we shall understand that obeying these rules makes things more agreeable?

I could make statements about this table, its height, hardness etc.; & we should say these were about <u>table</u>, & <u>not</u> about its appearance.

But I could ask what arrangement of parallel lines, will make them <u>look</u> as if they converged.

I could also talk of causal connections between visual appearances themselves: e.g. whenever I see a red spot on a blue ground, I 2 minutes after see a green on a grey.

9:28

These last 2 are Psychology.

But not <u>all</u> statements about appearances are <u>therefore</u> Psychology: e.g. our statement about nature of visual space – that[42]

When I say "This bass moves too much" I don't mean merely "It gives me such & such an impression", because If I did I should have to be content with the answer "It doesn't give <u>me</u> that impression".

A says "Isn't this door top-heavy". B. "Yes, it is, these panels are too long: make them shorter, & you'll see the effect is better".

Is this a conversation about Psychology?

Suppose, when B says "When I move up the cross-bar, that gives a better effect" A says "No, it gives me a most disagreeable impression".

I must have learnt what's meant by "looking top heavy".

---

[42] Sentence left unfinished.

Mrs. Knight[43] says: looks top-heavy partly means "gives me this feeling"; not merely that moving up cross-bar will mend it – be a remedy.

That medicine is a remedy for stomach-ache, is a causal proposition.

What will alleviate feeling of top-heaviness? is not an aesthetic question.

Something else comes in: What?

Possibly there is no remedy for feeling of top-heaviness, whatever I do.

9:29 But suppose I move bar up, & say: Is this better? And you say: This makes it worse; I say: It makes it better. If this is medical or psychological, there's an end of the matter. But if it's aesthetic, I can go on: Hasn't it removed top-heaviness, & isn't reason why you don't think it better, because now whole door looks too large?

Mrs. Knight says: This is like: The powders have removed stomach-ache; but now produce pain in my head.

Wittgenstein takes a face

& says by changing positions & shapes of dots & lines, you can make it look stupid, or gay, or sorrowful. But if all that can be said is it gives this feeling to A, & that to B, that isn't Aesthetics. What I say, & am interested in, is: This phenomenon is light-hearted; or stupid, or sorrowful.

Thus you might say: If it is light-hearted, what is your investigation about?

Suppose I say of a face I draw: It smiles too much.

There's a question of bringing it closer to some ideal; & this doesn't mean that it's not yet agreeable enough. As I said, more like solving a mathematics problem.

So when one asks: What words will go with this melody?

What kind of activity is this? Surely not one of psychological investigation. It's more like that of painter, who isn't making psychological experiments

---

[43] Helen Knight was one of the three presenters at a symposium on 'The Limits of Psychology in Aesthetics', at the Joint Session of the Aristotelian Society and the Mind Association in July 1932, to which Wittgenstein may be responding in these lectures. See Reid, Knight, and Joad 1932.

with himself. And is doing something more like making one curve like another: you can see where the copy is wrong.

"Top-heavy" says <u>what</u> is wrong with the door, <u>not</u> what impression it gave to me.

6a

9:30   May 22 / 1933.

Relation of Psychology to Aesthetics. In what sense is Aesthetics not part of Psychology?

What is a <u>reason</u> in Aesthetics? A reason for having this word in this place rather than that; this musical phrase rather than that.

Reason = justification. What is a justification like?

Joachim suggested to Brahms to begin his IV Symphony not with first subject but with 2 introductory chords. Brahms refused.[44]

What could make one suggest this? What reason could be given for rejecting it?

Latter would be: You misunderstand me: I know why you suggested that; you think this is what I meant to say, but it wasn't.

It's not: This doesn't produce <u>feeling</u> I want to produce.

When an alteration is suggested, one may say

(1) It's all right as it is

(2) There's something wrong, but not what you think.

I might then (a) shew you what does make it right

(b) if I couldn't do this, do something to suggest the sort of thing that would.

In this case: I have an ideal before my mind.

What happens if I do find the solution? What does it mean to say "It's right"? Can I prove to anyone that it is?

9:31 You might say it means: I'm now satisfied; I'm in a state of equilibrium, not of tension.

This may be a good metaphor; but there isn't <u>one</u> feeling which characterises the thousand different cases of equilibrium.

---

[44] See Brahms 2000, 133–4, 161.

What reasons could I give for being satisfied?

They are in the nature of further descriptions.

By making a person hear lots of different pieces by Brahms, you can make him see what he's driving at.

All that Aesthetics does is to draw your attention to things: e.g. "This is a climax". It places things side by side: e.g. this prepares the way for that.

You can make a person understand a composer, by drawing attention to a contemporary author: e.g. Brahms is like Keller. Aesthetics may say: Try to find Keller in Brahms. Like: try to see this as a colour.

It may make you hear a thing differently: just as you may find the head in a puzzle-picture.[45]

A solution must speak for itself. If when I've made you see what I see, it doesn't appeal to you, there is an end.

And you might say: With this "appeal" Psychology comes in.

How about ideal Greek profile?

Reasons can be given for this – I mean "reasons" not "causes".

It's of the kind: If you didn't do this, it would look top-heavy.

You might say: "This reason must appeal to you".

I don't think "appeals to you" stands for any single state of mind.

The reasons have nothing to do with psychology. 9:32

At back of my mind I have: Aesthetic discussion is like discussion in a court of law. You don't say "This is bad or good", but try to clear up circumstances; & in the end what you say will <u>appeal to</u> the judge.

The equilibrium into which you get, when something appeals to you, can be investigated psychologically.

That European music has certain laws does tell you something about psychology of Europeans; just as that they have this sort of mathematics or physics.

They did create this sort of music, & that says something: but that it appealed to them means nothing.

---

[45] Moore's summary notes: <It may make you hear a thing differently, just as when you find the head in a puzzle-picture you see it differently.> (10:64)

"x has nothing to do with psychology" = "such & such a problem is not a psychological problem".

"This isn't right ending of this piece. What's wrong with it?"

Problem "What's wrong with it?" isn't a psychological problem.

Nor is the reason one gives for "This is the right end" a proposition of psychology.

Reason ~~may be~~ is of nature of Bach's "A piece mustn't slink away like a thief"[46], e.g. you mustn't suddenly change from 4 parts to 3.

"This is bad, because it <u>does</u> slink away."

Are same <u>sort</u> of reasons given elsewhere except in Ethics? Yes; in philosophy.

9:33 When people heard that earth was not centre of planetary system, this revolted people.

It is often very disquieting to think So & so has a unique place; & then you are quieted down by seeing it is just one among lots.

E.g. cardinal numbers; & then people point out rational numbers etc..

Here a reason consists in drawing your attention to something which removes an uneasiness.

What satisfies my puzzlement about Beltane, is not kind of causal explanation which Frazer gives – which is a hypothesis; but simply describing lots of things more or less like Beltane.

Goethe in *Metamorphose der Pflanzen*, suggests that all plants are variations on a theme.[47] What is the theme?

Goethe says "They all point to a hidden law".[48] But you wouldn't ask: What is the law? <u>That</u> they point, is all there is to it.

Darwin made a hypothesis to account for this.

---

[46] The ultimate source of this story is probably an early biographical account of how Bach instructed students in four-part choral harmony, although the thief analogy is not present there. See Forkel 1802, 40–1; translation in Forkel 1920, 97–8.

[47] '*Metamorphose der Pflanzen*', i.e. '*Metamorphosis of Plants*', is the title of both a treatise and a poem by Goethe. See Goethe 2009.

[48] 'And so the choir hints a secret law, a sacred mystery.' (Goethe 2009, 1; lines 6–7 of the poem)

But you might treat it quite differently. You might say what is satisfactory in Darwin is not the hypothesis, but the putting the facts in a system – helping us to overlook[49] them.

You may ask: What is in common to all music from Palestrina to Brahms? And one might answer: They start from tonic, go to dominant, & return to tonic.

If you say "This piece must be in strict time" this is not about physical time, but about appearance time. In <u>that</u> sense all aesthetic propositions are about states of mind.

What's meant by "S has understood this piece of music"?   9:34

If he says, it reminds me of home; it gives me a feeling of warmth: I say that shews he doesn't understand.

If he says: Oughtn't it to have been more stressed here? Yes, that shews he did understand.

What does a man say, when he says: "This ought to have been stressed."?

(1) He is not making a hypothesis to the effect: I should have felt better if it had been.

Suppose I hear a waltz played. I am old enough to know how a waltz used to be danced 30 years ago, & therefore how one ought to be played. I know a young man who can't play a waltz, because he's never seen one danced.

Now here I've given a <u>cause</u> of my dissatisfaction with his playing.

He & I have a different ideal; & these ideals have been caused in a certain way: these causes don't come into Aesthetics; the ideals do.

Psychology can give the <u>cause</u> why I have this ideal, rather than another.

---

[49] Wittgenstein sometimes uses the word 'overlook' in its normal English sense of 'look past' or 'fail to notice' (see 9:16). But on this occasion he is using it as a literal translation of the German verb 'übersehen', which is most often translated as 'survey' or 'overview'. Wittgenstein's use of 'overlook' here should therefore be understood to mean 'gain a synoptic view'. The following instance of this Germanic use of 'overlook' is from Wittgenstein's pocket notebook from 1931: 'There is an infinity of things which you must notice about the use of the simplest word. The grammar of every word is enormously complicated and therefore enormously difficult to overlook and it is just that you must try to do' (MS 153b, 5r). Ambrose records a similar use of the word in her notes of Wittgenstein's lectures for Easter Term, 1935: 'A person who found an object in a maze by climbing a tree and overlooking the maze would be said not to be playing the game, that finding it means going into the maze and searching for it.' (Wittgenstein 1979, 183)

Richards supposes if you have an ideal, there will be some law which accounts for fact that some departures don't matter, others are terrible.

If "terrible mistake" = "mistake which makes me wild", then you can give a cause why it makes me wild.

9:35 But ordinarily: Why is this terrible? asks for a reason, not a cause. E.g. I might say: He's missed most important point. You might ask: Why is it important? And again give reasons.

You can give causes for calling it important.

Why does one feel that so & so is the climax?

Because at this point in the dance people began to turn round: a historical cause.

You can get 2 quite different kinds of satisfaction from this sort of explanation. (1) From knowledge that so & so is the cause; which will enable you to know that same will happen in another case. (2) A much stronger satisfaction from fact that I have supplied you with a parallel case: dance as well as piece of music.

Some people recently have given causal explanations of a sort – of which Freud's are examples. E.g. his explanation of "anxiety" is what happened at birth. Every experience of anxiety referred to this.[50]

Again Freud says sleep is a reproduction of situation one was in before birth: e.g. one draws up one's legs like a foetus.[51] There is something appealing in this: it makes a connection which impresses one. Can this connection be verified? It's clear that there are things in common between sleep & position of foetus.

Freud says: A human being can't stand day; he always puts himself back into position in which he was born.[52] Can he say that his being born before

---

[50] See Freud 1953a, 399–402 and Freud 1957a, 133 ff. Wittgenstein gave Drury a copy of *The Interpretation of Dreams* in the late 1930s, describing it as 'the most important of Freud's writings' (Drury 1984, 136. In Flowers 1999, 3 222; 2016, 2 809).

[51] See Freud 1957, 222.

[52] 'Sleep is a state in which I want to know nothing of the external world ... when I go to sleep I say to the external world: "Leave me in peace: I want to go to sleep." ... Our relation to the world, into which we come so unwillingly, seems to involve our not being able to tolerate it uninterruptedly. Thus from time to time we withdraw into the premundane state, into existence in the womb. At any rate, we arrange conditions for ourselves very like what they were then: warm, dark and free from stimuli. Some of us roll ourselves into a tight package and, so as to sleep, take up a posture much as it was in the womb.' (Freud 1963, 88)

birth in that position is <u>cause</u> of our adopting position in sleep? ~~No~~ It might be so discovered by experiment or observation, e.g. if animals which slept stretched out, were also stretched out in womb, etc.. We could then predict.

9:36

Suppose we discovered that what people painted in the heroic age of their painting were always shapes they saw at a certain period of development. E.g. suppose Aryans at a certain stage saw certain trees, & then in heroic age always painted trees in that. Ideal is always taken from there – just like Freud's: man marries woman like his mother.

This would give a <u>causal</u> explanation of racial ideals.

I say 2 things

(1) You may call this Psychology, if you like. But it is Natural History of Man.

(2) It's not Aesthetics.

I think one thing is clearer: one could sum up: Aesthetic reasons are given in the form: getting nearer to an ideal or farther from it. Whereas Psychology gives causes why people have an ideal.

6b

9:37   May 26 / 1933.

Aesthetics & Psychology.

There is an investigation which has been made which is in a sense Aesthetics & which is psychological – Freud's psychological investigation of, What is nature of a joke (Witz)[53]?

Sort of answer which he gives is: ~~A joke starts a sub-conscious train of thought,~~ Psychological process started by joke has 2 strata: (1) it starts understanding the words – in sense in which somebody who doesn't see the joke understands them (2) another sub-conscious process; & (1)[54] suddenly says what the other thinks – the other is suddenly found out.

In what way can or does such a theory satisfy us?

2 absolutely distinct ways

(1) that, like any scientific theory, it helps us to predict certain things. It then satisfies us only so far as future experience confirms it.

(2) that, if we hear this theory, we say: Oh, yes, that's what happens. This is a satisfaction we derive from it in an unhypothetical sense. You can say it is a paraphrase of the joke itself.

I say all Aesthetics is of nature of giving a paraphrase, even if same words also express a hypothesis. It is giving a good simile.

So of a piece of music, you might say: This is like question & answer.

9:38   Now Freud's investigation has 2 sides: it is aesthetic only in so far as it isn't hypothetical. He commits the mistake of supposing there is something common to all jokes, & that this is the meaning of "joke".

His explanation has a merit in making a bridge between what happens in jokes & in dreams, & in dreams & certain mental diseases.[55]

---

[53] The German word 'Witz' is usually translated as 'joke', but see also the footnote at 9:43 below discussing translation difficulties.

[54] It is likely that Moore wrote '(1)' mistakenly, and that Wittgenstein meant 'one' in the sense of an arbitrary person.

[55] See Freud 1963, 88–9, and chapter VI.

The joke allows you to do covertly, what it wouldn't be seemly to do openly.[56]

Now not every joke does so: "joke", like "proposition" etc., have a rainbow of meanings.

But in what way is his explanation a hypothesis? How could it be used to predict?

You might say: It would enable you to construct a joke; just as chemistry enables you to construct an explosive.

Suppose you say: "These words produce a sub-conscious train of thought; e.g. the thought that you would like to slander someone; & then you suddenly do".

Now a "subconscious train" is a hypothetical entity, like invisible masses to account for a thing's rolling at an unusual velocity; and can only give kind of satisfaction an hypothesis gives – it works or it doesn't.[57]

There's no such thing as an immediate recognition of[58] an hypothesis ~~as an hypothesis~~; but there is an immediate pleasure in seeing a neat way of representation.

E.g. to explain the odd way something moves, we may suggest a mechanism which both serves as an hypothesis, & enables you to overlook[59] a system at a glance.

So Frazer tells us lots of interesting stories, & joins them up by threading them on a hypothesis; but what satisfies is not the hypothesis. 9:39

Aesthetic craving for an explanation is not satisfied by a hypothesis.

This is what I mean by saying Aesthetics is not Psychology.

You might wish to call this Psychology too: but in fact to say so & so is Psychology, is to say the explanation is given by an experimental science like Physics. People hope that Psychology will make actions & feelings all predictable.

What I dislike about Psychology is perhaps only a muddle – a tendency to explain away.

E.g. "Science is greater than Art, because it shews you the general, not merely the particular".

---

[56] See: Freud 1960, 96–7.
[57] See the discussion of Hertz on invisible masses above, at 7:103.
[58] Moore later added: <truth of?>   [59] See footnote at 9:33 above on 'overlook'.

"Psychology" has many meanings, but it may be used to mean a Physics of the soul; & I think idea was this: Wherever there is a puzzle, you have problem of science: science will solve it for you. So too Mathematics has been treated as if it were a science.

In Mathematics, Ethics, Aesthetics, Philosophy, answer to a puzzle is to make a synopsis possible.

"Why is this note absolutely necessary?" Explanation would look like this: If you wrote out the tune in chords, you would see to which chord the note belongs. I.e. it hints at placing side by side with the tune a certain chorale.

You might say: Couldn't he have gone on to ask: Why this chord? My answer is: He didn't; this satisfied him.

9:40 Suppose someone said: At this point melody seems to fall over. I might say: Yes, that's where the dominant is reached.

This is an answer to: <u>Why</u> does it seem to fall over here? or <u>How</u> is this effect of falling over produced?

But this doesn't mean: What <u>machinery</u> produces this?

"It goes to the dominant" may mean nothing. Then I play a series of chords; & the man says: Oh yes, of course.

Why does "He always leaves out the 6/4 chord" satisfy me as an explanation of the peculiarity of way Bruckner ends his Scherzos?

The idea of Psychology explaining Aesthetic experiences I once had myself, & made useless experiments on rhythm in the laboratory.[60]

Why did I? I had a natural propensity to think about ideas which arise in music; & I thought what was wanted was to make experiments in a laboratory.

My idea was to investigate nature of rhythm, because you can produce it quite exactly by machinery. I was looking forward to talking with my subjects about something which interested me. To most people the rhythm meant nothing: one lady said: "It makes me feel like a butterfly with a pin through me".

<u>Why</u> is this interesting? If you were merely looking for <u>effects</u> of rhythm, here you've got one.

But I was looking for utterances inside an aesthetic system.

---

[60] See McGuinness 1988, 127–8; Monk 1990, 49–50; Wittgenstein 2003, 359–60.

If I ask "Why do you like this tune?" & answer is "Because it reminds me of my grandmother", this doesn't interest me.

If you hear music in one of the ancient modes, an ending doesn't at first seem like an ending. But one can be made to understand it in various ways:

(1) you could point out similar things in our modern keys

(2) you could leave out the tonic: & say: You've got to imagine it. Just as "rien"[61] is now a negation, but originally wasn't.

In Latin "Miles est bonus"[62] & "Mater est bona"[63], where "bonus"[64] sounds different from "bona"[65]. I could explain this to a German, by translating instead of by "gut"[66] & "gut", by "ein guter"[67] & "eine gute"[68].

What sort of thing is not understanding a church mode? & therefore "understanding"?

What makes you "understand" is a typical aesthetic explanation.

When I made those experiments, what would have satisfied me was <u>comparison</u>, within a system. You want to compare notes but not <u>any</u> notes; only those which are illuminating.

I did find out <u>one</u> thing, moderately interesting.

We wound a machine which didn't stress any notes.

$|\grave{||}-|-|\grave{||}-|-$

. When this was done, every one heard an accent on the ~~last~~ /first/ of the three. (Perhaps not exactly this; but[69]

1. You do hear some stresses, though machine doesn't give them

2. You can find laws which regulate what stress you hear. e.g. you try to divide into bars.

You tend <u>not</u> to stress 2 consecutive beats.

If you construct a rhythm in such a way that 2 tendencies conflict, a curious effect is produced – that of a constant stumbling.

---

[61] French for 'nothing', but derives that meaning from its role in the 'ne ... rien' construction.
[62] Latin for 'The/a soldier is good' (with 'good' in the masculine).
[63] Latin for 'The/a mother is good' (with 'good' in the feminine).
[64] Latin for 'Good' in the masculine.   [65] Latin for 'Good' in the feminine.
[66] German for 'good'.   [67] German for 'a good' in the masculine.
[68] German for 'a good' in the feminine.   [69] Sentence left unfinished.

7

9:43   May 29 / 1933.

Freud on "Wit"[70]. He has something to say.

It is interesting from philosophical point of view: a very good book for looking for mistakes.

He says: It's characteristic of a joke that, if you laugh, you don't know why you laugh.[71] This is true /important/; but comes near a muddle between cause & reason; <u>for</u> Freud thinks we can find out why he laughs by analysing – psycho-analysis.

General technique of psycho-analysis is that of questioning person analysed. If they analyse a dream, they question you about each feature, so as to find your associations with it. And they announce result as: <u>This</u> is the thought which underlies the dream.

<u>Note</u>: Whether analysis is successful or not is shewn by person analysed <u>agreeing</u> to analysis: i.e. to say: Yes, that did underlie.

There is nothing in physics corresponding to this.

Take a joke: analyst suggests: Wasn't it as if someone had said so & so, & wasn't this what produced queer effect on you? And: when subject agrees, he must be agreeing that this is the <u>reason</u> (not the cause).

Now his agreeing doesn't shew that he <u>thought</u> of the reason at the time; he didn't. To say he was doing so sub-consciously is a mere picture: it tells us <u>nothing</u> as to what was happening <u>when</u> he laughed. It may be a good expedient to talk of sub-conscious processes; but it gets its meaning from the actual verifying phenomena; which are what are interesting.

---

[70] This is presumably Wittgenstein's translation of the German 'Witz', usually translated as 'joke'. See the Editor's Preface to *Jokes and Their Relation to the Unconscious*: 'A major problem faces us with the very title of the book, "*Der Witz*". To translate it "Wit" opens the door to unfortunate misapprehensions. In ordinary English usage "wit" and "witty" have a highly restricted meaning and are applied only to the most refined and intellectual kind of jokes. The briefest inspection of the examples in these pages will show that "*Witz*" and "*witzig*" have a far wider connotation. "Joke" on the other hand seems itself to be too wide and to cover the German "*Scherz*" as well ...' (Freud 1960, 7)

[71] See Freud 1960, 102.

We've only discovered new laws: not new regions of the soul, as Freud suggests. 9:44

Freud says: Those who doubt subconscious processes, must be unacquainted with phenomena of post-hypnotic suggestion.[72]

Now in such a case we should say: It's exactly as if someone had been saying to himself all the time: I've got to shout "Hurrah" at 5 o'clock.

So, too, when I was terribly tired after marching in the war, I went to bed at 9 & had to wake at 12. I used to find myself shaking my head violently at 12 – exactly as if someone else had been shaking me.

Freud thinks it's part of essential mechanism of a joke to conceal something, & to make it possible for subconscious to express itself. Jokes are abbreviated – concentrated statements, & by abbreviation conceal e.g. a nasty remark against someone.[73] E.g. /Lecture on Anthropological:/ In most islands there are many more women than men; in one there are fewer, so that even N—benites[74] would be welcome there. Some of the ladies get up, & he says: Don't hurry, boat only leaves on Thursday. Here he deals a blow, under concealment.[75]

Freud thinks analysis brings out concealed meaning.

Now being clear why you laugh is not being clear about a cause, &, if it were, it would not need patient's consent.

E.g. compare a doctor's statement that your eyes are bad, because you do so & so. This can only be shewn right or wrong by experiment, not by patient's consent.

Everyone says: I must know why I did it.

Second confusion consists in saying that the reason is a cause seen from inside. 9:45

What people are thinking of is something like a clock of which you see the wheels, & one of which you don't.

---

[72] See Freud 1960, 162.   [73] See Freud 1960, 100–3.
[74] Uncertain word. It clearly begins with an 'N' and probably ends in 'benites' or 'lenites', with approximately three letters in between.
[75] Moore's summary notes: <E.g. (Lectures on Anthropology) While in most islands many more women than men, in one there are fewer. And when ladies get up, joker says: No hurry, boat only leaves on Thursday – concealed nasty remark> (10:66)

But do you really see the causal connection? It is perfectly <u>imaginable</u> that one wheel should not move the other. A cause is neither seen from within nor from without, but found by experiment.

A reason is found by questioning; or e.g. by noticing that he takes my pen, though he <u>said</u> his reason for coming was to see me. But the reason found in one of these ways, is a reason in a different sense from that found in the other.

The psycho-analytic investigation as to <u>Why</u> a person laughs, is of one of 2 kinds.

(1) We might experiment, & find: People always laugh, under these circumstances.

(2) Psycho-analytic way.

And Aesthetic investigations are analogous to (2). Freud on "Wit" is a good example of an Aesthetic investigation.

But then is not Psychoanalysis Psychology?

To reply to this objection, I should have to stress a difference within Psychology.

Aesthetics like Psychoanalysis doesn't explain anything <u>away</u>.

Many people want to say: Effect of a lyric poem <u>is</u> just so & so.

9:46 But it <u>is</u> what it is.

Can one be mistaken in such a case?[76]

We have to go into the question what's <u>meant</u> by being mistaken; which is something different from what's meant in science.

One can change one's mind about the reason.

Russell says other people know reasons of our actions better than we do.

This is like saying: Dentist knows our tooth-ache better than we do.

It is an ambiguity in "knowing".

"I did it from benevolence." "You did it from self-advertisement."

Here the meaning is determined by <u>both</u> criteria, if they contradict.

Relation between analysis of a joke & experimental method of Psychology.

---

[76] Moore added on the facing page: <What led us to say it was a mistake? What chances are that in future we may change again and say it wasn't?>

Criterion of correctness of an aesthetic analysis must be agreement of person to whom I make it.

Freud's remark that we don't know why we laugh /when hear a joke/ points to the puzzle which gives rise to aesthetics.

But aesthetics does not lie in finding a mechanism.

One might say a science is not <u>only</u> concerned in finding causal connections. This is true. E.g. suppose one shews path which moon describes round sun: something like ⟨⟩.

If this had been observed: someone might say: Explanation is that there is a body we can't see, which goes round sun in a circle, & round which moon goes.

9:47

Now this is in fact not a <u>causal</u> explanation; but merely a mathematical transformation. Copernicus's view was in fact this.

So Freud's discoveries are in fact merely of striking ways of expressing certain facts, & seeing them in a system: <u>not</u> causal explanations.

Ursell: Is the subconscious comparable to the sun? Wittgenstein: I should say rather to an electron.

Compare: A box which I both see & touch; sun, which I see & don't touch; a molecule which I neither see nor touch.

Motion of a molecule means something quite different from that of a box.

It's absurd to say I can't see an electron because it's too small.

It's not just <u>false</u> to say "I see an electron vibrating (schwingen)[77]", but it's <u>nonsense</u> to say either that or that I don't.

Suppose we observed heavenly bodies moving in epicycloids: & someone says: That shews that there <u>are</u> heavenly bodies which we don't see. This is like subconscious thoughts.

If you talk of conscious & subconscious thoughts, you are thinking of a body which you see, & one which is hidden but is there.

When you see the moon alternately appearing & disappearing, One person might say: there's a yellow patch existing, then ceasing to exist: Another: The moon's there all the time, but now it's seen, now <u>not</u> seen.

9:48

---

[77] German for 'vibrate' or 'oscillate'.

Subconscious is like hypothesis of body: physical bodies are hypothetical entities just as are subconscious thoughts.

I tend to produce confusions by saying: In "subconscious thoughts", "thoughts" is used in a different sense.

Truth is we can either play 2 separate games in such a case or one big game.

All that matters is: in which way do we describe the phenomena.

If I say: These were his conscious thoughts; these were his unconscious thoughts, then I'm only playing one game with "thought", & describing one kind of phenomenon by adding "conscious", another by adding "unconscious".

But I might mean by "thought" something

Freud says he can deduce subconscious thoughts from dreams: & I might use "thought" to mean only what can be deduced from dreams.

So with "tooth-ache" I may play 2 different games.

(1) My criterion for "Ursell has tooth-ache", is what I observe & what he says.

For I have tooth-ache, they are not.

And I can use "tooth-ache" as determined by this criterion.

That's one thing.

(2) Again I could talk of my tooth-ache only, & never of others; & then there would be no behaviouristic criterion.

But (3) I might use both criteria, as I do several different ones in "This happened before that".

The mistake of supposing that we only use tooth-ache for (1) or for (2), lies in supposing that there's something to which you can point as the meaning of a word.

I construct language-games and put them side by side with actual uses of a word.

And I think it's useful to do such a thing as construct a game in which "before" means only what it means in memory, although perhaps we never so use it.

Meaning of a word is defined by way we use it, & therefore not by any feeling which we have, when we say it or hear it.

If I say: "before" & "after" mean something different, when you use memory as criterion, & when you use documents, I'm referring to 2 games, which are never played in their purity. In a particular case where you use "before", if I want to find out what game you are playing, you may tell me: "Both", & this I understand.

So of question: When did a given dream take place? This is no question, unless we have a means of deciding: so let's ask: What are our means of deciding?

The confusion between getting to know the cause & the reason for laughing, has caused the extremely pernicious effect which psychoanalysis has had – why the pupils of Freud have made such an abominable mess. It's because what Freud says sounds as if it were science, but is in fact a wonderful representation.

9:50

Supposing I said: If we study the occurrence of one element in a dream, e.g. a window, it may mean anything, or its opposite. What follows is that there is so far no method of investigating dreams. It is /not/ like rules which will tell you causes of stomach-ache.

If I have genius of Freud, & analyse dreams, you may say: I dare say this was what was meant. What strikes you in Freud, the enormous field of psychological facts which he arranges. But this doesn't make it possible for anyone to analyse a dream. It's all excellent similes: e.g. of dream to a rebus.[78]

Freud's writings are an excellent field for philosophy, because there are so many cases in which one can ask: How far is this a hypothesis? How far a good way of representing a fact? On this Freud is constantly unclear.

---

[78] See Freud 1953, 277–8 and 1953a, 408–9.

Appendix: Moore's short paper on Wittgenstein on grammar

1. Moore's essay, revised version

February 26 / 1932

I am in a very great muddle about the way in which Dr. Wittgenstein uses the expressions "rule of grammar" or "grammatical rule". And all I have tried to do is to ask some questions, which puzzle me, about it. I am in such a muddle that I haven't been able even to arrange my questions well, & it's very likely that some of them will be questions of no importance & some of them questions to which I ought to be able to find the answer for myself. But whether I ought or not it is a fact that I'm not sure what the answer to any of them is; & I hope there may be at least some of them which are worth discussing.

We all understand the expressions "rule of grammar" or "grammatical rule" perfectly well, in at least this sense, that there are hosts of cases in which we should feel no doubt whatever that something which was offered to us as an example of a grammatical rule really was a grammatical rule: we could find plenty of examples in any grammar book. I will give two examples now, about which there doesn't seem to me to be any doubt whatever. Consider the words: "You can't say "Three men was working together in a field", you must say "Three men were working together in a field"." It seems to me there's no doubt whatever that these words do express a rule of English grammar – a very trivial & very specific one, no doubt, but still a rule. Or take this, which obviously has a certain connection with the last: "If the subject-noun of a sentence is in the plural, the verb must be in the plural too: you can't use a singular verb with a plural subject". This last rule can, I think, obviously be used in a sense to justify the first. If a child, to whom you were teaching English grammar were to ask: "Why can't I say "Three men was working together"?" a perfectly sensible answer would be: "Because "men" is plural & "was" is singular; "men" is the subject of your sentence & "was" its verb; & you can't put the verb of your sentence in the singular if its subject is in the plural". This seems to me the sort of justification for a particular rule, which actually is given, & rightly given, in teaching grammar; & it gives an example of a grammatical rule which can be justified; but only of course of a ~~explanation~~ justification of a grammatical rule by appeal to another grammatical rule which it exemplifies.

2   Now one of the most obvious & striking things about the way in which Dr. Wittgenstein uses the expressions "rule of grammar" or "grammatical rule" is that he often makes statements of the form "So & so is a grammatical rule", when the so & so in question is not the sort of thing you would find given in any grammar-book as an example of a grammatical rule; when most people certainly would not recognise that it was a grammatical rule at all, as they would do in the 2 cases I have given; & when, on the contrary, the statement that it was a grammatical rule would seem to them highly paradoxical. To make things definite I'd better give an example at once, & I'll take an example which was suggested by what Mr. Guest gave as an example of a grammatical rule last time, though I'm not sure that it's the same as he meant to give. Consider these words: "2 different colours can't both be in the same place in visual space at the same time". I think Dr. Wittgenstein would say that these words express a rule of grammar; or (what, I think, comes to the same thing) I think he would say these words: "That 2 different colours can't both be in the same place in visual space at the same time is a rule of grammar".[1] Now I don't think you would find this given in any grammar-book as a rule of grammar; I don't think most people would recognise that it was a rule of grammar at all, as they would in the case of the 2 instances I gave above; & I think to most people the statement that it was would seem highly paradoxical. It certainly does seem very paradoxical to me. And one thing I certainly don't know (though perhaps I ought to) is whether, when Dr. Wittgenstein says that this is a

---

[1] According to John King's notes, as edited by Desmond Lee, Wittgenstein had said something very similar two class meetings before the one in which Moore presented his paper. 'What does it mean to say "I can't imagine red and blue in the same spot at the same time"? It sounds as if it were a statement about psychology. But in fact it is nonsense to suggest we can even try to imagine it. It is impossible, though not in the sense in which we say that it is impossible to lift a man with one hand. When you say you can't imagine red and blue together on the same spot, this is a rule of grammar.'
(Wittgenstein 1979, 94)

King's original notes read as follows: '"I can't imagine Red and Blue in the same spot." This is psychology. It is nonsense to say "try to imagine this." It is not impossible in the same way in which we say it's impossible to lift a man with one hand. When you say you can't imagine green and red together, it is again a rule of grammar.'
(King, unpublished lecture notes, 35–6)

rule of grammar, he is using the expression "rule of grammar" in precisely the same sense in which I used it above of my 2 examples, & is saying that this, though it doesn't appear to be, really is a rule of grammar in precisely that sense; or whether he is using the expression "rule of grammar" in some different sense, though perhaps having something in common with that in which I used it: &, if he is doing the latter, then I certainly do not know in exactly what sense he is using it.[2] These are some questions about which I am puzzled & about which I should like to be clear.[3]

And the next question I want to ask is whether "2 colours can't ..." really is a rule of grammar in precisely the same sense in which we all recognise that the 2 examples I gave are rules of grammar.[4] And here I've got 2 subordinate questions to ask, upon which it seems to me that the answer to this one must at least partly depend. I shall give 2 reasons, which seem to me good ones, for answering "No" to the principal question. But I don't feel sure that either of these reasons are good reasons, & to the principal question my subordinate questions are: Are these 2 reasons good ones for saying No, or are they not?[5]

3

---

[2] Crossed-out passage: <Perhaps these are unimportant questions; but I do not think they are: for I think it is important to know whether what Dr. Wittgenstein means by saying that "2 colours can't both be in the same place at the same time is a rule of grammar" is true, & I don't see how we can know this, until we know how he is using the expression "is a rule of grammar". Perhaps it is only I who don't know, but I don't believe that is the case.> We have included some of Moore's significant but shorter deletions in the main body of this text, struck-through. When Moore crossed out longer passages, we have included them in footnotes.

[3] This sentence is written in the margin next to a crossed-out passage (reproduced in the previous footnote), suggesting that Moore intended it as a replacement for that passage.

[4] At this point Moore's revised essay departs from the earlier version. The first half of the first sentence of the earlier version is crossed out on page 2, as it is not part of the revised version; the second half begins on page 2a. See below for the second half of the earlier version.

[5] Crossed-out paragraph: <When we say that "You can't say "Three men was working"" is a rule of grammar, or that "You can't use a singular verb with a plural subject" is a rule of grammar, it seems to me clear that in each case we are talking about a certain kind of combination of words, & are saying that anybody who used a combination of that kind, would be speaking or writing ungrammatically. In the first case, we are describing the kind of combination we mean by mentioning the actual words, & giving an example of the form of combination; in the second case we are neither mentioning any actual words nor giving an example of a form of combination, but are giving a general description of certain kinds of words as "singular verbs" & "plural nouns", & are saying that any one who

My first reason is this. It seems to me that the expression "2 different colours can't be in the same place at the same time" only could express a rule of grammar in the same sense in which my 2 examples do, if ~~both of the 2 following conditions were satisfied. Namely (1) that~~ this expression meant precisely the same as the following: "If you are using B as the name of one colour & R as the name of another, you can't say: "It is both the case that B is in this place now, & also the case that R is in this place now"." & ~~(2) that it not only meant the same as this, but meant the same as this latter, even if in this latter you are using "you can't say" in the same sense in which I used it in my 2 examples~~. And it doesn't seem to me that "2 different colours can't be . . ." does mean the same as this latter expression, because in this latter you are obviously talking about names of colours whereas in the former it seems to me you are talking about colours & not about names of colours. If I say "blau" is the German for "blue", I am obviously talking about the word "blau" & the word "blue". But, if I say: "This ink looks blue to me", then it seems to me that though I am using the word "blue", I am not talking about it. In the same way if I say "2 colours can't be in the same place at the same time", it seems to me that I am not talking about names of colours; whereas if I say "If B is the name of one colour & R of another, you can't say: "B & R are both in this place now"", I am talking about names of colours. But I recognise that I may easily be wrong about this: that there are cases in which you may easily make the mistake of thinking that you are not talking about names or words, but only using them, when in fact you are not only using but also talking about them.

My second reason is this. It seems to me that "2 colours can't be in the same place at the same time" does mean precisely the same as each of the 4 following expressions, all of which contain expressions very commonly used in philosophy: namely "You can't imagine 2 different colours in the same place at the same time", "It is inconceivable that 2 different colours should be in the same place at the same time", "It is not thinkable that 2 different colours . . .", "It is logically impossible that 2 different

were to combine any singular verb with any plural noun, in the way of which we give a general description by saying that it is using a plural noun as subject to a singular verb, would be speaking or writing ungrammatically. And so far as I can see any assertion of the form "So & so is a rule of grammar", if used as it is used in these 2 cases, is always an assertion with regard to some kind of combination of words to the effect that anybody who were to use any combination of that kind would be talking ungrammatically.>

colours ...". And it seems to me quite clear that, as Dr. Wittgenstein pointed out last time,⁶ in these expressions "You can't imagine ...", "You can't conceive ...", "You can't think ...", the "can't" has a totally different meaning from that which "can't" has when it expresses a physical or psychological impossibility: as, for instance, in "You can't count up to a hundred in a second": in the latter case it expresses a fact or hypothesis which can be tested by trying – confirmed or rendered doubtful by experience – whereas in "It's impossible to think that 2 colours are both in the same place at the same time" it doesn't at all. And in this respect the "can't" in "You can't say: Three men was working together", is obvious like the "can't" in "You can't think that 2 colours are in the same place at the same time": here too you obviously don't mean that it's physically impossible to say the words: it isn't, for I've just said them over & over again; & some of the commonest cases in which you'd say "You can't say that" would be to a boy who had actually said it: just as in chess or another game you would say "You can't do that" to a person who had actually done it. But, though the "can't" in "You can't say "3 men was working"" seems to me just like the "can't" in "You can't think that 2 colours" in this respect, it doesn't seem to me that "You can't say: "Three men⁷ was working together"", means at all the same as "You can't think that 3 men was working together" or "It's logically impossible that 3 men was working together". It seems to tell you nothing about what you can think, but only something about what you can say. And hence it would seem that, even if "2 colours can't be in the same place at the same time" does mean the same as "Whatever 2 colours B & R may be the names of, you can't say "B & R are both in this place now"", yet "you can't say" can't mean the same here as it does in my examples, since here it means the same as "you can't think that those 2 colours are both in this place now", whereas in my example it doesn't.⁸ And then I should add: It's only where "you can't say"

---

⁶ See note above.
⁷· Most of the words from here to the end of this sentence are covered by wavy lines in the manuscript, similar to the ones used to delete passages elsewhere in this manuscript, but much fainter. It is possible that Moore decided to delete this material; but as the marking is so faint, and the entire sentence only makes sense if the words in question are included, we have chosen to retain these words.
⁸ Crossed-out sentence: <But here again I can see reasons for suspecting I may be wrong: that "You can't say "Three men was working together" may really mean the same as that something is logically impossible.>

means the same as it does in my 2 examples, & doesn't mean the same as "you can't think", that an expression beginning with "You can't <u>say</u>" will express a rule of grammar in the sense in which my 2 examples are rules of grammar. If "you can't say" <u>does</u> mean the same as "You can't think", then though perhaps what is expressed e.g. by "You can't <u>say</u> that 2 colours are both in the same place at the same time" may perhaps be a rule of grammar in <u>some</u> sense, it won't be a rule of grammar in the <u>same</u> sense in which my 2 examples are. Is this a good reason for saying that "2 colours can't be in the same place at the same time" is <u>not</u> a grammatical rule in the same sense in which my 2 examples are? I don't feel at all sure that it is – very far from sure, for I suspect that I am horribly muddled; and yet I can't see that it isn't a good reason.

2. Moore's essay: conclusion of early version

And the next question I want to ask is whether "2 colours can't ..." really is a rule of grammar in precisely the same sense in which we all recognise that the 2 examples I gave are rules of grammar.[9] I don't think it is; &, as I've said, I don't know whether Dr. Wittgenstein thinks it is or not; but, perhaps I may be wrong, & it really is. I think it's worth asking whether it is.

Consider, first, the ~~rule~~ expression: "You can't say: "Three men <u>was</u> working together in a field"." Obviously this does resemble an expression which was discussed last time, in connection with Mr. Guest's paper, namely this "You can't imagine 2 colours in the same place in visual space at the same time" in <u>one</u> respect. Dr. Wittgenstein pointed out that the "can't" in "you can't imagine" does not mean the same as the "can't" in e.g. "you can't count up to a hundred in a second": the first sentence, does not like the second, express a psychological ~~or physical~~ fact or hypothesis, the truth of which could be tested by trying – which could be confirmed or rendered doubtful by experience. It is obvious, I think, that similarly the "can't" in "You can't say "Three men <u>was</u> working"", doesn't mean that it's physically impossible for you to say these words; for it certainly is physically possible to say them: I have said them again & again; &, if you consider the kind of situation in which you could use the expression, it's plain that many of them would be cases in which the person you addressed had actually said them: in teaching a child grammar, it would often be because he had actually said "Three men <u>was</u> working" that you would say to him "You <u>can't</u> say that".

But what, then, does: "You can't say "Three men <u>was</u> working"" mean? So far as I can see it means the same as: "If you were to say "Three men <u>was</u>" you would be talking ungrammatically": & this again means the same as "To say "Three men <u>was</u>" is not good English". But, then, what is the test as to whether so-&-so is good English or not? It seems tempting to say that the test is whether well-educated Englishmen do actually use the

---

[9] This sentence, the beginning of the fourth paragraph of both the early version and the revised version, is repeated here, in order to make clear the point at which the two versions diverge.

[10] This page, and the following page, are described as pages 6 and 7 in the Cambridge University Library catalogue of Moore's papers. However, unlike the first five pages, which are numbered in black ink, these sheets are not actually numbered.

expression in question or not; & I cannot see that it isn't true that what is actually meant by "You can't say "Three men was working"" isn't merely "Well-educated Englishmen don't usually say "Three men was"." I.e. it is after all a statement the truth of which can be confirmed or rendered doubtful by experience. And this view seems to me confirmed by the fact that when I find in a Greek grammar the ~~statement~~ rule "A subject nominative in the neuter plural regularly takes a singular verb", this does seem to be merely a historical generalisation as to the actual practice of the ancient Greeks.

7 But though I can't see that the grammatical rule "You can't say "Three men was working"", isn't merely a historical statement as to the actual usage of well-educated Englishmen, I do see two things against it. One is this. (1) If this view were true, it would follow that the statement "Well-educated Englishmen don't usually say "Three men was working"" is a grammatical rule; & it doesn't seem natural to say that it is. The second is (2) that the "can't" in "You can't say that" does seem like the "can't" which may be used in stating a rule of a game. E.g. "You can't move a king more than one square at a time" is a rule of chess. If this were a mere historical generalisation, presumably the generalisation would be "People who are playing chess don't move a king more than one square at a time". But is this a historical generalisation at all? Isn't it a tautology? Isn't part of what is meant by saying that 2 people are playing chess just that they don't move a king more than one square at a time? The possibility suggests itself that "You can't move a king more than one square at a time" means "If you do, you won't be playing chess" & that this means "People so use the word "chess" that, if you do move a king more than one square at a time, they will say you're not playing chess"; which again would be a mere historical generalisation about the use of the word chess, but which doesn't seem to be a rule of chess.

I am utterly puzzled as to what is meant by saying that so-and-so is a rule of grammar or a rule of chess.

3a. Wittgenstein's response, John King's lecture notes.

<u>Wittgenstein's discussion class</u>

207. <u>Moore's paper</u> Rules of grammar. (1) cases where there is no doubt. "Three men was working". (2) "different colours can't be in the same place of the visual field." This is different from (1). Are the two senses of the rule of grammar not the same?

> "Two colours can't be in the same place"
> = can't imagine it
>   is inconceivable
>   is not thinkable
>   is logically impossible. ("can't" has a different meaning from the physically impossible)

208. <u>Wittgenstein</u> It ought to be expressed: "it does not have sense to say". usually badly expressed as a rule of grammar.

> "This table is as identical as the other."

cf. chess on a board, & same game with different moves.

There is a feeling that one misuse is vicious and the other is not.

"as identical as".

Moore's rules of grammar are the same: just that some have occurred in philosophical discussions and some haven't. If we raised discussion we should have to state the rule.

<u>difficulties arise over analogy.</u>

cf. the puzzle that we can't measure time. It is the use of analogy of the physical "can't".

We are inclined to say we can't think this, but could say correctly if there was such an experience. To say it's logically impossible makes it sound like a proposition.

If we say we can't think of Red and Blue together in visual space, we have a feeling of trying, as in the physical world. Somehow cheat yourself and think that it is done.

Grammatical rules are all of the same kind; but not the same mistake if man makes one as if he makes the other. Because man using "<u>was</u>" uses it just as "<u>were</u>" makes no confusion: whereas analogy with things which are in the same place at the same time. cf. Two people in a chair.

When we say "can't think that two colours" etc. – we make mistake of thinking as proposition & then see that it is not. We would never try to say the above unless we were misled by analogy.

Misleading to say "can't imagine", because it leads to wrong analogy. Must say "it has no sense to say".

The rule about Red & Blue existing is a rule about the use of word "and".

Question of Criterion.

41   We only say "was" makes nonsense if other man had said it was a philosophical problem.

What is general criterion for a proposition?

    a proposition can be true or false.

Part of the proposition is the propositional calculus. Not all of grammar. We could ask what are games just as we ask what are propositions.[11]

---

[11] King MS, 39–41.

3b. Wittgenstein's response, Desmond Lee's edition of King's notes.

Moore read a brief paper to introduce a discussion on Rules of Grammar. He gave two examples.

(1) Where there is no doubt. "Three men was working". Here it is clear what the rule is and how it has been broken.

(2) "Different colours cannot be in the same place in a visual field at the same time." This differs from example (1). Are the two examples rules of grammar in the same sense? If we say "Two colours can't be in the same place", we may mean that we can't imagine it, that it is inconceivable or unthinkable, or that it is logically (as distinct from physically) impossible.

W.'s reply.

The right expression is "It does not have sense to say - - -"; but we usually express it badly by speaking of a rule of grammar. So it does not have sense to say "This table is as identical as the other". Compare using the same board and the same pieces as we use for chess, but making moves which the rules do not provide for.

We have a feeling that the first misuse referred to by Moore is harmless but the second vicious. But in fact both kinds of rule are rules in the same sense. It is just that some have been the subject of philosophical discussion and some have not. If we discuss a rule we have to state it.

These difficulties arise from false analogy. So the puzzle that we "can't" measure time is due to the analogy of the physical "can't". We are inclined to say that we *can't* imagine or think something, and imply that we *could* express it correctly if we had the experience. To say that something is "logically impossible" sounds like a proposition. So if we say we can't think of red and blue together in the same visual space, we have a feeling of *trying* to do so, as if we were talking about the physical world; we somehow cheat ourselves and think it *can* be done.

Grammatical rules are all of the same kind, but it is not the same mistake if a man breaks one as if he breaks another. If he uses "was" instead of "were" it causes no confusion; but in the other example the analogy with physical space (c.f. two people in the *same* chair) does cause confusion. When we say we can't think of two colours in the same place, we make the mistake of thinking this is a proposition, though it is not; and we would never try to say it if we were not misled by an analogy. It is misleading to use the word "can't" because it suggests a wrong analogy. We should say, "It has no sense to say - - -".

The rule about red and blue ((2) above) is a rule about the use of the word 'and'; and we would only say that 'was' ((1) above) makes nonsense if someone said it posed a philosophical problem.[12]

---

[12] Wittgenstein 1979, 97–8.

Biographies

Brahms, Johannes (1833–1897)
German composer and pianist, one of the greatest composers of the Romantic era. He spent much of his professional life in Vienna, and was a friend of the Wittgenstein family. For some discussion of his connection with the Wittgenstein family, see McGuinness 1988, 19–20.

Beethoven, Ludwig van (1770–1827)
German composer and pianist. A crucial figure in the transition between the Classical and Romantic eras in Western music. 'Wittgenstein regarded Beethoven as *exactly* "the sort of man to be"' (Monk 1990, 86). In a letter to Russell, Wittgenstein called Mozart and Beethoven 'the actual sons of God' (Wittgenstein 2012, 34).

Brouwer, Luitzen Egbertus Jan (1881–1966)
Dutch mathematician and philosopher, and the founder of mathematical intuitionism; professor at the University of Amsterdam from 1912 to 1955. In March 1928, he visited Vienna to give a lecture on 'Mathematics, Science and Language', which Wittgenstein attended with Friedrich Waismann and Herbert Feigl, and which according to Feigl, 'marked the return of Wittgenstein to strong philosophical interest and activities' (Monk 1990, 249).

Bruckner, Anton (1824–1896)
Austrian composer, widely regarded in Germany and Austria as the greatest symphonist of the nineteenth century. He was a professor at the Vienna Conservatory from 1868 to 1891, and also taught at the University of Vienna.

Drury, Maurice O'Connor (Con) (1907–1976)
Irish doctor and psychiatrist. Drury first met Wittgenstein at a meeting of the Moral Sciences Club in 1929 and attended Wittgenstein's lectures until he graduated in 1931. They became close and life-long friends. He also wrote a book and a number of articles on Wittgenstein's life and work.

Frazer, Sir James George (1854–1941)
Scottish anthropologist, often considered as a founding father of modern anthropology. He graduated in classics at Trinity College, Cambridge, in 1878, and was a Fellow of Trinity from 1879 to 1941. In 1931, Wittgenstein and Drury (q.v.) read Frazer's *Golden Bough* together. Drury later recalled that he and Wittgenstein 'got the first volume of the full edition and we continued to read it for some weeks.

He would stop me from time to time and make comments on Frazer's remarks' (Wittgenstein 1993, 115). The first part of Wittgenstein's 'Remarks on Frazer's *Golden Bough*' (Wittgenstein 1993, chapter 7) dates from the first half of 1931.

Gauss, Johann Carl Friedrich (1777–1855)
German mathematician who made extraordinary contributions to many fields.

Goethe, Johann Wolfgang von (1749–1832)
One of the most celebrated German novelists, playwrights, poets, and natural scientists. There are an extraordinary number of quotations from Goethe, and references to Goethe, throughout Wittgenstein's writing (see Biesenbach 2014, 209–35, 551–4, 673–5 for a compilation). 'To say what Ludwig admired in Goethe would almost be to say what he found remarkable or worthwhile in life, so many are the themes and attitudes from Goethe that recur in his thought' (McGuinness 1988, 34–5).

Guest, David (1911–1938)
Student at Trinity from 1929 to 1930 and 1931 to 1933. One of a group of students who gathered around Wittgenstein in the autumn of 1929. The minutes of the Moral Sciences Club for 26 November 1931 record that he gave a paper on 'Atomic Propositions . . . in which he attempted to show that there were no such things'. He also gave a paper in Wittgenstein's class, probably on 12 February 1932, to which Moore referred in his own short paper on Wittgenstein on grammar (see Appendix above). He became a Marxist while at Cambridge. He volunteered for the International Brigade in the Spanish Civil War and died in the battle of Ebro. See Guest 1939 for further information about his life.

Haldane, John Burdon Sanderson (1892–1964)
English biologist, geneticist, mathematician, popularizer of science, and a central figure in the unification of Mendelian genetics and Darwinian natural selection. Between 1922 and 1932 he taught biochemistry at Trinity College, Cambridge.

Haeckel, Ernst (1834–1919)
German naturalist and professor of zoology at Jena, and an exponent of materialistic monism. His book of popular science and philosophy, *The Riddle of the Universe*, was widely read in the early twentieth century.

Helmholtz, Hermann von (1821–1894)
German physicist, physiologist, and mathematician who was a pioneering writer on non-Euclidean geometries. Russell responded to his work on the topic in his doctoral dissertation; Schlick and Reichenbach both wrote on Helmholtz's views about geometry in the early 1920s.

Hertz, Heinrich (1857–1894)
German physicist, and the discoverer of radio waves. A student with Helmholtz, he was later a professor of physics at the University of Bonn. The standard unit of frequency, the hertz (Hz, one cycle per second), is named in his honour. Wittgenstein was fond of quoting a favourite passage from Hertz's *The Principles of Mechanics* (see 7:17). Wittgenstein 'had a great admiration ... for the introduction to Hertz's *Mechanics*' (Lee 1979, 218; Flowers 1999, 2 195).

James, William (1842–1910)
American psychologist and philosopher, a professor at Harvard University from 1876 to 1907, and the most influential American philosopher of the early twentieth century. His first major work was *Principles of Psychology* (1890), which Wittgenstein discussed at length in his teaching and writing in the 1940s. Drury, one of Wittgenstein's closest friends, recalled that 'Wittgenstein had a great admiration for James, and *The Varieties of Religious Experience* was one of the few books he insisted I must read' (Drury 1967, 68).

Joachim, Joseph (1831–1907)
Famous violin virtuoso, conductor, and composer, and a cousin of Fanny Wittgenstein, Wittgenstein's grandmother. Joachim was adopted by Wittgenstein's grandparents at the age of twelve. He later introduced them to Johannes Brahms (q.v.), who became a close friend of the Wittgenstein family.

Johnson, William Ernest (1858–1931)
English logician who taught at King's College, Cambridge, for nearly thirty years. He is mainly remembered for his *Logic* (1921–1924), in three volumes. Johnson was Wittgenstein's logic teacher for a short period when Wittgenstein first arrived in Cambridge in 1912; they remained good friends.

Keller, Gottfried (1819–1890)
Swiss novelist, author of short stories, and poet. Best known for his semi-autobiographical novel *Green Henry*. Keller was 'one of the few great writers whom Wittgenstein revered wholeheartedly, indeed passionately' (Engelmann 1967, 86).

Knight, Helen (1899 – d. 1980s)
One of the note-takers at Wittgenstein's lectures for the *Blue Book* during the 1933–1934 academic year. She published a number of articles in the 1930s, mostly on aesthetics and ethics. She moved to Melbourne in the mid-1950s, where she was part of a group of Wittgensteinians that included Douglas Gasking and Camo Jackson. For more about her life and Wittgenstein's reception in Australia, see Marshall 2014, 105–6.

Lichtenberg, Georg Christoph (1742–1799)

German experimental physicist, astronomer, philosopher, satirist, and aphorist. A professor at the University of Göttingen, he is best known for his posthumously published notebooks of aphorisms. He corresponded widely with figures such as Kant and Goethe, and was an important influence on Schopenhauer, Freud, Nietzsche, and Kierkegaard. Wittgenstein gave Russell a copy of a second-hand edition of a collection of Lichtenberg's aphorisms in 1913. Decades later, he told von G.H. Wright that Lichtenberg was 'terrific' (McGuinness 1988, 37).

Lodge, Sir Oliver Joseph (1851–1940)

English physicist, pioneer of wireless telegraphy, and Fellow of the Royal Society, who had collaborated with Hertz (q.v.). He was also an advocate of spiritualism and took a scientific approach to proving the immortality of the soul. Wittgenstein kept a collection of articles and clippings which he considered to be particularly revealing examples of popular stupidity or nonsense. This collection included a story from the *Montreal Star*, dated 22 October 1931, about Lodge's belief 'that the mind of Edison was directing work from beyond the grave' (Wittgenstein 2012, 195).

Ogden, Charles Kay (1889–1957)

English linguist, philosopher, and writer. Co-founder, in 1909, of the Heretics Society in Cambridge, a forum opposed to traditional authority and religious dogma. Speakers included John McTaggart, Bertrand Russell, George Bernard Shaw, G.K. Chesterton, J.B.S. Haldane, Virginia Woolf, and Wittgenstein. Ogden co-authored *The Meaning of Meaning* (1923) with I.A. Richards (q.v.). In 1928, they invented Basic English, a practical, easily learned 850-word language. With the aid of Frank Ramsey (q.v.), Ogden produced the first English translation of Wittgenstein's *Tractatus*. Ogden was the general editor of the International Library of Psychology, Philosophy, and Scientific Method, which published not only the *Tractatus*, but also books by Russell, Ramsey, Carnap, I.A. Richards, and other influential philosophers, social scientists, and literary critics.

Palestrina, Giovanni Pierluigi da (1525–1594)

Italian Renaissance composer of sacred music and the best-known sixteenth-century representative of the Roman School of musical composition.

Ramsey, Frank (1903–1930)

Cambridge philosopher and mathematician who made important contributions to mathematical logic, probability theory, the philosophy of science, and economics. He visited Wittgenstein in Austria in September 1923, and was one of the first commentators on Wittgenstein's early work. According to Monk, Ramsey 'was not only Wittgenstein's most valued partner in philosophical discussion, but also his closest friend' during the first year after his return to Cambridge (Monk 1990, 258). See also Ramsey 1990, a collection of his philosophical papers, and Wittgenstein 2003, 15, for Wittgenstein's thoughts about Ramsey shortly after his death.

Richards, Ivor Armstrong (1893–1979)
Cambridge philosopher and literary critic. An acquaintance of Wittgenstein's who attended Wittgenstein's lectures in Michaelmas Term, 1932 and possibly those of other terms as well. He wrote about his experience of Wittgenstein's lectures in his poem, 'The Strayed Poet'. Co-author, with C.K. Ogden (q.v.), of *The Meaning of Meaning* (1923). Wittgenstein received a copy of the book shortly after its publication. He wrote to Russell that he had 'rarely read anything so stupid' (Wittgenstein 2012, 137).

Sheffer, Henry M. (1882–1964)
American logician who taught at Harvard from 1916 to 1952. He introduced, in 1913, what is now known as the Sheffer stroke. Sheffer showed that the truth-functions of propositional logic could all be defined from a single function, either 'not both … and …' or 'neither … nor …'. The Sheffer stroke became well known due to its use in the second edition of Whitehead and Russell's *Principia Mathematica*.

Skinner, Francis (1912–1941)
Mathematics undergraduate at Trinity from 1930 to 1933, and a postgraduate fellow during 1933–1936. He was one of the small group of students to whom Wittgenstein dictated the *Blue Book* and the *Brown Book*, and he worked with Wittgenstein on a number of other dictations during the 1930s. He was Wittgenstein's closest friend during these years; they lived together in the late 1930s. For further information about their friendship, see Pascal 1979 and Monk 1990.

Skolem, Thoralf (1887–1963)
Norwegian mathematician who made important contributions to mathematical logic and set theory.

Stevenson, Charles L. (1908–1979)
American student of Moore and Wittgenstein, best known for his pioneering work in metaethics and emotivism. He earned a BA in English literature from Yale in 1930, a BA in philosophy from Cambridge in 1933, and his PhD from Harvard in 1935. He later taught at Yale and the University of Michigan, and published his landmark *Ethics and Language* in 1944. Many of his most important articles in ethics are reprinted in *Facts and Values*.

Tarski, Alfred (1901–1983)
Polish-born American mathematician, philosopher, and philosopher of logic, widely regarded as one of the greatest logicians of the twentieth century. He is

best known for his work on the concepts of truth and consequence in the 1930s, culminating in his 'The Concept of Truth in Formalized Languages' (1933). He is also famous for his work on set theory, model theory, and algebra.

Ursell, Harold (1907–1969)
British mathematician, a Trinity Fellow from 1929 to 1933, and a close friend of Wittgenstein's. He taught at Leeds University from 1933 to 1967, after which he was a professor at the University of Calgary. For further information, see Young 1970.

Young, Laurence Chisholm (1905–2000)
Fellow of Trinity College from 1931 to 1935 who attended Wittgenstein's lectures on 'Philosophy for Mathematicians' throughout the 1932–1933 academic year (Young 1981, 63). He was a mathematics professor at the University of Cape Town from 1938 to 1948, and at the University of Wisconsin, Madison, from 1948 to 1975.

Moore's abbreviations

32	1932
33	1933
∴	therefore (but not as part of a proof)
acc.	according
aesth., aesthet.	aesthetics
Ap.	April
appar.	apparent
arg.	argument
ass., assoc., associat.	associative, association
Aug.	Augustine
b.	blue
bec.	because
Beeth.	Beethoven
bic.	bicycle
blg.	belong
C., Camb.	Cambridge
c., col.	colour
cd.	could
chap.	chapter
comb.	combination
comp.	compare
consec.	consecutive
constr.	construction
contr.	contradiction
corr.	corresponds, corresponding, correspondence
ct.	court
def.	definition (but not as part of a proof), define, definite
descr.	description
diam.	diameter
dict.	dictionary
dim.	dimensional
dist.	distinguished, distribution
distr.	distribution, distributive
distrib.	distributive
Eng.	English
esp.	especially

ex. mid.	excluded middle
exp., expect., expectat.	expectation
expl., explan.	explanation
F.	Frege, Frazer, Freud
Feb.	February
fig.	figure
ft.	foot, feet
G.	Goethe
g.	green
gen.	general
gener.	generally
geom.	geometry
Germ.	German
Gk.	Greek
gramm., grammat.	grammatical
H.	Haldane
hr.	hour
imag.	image, imagination
implic.	implication
imposs.	impossibility, impossible
in.	inch
indef.	indefinite
indep.	independently
inf., infin.	infinite
introd.	introduction
J.	Johnson
Jan.	January
k.	king
K.P.	King's Parade
lab.	laboratory
lang.	language
lbs.	pounds
lect.	lecture
M.	Moore
MS.	manuscript
math., mathem.	mathematics, mathematical
maths.	mathematics
mean.	meaning
min.	minute
Mon.	Monday
Mrs. K.	Mrs. Knight
mut. mutand.	mutatis mutandis

nec., neces., necess.	necessarily, necessary, necessity
Nov.	November
o.	orange
O. & R.	Ogden & Richards
opp.	opposed, opposite, opposites
ord.	ordinary
p.	purple
p.c.	primary colours
p.e.	present experience
P.M., Princ., Principia	*Principia Mathematica*
p.p.	primitive propositions
pent.	pentagon
perh.	perhaps
phenom.	phenomenon
phil., philos.	philosophical, philosophy, philosopher
phot.	photograph
poss.	possibility, possibly
pred.	predicate
presupp.	presupposition
prim.	primary, primitive
prob.	probable, probability
progr.	programme
prop.	proposition, propositional
propl.	propositional
psych.	psychical; psychology; psychological
psychol., psycholog.	psychology; psychological
q.	queen
r.	red
R., Russ.	Russell
reg.	regular
repr.	represented
S.	Sheffer, Smith
s.p.	same place
s.t.	same time
shd.	should
sq. ft.	square feet
sq. yds.	square yards
st.	straight
symph.	symphony
taut.	tautology
thermodyn.	thermodynamics
Tract.	*Tractatus*

trans., transl.	translated, translating
transit.	transitive
tri.	triangle
Trin.	Trinity
U.	Ursell
usu.	usual, usually
w.	white
W., Wittg.	Wittgenstein
wd.	word
wh.	which, what
wig.	wiggle
y.	yellow
yds.	yards

Bibliography

Ambrose, Alice 1972 'Ludwig Wittgenstein: A Portrait'. In Alice Ambrose and Morris Lazerowitz (eds.) *Ludwig Wittgenstein: Philosophy and Language*, 13–25. London: Allen and Unwin; New York: Humanities Press. In Flowers 1999, 2 263–72; Flowers 2016, 2 550–9.

Ammereller, Erich and Eugen Fischer 2004 *Wittgenstein at Work: Method in the Philosophical Investigations*. London: Routledge.

Augustine 1993 *Confessions*. Trans. F.J. Sheed. Indianapolis: Hackett.

Baker, Gordon 1979 'Verehrung und Verkehrung: Waismann and Wittgenstein'. In Luckhardt 1979, 243–85.

Baker, Gordon and Peter Hacker 1980 *An Analytical Commentary on Wittgenstein's* Philosophical Investigations. Chicago: University of Chicago Press. (Revised second edition, Oxford: Blackwell, 2005).

Baker, Gordon and Peter Hacker 1980a *Wittgenstein, Meaning and Understanding. Essays on the* Philosophical Investigations. Chicago: University of Chicago Press. (Revised second edition, Oxford: Blackwell, 2005).

Bengel, John Albert 1858 *Gnomon of the New Testament*, vol. I. Trans. Andrew R. Fausset. Edinburgh: T. & T. Clark.

Biesenbach, Hans 2014 *Anspielungen und Zitate im Werk Ludwig Wittgensteins*. Sofia, Bulgaria: Sofia University Press.

Boswell, James, John Wilson Croker, and John Wright 1846 *The Life of Samuel Johnson: Including a Journal of His Tour to the Hebrides*, vol. 2. London: H.G. Bohn.

Brahms, Johannes 2000 *Symphony No. 4 in E Minor, Op. 98: Authoritative Score, Background, Context, Criticism, Analysis*. Ed. Kenneth Hull. New York: W.W. Norton.

Britton, Karl 1955 'Portrait of a Philosopher'. *The Listener* 53 #1372, 16 June 1955, 1071–1072. In Fann 1967, 56–7. In Flowers 1999, 2 205–6; Flowers 2016, 2 491–7.

Brouwer, L.E.J. 1908 'De onbetrouwbaarheid der logische principes' [The unreliability of the logical principles]. *Tijdschrift voor Wijsbegeerte* 2, 152–8. English translation in Brouwer 1975, 107–11.

Brouwer, L.E.J. 1923 'On the Significance of the Principle of Excluded Middle in Mathematics, Especially in Function Theory'. Reprint in van Heijenoort 1967, 334–45.

Brouwer, L.E.J. 1975 *Collected Works. I: Philosophy and Foundations of Mathematics*. Ed. A. Heyting. Amsterdam: North-Holland.

Cann, Kathleen 1995 'The Papers of George Edward Moore (1873–1958) Cambridge University Library Add. MSS 8330 and 8875'. *Wittgenstein Studien* 2 (1).

Carroll, Lewis 1992 *Alice in Wonderland: Authoritative Texts of Alice's Adventures in Wonderland, Through the Looking-Glass, The Hunting of the Snark, Backgrounds, Essays in Criticism.* Ed. Donald J. Grey. Second edition. New York: Norton. (First published in 1871).

Citron, Gabriel 2013 'Religious Language as Paradigmatic of Language in General: Wittgenstein's 1933 Lectures'. In Venturinha 2013, 19–36.

Conant, James 2011 'Wittgenstein's Methods'. In Kuusela and McGinn 2011, 620–45.

Darwin, Charles 1998 *The Expression of the Emotions in Man and Animals.* Oxford: Oxford University Press.

Diamond, Cora 1991 *The Realistic Spirit: Wittgenstein, Philosophy and the Mind.* Cambridge, MA: MIT Press.

Diamond, Cora 2004 'Criss-Cross Philosophy'. In Ammereller and Fischer 2004, 201–20.

Dickinson, G. Lowes, Dean Inge, H.G. Wells, J.B.S. Haldane, Sir Oliver Lodge, and Sir Walford Davies 1939 *Points of View: A Series of Broadcast Addresses.* London: G. Allen & Unwin.

Drury, M.O'C. 1967 'A Symposium: Assessments of the Man and the Philosopher. II'. In Fann 1967, 67–71. In Flowers 1999, 4 149–53; Flowers 2016, 2 1043–7.

Drury, M.O'C. 1984 'Conversations With Wittgenstein'. In Rush Rhees (ed.) *Recollections of Wittgenstein,* 97–171. Oxford: Oxford University Press In Flowers 1999, 3 188–252; Flowers 2016, 2 776–837.

Drury, M.O'C. 1984a 'Some Notes on Conversations With Wittgenstein'. In Rush Rhees (ed.) *Recollections of Wittgenstein,* 76–96. Oxford: Oxford University Press. In Flowers 1999, 3 171–87; Flowers 2016, 2 758–75.

Engelmann, Paul 1967 *Letters from Ludwig Wittgenstein, With a Memoir.* Oxford: Blackwell.

Engelmann, Mauro 2011 'What Wittgenstein's "Grammar" is *Not* (On Garver, Baker and Hacker, and Hacker on Wittgenstein on "Grammar")'. *Wittgenstein-Studien,* 2 (new series), 71–102.

Engelmann, Mauro 2013 *Wittgenstein's Philosophical Development: Phenomenology, Grammar, Method and the Anthropological View.* Basingstoke, Hampshire: Palgrave Macmillan.

Erbacher, Christian 2015 'Editorial Approaches to Wittgenstein's Nachlass: Towards a Historical Appreciation'. *Philosophical Investigations* 38 (3), 165–98.

Euclid 2006 *The Elements, Books I–XIII.* Trans. Sir Thomas L. Heath. New York: Barnes and Noble.

Fann, K.T. 1967 *Ludwig Wittgenstein: The Man and His Philosophy.* New York: Dell Publishing.

Fitzgerald, Robert 2007 *Rowntree and the Marketing Revolution, 1862–1969*. Cambridge: Cambridge University Press.

Flowers III, F.A. (ed.) 1999 *Portraits of Wittgenstein*, 4 vols. Bristol: Thoemmes Press.

Flowers III, F.A. and Ian Ground (eds.) 2016 *Portraits of Wittgenstein*: 2 vols., second edition. London: Bloomsbury.

Forkel, Johann Nikolaus 1802 *Über Johann Sebastian Bachs Leben, Kunst und Kunstwerke*. Leipzig: Hoffmeister und Kühnel.

Forkel, Johann Nikolaus 1920 *Johann Sebastian Bach: His Life, Art and Work*. Trans. Charles Sanford Terry. London: Constable and Co.

Frazer, Sir James George 1911 *The Golden Bough: A Study in Magic and Religion. Part I: The Magic Art and the Evolution of Kings*, vol. 1. London: Macmillan.

Frazer, Sir James George 1915 *The Golden Bough: A Study in Magic and Religion. Part VII: Balder The Beautiful*, vol. 1. London: Macmillan.

Frazer, Sir James George 1922 *The Golden Bough: A Study in Magic and Religion*. One volume abridged edition. New York: Macmillan.

Frazer, Sir James George 1934 *The Fear of the Dead in Primitive Religion: Lectures Delivered on the William Wyse Foundation at Trinity College Cambridge*, vol. 2. London: MacMillan.

Frege, Gottlob 1879 *Begriffsschrift*. References are to the reprint in van Heijenoort 1967, 1–82.

Frege, Gottlob 1893 *Grundgesetze der Arithmetik*. Jena: Herman Pohle.

Freud, Sigmund 1953 *The Interpretation of Dreams (First Part)*. Volume IV of *The Standard Edition of the Complete Psychological Works of Sigmund Freud*. Trans. James Strachey. London: Hogarth Press.

Freud, Sigmund 1953a *The Interpretation of Dreams (Second Part)*. Volume V of *The Standard Edition of the Complete Psychological Works of Sigmund Freud*. Trans. James Strachey. London: Hogarth Press.

Freud, Sigmund 1957 'A Metapsychological Supplement to the Theory of Dreams'. In Volume XIV of *The Standard Edition of the Complete Psychological Works of Sigmund Freud*, 217–36. Trans. James Strachey. London: Hogarth Press.

Freud, Sigmund 1957a 'Inhibitions, Symptoms and Anxiety'. In Volume XX of *The Standard Edition of the Complete Psychological Works of Sigmund Freud*, 77–178. Trans. James Strachey. London: Hogarth Press.

Freud, Sigmund 1960 *Jokes and Their Relation to the Unconscious*. Volume VIII of *The Standard Edition of the Complete Psychological Works of Sigmund Freud*. Trans. James Strachey. London: Hogarth Press.

Freud, Sigmund 1963 *Introductory Lectures on Psycho-Analysis*. Volume XV of *The Standard Edition of the Complete Psychological Works of Sigmund Freud*. Trans. James Strachey. London: Hogarth Press.

Gasking, D.A.T. and A.C. Jackson 'Ludwig Wittgenstein'. 1951 *Australasian Journal of Philosophy* 29, 73–80. In Flowers 1999, 4 141–6; Flowers 2016, 2 1035–40.

Geach, Peter (ed.) 1988 *Wittgenstein's Lectures on Philosophical Psychology, 1946–47*. New York: Simon & Schuster.
Glock, Hans-Johann 1996 *A Wittgenstein Dictionary*. Oxford: Blackwell.
Goethe, Johann Wolfgang von 2009 *Metamorphosis of Plants*. Trans. Gordon L. Miller. Cambridge, MA: MIT Press.
Guest, Carmel Haden (ed.) 1939 *David Guest: A Scientist Fights for Freedom (1911–1938) A Memoir*. London: Lawrence & Wishart.
Haeckel, Ernst 1900 *The Riddle of the Universe at the Close of the Nineteenth Century*. Trans. Joseph McCabe. New York: Harper & Brothers.
Haldane, J.B.S. 1929 'Points of View'. *The Listener*, 1 #43, 6 November 1929, 601–626. Reprinted in Dickinson et al. 1939, 73–89.
Hamann, Johann Georg 1956 *Briefwechsel*, vol. 2 (1760–1769). Ed. Arthur Henkel and Walther Ziesemer. Wiesbaden: Insel-Verlag.
Hamann, Johann Georg 2007 *Writings on Philosophy and Language*. Ed. Kenneth Haynes. Cambridge: Cambridge University Press.
Helmholtz, Hermann von 1881 *Popular Lectures on Scientific Subjects, second series*. Trans. E. Atkinson. London: Longmans, Green & Co.
Hertz, Heinrich 1899 *The Principles of Mechanics Presented in a New Form*. Trans. D.E. Jones and J.T. Walley. New York: Macmillan. (New York: Dover reprint with same pagination, 1956).
Hilmy, S. Stephen 1987 *The Later Wittgenstein: The Emergence of a New Philosophical Method*. Oxford: Blackwell.
Hintikka, Jaakko 1991 'An Impatient Man and His Papers', *Synthese* 87, 183–201. Reprinted as chapter 1 of Hintikka 1996.
Hintikka, Jaakko 1996 *Ludwig Wittgenstein: Half-Truths and One-and-a-Half-Truths*. Dordrecht: Kluwer.
James, William 1904 'Does "Consciousness" Exist?' *Journal of Philosophy, Psychology, and Scientific Methods* 1, 477–91. Reprinted in James 1912, 1–38.
James, William 1912 *Essays in Radical Empiricism*. Ed. Ralph Barton Perry. London: Longmans, Green & Co.
Johnson, W.E. 1921 *Logic, Part I*. Cambridge: Cambridge University Press. (New York: Dover reprint, 1964).
Keller, Gottfried 1985 *Green Henry*. Trans. A.M. Holt. London: John Calder.
Kenny, Anthony 1976 'From the Big Typescript to the *Philosophical Grammar*'. *Acta Philosophica Fennica* 28, 41–53. Reprinted in Kenny 1984, 24–37.
Kenny, Anthony 1984 *The Legacy of Wittgenstein*. Oxford: Blackwell.
Kenny, Anthony 2005 'A Brief History of Wittgenstein Editing'. In Pichler and Säätelä 2005, 341–55.
Kienzler, Wolfgang 1997 *Wittgensteins Wende zu seiner Spätphilosophie 1930–1932* [Wittgenstein's Turn to His Late Philosophy 1930–1932]. Frankfurt am Main: Suhrkamp.

Kienzler, Wolfgang 2001 'About the Dividing Line between Early and Late Wittgenstein'. In G. Oliveri (ed.) *From the* Tractatus *to the* Tractatus *and Other Essays* (*Wittgenstein Studien* 2-2000), 125-30. Frankfurt am Main: Peter Lang.

Kierkegaard, Søren 1987 *Either/Or: Part II*. Trans. Howard V. Hong and Edna H. Hong. Princeton: Princeton University Press.

King, John. Unpublished lecture notes. Add. 506. 'Philosophy with Wittgenstein'. Cambridge: Wren Library.

Klagge, James 2003 'The Wittgenstein Lectures'. In Wittgenstein 2003, 331-72.

Kuusela, Oskari 2008 *The Struggle Against Dogmatism: Wittgenstein and the Concept of Philosophy*. Cambridge, MA: Harvard University Press.

Kuusela, Oskari 2011 'The Development of Wittgenstein's Philosophy'. In Kuusela and McGinn 2011, 597-619.

Kuusela, Oskari and Marie McGinn (eds.) 2011 *The Oxford Handbook of Wittgenstein*. Oxford: Oxford University Press.

Lee, Desmond 1979 'Wittgenstein 1929-1931'. *Philosophy* 54, 211-20. In Flowers 1999, 2 188-97; Flowers 2016, 2 476-85.

Lewy, Casimir 1976 *Meaning and Modality*. Cambridge: Cambridge University Press.

Lichtenberg, Georg Christoph 1971 *Schriften und Briefe, Volume 2: Sudelbücher II, Materialhefte, Tagebücher*. Ed. Wolfgang Promies. Munich: Carl Hanser.

Lichtenberg, Georg Christoph 2000 *The Waste Books*. Trans. R.J. Hollingdale. New York: New York Review of Books.

Lodge, Sir Oliver 1929 *Phantom Walls*. London: Hodder and Stoughton.

Lodge, Sir Oliver 1930 *Conviction of Survival: Two Discourses in Memory of F.W.H. Myers*. London: Methuen & Co.

Luckhardt, C. Grant (ed.) 1979 *Wittgenstein: Sources and Perspectives*. Hassocks, Sussex: The Harvester Press.

Lütterfelds, W. (ed.) 2007 *Wittgenstein Jahrbuch 2003/2006*. Frankfurt: Peter Lang.

Malcolm, Norman 1984 *Ludwig Wittgenstein: A Memoir. With a Biographical Sketch by G.H. von Wright*. Second edition. London: Oxford University Press. (First edition, 1958).

Marshall, Graeme 2014 'The Influence of Wittgenstein: 1940s'. In G. Oppy and N.N. Trakakis (eds.) *History of Philosophy in Australia and New Zealand*, vol. 1, 89-120. Springer.

Mauthner, Fritz 1923 *Beiträge zu einer Kritik der Sprache. Erster Band* [Contributions to a Critique of Language. Volume One]. Third edition. Leipzig: Felix Meiner.

McGuinness, Brian 1979 'Wittgenstein and the Vienna Circle'. Editor's preface in Waismann 1979, 11-31. In Flowers 1999, 2 161-71; Flowers 2016, 1 447-58.

McGuinness, Brian 1988 *Wittgenstein: A Life. Young Ludwig 1889–1921*. London: Duckworth.
McGuinness, Brian 2016 'Arthur MacIver's Diary: Cambridge (October 1929 – March 1930)'. *Wittgenstein-Studien* 7, 201–256.
Monk, Ray 1990 *Ludwig Wittgenstein: The Duty of Genius*. New York: The Free Press.
Moore, G.E. 1955 'Wittgenstein's Lectures in 1930-33'. First published in three parts in *Mind* in 1954–1955. References are to the reprint in Wittgenstein 1993, 45–114.
Moore, G.E. 1962 *Commonplace Book: 1919–1953*. Ed. Casimir Lewy. London: George Allen & Unwin.
Moore, G.E. 1968 'An Autobiography'. In Paul Arthur Schilpp (ed.) *The Philosophy of G.E. Moore*, 3–39. La Salle, IL: Open Court. Extract in Flowers 1999 1, 149; Flowers 2016, 1 153.
Moore, G.E. 2007 'Wittgenstein's Expressions "Rule of Grammar" or "Grammatical Rule"'. Ed. Josef Rothhaupt and Aidan Seery. In Lütterfelds 2007, 201-7.
Moore, G.E. Add. 8330, 1/5 'Extracts from diaries 1929–1939'. Cambridge: Cambridge University Library.
Moore, G.E. Add. 8875, 10/7/4–9 'Notes of lectures in Cambridge 1930-1933'. Cambridge: Cambridge University Library.
Moore, G.E. Add. 8875, 10/7/10 'Summaries of Wittgenstein's lectures, c.1953?' Cambridge: Cambridge University Library.
Moore, G.E. Add. 8875, 15/10 'Wittgenstein's use of "grammar"'. Cambridge: Cambridge University Library.
Moore, G.E., H.W.B. Joseph, and A.E. Taylor 1932 'Symposium: Is Goodness a Quality?' *Proceedings of the Aristotelian Society, Supplementary Volumes* 11, 116–68.
Nahim, Paul J. 1998 *An Imaginary Tale: The Story of $\sqrt{-1}$*. Princeton: Princeton University Press.
Nedo, Michael 1993 'Ludwig Wittgenstein: A Chronology'. In Michael Nedo (ed.) *Ludwig Wittgenstein: Wiener Ausgabe. Einführung* [Ludwig Wittgenstein: Vienna Edition. Introduction], 11–47. Vienna and New York: Springer. In Flowers 1999, 1 30–62; Flowers 2016, 1 31–65.
Ogden, C.K. and I.A. Richards 1923 *The Meaning of Meaning: A Study of the Influence of Language Upon Thought and of the Science of Symbolism*. London: Routledge & Kegan Paul. (New York: Harcourt, Brace and World reprint. Eighth edition, 1946).
Pascal, Fania 1979 'Wittgenstein: A Personal Memoir'. In Luckhardt 1979, 23–60 and Rhees 1984, 12–49. In Flowers 1999, 2 222–48; Flowers 2016, 2 508–35.
Paul, Denis 2007 *Wittgenstein's Progress: 1929–1951*. Bergen: Publications from the Wittgenstein Archives at the University of Bergen #19.
Pichler, Alois 2004 *Wittgensteins* Philosophische Untersuchungen: *Vom Buch zum Album* Studien zur Österreichischen Philosophie 36 (ed. Rudolf Haller). Amsterdam and New York: Rodopi.

Pichler, Alois and Simo Säätelä (eds.) 2005 *Wittgenstein: The Philosopher and his Works*. (Second edition, 2006. Frankfurt am Main: ontos verlag).
Plato 1997 *Complete Works*, ed. John Cooper. Indianapolis: Hackett.
See Plato, *Euthyphro*. Trans. G.M.A. Grube, 1–16.
See Plato, *Republic*. Trans. G.M.A. Grube, revised by C.D.C. Reeve, 971–1223.
See Plato, *Theatetus*. Trans. M.J. Levett, revised by Myles F. Burnyeat, 157–234.
Ramsey, Frank 1990 *Philosophical Papers*. Ed. D.H. Mellor. Cambridge: Cambridge University Press.
Reid, Louis Arnaud, Helen Knight, and C.E.M. Joad 1932 'Symposium: The Limits of Psychology in Aesthetics'. *Proceedings of the Aristotelian Society, Supplementary Volumes* 11, 169–215.
Rhees, Rush (ed.) 1984 *Recollections of Wittgenstein*. Revised edition. Oxford: Oxford University Press. (Previously published in 1981 as *Ludwig Wittgenstein: Personal Recollections*. Oxford: Blackwell).
Room, Adrian 2005 *Placenames of The World: Origins and Meanings of the Names for 6,600 Countries, Cities, Territories, Natural Features and Historic Sites*. Second edition. Jefferson, NC: McFarland & Co.
Rothhaupt, Josef 2007 'Moores Statement über "Wittgenstein's expressions 'rule of grammar' or 'grammatical rule'"'. In Lütterfelds 2007, 209–29.
Rothhaupt, Josef 2016 'Wittgensteins "Bemerkungen über Frazers The Golden Bough"'. In Lars Albinus, Josef G.F. Rothhaupt, and Aidan Seery (eds.) *Wittgenstein's Remarks on Frazer: The Text and The Matter*, 11-83. Berlin: De Gruyter.
Russell, Bertrand 1903 *The Principles of Mathematics*. Cambridge: Cambridge University Press.
Russell, Bertrand 1905 'On Denoting'. *Mind* (new series) 14 (56), 479–93.
Russell, Bertrand 1919 *Introduction to Mathematical Philosophy*. London: George Allen & Unwin. (Online Corrected Edition version 1.0, based on the 'second edition' (second printing) of April 1920. http://people.umass.edu/klement/russell-imp.html).
Russell, Bertrand 1921 *The Analysis of Mind*. London: George Allen & Unwin.
Russell, Bertrand 1927 *Outline of Philosophy*. London: George Allen & Unwin.
Schilpp, Paul Arthur 1963 *The Philosophy of Rudolf Carnap*. La Salle, IL: Open Court.
Schulte, Joachim 1998 Review of Wolfgang Kienzler *Wittgensteins Wende zu seiner Spätphilosophie 1930–1932*. *European Journal of Philosophy* 6, 379–85.
Schulte, Joachim 2002 'Wittgenstein's Method'. In Rudolf Haller and Klaus Puhl (eds.) *Wittgenstein and the Future of Philosophy: A Reassessment after 50 Years*, 399–410. Vienna: Hölder-Pichler-Tempsky.
Schulte, Joachim 2011 'Waismann as Spokesman for Wittgenstein'. In B.F. McGuinness (ed.) *Vienna Circle Institute Yearbook, Vol. 15*, 225–41. Dordrecht and New York: Springer.

Skolem, Thoralf 1923 'The Foundations of Elementary Arithmetic Established by means of the Recursive Mode of Thought, Without the use of Apparent Variables Ranging Over Infinite Domains'. In van Heijenoort 1967, 303–33.

Sluga, Hans and David Stern (eds.) 1996 *The Cambridge Companion to Wittgenstein*. First edition. Cambridge: Cambridge University Press.

Smith, Jonathan 2013 'Wittgenstein's *Blue Book*: Reading Between the Lines'. In Venturinha 2013, 37–51.

Stern, David G. 1991 'The "Middle Wittgenstein": From Logical Atomism to Practical Holism'. *Synthese* 87, 203–26.

Stern, David G. 1995 *Wittgenstein on Mind and Language*. Oxford: Oxford University Press.

Stern, David G. 1996 'The Availability of Wittgenstein's Philosophy'. In Sluga and Stern 1996, 442–76.

Stern, David G. 2004 *Wittgenstein's* Philosophical Investigations: *An Introduction*. Cambridge: Cambridge University Press.

Stern, David G. 2005 'How Many Wittgensteins?' In Pichler and Säätelä (eds.) 164–88; 2006, 205–29.

Stern, David G. 2007 'Wittgenstein, the Vienna Circle, and Physicalism: A Reassessment'. In Alan Richardson and Thomas Uebel (eds.) *The Cambridge Companion to Logical Empiricism*, 305–31. Cambridge: Cambridge University Press.

Stern, David G. 2013 'Wittgenstein's Lectures on Ethics, Cambridge 1933'. *Wittgenstein Studien* 4, 191–206.

Stern, David G. forthcoming 'Wittgenstein in the 1930s'. In Hans Sluga and David G. Stern (eds) *The Cambridge Companion to Wittgenstein*, revised second edition. Cambridge: Cambridge University Press.

Stern, David G., Gabriel Citron, and Brian Rogers 2013 'Moore's Notes on Wittgenstein's Lectures, Cambridge 1930–1933: Text, Context, and Content'. *Nordic Wittgenstein Review* 2, 161–79.

Tarski, Alfred 1933 'The Concept of Truth in Formalized Languages'. First published in Polish in 1933. English translation in *Logic, Semantics, Metamathematics* (1956), 152–278. Oxford: Clarendon Press.

van Heijenoort, Jean (ed.) 1967 *From Frege to Gödel*. Cambridge, MA: Harvard University Press.

Venturinha, Nuno (ed.) 2013 *The Textual Genesis of Wittgenstein's* Philosophical Investigations. London: Routledge.

von Wright, G.H. 1984 'A Biographical Sketch'. In Malcolm 1984, 3–20.

Waismann, Friedrich 1979 *Wittgenstein and the Vienna Circle: Conversations Recorded by Friedrich Waismann*. Ed. B. McGuinness, trans. J. Schulte and B. McGuinness. Oxford: Blackwell. First published in German in 1967.

Wallgren, Thomas 2013 'The Genius, the Businessman, the Sceptic: Three Phases in Wittgenstein's Views on Publishing and on Philosophy'. In Josef Rothhaupt and Wilhelm Vossenkuhl (eds.) *Kulturen Und Werte: Wittgensteins 'Kringel-Buch' als Initialtext*, 113–40. Berlin: Walter de Gruyter.

Whitehead, Alfred North and Bertrand Russell 1927 *Principia Mathematica*, 3 vols. Second edition. Cambridge: Cambridge University Press. (First edition, 1910).

Wittgenstein, Ludwig 1922 *Tractatus Logico-Philosophicus*. Trans. [on facing pages] C.K. Ogden. London: Routledge and Kegan Paul. (Second edition, 1933).

Wittgenstein, Ludwig 1953 *Philosophical Investigations*. Trans. [on facing pages] G.E.M. Anscombe, P.M.S. Hacker, and Joachim Schulte. Oxford: Blackwell. (Revised fourth edition, ed. P.M.S. Hacker and Joachim Schulte, 2009).

Wittgenstein, Ludwig 1958 *The Blue and Brown Books: Preliminary Studies for the 'Philosophical Investigations'*. References are to the *Blue Book* or *Brown Book*. Oxford: Blackwell. (Second edition, 1969).

Wittgenstein, Ludwig 1964 *Philosophical Remarks*, first published as *Philosophische Bemerkungen*, German text only. Ed. R. Rhees. Oxford: Blackwell. (Second edition, 1975, trans. R. Hargreaves and R. White. Oxford: Blackwell).

Wittgenstein, Ludwig 1966 *Lectures and Conversations on Aesthetics, Psychology and Religious Belief*. Ed. Cyril Barrett. Oxford: Blackwell.

Wittgenstein, Ludwig 1969 *Philosophical Grammar*, first published as *Philosophische Grammatik*, German text only. Ed. R. Rhees. Oxford: Blackwell. (Trans. A. Kenny, 1974. Oxford: Blackwell).

Wittgenstein, Ludwig 1976 *Wittgenstein's Lectures on the Foundations of Mathematics, Cambridge 1939*. Ed. Cora Diamond. Ithaca, NY: Cornell University Press.

Wittgenstein, Ludwig 1979 *Wittgenstein's Lectures, Cambridge 1932–1935: From the Notes of Alice Ambrose and Margaret MacDonald*. Ed. Alice Ambrose. Chicago: University of Chicago Press.

Wittgenstein, Ludwig 1979a *Notebooks, 1914–1916*. Ed. G.H. von Wright and G.E.M. Anscombe, trans. [on facing pages] G.E.M. Anscombe. Oxford: Blackwell. (First edition, 1961. Third edition, 1998).

Wittgenstein, Ludwig 1980 *Wittgenstein's Lectures, Cambridge 1930–1932: From the Notes of John King and Desmond Lee*. Ed. Desmond Lee. Chicago: University of Chicago Press.

Wittgenstein, Ludwig 1993 *Philosophical Occasions*. Ed. James Klagge and Alfred Nordmann. Indianapolis: Hackett.

Wittgenstein, Ludwig 1993– *Wiener Ausgabe* [Vienna Edition]. Ed. Michael Nedo. Vienna: Springer.

Wittgenstein, Ludwig 1995 *Ludwig Wittgenstein, Cambridge Letters: Correspondence with Russell, Keynes, Moore, Ramsey and Sraffa*. Ed. Brian McGuinness and G.H. von Wright. Oxford: Blackwell.

Wittgenstein, Ludwig 2000 *Wittgenstein's Nachlass: The Bergen Electronic Edition*. Oxford: Oxford University Press.
Wittgenstein, Ludwig 2003 *Ludwig Wittgenstein: Public and Private Occasions*. Ed. James Klagge and Alfred Nordmann. Lanham, MD: Rowman & Littlefield.
Wittgenstein, Ludwig 2005 *The Big Typescript*. Ed. C. Grant Luckhardt and Maximilian A.E. Aue, translation on facing pages. Oxford: Blackwell.
Wittgenstein, Ludwig 2012 *Wittgenstein in Cambridge: Letters and Documents 1911–1951*. Revised fourth edition. Ed. Brian McGuinness. Oxford: Blackwell.
Wittgenstein, Ludwig 2014 *Lecture on Ethics*. Ed. Edoardo Zamuner, Ermelinda Valentina Di Lascio, and D.K. Levy. Malden, MA: Wiley-Blackwell.
Wittgenstein, Ludwig and Friedrich Waismann 2003 *The Voices of Wittgenstein: The Vienna Circle*. Ed. Gordon Baker, trans. Gordon Baker et al. London: Routledge.
Young, Laurence C. 1970 'Harold Douglass Ursell'. *Bulletin of the London Mathematical Society* 2 344–6.
Young, Laurence C. 1981 *Mathematicians and Their Times*. North-Holland mathematics studies. New York: North-Holland Publishing.

Index

abstract (as opposed to concrete), 319
absurdity, 70, 79, 82, 215, 247, 270, 272, 274
accidentals, 94, 98, 106
accordance (in accordance with), 75, 93, 122, 247, 278, *See also* following, *See also* grammar, *See also* rules (grammatical)
actions
   behaviourism and, 109, 115, 206-7, 209-10, 266, 270, 286
   causal explanations and, 29, 80, 109, 200-1, 326, 331
   descriptions of, 205
   ethical or aesthetical qualities of, 332
   grammatical description and, 134-5, 139-40, 146-7
   justifications of, 140-2, 196, 198, 201, 203
   linguistic cues and, 5
   signals and, 5-6, 9, 72, 109
   understanding and, 9, 72, 75-8, 95
   voluntary, 197, 201
addition, 62
adjectives, 6-7, 139, 184, 221-2, 290
aesthetics, xxviii, xl, 325-6, 332-3, 335, 338, 343, 346, 348-9, 352-6, 362-3, *See also* description, *See also* grammar, *See also* music, *See also* proof, *See also* reasons, *See also* showing
affirmation, 57, 70, 110, 321-2
after-images, 17
agreeability, 333, 337-8, 340, 346-8
agreement, 234, 363
ales, 152-3
algebra, 160, 241-2
all, 42, 51, 55, 80, 104, 164-6, 170-3, 203, 221, 228-30, 343, 347, *See also* and so on, *See also* infinity, *See also* series

alphabet, 82, 85
ambiguity, lv, 78, 89, 140, 255, 277, 333-4, 362, *See also* blurriness, *See also* unclarity, *See also* vagueness
Ambrose, Alice, x, xvi-xvii, xx-xxi, xxviii-xxix, xliv-xlvi, 320, 353
analogies
   continuing a series and, 237, 240-1
   experiential correlations and, 271-2, 287-8
   false, xl-xli, 34-5, 123, 241, 246, 260-1
   other minds and, 286
analysis (logical), xxviii, 85, 87, 122-3, 189, 249-50, 252, 255, 257-8, 265-6
and, 48-9, 60, 104, 107, 115-16
and so on, 53-5, 172, 196, 215, 217, 219, 235, 238, 244, 277, *See also* infinity, *See also* π, *See also* series
Annalen der Naturphilosophie, xiii
anthropology, xxviii, 325-6, 331, 343-5, 352, 357, 360-1
any, 80
aphorisms, 381
appeal, 351
apples, 211-12
application. *See* use
a priori, 30, 261, 263, 314
apriori, the, 261-3, 314
arbitrariness
   grammar and, 17, 28-9, 52, 98, 109-10, 112-13, 131, 133, 135, 139, 147, 153-4, 180, 183, 185, 191-2, 194, 210, 212-14, 249, 256-7, 262, 265-6, 276, 279-80, 323, 358-9
   measurement and, 210-11
   necessity and, 130
   symbols and, 5-6, 41, 90, 92, 96
architecture, 68

arithmetic, xli, 53, 63, 162, 165, 189, 211, 213, 237–8, 240, 250–1, 257, 259, See also mathematics, See also tautologies
arrows, 33, 57, 122, 134–5, 139, 141, 260
aspects, 48, 142, 327, See also grammar, See also seeing
assertion, 132
association, 71, 90, 104, 162
associative law, 53, 56–7, 162–4, 166, 171–2
atomic propositions, xxviii, 131, 189–90, 214, 249–50, 252–3, 255, 380
attention, 352
Augustine (Saint), 120
Austrian general, 321
autonomous (in thought and grammar), 51, 108, 143
axioms, 189, 241

Bach, Johann Sebastian, 352
Baker, Gordon, xlvii
bearers (of names), 151, 177–9
beauty. See aesthetics
Beethoven, Ludwig van, 341, 379
Begriffsschrift (Frege), 48
behaviourism, xl, 109, 115, 206–7, 209–10, 266–7, 269–70, 286
Beltane Fires, 327–31, 343, 352
Bengel, Johann Albrech, 320
Bergen Electronic Edition, xxxiii
Bergen Wittgenstein Archive, lvi
Berkeley, George, 232, 274
between, 10, 17, 20, 25, 28, 31, 33–4, 41, See also boundaries, See also comparison, See also expectation, See also internal relations, See also proof
Biesenbach, Hans, 303
The Big Typescript (Wittgenstein), ix, xxiii, xxv–xxvi, xxxi–xxxii, xxxiv, xlvii, 164, 168–9
bisection, 31, 235, 237–8, 240
blackboard (Wittgenstein's use of), liv–lv
blasphemy, 321
Blue Book (Wittgenstein), xxi, xxxi–xxxii, xlvi, 381, 383

blurriness, 292–3, 299, 310–11, 323, See also boundaries, See also colours, See also visual field
boat-races, 309–11
body, the, 267, 274, 282–3, 285, 287–90, 292, 308, 319, 363
boundaries, 17, 27, 34, 87, 126–7, 183–4, 205–7, 222, 255, 258, 279–80, 292–3, 299, 323
Brahms, Johannes, 350–1, 353, 379, 381
brain, the, 74, 291
Braithwaite, Richard, xv
breath, 74, 319
Briand, Aristide, 79
Britton, Karl, xix, xxvi
Brouwer, Luitzen Egbertus Jan, 58, 379
Brown Book (Wittgenstein), xxxi–xxxii, 383
Bruckner, Anton, 358, 379

Cadbury, 262
calculation, 67, 145–6, 149–50, 152, 169–71, 184, 187–8, 191, 196, 201, 203–5, 207–10, 243, 249, 251, 259, 376
Cambridge University
  academic calendar of, xxii
  Moral Sciences Club of, xii, xiv, xx, 379–80
  Wittgenstein papers and, l
  Wittgenstein's relation to, ix, xxxiii
Cambridge University Reporter, xv, xxv
can (able to), 75–6, 122
Carroll, Lewis, 7, 70, 184
causes
  actions and, 80, 109
  explanations as, 85, 96, 106, 326, 331
  grammatical systems and, 263–4
  guiding and, 90, 139–40
  language as, 9
  reasons and, xxviii, 116, 140–1, 196–7, 200–1, 208–10, 284, 341–2, 346, 348, 352–3, 360–2, 365
  rules and, 180
  sciences and, 87–8, 104, 263, 335, 341–3, 345, 348, 353, 355, 363

thinking and, 79
understanding and, 80
certainty, 76, 82, *See also* doubt
certified formally, 30
chain. *See also* justifications, *See also* proof,
    See also reasons, *See also* series
  of equations, 53, 55, 57
  of reasons, 203, 210
chairs, 42, 121, 183, 185, 201, 234, 256, 259,
    272, 277, 280–1, 289–90, 295, 299,
    310–11, 316, 319
chess, 52, 63, 111–13, 115, 120, 179–80, 182,
    195–6, 238–40, 256–7, 277, 313, 320,
    343, 374
child (teaching of), 11, 69, 80, 103, 121, 179,
    255, 257, 285, 290, 327, 367, 373, *See
    also* language, *See also* teaching
Chinese, 308, 312, 336
church mode, 359
circles, 124, 221–2
classification, 23, 215, 250–1, 281, 310,
    320
clumsiness, 231
colours
  after-images and, 17, 77
  grammar of, 16, 20–1, 24–30, 34, 41,
    70–1, 77–8, 86, 89, 105, 108, 110, 112,
    136, 145–6, 150, 178, 180, 184–5, 192,
    204, 215, 272, 311, 317, 351, 367
  images of, 143–4
  meaning of, 70, 79, 196–7
  mixtures of, 25–6, 28, 34–5, 332, 375
  primary colours, xli, 22, 25, 31, 42, 51–2,
    215, 221
  representational theories and, 20
  similarity and, 10, 43
  specimens of, 15
  teaching of, 76, 341
commands, 72, 76, *See also* obeying (of
    orders), *See also* orders
commitment, 90, 93, 96, 98–9, 109–10
Commonplace Book (Moore), xxxix
comparison, 72, 167–9, 171–2, 179, 200,
    203–4, 208, 230–2, 234, 237–8, 336–7,
    343, 351, 359, 365
  intention and, 83

logical multiplicity and, 13, 122–3
pictures and reality, 5, 10–11
projection and, 81
compass. *See* rule and compass
complexity (of propositions), 152–3
complex numbers, 41, 110, 169, 304
concepts. *See* logic
concrete (as opposed to abstract), 319
confusion, 63, 85, 89, 177, 179, 183,
    187, 214, 217, 221, 235, 241, 243,
    268–9, 309, 332–3, 335, 361, 364–5,
    375, 377, *See also* vagueness, *See also*
    unclarity
conjunction. *See* and
conscious(ness). *See also* unconscious, the
  jokes and, 356–7
  of rules and reasons, 111, 115, 120, 325–6,
    360–1, 363–4
  state of being, 75, 287, 290, 309, 319
consequences, 93, 96
constructions, 228–30, 232–3, 235–7, 240–1,
    See also geometry, *See also* rule and
    compass
content, 252
contradictions. *See also* logic, *See also*
    tautologies
  hidden contradictions and, 193, 204, 223,
    241, 244, 249, 258
  law of, 180, 190–2, 195
conventions, 180
  grammar's relation to, 18, 28–30
  stage-setting and, 13–14, 93–4, 145
  teaching of, 11, 80, 94
conversations, 311, 347
coordinate systems, 15, 43
Copernicus, Nicolaus, 363
copula, 183
copying, 84, 90–1, 93, 153–4, 341
Cornforth, Maurice, xlii
correctness, 363
  grammatical rules and, 192, 363
  intentions and, 9, 98
  measurement and, 17
  projection and, 91, 93, 96
  proofs and, 159–60, 166
correlations, 271–2

counting, 31, 167–8, 172, 204, 211, 229–30, 242, 253, 255
criteria
  of correctness, 93, 143, 152, 167–9, 285
  direct experience and, 283–4, 286
  inference and, 130
  memory and, 148, 296–7
  nonsense and, 82, 267–8, 270, 279
  reasons and, 197, 362–3
  symptoms and, xxviii, 144, 267, 285–6, 313–16, 333, 364
  verification and, 276, 287, 294–9, 309–11, 339
crotchets, 96, 98–9
cubes, 124, 136, 180

dancing, 329–30, 353–4
darkness (and light), 20
Darwin, Charles, xxviii, 331, 352–3, 380
death, 246–7, 321
decay, 340–1
decisions, 183, 276, 288–9, *See also* judgement, *See also* other minds, *See also* series
deduction, 181, 190, 210–11, 213–15, 218, 259, *See also* inference, *See also* logic
definitions
  in explanations, 117, 177–9
  of games, 277, 323, 343
  grammar and, 29–30, 109, 150, 183
  nonsense and, 50–1
  ostensive, 30, 71, 75, 79, 105, 107, 150–1, 192–3
  propositions and, 255, 257
  series of projections and, 53, 57
  Skolem's proof and, 162, 164
degrees of freedom, 16, 61, 99, 126, 157, 245
description, 112
  aesthetics and, 342
  application of language and, 29, 133–5
  beforehand, 49, 89, 93, 152, 159, 212, 228, 250, 252, 255, 263, 322
  equations and, 111, 124
  expectations and, 6, 8, 11, 85, 87, 206, 229–30

  grammar and, 14, 22–3, 59–60, 109–10, 112, 124, 133–5, 185, 229–30, 236, 364
  as philosophical method, 88–9, 103, 109–10, 326, 331
  rule-following and, 91–2, 170
  of sensory experience, 274
  symbolism and, 76, 79–80, 84, 143, 147, 150
desks, 14
development of π. *See* series
Diamond, Cora, xxx
dictionary, 215, 252
differential gear, 126
digestion, 74, 107
Ding an Sich (Thing in Itself), 320
direction (of time), 260–1
discomfort, xlv–xlvi, 103, *See also* satisfaction (of needs), *See also* tooth-aches, *See also* uneasiness
discoveries (mathematical), 46–9, 131, 157–8, 171, 231, 235, 237–8, 244, 252
discursive proof, 163, 308–9
discussion classes (Wittgenstein's), xv–xviii, xx, xxii–xxiii, xxvi–xxvii, xxxvii, xxxix, 68–9
disjunction, 42, 49, 123, 157, 172, 207, 209–10, 280, *See also* or
distributive law, 53
division, 164–5
doors, 337, 340
doubt, 371
  of ability to do something, 82
  grammatical limits to, 27, 279, 367
  hypothesis testing and, 373
  order-following and, 76, 122, 140–1
  proposition's definition and, 33, 72–3
  quieting of, 200, 203
  religion and, 321
  unconscious/subconscious processes and, 361
dreams, 290, 293, 298, 309, 356, 364–5
drugs, 9, 35, 71, 94, 105
Drury, Maurice O'Connor, xx, 29, 71, 145, 149, 379–81

dwell, 319
dynamics, xlv, 67

editorial practices, xlix–li, liii–lv
effigies, 326–31
Either/Or (Kierkegaard), 246
elasticity, 309, 333
Elements (Euclid), 17
elliptical sentences, 256
emotions, xxviii, 120, 331–2, *See also* expressions, *See also* hatred, *See also* psychology, *See also* thoughts
end, coming to an, 99, 203, 210, 235
engineering, 68
entailment, 49, 129, 133, 187, 189, 214–15, 218–19
equations
 aspects of, 48
 chains of, 53, 55, 57
 as conventions, 61–2, 188, 191–2, 245
 propositions and, 111, 124, 313
 understanding of, 173
Erbacher, Christian, xlix
ethical expression, 318
ethics, xxviii, xl, 247, 318, 322, 325–6, 331–5, 338, 343
Ethics and Language (Stevenson), 383
Euclid. *See Elements* (Euclid)
Euclidean geometry
 completeness of, 240
 generality and, 53
 as grammar, 17, 36, 47, 124, 180
 proofs in, 236–7
 visual space and, 35, 50, 220, 271
evidence. *See* criteria
examples, 97–8, 172–3, 179, 198, 228–9, 231, 234, 242, 245, 250–2, 279–80, 323, *See also* constructions, *See also* rules (grammatical), *See also* series
excluded middle, law of, 58
existence, 14–15, 22, 41, 104, 159, 170, 245, 250, 274, 294
existential theorems, 159
expectation
 description and, 85–6, 88–9, 205

 as foreshadowing, 80, 82, 84–5, 89–90, 96, 105
 justifications of, 195
 language-use and, 11, 44, 207
 logical notation and, 250–2
 of philosophy, 103
 projection and, 105–6
 symbolism and, 202–3
 thought-reality correspondence and, 10, 11, 10, 11, 10, 72, 74, 104, 148, 149
experience. *See* grammar, *See* logic, *See* rules (grammatical), *See* primary experience, *See* tactile experience
experiential propositions, 111, 181–2, 274, 279–80, 314, 316
experiments, 315, 335
 causes and, 199, 202
 grammar and, 103, 122, 195, 220, 294, 296
 measurement and, 47, 263–4, 311
 psychological, 346, 355, 359, 361, 363
 the, 271, 275
explanations
 actions and, 29, 154
 causes and, 85, 87, 326, 331
 definitions and, 117, 178
 description and, 79–80
 drugs and, 71, 99, 105
 examples as, 234
 explaining away, 362
 finality and, 70–1
 forgetting of, 77
 grammar and, 52, 111–12, 116–17, 198, 314, 317
 of language, 80, 84–5, 94–5, 105, 116, 120, 152–3, 250
 logic and, 114–15
 multiplicity and, 99, 111, 116, 139, 310
 norms of, 262–4
 pointing and, 14, 145
 psychical effects of, 70
 reasons and, 331
 of rules, 141, 237
 showing and, 76–7, 80, 84, 94–5, 99, 109, 114–15, 228, 234–6, 310, 312, 353–4, 359, 363

explanations (cont.)
    sufficiency of, 94
    truth functionality and, 60, 116–17
expressions
    descriptions and, 85–6
    of grammatical rules, 21–2, 24, 27, 73, 83–4, 92, 111, 135, 202–3
    of intention, 83
    method and, 68
    of pain, 285, 288–9
    philosophy's investigations of, 8–9, 12
    of thought, 8, 72, 79, 89, 104
    of wishes, 325–6
extensions
    laws and rules and, 32, 230, 235, 265
    of π, 166, 169–70
external relations, 85, 241
eye, the, 37, 105, 268, 270, 274, 283, 286, 290, 293, 295, 299, 337, 361, *See also* seeing, *See also* visual field

faces, 337–8
facts, 84–8, 96, 105, 151–3, 190, 200, 207–8, 252, 294
fallacies, 25, 88, 157, 217, 238, 294, *See also* analogies, *See also* grammar, *See also* logic
false analogies
    infinity and, 164, 166, 217
    logic and, 27, 117–18, 180, 218, 221, 253, 260
    negation and, 122–3, 125
    pain attribution and, 267–8
    propositions and, xli, 152–3
    scientific explanations and, 375, 378
    series and, 230–1
    substantives and, 195, 199, 313, 318–19, 331, 335
    thinking and, 74
    time and, 260–1, 299, 317
    the unconscious and, 289–90
    visual space and, 35
fear, 72, 74, 210
Feigl, Herbert, 379
finding, 157, 159–60, 166, 168, 204, 219, 223, 228–9, 236, 241–3, 249–50, 252, 262, 281

finite numbers, 46, 52
finite series, 166, 242
finite sets, 172
First World War, xiii
fitting, 86–7, 111–12, 340, 348
flow (of time), 260–1, 264, 317–18
following, 186, 188–92, 194, 196–7, 205–6, 218, 230–1, 238, 284, 294–5
footrules, 44, 152, 195, 211
foreshadowing, 80–2, 105
forgetting, 77, 94, 200, 310, 319
formally certified, 30
foundations of mathematics, 250
Frazer, James George, xxviii, 325–31, 343–5, 352, 357, 380
freedom. *See* degrees of freedom
Frege, Gottlob, 21, 42, 48, 60, 63, 114–15, 117, 131, 143, 181, 222, 251, 253, 259
French (language), 79, 104
Freud, Sigmund, xxviii, 287, 289–90, 354–6, 360–5, 381
fulfilment. *See* satisfaction (of needs)
fundamental, the, 87, 92, 103, 131, 169, 255
future, 45, 86, 96, 191, 250–1, 264, 275, 299–300, 356, *See also* expectation, *See also* infinity, *See also* series, *See also* time

Galileo Galilei, xlv, 67
games
    common features of, 323, 325
    definitions of, 277, 280, 323, 343
    discoveries of, 252
    grammar as, 28, 51–2, 63, 116, 331, 333, 335, 338
    justifications within, 281
    language games and, 130–1, 203, 207, 255–9, 276–7, 280, 331, 335, 337–8, 343, 364–5
    logic as, 182–3
    reasons in, 203
    rules of, 28, 56, 115, 124, 130–1, 179, 185, 196, 264–5, 277
    substitutions and, 111–12
Gauss, Johann Carl Friedrich, 304, 380

generality, 6, 33–4, 41–2, 46, 49, 51–3, 55, 92, 97–8, 165–6, 171–2, 190, 214, 216, 221, 228–30, 234, 244, 280, 343, 358, 374
geometry. See also bisection, See also pentagons, See also rule and compass, See also triangles, See also trisection
    constructions in, 228, 230, 233, 237, 240–1
    Euclidean, 17, 26, 35–6, 47, 49–51, 53, 124, 180, 220, 236–7, 240, 271
    Helmoltz on, 380
German (language), 84, 121
gestures, 71, 107, 115, 134, 139, See also ostensive definition, See also pointing
God, 318–22, 329
Goethe, Wolfgang Johann von, 352, 380–1
Goldbach's Conjecture, 47
The Golden Bough (Frazer), 325–6, 331, 343–5, 380
good, 331–5, See ethics
government, 206
grammar
    aesthetics and, xl, 332–3, 335, 338, 340, 343, 346, 348, 352
    arbitrariness and, 17, 28, 52, 98, 109–10, 112–13, 131, 135, 139, 147, 153–4, 180, 183, 185, 191–2, 194, 210, 212–14, 249, 256–7, 262, 265–6, 276, 279–80, 323, 358
    boundaries of, 238–9, 284
    as calculus, 62–3, 131–2, 140, 145–6, 152, 169–71, 180, 184–5, 187–8, 191–2, 196, 203–4, 207, 209–10, 243, 249, 251, 259, 376–7
    classification and, 215
    of colours, 21, 26, 28, 34–5, 41, 70, 72, 86, 89, 93, 105, 108, 110, 112, 136, 150, 178, 184–5, 192, 204, 215, 282, 311, 317, 351, 367
    commitment and, 90, 93–4, 96, 98–9, 109–10, 122, 133, 135
    completeness of, 46, 49, 92–3, 131–2, 136, 144, 146, 237, 252–3, 256, 265
    conventions and, 28, 145–6
    criteria and, 294, 362–3
    definitions and, 29, 109, 150
    degrees of freedom and, 16, 60, 99
    of direct experience, 266, 273, 282–3
    discoveries and, 289–90
    ethics and, xl, 318, 320–2, 325, 331, 333
    Euclidian geometry and, 17, 35–6, 47, 124, 180
    expectations and, 84, 86, 314
    explanations and, 92, 94, 99, 115, 117, 198
    expressibility of, 21–2, 24, 27
    first-person attribution and, 267, 273, 282–3
    Freud's work and, 362–3
    games and, 28, 51–2, 56, 63, 179, 281–2, 323
    infinity and, 22, 32–3, 35, 304
    justifiability of, 29, 36–7, 51–2, 128–32, 135, 139–40, 146–7, 188, 195
    language and, 111–15, 144, 253, 255, 260, 277–8, 333
    mathematical proofs and, xxviii, 17, 21, 26–7, 51, 56–7, 62, 131–2, 157–8, 192, 211–12, 217, 230–1, 236, 242, 252, 310, 318
    meaning and, xli, 10, 111, 136, 150–1, 177–9, 203, 253, 302–3, 309, 313, 317
    Moore's essay on, xxxvii–xxxviii, 365, 375
    Moore's summary notes on, xxxvii
    multiplicity and, 16, 20, 63, 99, 115, 139, 143–5, 170, 172–3, 198, 257, 310
    of music, 27
    ordinary, 318
    philosophical investigations of, 8–9, 89–90, 235, 280–1
    pictures and, 29, 41, 51, 141, 143, 302, 310
    possibility and, 18, 20, 22, 30, 33
    proofs and, 157, 166, 223, 231, 233–5
    propositions and, xxiv, 24, 29–31, 70, 90, 181, 186
    psychology and, 16
    reality and, 112–13

grammar (cont.)
  reasons and, 195–7, 203, 314
  of religion, 318, 322
  Russell's thoughts on, xxxiii
  science–philosophy distinctions and, 29, 314
  sense–nonsense distinction and, 109–11, 124, 127, 141, 274–5, 281–2, 363, 375–8
  showing and, 30, 35–6, 60–1, 109, 132, 134–6, 274–7, 284, 303, 311–12, 321, 333, 338
  stage-setting and, 17, 49, 61–2, 193, 313
  substitutions and, 21–4, 28, 71, 76–7, 141, 285, 324
  symbolic systems and, 77–8, 130, 133, 135
  system and, 152, 198, 359
  of time, 260–1, 264–6, 299–300, 310–11, 317
  of tooth-aches, 266–70, 273–5, 277, 279, 282, 284–6, 288–9, 291
  translation and, 51, 81, 106, 121, 184
  variables and, 21, 24, 28
  verification and, 314–16
  Wittgenstein's response to Moore on, 375, 378
Green Henry (Keller), 319, 381
guesses, 29
Guest, David, 367, 380
guiding, 90–1, 93–7, 99, 106, 108, 139–40, *See also* orders, *See also* reading

Hacker, P.M.S., xlvii
Haeckel, Ernst, 319, 380
Haldane, John Burdon Sanderson, 291–2, 380
hallucinations, 104
Hamann, Johann Georg, 320
Hardy, G.H., xxxiv
harmony, 89, 91, 335, 347
hatred, 289–90
having. *See* body, the, *See* tooth-aches
hazes, 69, 103
Helmholtz, Hermann von, 303–4, 380–1

Heretics Society, xiv
Hertz, Heinrich, 203, 262, 381
hidden contradictions, 193, 204, 223, 241–2, 244, 249, 258
hints, xlvi–xlvii, *See also* philosophy
history, 343, 345, 354, 374
human beings, 74, 231, 340–1, 343
hunger, 86
hypotheses, 44–5, 47, 50, 63, 76, 114, 118, 201–2, 210, 253, 262, 300, 309, 352–3, 355–7, 363, 365, 371

idealism, xl, 270, 275, 294–6, 310, 338–40, 343, 348, 350–1, 353
identical, 112
identity, 61, 120, 180, 216, 241
idleness, 260, 295, 300
idols, 319, *See also* dwell
images. *See* pictures
imagination
  gaps in, 233
  inference and, 127
  interpretation and, 148–9
  meaning and, 154, 358–9
  nonsense and, 112
  pictures and, 15, 115, 148, 301–2
  sense and nonsense and, 17–18, 43, 181–2, 275, 299, 301, 371, 375
immortality of the soul, 245–7
implication, 118, 127, 187, 189, 219
impressions, 180, 313, 330–1, 343, 347–8
incompatibility, 204
individuals, 215, 250, 317
induction, xxvi, 37, 50, 53, 55, 57, 159, 164, 210
infantile mathematics, 161
inference, 117–18, 125–9, 131–2, 135, 139–40, 191–2, 195, 203–4, 210, 214, 216, 218
infinite regress, 128, 135, 154, 191, 196–7, 210, 235
infinity
  colour scales and, 30–1
  counting and, 31
  degrees of freedom and, 126, 157, 245, 300

games and, 52
grammatical rules and, 22, 31–7, 43, 50, 52, 131–2, 228–9, 270, 304
logical spaces and, 49, 255
periodicity and, 33–4, 58–9, 157, 244–5
possibility and, 31–2
prime series and, 5
series and, 43–4, 46, 49, 52, 54–5, 157, 164, 166, 168–73, 183, 196, 217, 219–20, 229, 231–2, 242, 264, 281, 343, 347
tautologies and, 126–7
time and, 45
Wittgenstein's Trinity Fellowship applications and, xiv, xxxiii
information-time, 264
Inman, John, xxix
instinct, 70, 107
integers, 41
intellect, xlvi–xlvii, 87, 152, *See also* discomfort, *See also* mind, *See also* thoughts, *See also* uneasiness
intention. *See also* actions, *See also* mind, *See also* orders, *See also* thoughts, *See also* volition
actions and, 197–8, 200, 228
guiding and, 90–1, 93
pictures and, 9, 210
portraiture and, 83
rules and, 94, 96–8, 308
verification and, 96, 98
internal relations, 31, 41, 57–8, 82–3, 85, 115, 127–9, 132–4, 146, 187
interpretation, 71–2, 74–5, 83–4, 97, 99, 116, 146, 148, 235, 321
Interpretation of Dreams (Freud), 354
introspection, 115
intuition, 309, 313–14
invisible masses, 262–3, 314, 363
is, 8, 121, 136, 149, 177–8, 317, *See also* copula, *See also* existence

James, William, 319, 381
jingle, 184
Joachim, Joseph, 381

Johnson, Samuel, 274
Johnson, William Ernest, 30, 81, 381
jokes, 356, 358, 360–1, 363, 365
Jokes and Their Relation to the Unconscious (Freud), 360
Joseph, H.W.B., 324
judgement, 92, 98, 109
justifications. *See also* causes, *See also* grammar, *See also* proof, *See also* reasons
of actions, 140–2, 146–7, 196, 198
of grammar, 106, 111, 116, 128–9, 131, 188, 195
inductive proof and, 54–5
inference and, 127–9, 131–2, 135, 139–40
rule-following and, 96–9, 115, 281, 348, 352

Kant, Immanuel, 319, 381
Keller, Gottfried, 319, 351, 381
Kienzler, Wolfgang, xxxiv
Kierkegaard, Søren, 246–7, 381
kinds, 23, 182–4, 222
King, John, xxiv–xxv, xxviii–xxix, xli, 367–8, 375–8
King Lear (Shakespeare), 336–7
Knight, Helen, 324, 348, 381
knowledge. *See also* doubt, *See also* mind, *See also* rules (grammatical), *See also* teaching, *See also* understanding
grammar of, 284–5
mathematical discoveries and, 46–7
meanings of, 208, 362
pain-attribution and, 266, 268
sense data and, 29, 47
knowledge, foundations of, 5, 8, 73

language
actions and, 5–6, 9, 72, 253, 255
arbitrariness of, 17, 28
behaviour and, 206–7
boundary of, 87, 112, 238–9, 250
definitions of, 5
description's capability and, 6–7, 11, 69, 85–7, 89, 149–50

language (cont.)
   drugs and, 9
   explanations and, 70-1, 84-5, 94-5
   as games, 130-1, 203, 207, 255-9, 276-7, 280, 304, 331, 335, 337-8, 343, 364-5
   grammar and, 111, 113-15, 145-6, 200, 204, 253, 255, 260, 277-8
   guiding and, 91, 96
   hypotheses and, 44
   imagination and, 15
   the inexpressible and, 87
   infinite possibility and, 31-2, 183, 186
   instinct and, 5
   jokes and, 356, 360
   justifications of, 106, 111, 130, 141
   meaning and, 6-8, 14-15, 63, 67, 70, 72-3, 78, 89, 104, 281-2, 300-1, 313, 316-17, 340
   multiplicity and, 6-7, 14-16, 18, 20, 22, 115, 143-5
   names and, 90
   ordinary, 92, 103, 141, 188, 207, 222, 228, 257, 274, 289
   ostensive definitions and, 30, 71, 75, 79, 105, 107, 150-1, 192-3
   other minds and, 75
   philosophy and, xli, 85, 259-60, 317
   picture qualities of, 5, 16, 20, 26, 41, 296, 299, 301
   prescriptions and, 5-6, 9
   private language and, 276
   propositions as parts of, 5, 41, 131, 202
   signals and, 94
   signs and, 76
   as sounds, 86, 92, 95
   substitution and, 7, 11, 22-4, 71, 75-6, 111-12, 116-17, 123, 133-4, 141, 151, 249, 257
   teaching and, 11, 14-15, 109, 179, 205, 250, 310, 337, 341, 347
   thinking and, 8, 79, 82, 107-8, 112
   translation and, 51, 73, 77, 144-5
   truth functionality of, 20
   understanding of, 9-10, 15-16, 77, 90

laws, 33, 44-5, 54-5, *See also* nature, *See also specific laws*
leading. *See* guiding
learning. *See* teaching
Lee, Desmond, x, xvi, xviii, xxviii, xxxviii, xli, 19, 47, 367-8, 377-8
length, 14, 207, 210-14, 220, 264, 294, 310
levers, 6
Lichtenberg, Georg Christoph, 287, 381
life (ordinary), 141, 146, 208, 260, 311
lifting my arm, 198, 201
light and darkness, 20
limit(s). *See also* boundaries
   of logical possibility, 99, 126, 262, 302
   mathematical, 37, 217, 245
   projection and, 300-1
linguistics, 317-18
Littlewood, J.E., xxxiii
locomotion, 37, 43-4, 50
Lodge, Oliver Joseph, 246-7, 382
logic. *See also* infinity, *See also* multiplicity, *See also* negation, *See also* use
   generality and, 49-50
   grammar and, 113-14, 131-2, 180, 183, 186, 214
   inference and, 117-18, 125-9, 131-2, 135, 139-40, 203-4, 210, 216, 218
   language games and, 255-6
   logical analysis and, xxviii, 16, 85, 88, 122-3, 189, 249-50, 252-3, 255, 257-8, 265-6
   logical concepts and, 21-2, 24-5, 52, 249-50, 253, 280
   logical constants and, 47, 60
   logical products and, 37, 41-3, 49-50, 52, 172, 189, 215-17, 219, 221-2, 249
   logical sums and, 41, 43, 46, 49, 189, 215-17, 219, 221
   metalogic and, 141, 316
   methods and, 46
   multiplicity and, 6, 9, 11, 13-16, 20, 22, 46, 58, 63, 123, 139
   notations and, lv, 46, 48, 112, 114, 222, 250-1

propositions and, 110, 216–17, 249
Russell's theories and, xi–xii, xxxiii, 14, 23, 42, 76, 113–14, 186, 188–9, 222–3, 250–1
saying/showing and, 30, 49, 86–7, 112, 181, 214
as science, 219, 259
tautologies and, 60, 63, 126–7, 132, 186–8, 190, 245
thoughts and, 20, 41
use theories and, 21
variables and, 21–2, 24, 28, 46, 50, 52, 61, 140
Logic (Johnson), 381
logical laws, 181, 190, 195
Logisch-philosophische Abhandlung (Wittgenstein), xiii
Luther, Martin, 320

MacIver, Arthur, xvi
magic, 94, 132, 325–6
magic lanterns, 287–8, 296–7, 299
Malcolm, Norman, xvii, xxx
many, 220
marginalia. See Moore, G.E.
materialistic monism, 380
mathematics. See also algebra, See also arithmetic, See also geometry, See also logic
arbitrariness and, 212–13
completeness of, 237–40
experiments and, 47
foundations of, 250
as game, 51, 211, 259
grammar and, 18, 26, 28, 51, 170–1, 217, 223, 237–8
induction and, 50, 53, 55, 57–8
infantile, 161
inference and, 128–9, 131, 214
infinity and, xxiv, 22, 31, 264
limit concept and, 37, 217, 245
mathematical discoveries and, 46–7, 49, 244, 252
number theory and, 23, 167, 169
ordinary, 58
periodicity and, xxvi, 164–5, 243

philosophy of, 69, 103
proofs and, xxviii, 35, 53–4, 57–8, 157–63, 166–7, 170, 231, 236–7, 241, 245
propositions of, 5, 69, 217, 324
Russell on, 62
science and, 219, 346, 358
tautologies and, 59, 61–3
teaching of, 228–9, 240, 250
theorems of, xxviii, 62, 159, 169, 223
translations and, 50
Mauthner, Fritz, 321
McTaggart, John, 382
meaning. See also grammar, See also language, See also logic, See also not, See also sense
associative theories of, 71, 90, 104
carrying of, 145, 149–52, 177
correspondence theories of, 122–3, 136, 144–5, 195, 313
description and, 79–80, 179
examples and, 251–3
Freud on, 360–1
grammar and, xli, 10, 20, 28–9, 78, 90, 96, 136, 150–1, 177–9, 192, 203, 214, 256–7, 301–3, 309, 313, 323
induction and, 53
learning of, 70, 72, 332
mathematics and, 46–7
names and, 151
of not, 70, 80
as object, 136
philosophy's role with respect to, 8, 67, 89, 104, 316–17
pointing and, 42, 115, 364
proofs and, 159
psychology and, 308
sense concept and, 70, 76, 107, 151–2, 177, 195, 251–2, 300–1, 308, 313
signs and, 79–80
symbolism and, 6, 8, 14–15, 20, 24, 62–3, 76–9
symptoms and, 164
translation and, 50, 73
understanding of, 9–10, 72, 75–7, 79

meaning. (cont.)
  use of language and, 8–9, 41, 67, 77, 179, 222, 249, 259, 277, 281–2, 290, 300, 312–13, 317, 324, 333, 340, 365, 369
  verification and, xxviii, xlii–xliii, 17, 209, 242, 244–5, 308–9, 311, 314, 323
The Meaning of Meaning (Ogden and Richards), 382–3
measurement, 17–18, 47–8, 61, 195, 207, 210–14, 220, 232, 240, 246–7, 260–1, 263, 294, 296–7, 310–11, 336
measuring-rods, 12–15, 211, 296
mechanisms, 6, 79, 86, 94, 96, 144, 253, 255, 263, 294–5, 300, 314, 357–9, 363
memory, 15, 72, 77, 79, 105, 143, 148, 201, 238, 240, 264, 293–4, 296, 299, 309–11, 321, 341, 365, See also following, See also teaching, See also time
mental states, 74, 309, 352, See also mind, See also psychology
metalogic, 141, 316
Metamorphose der Pflanzen (Goethe), 352
metaphor, 321, 350, See also analogies, See also language, See also pictures
method. See also discoveries (mathematical), See also philosophy, See also Wittgenstein, Ludwig
  for mathematical discoveries, 46, 171, 223, 228, 235, 237–8, 249, 281
  in philosophy, 67–8, 88, 200
Michelangelo, 300
mind. See also psychology, See also rules (grammatical), See also thoughts, See also volition
  expressions of, 8, 72, 79, 107
  false analogies of, 74–5
  internal processes and, 188, 191, 196, 201, 205, 208–9, 283
  interpretation and, 75, 148
  other minds and, 75, 82, 207, 267–8, 274–5, 282, 286
  understanding and, 255–6
Mind, x, xxi–xxii, xxv, xxxvi–xxxviii, xl–xli, xlv, li
Mind Association and the Artistotelian Society, xiv, 323–4, 348

mirrors, 199, 240, 267–8, 270–2, 274, 283, 285, 310
mistakes, 89–90, 98, 245–6, 256–7, 281, 304, 353, 362, 371, 376
models, 84, 90–1, 93, 97, 143, 151
molecular propositions, 139, 189, 214–16, 218, 249, 252–3
money, 245
Monk, Ray, 383
Monte Cassino POW camp, xiii
Montreal Star, 382
moon, the, 11–12, 184, 363
Moore, G.E.
  on grammatical rules, 365, 367–9, 371, 373–5
  marginalia of, xxxv, xxxvii, 10–12, 15, 27, 43–4, 53–5, 58, 76, 105, 110, 113, 118, 121, 124, 126–7, 129, 132, 135–6, 144–5, 151, 166, 168, 170, 172, 178, 181, 188, 190–3, 215, 221, 243, 247, 263–4, 266, 268, 274, 276, 279, 284–6, 297, 303, 311–12, 357, 362
  Moral Sciences Club and, xii, xiv, xx
  note-taking practices of, xxi, xxvii–xxx, xxxv–xxxvii, xxxix, xlix–l, lii–liv, 54, 56
  relation of, to Wittgenstein, x, xv, xlvi–xlvii
  summary notes of, xxxvii, l, lii–liv, 7, 12, 16–17, 22, 29, 31, 34, 48, 52, 56, 62, 67, 75, 80–2, 88–9, 97–8, 107, 109, 113–14, 116, 120, 122, 135, 139–40, 144, 147–9, 154, 159, 168, 170, 172, 185, 189, 191–2, 194–5, 197, 200–1, 204, 209, 220, 222, 232–3, 235–6, 238, 242–5, 247, 256, 262, 276, 279–80, 300, 313–14, 316, 319–21, 351, 361
  Wittgenstein's lectures and, ix–xi, xv, xviii–xxi, xxviii, xlv–xlvi, 380
Moral Sciences Club, xii, xiv, xx, 379–80
Morrell, Ottoline, xi
motive, 326, 331, See also reasons, See also volition
mouths, 285

moving my arm, 198, 201
muddles, 69, 266, 357, See also puzzle(s)(d)
multiplication, 228-9, 231, 235, 244, 257
multiplicity, 111, 115, See also logic
  grammar and, 63, 111, 115-16, 144, 172-3, 257
  of symbols, 6, 9, 11-12, 14, 18, 20, 99
music. See also pianolas
  aesthetic discussions of, 336, 340, 342, 346, 348, 352, 358
  grammar of, 27
  meaning and, 313
  notion of, 11
  reading of, 93-4, 96-9, 106, 141, 181, 301
must, 211-12, 253, 262-3, 275, 314, 335

Nachlass (Wittgenstein), xxxii, 79
names (proper), 41-2, 52, 60, 90, 104-5, 107, 112, 139-40, 144, 151, 177-9, 222, 285, 289, 296, 369, See also bearers (of names)
Napoleon, 179
nature, 29, 108, 122, 127, 194, 203, 213-14, 263-4, 271, 291, 327-9
necessity, 130, 197, 275, 358, See also must, See also proof
negation, 67, 70, 80, 110-11, 116-17, 120-3, 125, 130, 133, 185, 217, 280, See also not
neighbours, 287-8, 299
new facts, 75, 88
news, 244-5
Nietzsche, Friedrich, 381
nimbus, 68
non-contradiction, law of, 180, 190-2, 195
nonsense
  comparison to reality and, 14
  criteria of, 270, 279, 300
  definitions of, 51
  doubt and, 140-1
  grammatical rules and, 21-2, 25, 28, 30, 109-10, 124, 180-2, 186, 222, 275, 281-2, 284-5, 363, 375-8
  imagination and, 18, 43, 112, 299, 304

infinity and, 31, 34, 57-8, 300
mathematical proofs and, 47, 233, 236
pain attribution and, 267-8, 275-6
proper names and, 41-2
Russell on, xxxiii, 14
substitution and, 7, 11-12, 21-3
symbols and, 76
tautologies and, 132
use and, 281
verification principle and, xlii-xliii
norms, 262-4
not, 48, 60, 70, 72, 78, 80, 114-17, 120-3, 125, 133, 136, 145, 180, 189, See also negation
notation
  language and, 249, 270, 284
  logical, 41, 46, 112, 114, 116, 129-30, 187-8, 222, 250-1
  mathematical, 163
  name-notation and, 223
now, 296-7
numbers
  cardinals numbers as, 23-4, 27, 62, 168, 171-2, 183-4, 228-31, 234, 236, 238, 352
  complex numbers and, 41, 110, 168-9, 171, 304
  grammar of, 21, 24-5, 53, 110, 234-5, 310, 318
  infinity and, 32, 164-5, 167, 183
  integers and, 41
  irrational numbers and, 27, 52, 58, 168-9, 171
  π and, 18, 58-9, 158, 167-9, 243-5
  primes and, 5, 22, 47, 168-70, 229, 231-2
  realism and, 5

obeying (of orders), 72, 76, 90, 108, 146, 181, 196-7, 205-6, 256, 280, 304
observation-time, 264
Ogden, Charles Kay, 71, 382
or, 60, 116, See also disjunction
orders, 72, 76, 90, 108-9, 144, 146, 181, 196-7, 205-6, 256, 280, 304

ordinary
  grammar, 318
  language, 92, 103, 141, 188, 207, 222, 228, 257, 274, 289
  life, 141, 146, 208, 260, 311
  mathematics, 58
  names, 60
oscillation, 301
ostensive definition, 30, 71, 75, 79, 105, 107, 150–1, 192–3, *See also* meaning, *See also* pointing
other minds, 75, 82, 207, 267–8, 274–5, 282, 286
Outline of Philosophy (Russell), 294
overlook, 353, 357

pain. *See* tooth-aches
Palestrina, Giovanni Pierluigi da, 382–3
paradigms, 180, 194
paradoxes, 22, 117–18, 122, 141, 368–9
paraphrase, xxxvii, lii, 356, *See also* jokes, *See also* language
particles, 296, 301
Pascal, Fania, xx
past, 71, 120, 264–5, 294, 299, 309, *See also* memory, *See also* time
pattern-books, 153
pentagons, 228–30, 232, 235–7, 240–1
periodicity, xxvi, 31, 58–9, 157, 164–5, 243, 245, 281
permission to sit in a chair, 319, *See also* chairs
phenomenology, 16
Philosophical Grammar (Wittgenstein), ix, xxxi, xxxv, 164
Philosophical Investigations (Wittgenstein), ix, xviii, xxxi, xliii–xliv, xlvii, liii, 203
Philosophical Remarks (Wittgenstein), ix, xxiii, xxxi–xxxv
philosophy
  essential terms and, 259
  ethics and, 247
  language as subject matter of, xli, xlvi, 8, 375, 378
  meaning and, 8, 67, 89, 104, 316–17
  philosophical problems and, xviii, xliv, xlvi–xlviii, 8, 69, 200, 250, 281–2, 316–17, 376
  science's relation to, xxiv, xxviii, xlv, 67–9, 73, 75, 88–9, 103, 194–7, 200–1, 203, 210, 220, 232, 238, 245–7, 249–50, 294, 311, 313, 316–18, 321, 340, 342, 346, 350, 352–3, 355–6, 360–2
  symbolism's unclarity and, 8
  Wittgenstein's teaching methods and, xvii, xli, xliv–xlviii, 67, 69, 74, 87–8, 141, 200, 203, 232, 280
philosophy of mind. *See also* expressions, *See also* mind, *See also* thoughts, *See also* volition
  ego and, xxviii
  idealism, xxviii
  language and, xli, 69
  solipsism and, xxviii
  visual field and, xxviii
photography, 20
physics, xi, 36, 67, 88, 122, 181, 207, 264, 314–16, 336, 357, 360
π, 18, 58–9, 158, 167–9, 243–5
π′, 58–9, 167, 169
pianolas, 96, 181
pianos, 94, 96–8, 106
pictures
  definitions of, 9
  drawing of, 206
  expectation and, 10, 44
  false analogies and, 74, 88–9
  grammar as, 29, 51, 141, 143–4, 310
  imagination and, 143, 149, 301–2
  interpretations of, 146
  language-use and, 5, 9, 14–15, 20, 41, 112, 116, 296, 300–1
  magic lanterns and, 287–8, 296
  memory and, 72, 77, 143, 145
  multiplicity and, 6–7, 11–12, 14–16, 22
  musical performance and, 93–4
  nonsense's criteria and, 18
  portraiture and, 82–3, 127
  symbolic order and, 5–6, 12, 26, 48–9, 104, 141–2, 147–8, 299

thinking as series of, 79
plans, 72-3, 75, 90
Plato, 194, 232, 332, 343
pleasure, 247, 333, 335, 338-41, 346, 350, 357
pointing, 42, 71, 76, 93, 105, 134, 145, 151, 223, 286, 310, 317-19, 364
pointing beyond, 80, 228-9
portraits, 82, 127
possibility, 12-13, 18, 20, 23, 27, 30-3, 35-7, 42, 44-6, 48-50, 52, 59, 63, 92, 97, 99, 106, 111, 113, 122-3, 128-9, 131, 136, 140-1, 158, 172, 229, 241-2, 247, 249-50, 257, 262, 264, 268, 275-6, 284, 370, See also colours, See also grammar, See also necessity, See also rules (grammatical)
postulates, 213
potential, 336
practice, 322
   philosophical method and, xlviii-xlix
prayer, 321
precision, 258, 310-11, 323, See also blurriness, See also vagueness
pre-description, 212, 250-3, 255, 263, See also description
predicates, 6, 42, 110, 133-4, 183, 253, See also description, See also grammar, See also names (proper)
prescription, 5-6, 9, 11, 167, 169
present, the, 293-4, 297-9
presupposition, 15, 29-30, 42, 49, 70, 81, 85-6, 105, 111, 182, 192-3, 304, 347, See also meaning, See also propositions
pretending, 217, 235, 255, 267, 280, 328, 331, 343, See also imagination
Priestley, Raymond E., 19
primary experience, 274, 283
prime numbers, 5, 22, 47, 168-70, 229, 231-2
primitive ideas, 49
primitive propositions, 55
Principia Mathematica (Russell and Whitehead), lv, 190, 249-51, 383
The Principles of Mechanics Presented in a New Form (Hertz), 203, 381

Principles of Psychology (James), 381
privacy, 268-9, 273, 275-6
probability, 247, 314-16
prohibitions, 109-10
projection, 81-5, 90-1, 93, 95-9, 105-6, 108-9, 147-8, 233-4, 287-8, 300-3
promises, 157-8
proof
   aesthetics and, 350-1
   discursive, 308-9
   Euclidean, 237
   of existence, 22, 159, 245
   foundations of knowledge and, 5
   games and, 238, 240
   generality and, 50
   grammar and, 46-7, 56, 234-5, 277
   hidden contradictions and, 223, 241-2, 244
   inductive, xxvi, 51, 53, 55, 57, 159, 164
   infinite series and, 157, 173
   mathematics and, xxviii, 35, 53-4, 157, 159-61, 166-7, 170-3, 210, 223, 241
   meaning and, 246-7
   soul's immortality and, 245-7
proper names, 41-2, 104-5, 107, 112, 139-40, 151, 178-9, 222, 285, 289, 296, 369
prophecies, 211-12, 252
propositions
   actions and, 29, 95
   analyses of, 16
   atomic, xxviii, 131, 189-90, 214, 249-50, 252-3, 255, 380
   causation and, 79
   commitment to, 90
   complexity of, 152-3
   criteria of, 376-7
   definitions of, 104, 107, 110, 113-14, 139, 257, 280
   elementary, 139-40
   expectations and, 85
   experiential, 111, 181-2, 274, 279-80, 314, 316

propositions (cont.)
    expressions as, 8–9, 12, 72, 79, 85–6, 88–9, 92, 104, 331
    grammatical rules and, xxiv, 21, 27, 31, 33, 71, 114, 121, 124, 126, 141–2, 181, 186, 255, 277, 316
    hypotheses and, 44–5, 50, 118, 202, 210, 253
    infinity and, 22, 183, 186
    internal relations and, 57
    logical propositions, 186, 249
    mathematical proof and, 51, 53, 69, 279
    of mathematics, 5, 131–2
    meaning and, 6, 70, 72, 74, 152
    measuring-rods and, 12–14
    molecular, 139, 189, 214–16, 218, 249, 252–3
    pictorial properties of, 5–6, 9, 14, 116, 127, 141–2, 144, 148
    predicates and, 6–7
    primitive, 181, 186, 188, 191–2
    saying and, 107
    senses of, 17–18, 20, 22, 51, 61–2, 70, 76, 80, 104, 116, 127, 132, 177, 214, 221, 251–2, 313
    substitution and, 7, 11, 21, 23, 133–4, 249
    symbolism's functioning and, 15–16, 62–3, 80
    thinking and, 79, 92
    truth functionality and, 20–1, 28, 30, 33, 44, 70, 77, 112, 114, 117–18, 139–40, 255, 257, 279–80, 376–7, 383
    uses of, 255, 280, 308
    verification and, xlii–xliii, 17, 20, 44, 118, 144, 181, 201–2, 207–8, 245, 282
    words and, 85
pseudo-concepts, 30, 52
psychoanalysis, xxviii, 75, 360–3
psychology, xi, 16, 104, 132, 200, 287, 294, 308–9, 321, 336, 340–2, 346–8, 350–3, 356–7, 360, 362–3
publications (lectures as), xxxi
punishment, 325–6
puzzle(s)(d), 5, 8, 123, 317–18, 342, 345, 351, 353, 358, 363, 367, See also confusion
Pythagorean theorem, 47

qualities, 338, 343
questions, 58

race, 355
railways, 80, 94, 188, 319
raising my arm, 198, 201
Ramsay, John, 327–8
Ramsey, Frank, xiii–xiv, 61–2, 250
rapping, 5, 7, 80, 94–5
reading. See also guiding, See also pianolas
    backwards, 184
    behaviourism and, 109
    of books, 75, 97, 109, 145, 154, 244
    in descriptions, 108
    of music, 93–4, 96–9, 106, 141, 181, 301
    of reports, 244, 309
    of rules, 97, 135
    of thoughts, 75
    of trees, 121
realism, xl, 5, 270, 275, 293–4, 299
reality, 5–6, 10, 14, 16, 18, 20, 28, 51, 60, 72, 89, 91–2, 105, 110, 112–13, 148, 184–5, 213, 264–5, See also actions, See also comparison, See also description, See also following, See also harmony, See also language, See also multiplicity, See also nature, See also pictures
reasons
    in aesthetics, 350, 353, 355–6, 358, 360
    causes and, xxviii, 140–1, 196–7, 200–1, 208–10, 284, 342, 346, 350–3, 360–2, 365, 367
    coming to an end of, 99, 203, 210, 235
    consciousness of, 360–1
    emotional expressions and, 331
    grammar and, 112, 146, 195–8, 203, 209–10, 314
    for grammatical rules, 29
    infinite regress of, 196–7, 210
    joking and, 356, 360
rebus, 365, 367
recognition, 82, 143, 192, 232, 234, 237, 241, 281, 341, 357
recursion, 159–60, 162

reference (in symbolic systems), 58, 81, 135, 139–40, 148, 201, 239–40, 259–60, 282, 285, 291, 310, 340, *See also* justifications, *See also* projection, *See also* proof, *See also* rules (grammatical)
regress. *See* infinite regress
regularity (in measurement), 247
religion, xiii, xxviii, 318, 322, 325–6, 331, 343, 345, 353
representation. *See* language, *See* meaning, *See* pictures, *See* symbols
Rhees, Rush, xlviii–xlix, 164
rhythm, 260, 358, 360
Richards, Ivor Armstrong, xvii, 71, 353, 383
The Riddle of the Universe (Haeckel), 380
rivers, 260–1, 264–5, 318
roots, 159
Rothhaupt, Josef, xxxviii, 326
Rowntree's, 262
rule and compass, 228, 230, 233, 237, 240–1
rules (grammatical)
  arbitrariness and, 17, 28, 99, 109–10, 145, 183, 185, 191–2, 194, 262, 265–6, 280, 323
  as calculus, 62–3, 131–2, 140–1, 157–8, 178–9, 188, 192, 196
  causal pictures of, 180
  ethics and, 323, 325
  examples and, 228–9, 231, 242, 250, 277
  explanations and, 117, 120
  following of, 90–1, 93–4, 97–8, 121–2, 134–5, 167, 170, 186, 191–2, 194, 203–6, 217, 219, 230, 232, 235, 237–8, 294–5
  games and, 28, 111, 113, 115, 120, 264–5
  generality and, 6
  grammar of, 180–1, 256–7
  inference and, 127–9, 131, 133, 135, 181, 191–2, 195, 210, 214, 216
  infinity and, 164, 166
  intention and, 94, 97
  of interpretation, 72–3, 99, 242
  logical kinds and, 113–14
  logical products and, 172
  mechanistic metaphors and, 97, 106, 212
  Moore on, 365, 367, 375
  of negation, 120
  of projection, 81, 83–4, 91, 147–8, 233–4, 300
  as reasons, 195–6
  stateability of, beforehand, 93, 152, 159
  substitutions and, 7, 11–12, 21, 24, 182, 186, 314
  teaching of, 121–2, 206
  of translation, 135
  use and, xxviii, 131–2, 135, 140, 153–4, 178, 191, 200, 256, 258, 265, 277–8
  verification and, 152, 294
  visibility of, 33, 97–8, 111, 120, 122, 127–8, 133–5, 139–40, 147–8, 159, 167, 202, 228, 230, 234, 313
Russell, Bertrand. *See also Principia Mathematica* (Russell and Whitehead)
  Helmholtz and, 380
  Heretics Society and, 383
  individuals and, 215, 250
  logic of, 23, 41–2, 48, 60, 62, 76, 85, 112, 116–17, 125, 132, 181, 186, 188–9, 214, 220, 222, 250, 252–3, 259, 383
  number theory of, 21
  type theory of, xii, 30
  Wittgenstein's critiques of, xxviii, 14, 117–18, 129–30, 190–2, 215, 222–3, 250–1, 253, 259, 294–6, 300–1, 362
  as Wittgenstein's mentor, ix, xi–xii, xxxiii–xxxiv

sacrifice (human), 327–8, 331
samples. *See* colours, *See* copying
satisfaction (of needs), xlvi, 21–2, 37, 80, 86, 88–9, 105–6, 198, 202, 207–8, 210, 228, 235, 342, 350–1, 353–4, 357–8
saying
  grammatical rules and, 61–2, 109–10, 120, 124, 126, 152
  limits of, 92, 107
  pain's expression and, 285
  philosophy's goals and, 69
  propositions and, 30
  showing and, 61, 112, 181
  tautologies and, 125–6, 186–90
Schlick, Moritz, xiv, xlii
Schopenhauer, Arthur, 381

Schulte, Joachim, xxxiv, xliii
science. *See also* physics, *See also* psychoanalysis, *See also* psychology
  anthropology and, xxviii
  causal accounts and, 326, 331, 343, 345, 348, 353, 356, 360, 362–3, 365, 367
  magic and, 325–6
  mathematics' relation to, 219, 358
  philosophy's contrasts with, xxiv, xxviii, xlv, 67, 73, 75, 87–9, 103–4, 194–5, 200–1, 203, 210, 220, 232–3, 238, 245–7, 249–50, 294, 311, 313, 316–18, 321, 340, 342–3, 346, 350, 353, 355, 361–2
  possibility and, 35
scores (musical), 93, 96, 99, 106, 141, 301, *See also* guiding, *See also* music, *See also* reading
Scott, Walter, 327–8
seeing, 10, 12, 27, 30, 36, 44, 46, 56, 116, 133–5, 139–40, 159–60, 167, 200, 202, 270–1, 274, 290–1, 296, 363
seeming, 278–9
self, 178, 267–73, 282–3, 285–92, 296, 308, 310, *See also* subject, the
self-evidence, 181, 186, 200
sense
  doubt and, 140–1
  grammar and, 109, 111, 141, 214, 276–7, 279, 300
  imagination and, 18, 43, 112, 299, 304
  infinite series and, 228–9, 245
  meaning and, 70, 76, 107, 151–2, 177, 195, 251–2, 300–1, 308, 313
  privacy and, 268–9
  propositions and, 69–70, 76, 81, 104, 108, 151–2, 221, 280
  verification and, 167
sense data, 29, 47, 144, 180, 205–6, 268–72, 285, 292, 315, 335
series
  of constructions, 228, 230, 232–3, 235, 237, 240–1
  definitions and, 54
  explanations and, 235
  finite, 166, 242

  generality and, 6, 34, 323, 325
  grammar and, 41, 229
  induction and, 37, 53–5, 164
  infinite, 32, 43–4, 46, 50, 57–8, 157, 164, 168–9, 171–2, 183, 196, 217, 219–20, 228–32, 242, 281, 347
  laws' representation of, 33–4
  meaning and, 323, 325, 356–7
  periodicity and, xxvi, 243
  time and, 44–5
sets, 170
shadows, 222
shadowy entities, 81–2, 84–5, 105
Shaw, George Bernard, 383
Sheffer, Henry M., 46, 48, 112, 129, 216, 383
short-hand, 80
showing. *See also* proof
  aesthetics and, 350
  description and, 49
  explanation and, 76, 84, 310, 312, 353
  expressions and, 89
  grammar and, 30, 78, 112, 132, 277, 303, 311, 321, 333, 338
  infinity and, 36
  philosophical investigations and, 69
  proofs and, 245, 247
  rule-following and, 97–8, 127–9
  saying and, xii, 61
  teaching and, 228
  translation and, 73, 77–8
  of understanding, 72–3
signals, 5, 80, 94, 117
significance. *See* meaning, *See* understanding
signs, 76–9, 132, 134–5, 145–6, 152–4, 242, 280
similarity, 10, 42, 81–5, 89–90, 98, 105, 121, 147, 179, 184, 231, 234, 240, 250, 262, 281, 288–9, 311, 337, 343
simile, xx, 13, 33, 68, 74, 194, 261, 275, 318, 356, 365, 367, *See also* analogies, *See also* language, *See also* metaphor
simulation, 109
sining, 301
Sistine Chapel, 300

skill (in philosophy), xlv, xlviii, 67
Skinner, Francis, 234, 383
Skjolden, xii
Skolem, Thoralf, 162-3, 383
Socrates, 332
Sognefjord, xii
solipsism, xl, 270, 272-5, 284
some, 80
souls, 74, 245-7, 318-19
sounds, 86, 92, 95-6, 110, 151, 291
space
   Euclidean, 17, 50
   grammar of, 27, 31, 34, 36-7, 113-14, 136, 317
   logical multiplicity and, 13-15, 47-9, 58, 111, 122, 150-1, 308
   meaning of, 8
   measurement of, 210-13, 220
   movement and, 43-4
   realism and, 5
   Sheffer and, 46
   stage-setting and, 49
   time's relation to, 6
Spanish Civil War, 380
special cases, 6, 42, 50, 61, 97-8, 122-3, 200, 205, 218-19, 234, 279-82, 323-4, 358
spirals, 56-8
spirit, 74
stage-setting, 14-15, 17-18, 62, 193, 313
standards, 210-11, 214
Stevenson, Charles L., 296, 383
Stonborough, Margarete, xiii
structure. *See also* systems
   of logic, 252
   of nature, 29
   of propositions, 252-3
   showing of, 61-2, 333
subconscious. *See* unconscious, the
subject, the, 267, 273-4, 282-3, 285, 287-92, 308
substantives, 7, 139, 194, 199, 257, 313, 318-19, 323, 325, 331, 335
substitution (of symbols), 11-12, 21, 23-4, 28, 50, 71, 76, 111-12, 116, 123, 141, 151, 170, 249, 257, 324

substrates, 29, 42, 222
summary notes. *See* Moore, G.E.
superstition, 210, 327-8
symbols
   arbitrariness of, 17, 28, 111-12, 153-4
   definitions of, 105
   explanations of, 84, 94-5, 99, 105, 109
   Frege on, 63
   grammar and, 77-8, 89-90, 92-3, 99, 130, 133, 135-6, 139-40, 143, 152, 182
   imagination and, 15
   interpretations and, 72, 81
   logical operations and, 60, 131-2
   measurement and, 14-15
   multiplicity and, 6, 10-11, 13-16, 20, 59, 99, 123, 139, 143, 172-3
   philosophy's practice and, 8, 108
   pictorial arrangements and, 5-6, 13, 26-7, 147
   pointing and, 14
   reality and, 5-6, 10, 14, 16, 18, 20, 28-9, 51, 60, 72, 89, 92, 105, 110, 112-13, 184-5
   series and, 33-4
   signs and, 76-9
   stage-setting and, 14-15, 17-18
   thought and, 72, 75, 104
   understanding of, 10, 71-2, 79-81
   uses of, 14-15, 28-9, 77, 154
symptoms, xxviii, 164, 286, 313-16, 333, 339
synopsis, 75, 87, 358
systems, 17, 46, 49, 80, 86, 90, 93, 96, 111-12, 122, 134-5, 139, 145, 148, 152, 158, 160, 185, 198, 200, 359, *See also* grammar

tactile experience, 272
Tarski, Alfred, 131, 383-4
taste, 325, 346
tautologies, xxviii, 59, 61-3, 126-7, 132, 186-90, 245
tea, 74, 195, 252, 264
teaching
   to a child, 11, 69, 80, 103, 121, 179, 255, 257, 285, 290, 327, 367, 373

teaching (cont.)
  of conventions, 11, 80, 94–5, 126, 128, 145, 147–8, 179, 205–6, 228–9, 240, 250, 347
  examples and, 97–8, 172–3, 255, 280
  of language, 70–1, 76, 80, 109, 121–2, 310, 332, 337, 341
  mathematics and, 228–9, 240, 250
  philosophical skill and, 67–8
temptation, 88–9, 152–3, 189, 205, 215, 230, 260, 274, 280, 285, 292, 294, 298, 313, 373
theology, 313
theorems (mathematical), 47, 62, 159, 169, 223, *See also* proof
Theory of Relativity, 284
thirst, 205–6
this, 42–3, 71–2, 81–2, 145, 180, 215, 318
thoughts
  expectation and, 10–11, 85
  explanations of, 87
  expressions of, 8, 12, 72, 74, 79, 85, 88, 92
  foreshadowing and, 80
  grammar and, 72, 111–12, 115, 180
  language's relation to, 8, 11, 18, 75, 79, 82, 107–8
  others' access to, 75
  physical space and, 292
  pictures as, 79, 148–9
  psychological views of, 104, 360
  reality's representation and, 20, 89, 91–2
  subconscious/unconscious, 287, 290, 309, 356–7, 360–1, 363–4
  temporality of, 74, 79
  thinkability and, 301, 303
  understanding and, 10
tidying, 69, 73, 103, 107, 109, 146, 177, 233
time, xli, 311
  Augustine on, 120
  before/after/earlier/later notions of, 113, 264, 264, 265, 265, 296, 311, 364, 365
  direction of, 260–1
  expectation and, 10, 13, 80–1, 84, 86, 88–9
  flow of, 260–1, 264, 317–18
  grammar of, 113–14, 260, 264–6, 310, 317
  hypotheses and, 44–5
  infinity and, 44
  information-time, 264
  meaning of, 8
  measurement of, 208, 211, 260–1, 265, 296–7, 310, 341–2
  memory and, 15, 264, 293, 296, 311
  in music, 353
  observation-time and, 264
  possibility's relation to, 18
  realism and, 5
  space's relation to, 6
  symbol's effects and, 6
  thinking and, 74, 76, 79, 104
Times, 244
time-tables, 235
tooth-aches, 115
  criteria of, 364
  first-person attribution and, xl, 207, 266–7, 269–70, 273–4, 276, 279, 282–9, 291, 308, 335, 362, 364
  second-person attribution of, xl
  symptoms of, 315
  third-person attribution and, xl, 207, 266–7, 269–70, 273, 275–6, 279, 282, 284–7
  unconscious, 290, 364
totalities, 42–3, *See also* grammar, *See also* systems
Townsend, R.D., xxix, 108
Tractatus Logico-Philosophicus (Wittgenstein), ix, xiii–xiv, xxviii, xlii–xliv, 23, 215–16, 219, 221, 250, 252, 260, 321, 382–3
training, 109
transcendence, 80, 105, 150–1
transformation, 242, 363, *See also* mathematics, *See also* projection, *See also* rules (grammatical), *See also* series
transitions, 323, 325–6, 331, 335, 338, 340, 343, 347
translation, 48, 50–2, 90, 108–9, 202–3, 323, 325
  grammar and, 51, 81, 106, 121, 145

projection and, 81, 84–5, 95, 108–9, 184, 255–6
showing and, 73, 77–8, 135
transubstantiation, 313
triangles, 160
Trinity Clock, 208, 311
Trinity Mathematical Society, xiv
trisection, 31, 210, 233–4, 236–8, 240–1
trivialities, xlvi, 8, 75, 87, 97, 247, 266, 367, See also philosophy, See also synopsis, See also Wittgenstein, Ludwig
truth/falsity
 false analogies and, 123, 125
 grammar's relation to, 28, 32–3, 70, 110, 116, 131–2, 184–5, 192, 257, 279–80
 inductive proofs and, 57
 inference and, 118, 125–6, 129, 131, 139–40, 187
 infinite series and, 157
 language and, 20, 104, 114, 255
 language games and, 256
 obedience of orders and, 72
 verification and, 20
Turner, Frederick Jackson, 343
type theory, xii, 23, 30, 182, 251

übersehen, 353, 357
unclarity, 8, 233, 250, 280
unconscious, the, 287, 289–90, 309, 356–7, 363
undecidability, 58
understanding
 definitions and, 70–1, 105
 descriptions of, 121–2
 examples and, 97–8, 172–3, 255, 280
 expectation and, 10
 explanation and, 94–5, 99, 105, 111, 116–17, 122, 359
 grammar and, 29, 111, 244
 mental processes as, 255, 313–14
 of music, 353
 new facts and, 75
 of orders, 72–3, 90, 109, 148
 of questions, 69
 rule-following and, 121–2, 265–6
 seeing and, 116, 120, 236

symbolism and, 76–8, 80, 84–5
of symbols, 9–10
uneasiness, xlvi, 87, 103, 196, 200, 203, 207–8, 210, 342, 352
unicorns, 236, 257
Ursell, Harold, 215, 232, 237, 247, 264, 267, 285, 287, 346, 363, 384
use
 of calculus, 187–8, 191, 196–7, 201, 205
 description of, 149–50
 grammatical rules and, 28–30, 53, 113, 115, 130–3, 135, 139–40, 178, 242, 247, 253, 255, 277, 281
 meaning and, xxviii, 8–9, 17–18, 67, 152, 179, 249, 281–2, 300–1, 308–9, 313, 317, 323, 325, 340, 365, 369
 measuring-rod and, 14
 symbolism's functioning and, 14–15, 28–9, 81, 130, 152–3, 178
 transcendence and, 150

vagueness, 69, 103, 205, 240, 255, 257–8, 277, 280, 282, 284, 301, 313, 323, See also blurriness, See also haze, See also unclarity
variables, 21–2, 24, 28, 46, 50, 52, 62, 140
The Varieties of Religious Experience (James), 381
verification
 counting and, 31
 criteria and, 284–7, 294–9, 310–11, 333
 experimental means of, 35–6, 96, 98, 118, 120, 201, 267, 284
 falsification and, 157, 166, 171–2, 201–2, 281
 formal certification and, 30
 hypotheses and, 44–5, 118, 354–5
 idealism and, 294
 of intention, 96, 98, 207–8
 of lies, 208
 mathematics and, 232
 meaning and, 167, 209, 242, 244, 246–7, 308, 311, 314–16, 323
 music and, 313
 other minds and, 207, 275–6, 282
 proofs and, 157–8, 166, 280

verification (cont.)
  propositions' sense and, 20, 44, 118, 144, 208, 245
  rules for, 152
  showing and, 89, 284
  stage-setting and, 17
  teaching and, 11
  Vienna Circle and, xlii–xliii
Vienna Circle, xiv
visual field, xxviii, 27, 35–7, 44, 50, 122, 184, 220, 270–2, 274, 291–3, 299, 368, 375
voices, 271–2, 285–9
volition, 197–201, *See also* intention
von Wright, G.H., xviii, xlviii–xlix, 383

Waismann, Friedrich, xiv, xli, xliii, 379
Ward, James, xi
water, 177–8, 198
Wessel, Caspar, 304
whistling, 198, 215, 302
Whitehead, Alfred North, 233, 383
will, 201
wishes, 72, 85, 105, 122, 197–8, 201–2, 204–8, 210, 257, 325–6
  descriptions of, 205
witchcraft, 329
Wittgenstein, Ludwig. *See also* Brown Book (Wittgenstein), *See also* Blue Book (Wittgenstein), *See also* Philosophical Remarks (Wittgenstein), *See also* Philosophical Investigations (Wittgenstein), *See also* Philosophical Investigations (Wittgenstein), *See also* Philosophical Grammar (Wittgenstein), *See also* Tractatus Logico-Philosophicus (Wittgenstein)
  death of, ix
  discussion classes of, xv–xx, xxii–xxiii, xxvi–xxvii, xxxvii, 68
  First World War and, xiii
  Moore's relationship to, xi, xv, xviii–xix, xxx, xxxii–xxxiii, 375–9
  Moore's responses to, 365, 367–71, 373–5
  Norway period of, xii
  pedagogical style of, xv, xxi, xxiii–xxiv, xxvi–xxvii, xxxvii–xxxviii, xli, xliv–xlvii, 19, 68, 144
  periodization of, ix, xliii–xliv
  philosophical method of, xli, xliv, xlvii–xlix, 67, 69, 74, 87–8, 141, 200, 203, 232–3, 280, 326, 331, 378
  Russell and, ix, xxviii, 129–30, 132
  students' lecture notes on, x, xxviii, xxx, xli
  writings of, xxxi, xxxv, *See also* specific works
Wittgenstein's Lectures on the Foundations of Mathematics, Cambridge 1939 (Diamond), xxx
Woolf, Virginia, 383
words, 85, 89, 94–5, 112, 143, 145
  actions' connection to, 5–6, 28
  justifications of, 90
  meaning and, 145, 149, 152, 177–9, 195, 249
  multiplicity of, 6
writing, 205–6, 208
www.wittgensteinsource.org, lvi

Young, Laurence Chisholm, 267, 384

For EU product safety concerns, contact us at Calle de José Abascal, 56–1°,
28003 Madrid, Spain or eugpsr@cambridge.org.

www.ingramcontent.com/pod-product-compliance
Lightning Source LLC
LaVergne TN
LVHW010252260326
834688LV00044B/1239